W9-CLH-812

Kentucky

Kentucky

Deborah Kohl Kremer

The Countryman Press ✳ Woodstock, Vermont

SECOND EDITION

Interior photographs by the author unless otherwise specified
Maps by Erin Greb Cartography, © The Countryman Press
Book design by Bodenweber Design
Composition by PerfecType, Nashville, TN

Published by The Countryman Press, P.O. Box 748, Woodstock, VT 05091

Distributed by W. W. Norton & Company, Inc., 500 Fifth Avenue, New York, NY 10110

Printed in the United States of America

10 9 8 7 6 5 4 3 2 1

Explorer's Guide Kentucky
978-1-58157-170-7

DEDICATION

To my parents, Paul and Peg Kohl: Thanks for being such great parents and proud Kentuckians. Those early road trips through the state really inspired me, but now I stay home when they predict sporadic showers. Love you both.

EXPLORE WITH US!

Welcome to the second edition of *Kentucky: An Explorer's Guide*. All attractions, activities, lodgings, and restaurants have been selected based on recommendations and personal experiences, never through paid advertising. This book is laid out in a user-friendly manner, but go ahead and familiarize yourself with the following information to make the most of it.

WHAT'S WHERE

This section is an alphabetical list of the state's highlights as well as important information you might need as you travel.

ALCOHOL

Kentucky's 120 counties all have different laws regarding the sale of alcohol. A *wet* county is one in which alcohol sales are permitted everywhere. A *dry* county allows no alcohol sales within the county borders. And, just to confuse the situation, some counties are *moist*. This means that selected restaurants in selected cities of a dry county are permitted to sell alcohol by the drink. So my advice is to always call ahead if you want a drink with dinner.

LODGING

The hours and price ranges listed after each entry are correct as of press time. This is subject to change at the owner's discretion. Please call ahead or check the website if you're ever in doubt.

Lodging prices
Less than $100 = $
$101–150 = $$
$151–200 = $$$
$201 and up = $$$$

DINING

Restaurants listed under the *Dining Out* heading are typically a little higher end. Those listed under the *Eating Out* heading are generally less expensive and casual.

Restaurant entrée prices
Less than $10 = $
$11–20 = $$
$21–30 = $$$
Above $30 = $$$$

KEY TO SYMBOLS

☿ **Weddings.** The wedding-ring symbol indicates establishments that frequently serve as venues for weddings and civil unions.

☙ **Special value.** The special-value symbol appears next to lodgings and restaurants that combine high quality and moderate prices.

✎ **Child-friendly.** The kids-alert symbol indicates those lodging places, restaurants, activities, and shops of special appeal to youngsters.

🐾 **Pets.** The dog-paw symbol shows those lodgings that accept pets (usually with a reservation and a deposit) as of press time.

♿ **Handicapped access.** The wheelchair symbol appears before lodgings, restaurants, and attractions that are partially or fully handicapped accessible.

((ⁱᵖⁱ)) **Wireless Internet.** This symbol shows establishments that offer WiFi or computer access.

ϒ **Beer/alcohol/wine.** This symbol appears beside establishments that serve alcohol.

I welcome your comments or corrections about places you discover or know well in Kentucky. Please email me at deb@deborahkohlkremer.com or address correspondence to Explorer's Guide Editor, The Countryman Press, P.O. Box 748, Woodstock, VT 05091; countrymanpress@wwnorton.com.

CONTENTS

MAPS

ACKNOWLEDGMENTS

Writing a book about a place as large and diverse as Kentucky is a job not to be tackled alone. Well armed with that knowledge, I went about alerting everyone that I knew, and some I didn't, that I was writing a book. Funny thing is, when people know that you're interested in their part of town, they can't wait to tell you about it. If you mention that you're on your way to Bardstown, chances are the next words out of your listener's mouth will be, "Bardstown? Did you ever try that little restaurant . . ." And if you are planning an outing at the track, you're likely to hear, "After the races, you need to stop and get a piece of pie at this little place . . ."

People are forever recommending places to eat, and luckily for me, that's one of my favorite activities.

In addition to my friends, relatives, neighbors, and business associates, who all recommended great places to go, I need to thank the total strangers, too. So to the guy in Paintsville who was fixing his front porch on a Sunday morning when I showed up lost and asked the direction to Prestonsburg . . . thanks for putting down your tools, coming across your yard, standing outside my car, and giving me fantastic guidelines. All he had to do was point, but the guy wanted to make sure we got there. And thanks to the woman in a parking lot in Russellville. When I asked if she knew of a particular bakery, she replied, "Well bless your heart, you are lost, honey. Just follow me and I'll take you there myself." And she did.

So as much as I attempt to list all the people who helped make this book possible, even after several tries I'll never be able to thank them all.

Specifically though, I do have to thank my parents, Paul and Peg Kohl, who are the best parents a girl could ever have. They raised me right and began teaching me about Kentucky at an early age. The combination of Mom's enthusiasm and Dad's sarcasm gave me just the right mix to be excited, but sometimes cynical in my writing endeavors.

To my sister Nancy Hoffman and her family, Jerry, Emily, Drew, and Chris Hoffman; as well as Ben, Deneen, Trey, and Bray Zimmerman; Jodi Karem; Sue Gladding Carpenter; Mike and Ann Wright; Missy Reynolds

ACKNOWLEDGMENTS

Witt; my friends at *Kentucky Monthly* magazine; Beverly Landrum Ralenkotter; Terry, Julie and Christian Bricking; Julie Kremer; and all the people who read the first edition and offered suggestions, recommendations, and opinions, I could not have done it without you.

But the group that certainly deserves the most accolades would be my husband, Nick, and my children, Ellie and Paul. Nick enjoys traveling the back roads as much as I do, and, God love him, he always orders desserts in the restaurants and shares with me. Ellie has helped me spread the word about the book, as well as told me her honest opinion of some of the restaurants and attractions we found along the way. Paul saw little details that I might have missed and reminded me to include them in my descriptions. So really, this book belongs to all four of us, not just me. As we spent weekends traveling around the state, stopping in antiques shops, visiting historical sites, touring horse farms, and generally eating our way across Kentucky, they were troupers. Although we all love the Bluegrass State, I'm sure there might have been a time or two when they wished they could've just stayed home. Thanks for not staying home. Thanks for all your help in writing this book. Thanks for being you.

■ INTRODUCTION

Writing a book about a place as vast and exciting as Kentucky is a dream come true for me. I've lived here all my life, and I've been writing about it for the last 20 or so years. It only makes sense that I finally put it into book form to share with you.

This book is divided up regionally, hopefully to aid you in your travels. You won't find any chain restaurants or chain lodging choices in this book, but all the biggies are well represented throughout the state if that is what you are looking for. The reasoning behind this is you can stay at a chain anywhere. But you are in Kentucky, and the best way to explore the state is by patronizing the antiques-filled, historic B&B mansion, the locals'

THE AUTHOR WITH SOME FAMOUS KENTUCKIANS

Nick Kremer

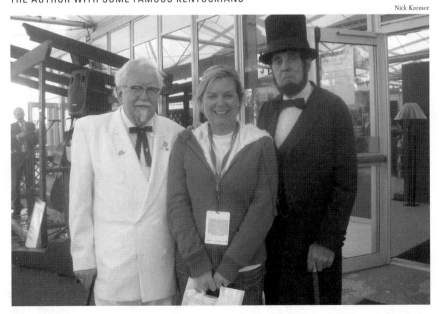

favorite greasy spoon, and the secluded barbecue joint just on the out-skirts of town.

Traveling through Kentucky will lead you high atop mountains, through gentle rolling plains of bluegrass, to major metropolitan cities, and to small towns that are so cute, you wish you could pinch their cheeks. I hope you will use this guide to take you to these amazing places.

After you visit the awe-inspiring mountains, canyons, lakes, or forests, and when you've made your way through the skyscrapers, tourist attractions, and shopping malls, then you'll be on your way to knowing Kentucky.

Because, you see, for the best part, you need to get out of your car and possibly your comfort zone. You have to talk to the people. Kentucky people are the abundant natural resource that gives the state its beauty. They give it character, life, and personality.

So whether you're in a bustling downtown or a local coffee shop, pull up a chair and ask the natives about their hometown. You'll see the sparkle in their eyes, the genuine kindness in their hearts, a sprinkle of southern hospitality in their voices—and then you'll know what Kentucky is all about.

Welcome to Kentucky. I hope you love it here as much as I do.

WHAT'S WHERE IN KENTUCKY

AIRPORTS AND AIRLINES
Kentucky is served by three primary airports, which include all the major airlines. Even though it sounds like it's in Ohio, the **Greater Cincinnati/Northern Kentucky Airport** (859-767-3151; www.cvgairport.com) is in Hebron. Serving the rest of the state are the **Louisville International Airport** (502-368-6524; www.flylouisville.com) and **Lexington's Bluegrass Airport** (859-425-3114; www.bluegrassairport .com). There are a scattering of small regional airstrips for private airplanes throughout the state.

ALCOHOL Kentucky alcohol laws vary by county, so you can't just have a drink anywhere. You need to know what county you are in to find out if they are wet—which means you can purchase alcohol anywhere that sells it—or dry, meaning you can't purchase alcohol within the county limits. Now, just to make sure you are paying attention, some counties offer limited consumption, which means that they may allow alcohol at a

specific restaurant, winery, or historic landmark. When in doubt, simply call the establishment and ask.

AQUARIUMS Sure, Kentucky is about 1,000 miles from the nearest ocean, but you can learn all about our friends from the sea at the state's only aquarium, **Newport Aquarium** (859-261-7444; www.newportaquarium.com). Surrounded by a million gallons of water, the aquarium offers huge exhibits that allow visitors to actually walk through the natural habitat of man-eating sharks, piranhas,

www.kentuckytourism.com

and alligators. Listen to classical music and enjoy the ballet of the jellyfish or sit and watch the antics of the penguins.

AREA CODE The area codes for Kentucky are 270, 502, 606, and 859. The central part of the state uses the newest area code, 859. If turned to text, 859 reads *UKY*, which the University of Kentucky is quite happy about.

ART MUSEUMS The state's oldest museum is the **Speed Art Museum** (502-634-2700; www .speedmuseum.org) in Louisville. With more than 12,000 pieces in its permanent collection, it is the state's largest, too. The second oldest is the **Owensboro Museum of Fine Art** (270-685-3181; www.omfa.museum). The **University of Kentucky Art Museum** (859-257-5716; www .uky.edu/ArtMuseum) also has a fascinating collection. Be sure to stop in while browsing around campus.

BED & BREAKFASTS Kentucky has a huge assortment of B&Bs to meet the needs of any traveler. Whether you're traveling with your children or your horses, Kentucky has inns that accept both. Choices include Victorian-era mansions in the historic district of a downtown, and secluded mountain hideaways where you can snuggle up with a quilt and a book next to a fieldstone fireplace and unwind. A great place to look first is the **Kentucky Bed and Breakfast Association** (www .kentuckybb.com).

BICYCLING With so much of Kentucky's countryside devoted to outdoor recreation, you can be sure there are lots of opportunities to bike. Several state parks offer biking trails (see www.parks.ky .gov) as well as the mountain bike trails in the **Daniel Boone National Forest** (www.fs.fed.us /r8). An organization called **Bike Kentucky** (www.bikekentucky .com) lists great trails on their website.

BIRDING Bird-watching is a popular attraction in Kentucky; after all, John James Audubon himself called Henderson home. Audubon, who painted and classified native birds throughout the early 1800s, supplied us with information that is still used today. Opportunities for birding are great at the **John James Audubon State Park** (270-826-2247; parks.ky.gov) in Henderson. The **Land Between the Lakes Recreational Area** (800-455-5897; www.lbl.org) offers 170,000 acres of unspoiled forest. Just outside Bardstown, in the tiny town of Clermont, you'll find the **Bernheim Arboretum and Research Forest** (502-955-8512; www .bernheim.org), offering more than 14,000 acres of bird lovers' paradise.

BOAT EXCURSIONS In Louisville, take a ride aboard a historic paddle-wheeler, the *Spirit* *of Jefferson* or the *Belle of Louisville* (502-574-2355; www .belleoflouisville.org). These grande dames of the Ohio River offer excursions and dinner cruises daily. In Northern Kentucky, **BB Riverboats** (859-261-8500, 800-261-8586; www.bbriver boats.com) offers sightseeing tours and meal packages year-round. The *Dixie Belle* **Riverboat at Shaker Village** (859-734-5411, 800-734-5611; www.shakervillageky.org) offers tours of the Kentucky River and the scenic palisades and cliffs that surround it.

BOAT RENTALS Known for its natural and human-made lakes,

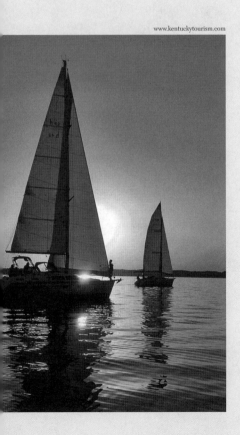

www.kentuckytourism.com

Kentucky offers boat rentals all over. In addition to **Lake Cumberland** (www.cumberlandlake .com), **Kentucky Lake** (www .kentuckylake.com), and **Lake Barkley** (www.lakebarkley.org), there are also marinas and docks at some of the smaller bodies like **Green River Lake** (www.green rivermarina.com).

BOOKS In the urban areas of the state, you find the big-box book sellers, but in the small communities you'll find the treasured old-time bookstores. Try **Bardstown Booksellers** (502-348-1256) or Louisville's **A Reader's Corner Bookstore** (areaderscorner.com), tucked into their respective historic downtown storefronts.

CAMPING Nearly all of Kentucky state parks (see parks.ky .gov) offer camping options that range from primitive tent sites to deluxe accommodations for the biggest rig. Another great place to rough it is the **Daniel Boone National Forest** (www.fs.fed.us /r8/boone), which is sprawled across 700,000 acres in 21 Kentucky counties.

CANOE AND RAFTING So many streams and lakes, so little time. You'll find canoe rentals at all the major marinas and docks. Head for **Sheltowee Trace Outfitters** (800-541-7238; www.ky -rafting.com) to hook you up with canoe and rafting trips on all the major waterways near Corbin. **Thaxton's Canoe Rental**

(gopaddling.com), with excursions along the Licking River, is easy to reach, just an hour north of Lexington and 30 minutes south of Newport.

CAVES As home to the world's largest cave, known as **Mammoth Cave** (270-758-2180; www.nps .gov/maca), Kentucky is the place to come for underground natural wonders. There are many caves in Western Kentucky but also a few lesser-known caves in the northeast region. Try **Carter Caves State Park** (606-286-4411; parks .ky.gov) to learn more about the caves there.

CHILDREN, ESPECIALLY FOR Kentucky is bursting at the borders with family-style fun, historical learning opportunities, and recreation. One location that focuses directly on the kids is the **Explorium** (859-258-3253; www .explorium.com). Formerly known as the Lexington Children's Museum, this great place changed their name because the emphasis is more on exploring than observing. Fun for adults, too.

CIVIL WAR Although Kentucky was officially neutral in the War Between the States, the Bluegrass State saw her share of action. Today there are many historic sites, driving tours, and museums that focus on how the war affected that area of the state. The largest battle, the **Battle of Perryville** (www.perryville.net), pitted 18,000

Confederates against 20,000 Union troops. Today Perryville is a historic site with a preserved battlefield, walking tours, and a museum with a fabulous movie that explains everything. In Northern Kentucky, you can see the site high atop a mountain where Union forces gathered to defend Cincinnati—but the Confederates, hearing they were outnumbered, turned back and headed home. Tour the **James A. Ramage Civil War Museum** (859-344-1145), which is on the grounds of this historic outlook. In Lexington, you can visit **Hunt Morgan House and Civil War Museum** (859-233-3290; www.bluegrasstrust .org), which has an impressive collection of Civil War artifacts as well as memorabilia that belonged to the infamous Confederate raider John Hunt Morgan.

CLIMBING One of the best places for rock climbing in Kentucky is the **Red River Gorge** (www.redrivergorge.com). Located in the east-central part of the state, this intricate canyon system features sheer limestone cliffs and more than 80 natural bridges.

COVERED BRIDGES The Bluegrass State, once dotted with more than 400 covered bridges, now has 13 remaining. Most are located in the northeastern section of the state. Flemingsburg, in Fleming County, is home to three and is known as the **Official Covered Bridge Capital of Kentucky**.

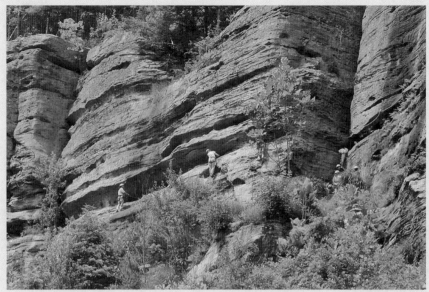

www.kentuckytourism.com

CRAFTS Kentucky's rich Appalachian heritage has resulted in generations of craftspeople who produce art in all forms and now sell their wares throughout the state. Berea, which is known as the Folk Arts and Crafts Capital of Kentucky, is home to the **Kentucky Artisan Center** (www .kentuckyartisancenter.ky.gov), a 25,000-square-foot facility offering a huge variety of crafts all under one roof. In Louisville, the **Mellwood Arts and Entertainment Center** (502-895-3650; www .mellwoodartcenter.com) is home to 200 art studios, galleries, and specialty shops where you can purchase crafts as well as watch the artists working in their studios.

DRIVE-IN MOVIES If drive-in movies were wild animals, they would be on the endangered list—

not quite extinct, mind you, but not as many around as there used to be. Although their predator, the multiplex, has been gobbling them up for years, there are currently 13 standing strong in Kentucky. Tucked into places where you would least expect them, like the **Twin Hills Drive-In Theatre** in Harrodsburg (859-734-3474) and the **Mountain View Drive-In** in Stanton (606-663-9988), they're all great places to go for family-style entertainment. There's a great website that can help you locate all of them: www.drive-ins.com.

EMERGENCIES Dial 911 anywhere in the state for emergency help.

FACEBOOK One of the most noticeable changes that's taken place since the publication of the first edition of *Kentucky: An Explorer's Guide,* which was published in 2010, is the growth in Facebook's popularity. So many stores and restaurants seem to be opting to forgo the traditional website and just use social networking. So, if you do not see a website listed for a place you are interested in, give them a search on Facebook. The benefit, in addition to being free, is that it is a great way for business owners to quickly post up-to-the-minute news whenever they want. A restaurant that does it well is **Mermaids Bar and Bistro** in Danville. Give them a "like" on Facebook.

FACTORY TOURS Many things are made in Kentucky, and luckily for us some of the manufacturers offer tours. You might be surprised to learn that **General Motors** builds Corvettes in Bowling Green (www.bowlinggreen assemblyplant.com) or that **Toyota** churns out Camrys in Georgetown (www.toyotageorgetown.com /tour.asp), but the Bluegrass State is home to other products, too. Winchester's **Ale-8-One** (859-744-3484; www.ale-8-one.com) offers tours of their soft-drink manufacturing plant. The **Louisville Slugger** (www.sluggermuseum.org) factory lets visitors see how a big hunk of wood can be transformed into a sleek baseball bat, headed for the major leagues.

FARMER'S MARKETS Rich farmland and a good climate have produced bountiful crops for Kentuckians for generations. This is evident in summer and fall as local farmers bring their wares to the farmer's markets held in most counties, and to the roadside stands that pop up in the farmers' own front yards and at busy intersections. Farmer's markets by county are listed on the **Kentucky Department of Agriculture** website: www.kyagr.com.

FISHING is available all over the state, but you're going to need a Kentucky State Fishing License to be legal. To get yours, just contact the Kentucky Department of Fish and Wildlife Resources at 800-858-1549.

FORTS Get a taste of the frontier life at **Fort Boonesborough State Park** and **Fort Harrod State Park** (parks.ky.gov). Once our forefathers made their arduous journey over the mountains and through the Cumberland Gap, the first settlements took root in the Bluegrass Region. Unfortunately the Native Americans in the area weren't waiting here with a bottle of champagne and basket of cookies to welcome them. The threat from the Indians was very real and very dangerous, so the settlers erected huge forts for protection. Today these state parks have re-created the forts to give visitors a feel for how these brave pioneers lived.

FREE FAMILY FUN You can see and do quite a bit in Kentucky

www.kentuckytourism.com

without ever spending a dime. There are endless opportunities to swim, fish, and hike at the Kentucky state parks (parks.ky.gov).

GARDENS The Kentucky climate is great for growing stunning flowers as well as tobacco. Outside Owensboro you'll find a breathtaking daylily and hosta farm called **Pinecliffe Gardens** (270-281-9791) where you can enjoy peak bloom season in mid-June. In Lexington, visit the **University of Kentucky Arboretum** (859-257-6955), where you can see 1,500 varieties of roses in bloom. Bet it smells heavenly.

GOLF With more than 300 courses to choose from, the Bluegrass State's beautiful courses are always nearby. The website www.golflink.com can help you find one near you, listed by city.

HIKING Kentucky has wonderful trails, whether you want the rugged terrain of the **Daniel Boone National Forest** or the flat, wooded trails of the **Land Between the Lakes** region. It's beautiful whichever end of the state you choose. Most parks offer trail maps that let you know how long the trail is and how difficult it might be.

HISTORIC HOUSES Touring a historic home is like a brush with greatness. There are lots of Lincoln-related cabins in the state, including Abraham's birthplace (www.nps.gov/abli) in Hodgenville. In Bardstown, you'll find the Rowan estate, also known as **My Old Kentucky Home** (parks.ky.gov). You can also tour White Hall, the 1800s-era home of Cassius Clay, which is near Richmond.

HORSE RACING What's a trip to Kentucky without a little horse racing to really get a feel for the place? **Turfway Park** (www .turfway.com) in Florence, **Keeneland** (www.keeneland.com) in Lexington, **Churchill Downs** (www.churchilldowns.com) in Louisville, and **Ellis Park** (ellis parkracing.com) in Henderson all offer live thoroughbred racing. If you're into harness racing, the **Red Mile** (www.theredmile.com) in Lexington is a great place to go. The schedules vary, so call ahead for post times.

KENTUCKY STATE FAIR For more than 100 years, the **Kentucky State Fair** has been drawing crowds to Louisville vying for the coveted blue ribbon in competitions ranging from homegrown produce to handmade quilts, bunnies, roosters, pigeons, and livestock. There are hundreds of categories and thousands of entrants; it really is unbelievable. People also come for the Thrillway rides, the Championship Horse Show, and the Pride of the Counties exhibit, where each of Kentucky's 120 counties gets its chance to brag.

LAKES In addition to the big three, **Lake Cumberland**, **Kentucky Lake**, and **Lake Barkley**, you'll find nice-sized lakes all over the state. Whether you're into houseboating, fishing, or waterskiing, Kentucky's lakes have you covered.

MAGAZINE *Kentucky Monthly* magazine is for sale at newsstands throughout the state. This magazine gives a glimpse into the life of Kentuckians, and usually shines a spotlight on a few restaurants or B&Bs in each issue. There is also a monthly calendar to tell you what's going on. Pick up the latest

www.kentuckytourism.com

Paul Kremer

copy at newsstands all over the state.

MAIN STREET Main Streets, the ever-present commercial centers of downtown cities across the country, are alive and well throughout Kentucky. Although some city centers have moved to the outskirts of town—where you'll find the chain stores and big-box retailers—there's still something special about walking down Main Street and browsing through the shops. In Danville, the historic downtown includes well-kept storefronts, charming shops, and pristine churches. In Covington, the area once populated by German immigrants is host to Mainstrasse. This neighborhood, sprinkled with galleries, antiques shops, and cool restaurants, has hints of the motherland apparent in the amazing architecture.

MUSEUMS Kentucky offers a variety of museums; you just have to look for them. Get a feel for the "Greatest Two Minutes in Sports" at the **Kentucky Derby Museum** (www.derbymuseum .org) in Louisville. You'll enjoy the interactive exhibits and huge mul-

Kentucky Monthly Magazine

tiscreen movie, where you can learn all about a Kentucky tradition that has been around since 1875. For a not-so-common museum experience, Lexington's **Headley-Whitney Museum** (www.headley-whitney.org) is known for their stunning collection of bibelots—small intricately jeweled baubles. The museum also houses unique art pieces, jewelry, and pieces from the Smithsonian.

NATIVE AMERICANS The **Trail of Tears Commemorative Park** (www.trailoftears.org) in Hopkinsville is dedicated to the remembrance of the Cherokee people who traveled the trail in the mandatory migration westward of the 1830s. Hopkinsville was a stop on the trail; the park pays respect to all who passed through, and those who did not make it.

POPULATION Kentucky is home to more than four million people. The largest concentration lives in the triangle that includes Louisville, Lexington, and Northern Kentucky.

POTTERY Thanks to the state's unique mix of limestone, clay, and probably something to do with bluegrass, artisans from Kentucky have been producing artistic and functional pottery here for generations. Although some of the studios are tucked away in the artists' homes, many are open to visitors. The city of Louisville is home to

Deborah Kohl Kremer

several, like **Louisville Stoneware** (louisvillestoneware.com), **M. A. Hadley Pottery** (hadley pottery.com), and **Pottery Rowe** (potteryrowe.com).

QUILTS For quilters, there is no better destination than the **National Quilt Museum** (www .quiltmuseum.org) in Paducah. The museum showcases quilts both old and new, and the exhibits tell the stories behind them. For those not so well versed in the art of quilting, this is a great place to learn about this intricate craft.

RAILROAD AND RAILROAD MUSEUMS The railroad is credited with bringing people, news, supplies, and life to Kentucky, so it is only fitting that there are several museums around the state that pay it homage. On the far eastern tip of the state is the **Elkhorn City Railroad Museum** (606-754-8300;

elkhorncityrrm.tripod.com). Centrally located in Versailles is the **Bluegrass Scenic Railroad and Museum** (859-873-2476, 800-755-2476; www.bgrm.org); tucked into the Big South Fork Recreation Area in Stearns, you'll find the **Scenic Railway** (606-376-5330; www.bsfsry.com), where you can take a 16-mile ride on the 100-year-old Kentucky & Tennessee Railroad.

SCENIC BYWAYS Hopping onto a well-marked scenic byway is a great way to see the natural beauty of Kentucky, all from the comfort of your car. There are three **National Scenic Byways** in the state: the **Country Music Highway**, the **Red River Gorge Scenic Highway**, and the **Wilderness Road Heritage Highway**. The state has also designated several **Kentucky Scenic Byways**, too. A great drive through horse country is along US 68 in the Lexington area. The route encompasses 106 miles of sprawling horse farms, complete with hand-laid fieldstone fences, chandeliered horse barns, and horses grazing in the rolling pastures. To find route information, go to www.kentuckytourism.com.

WELCOME CENTERS Kentucky is a welcoming state, and all that down-home hospitality has to start somewhere. So you'll find eight interstate highway welcome centers located near the state borders. Stop in to be welcomed by the friendly staff, and feel free to grab some brochures, use the clean restrooms, and buy a can of cola and a pack of M&M's before getting back on the road. The centers are:

Bullitt County Welcome Center, I-65 South (502-543-5900)

Christian County Welcome Center, I-24 West (270-439-7505)

Florence Welcome Center, I-75 / I-71 South (859-384-3130)

Franklin Welcome Center, I-65 North (270-586-6292)

Grayson Welcome Center, I-64 West (606-474-4333)

Shelby County Welcome Center, I-64 East (502-722-9383)

Whitehaven Welcome Center (Paducah), I-24 East (270-554-2077)

Williamsburg Welcome Center, I-75 North (606-786-4474)

WINERIES Napa Valley has nothing on Kentucky. The Bluegrass State's fertile soil, good climate, and determined winemakers are turning out wonderful "vino." **Ruby Moon Vineyard & Winery** (270-830-7660; www.ruby moonwinery.com), Henderson, produces award-winning wine at their wonderful vineyard. They also have a tasting room, a gift shop, and events like art shows on the grounds. The folks at **Elk Creek Vineyards** (www.elkcreek vineyards.com) in Owenton produce a huge selection of wines as well as offering tours, cooking classes, and some really great concerts on their scenic rolling pastures. In all Kentucky has more than 50 wineries; check out the Kentucky Grape and Wine Council (www.kentuckywine.com) to find them all.

ZOO Kentucky has one zoo: the **Louisville Zoo** (502-459-2181; www.louisvillezoo.org). It's a beautiful zoo, with wonderful adaptations that allow the animals to live in their native environments.

Eastern Appalachian Region

Eastern Appalachian Region

© The Countryman Press

INTRODUCTION: EASTERN KENTUCKY APPALACHIANS

T he rugged natural beauty of the eastern side of Kentucky is reflected vividly in the people and culture. The high mountains and the low scenic valleys, which are known as hollows to locals, include coal mines, state parks, and even the massive Daniel Boone National Forest. Although some of the terrain is jagged and rough, you'll find small storybook towns and people with enough charm to make it all feel smooth.

The Appalachian Mountains—pronounced *appa-LATCH-an* or *appa-LAY-sion*, depending on your location and who you're talking to—run in a north–south direction through Eastern Kentucky. The Appalachian lifestyle is tied to the mountains and the hardworking people who reside there. This culture is readily apparent in the crafts and folk art produced in the region. Another boon to the area is its ability to turn out nationally known country music artists. Tour the Country Music Highway, also known as US 23, to learn about these famous locals. As this scenic byway stretches through eight counties, it takes you through hometowns and birthplaces of superstars like Loretta Lynn, Billy Ray Cyrus, the Judds, and Dwight Yoakam.

With so much natural scenic beauty, it seems like there is a state park around every bend. The state of Kentucky created these parks to capture the mountains, lakes, and rolling plains before development took hold, resulting in one beautiful park after the next. Although most boast camping, boating, and fishing, some offer a unique magnet, like elk viewing, outdoor Broadway-style shows, and even black bear sightings, that you won't want to miss.

Sprinkle in a little history with your commune with nature by learning about legendary frontiersman Daniel Boone. One of Kentucky's first explorers, Boone led literally thousands of pioneers into Kentucky through the Cumberland Gap, in the southeast corner of the state. Today visitors will find that progress has been hidden, and the area near the gap looks as it must have when those brave pioneers found this convenient cut-through in the mountains. Hike or horseback ride along the historic Wilderness Road, which was cut down by Boone himself, and you can really see what our forefathers' first glimpses of Kentucky were like.

You will find nods of appreciation to Boone, who never actually wore a 'coonskin cap, all over the region. One of the largest tributes is the enormous Daniel Boone National Forest. This wooded wonderland covers 694,985 acres and most of Eastern Kentucky, touching 21 counties. It includes the stunning Red River Gorge Geological Area and Natural Bridge State Park, a mecca for hikers, rock climbers, and campers.

Eastern Kentucky, not known as the most affluent part of the state, is steeped in riches that money can't buy. It is bursting with natural beauty, recreational opportunities, a rich artistic culture, and mountainfuls of friendly people who can't wait to meet you.

ASHLAND AREA

Ashland is the welcome mat into Kentucky if you're arriving from the east—and what a warm welcome you'll receive. Ashland is a charmer, built around the lush, 47-acre Central Park, breathtaking 100-year-old homes, and a vibrant central business district made up of both new and old buildings that are well maintained.

When the Poage family arrived from Staunton, Virginia, in October 1799, they promptly named the area Poage's Landing. In 1854, the city name was changed to Ashland after statesman Henry Clay's Lexington estate.

The area became prosperous due to its prominent natural resources and proximity to the Ohio River, where these resources could be easily distributed. The Kentucky Iron, Coal and Manufacturing Company was incorporated on March 8, 1854, and they are credited with laying out the town of Ashland. The company purchased thousands of acres of coal, timber, and ore throughout the area; as the firm flourished, so did Ashland. Known today as AK Steel, the industry remains a major employer in northeastern Kentucky.

While downtown Ashland offers restaurants, art galleries, and shops, do venture into the surrounding communities like Russell and Flatwoods for even more mom-and-pop shops, one-of-a-kind eateries, and some real friendly folks.

About 30 miles west of Ashland, in Carter County, you'll find Grayson, known as the Heart of the Parks. It's located in the center of a triangle formed by three of the commonwealth's most beautiful state parks: Carter Caves, Greenbo Lake, and Grayson Lake. These parks offer outdoor recreation as well as a taste of the region's natural beauty.

GUIDANCE Ashland Area Convention & Visitors Bureau (606-329-1007, 800-377-6249; www.visitashlandky.com), 1509 Winchester Ave., Ashland. Open weekdays 9–5. You can't miss this visitors center, which is located on Winchester Avenue, the main route through town. The staff are eager to help with info, maps, and tips.

GETTING THERE Northeastern Kentucky is served by several state routes as well as Interstate 64, which runs east–west across the state, and the AA Highway, which runs from Alexandria to, you guessed it, Ashland. The nearest commercial airport is the **Tri-State Airport** (304-453-6165; www.tristateairport.com), located about 30 minutes from Ashland in Huntington, West Virginia. **Greyhound Bus Lines** serves the northeastern Kentucky area (800-231-2222; www.greyhound.com). The depot operates out of the Ashland Transportation Center, 99 15th St., in Ashland.

GETTING AROUND It is easy to get around the area by car. Streets are well marked, and parking in the downtown areas is free. Public transportation is available through the **Ashland Bus System** (606-327-2025; www.ashlandky.org/abs.htm), 99 15th St. Buses blanket the area weekdays 7–6 and Sat. 9–6.

MEDICAL EMERGENCY King's Daughters Medical Center (606-408-4000; www.kdmc.com), 2201 Lexington Ave., Ashland. Established in 1899, King's Daughters Medical Center (KDMC) is a 385-bed center that covers a 150-mile radius including southern Ohio, Eastern Kentucky, and western West Virginia.

ALCOHOL Both Carter and Boyd are dry counties, which means they prohibit alcohol sales. Alcohol sales by the drink are permitted in Ashland restaurants that seat more than 100 people, making it a wet city. If you want a drink with dinner, call ahead to make sure you are in the city limits.

✳ To See

✿ ✈ ♿ **Highlands Museum & Discovery Center** (606-329-8888; www.highlandsmuseum.com), 1620 Winchester Ave., Ashland. Open Wed.–Fri. 10–4, Sat. 10–6. Housed in the former Parsons Department Store, this interactive museum features exhibits where you can learn about the history of Ashland and Eastern Kentucky. Learn about caves, coal mining, and life on the river; lots of hands-on activities for kids. $5.50 adults, $4.50 seniors, $4.50 children ages 2 and over; under 2 free.

Jesse Stuart Foundation (606-326-1667; www.jsfbooks.com), 1645 Winchester Ave., Ashland. Call for hours. Visit this former post office, which was built in 1917, and learn about the career of world-renowned writer and area native Jesse Stuart. This former poet laureate published more than 460 short stories and used Northeastern Kentucky as the setting of many of his works. This foundation is dedicated to preserving his literary works, and visitors can enjoy viewing some of his personal belongings and signed manuscripts. The foundation sells works by Stuart, as well as books by other Appalachian authors.

❦ ♿ **Catlettsburg Floodwall Murals** (606-329-1007), Center St. in downtown Catlettsburg. Many of Kentucky's river cities boast intricately painted floodwall murals, and Catlettsburg is no different. Stop and get a closer look at these magnificent murals that tell the story of the history of Catlettsburg.

❦ **Northeastern Kentucky Museum** (606-286-6012), 1385 Carter Caves Rd., Olive Hill. Open weekdays 9–5, but call ahead to double-check. This area of Kentucky features caves, rugged terrain, and fossils, and this is the place to learn all about it. They have collections covering Indian artifacts, fossils, and war memorabilia. Tours of privately owned caves can be arranged here, too. Free.

✳ To Do

GOLF Sandy Creek Golf Course (606-928-6321; www.sandycreekgc .com), 9701 Meade Springer Rd., Meads. This public, 18-hole course measures 5,538 yards. Short and hilly, it has a few elevated greens, a chipping area, and a practice bunker.

Sundowner Golf Course (606-329-9093), 4135 KY 5, Ashland. This 9-hole, par-33 bent grass course has lots of obstacles and traps. It measures 2,009 yards and is somewhat hilly.

CATLETTSBURG FLOODWALL MURALS

Deborah Kohl Kremer

Hidden Cove Golf Course at Grayson Lake (606-474-9727; parks .ky.gov), 314 Grayson Lake Park Rd., Olive Hill. This public 18-hole, par-72 course hugs the shores of Grayson Lake.

✳ Green Space

Central Park (606-327-2007), bounded by Lexington and Central Ave., and 17th and 22nd Sts., Ashland. The crown jewel of the Ashland city parks sits right in the downtown area. This 47-acre gem is a perfect place to eat a picnic lunch surrounded by the 1,100 trees, with each identified and located on maps of the park. If you're looking for recreation, there are three separate children's playgrounds, several baseball diamonds, and tennis and volleyball courts. In summer the city offers outdoor concerts; in winter you can ice skate. It really is a year-round park.

Tygarts State Forest (606-286-4411; www.forestry.ky.gov), KY 182, Olive Hill. Adjacent to Carter Caves State Park is this lush 874-acre forest. They offer hiking and picnicking, but camping and ATV riding are not allowed.

STATE PARKS Grayson Lake State Park (606-474-9727; parks .ky.gov), 314 Grayson Lake Park Rd., Olive Hill. Enjoy this former camping area of Shawnee and Cherokee Indians, full of beautiful sandstone canyons and scenic terrain. There are 74 miles of shoreline on this 1,500-acre lake where you can rent fishing and pontoon boats, and enjoy the sand between your toes at the sand beach. The park offers a spacious 71-site campground (606-474-6856, 606-474-5815). They have utility hookups, a dump station, a bathhouse, and laundry facilities. The check-in station has a small store with some necessities like ice and firewood. Closed mid-Nov.–mid-Mar.

&. **Carter Caves State Resort Park** (606-286-4411, 800-325-0059; parks.ky.gov), 344 Caveland Dr., Olive Hill. This is the perfect park for nature lovers and spelunkers alike. Hidden under the park are 20 natural caves, with 4 open for touring. Tours are available for every level of caver. Bat Cave, the largest, is home to more than 40,000 Indiana bats that come to hibernate each winter. Each cave has its own natural wonders—but don't miss Cascade Cave, where you can enjoy the Cathedral Room and a 30-foot underground waterfall. Not all the natural beauty is underground, though. Carter Caves State Park has several natural bridges, one with a paved road on top. The park offers more than 20 scenic miles of trails for hiking, horseback riding, and mountain biking. The 45-acre **Smokey Lake** offers fishing, boating, and water sports. And if you have any time left, they also have an outdoor pool, a 9-hole golf course, tennis courts, and miniature golf. Stay on site at the **Lewis Caveland Lodge**, where you'll find 28 rooms, all with outdoor balconies where you can take in the scenery. The resort also offers 10 rustic cottages, 8 with wood-burning fireplaces, all equipped with modern conveniences such as dishwashers and microwave ovens. If outdoors is more your style, **Carter Caves Campground** has 89 campsites with utilities, a dump station, and a bath-house. They also have 30 tent sites that do not have water or electric. Closed mid-Nov.–mid-Mar. **Tierney's Cavern Restaurant** is open seven days a week. Breakfast 7–10, lunch 11:30–2, dinner 5–9; Sun. brunch is served 11–3. Enjoy fine dining while surrounded with caving artifacts, photos, and memorabilia. The menu offers steaks and seafood as well as appetizers and sandwiches. People come from miles away to enjoy the Sunday brunch, which is loaded with entrées like fried catfish, turkey and dressing, fried chicken, and Kentucky hot brown. $–$$

& **Greenbo Lake State Resort Park** (606-473-7324, 800-325-0083; parks.ky.gov), 965 Lodge Rd., Greenup. At the confluence of Clay Lick Creek and its tributaries, Buffalo Fork and Pruitt Fork, sits the 300-acre Greenbo Lake. Its name reflects the two counties, Greenup and Boyd, and recognizes the efforts of the citizens who worked so hard in the late 1940s to establish a recreational park in this area. Greenbo is a fisherman's dream, stocked full of largemouth bass, bluegill, crappie, catfish, and trout. In addition to boating and fishing, this 3,330-acre park offers more than 25 miles of trails for all levels of hikers. Along the trails you can enjoy the seasons as well as sightings of grouse, deer, squirrels, and many differ-ent birds. Stay in one of the 36 rooms of the **Jesse Stuart Lodge** over-looking beautiful Greenbo Lake. This lodge was named in honor of Jesse Stuart—a native of Greenup County and Kentucky's poet laureate. The lodge has a welcoming reading room where you can enjoy some of Stuart's works and personal artifacts. If you would rather camp, they offer 63 sites with utility hookups; or you can rough it on one of the 35 primitive sites. At the **Angler's Cove Restaurant**, open seven days a week 7 AM–9 PM, you can enjoy your meal with a relaxing view of the lake. The menu fea-tures tasty catfish and seafood entrées, legendary corn chowder, and fresh salads. $–$$

✳ Lodging

& **Ashland Plaza Hotel** (606-329 0055; www.ashlandplaza.net), 15th and Winchester Ave., Ashland. Known as the jewel in the crown of Ashland, this independently owned 141-room hotel feels like an upscale chain, but the personal service indicates otherwise. Spa-cious rooms, workout facilities, and a complimentary continental

breakfast make the Plaza a good choice. $$

The Presidents' House Bed & Breakfast (606-739-8118, 877-500-3452; www.bbonline.com), 2206 Walnut St., Catlettsburg. Just south of Ashland is this stately B&B in the former home of Levi Hampton, one of the first settlers in the Big Sandy Valley. Built in

1847, this five-guest-room-home has all the authentic historic touches, mixed with modern amenities to ensure a comfy stay. The innkeepers have one of the largest private collections of authentic presidential memorabilia and autographs, and it is all displayed meticulously. Full breakfast on weekends and deluxe continental during the week. $–$$

CAMPING Yatesville Lake State Park Campground (606-673-1492; parks.ky.gov), Louisa. This 47-site campground offers 27 full-hookup campsites and 20 primitive campsites. Sixteen of the sites are "boat-in" sites that can only be reached via the 2,300-acre lake, and four are "hike-in" sites offering complete seclusion. The campground also has a playground facility, nature trails, laundry room, restrooms, showers, and a dump station. Closed mid-Nov.–mid-Mar.

✳ Where to Eat

🍸 **Chimney Corner Café** (606-324-7500), 1624 Carter Ave., Ashland. Open Mon.–Fri. 11–10, Sat. 4–10. This restaurant has been a staple in Ashland for years, and locals turn to it when they want an upscale meal with reasonable prices. Thorough assortment of steaks, seafood, and chicken available. $$

Giovanni's Pizza (606-324-5157), 724 Greenup Ave., Ashland. With six locations in the area; you're probably already close to one. This pizza is a local favorite as well as a first stop for those revisiting the area. The pizza is delicious, but they also have good sandwiches, salads, and pasta dinners. At lunch, there's a pizza buffet where

CHIMNEY CORNER CAFÉ

Deborah Kohl Kremer

you can try all different kinds of pizza and pasta. You might want to wear loose clothing, because you'll be full when you leave. $

& Cafe Zeal (606-324-8565; www .theframeupgallery.com), 1436 Winchester Ave., Ashland. Open Mon.–Sat. 11–8. Located inside the Frame Up Gallery in downtown Ashland, Café Zeal offers a relaxing place for lunch right in the heart of downtown. Surrounded by soothing music and work by local artists, you'll enjoy the salads, sandwiches, desserts, and specialty coffee drinks while you unwind. The Italian cream cake consists of three layers of unbelievable happiness. $

& ⑂ Fat Patty's (606-325-7287; fatpattysonline.com), 1442 Winchester Ave., Ashland. Local chain with three locations, just one in Ashland. Specializing in burgers and overstuffed sandwiches, Fat Patty's is also proud to feature a full bar. Casual atmosphere and reasonable prices. $

Katie's Corner Cafe (606-325-5283), 1450 Greenup Ave, Ashland. Serving all three meals Mon.–Sat. Full range of menu items in this casual diner, even breakfast all day. Very casual, perfect for families or just a quick bite. Very reasonable prices. $

SNACKS Randy's Roadside Market and Deli (606-474-6455), 431 E. Main St., Grayson. Open 7 AM–9 PM every day. Disguised as a market, this is a favorite of locals for burgers and loaded hot dogs smothered in homemade chili sauce, coleslaw, and shredded cheese. They've been around for more than 20 years serving up hearty breakfasts, hand-dipped ice cream, and old-fashioned homemade shakes, too. $

✳ Entertainment

& Paramount Arts Center Theatre (606-324-3175; www .paramountartscenter.com), 1300 Winchester Ave., Ashland. Visit this historic art-deco-inspired theater from the 1930s. You can take in a tour, or take in a show; either way you'll see how an old-time theater is supposed to look. It was constructed by Paramount Pictures, whose plan was to have one of these theaters in each of the 48 states. Unfortunately, only three were completed, and Ashland's version is the only survivor. Shows vary throughout the year, so check the website to see what's coming. Paramount's claim to fame is that it was the location site of native Billy Ray Cyrus's "Achy Breaky Heart" video shoot.

GALLERIES Pendleton Arts Center (606-920-9863; www .pendletonartcenter.com), 1537 Winchester Ave., Ashland. Artists and craftspeople come to Pendleton to work on their art and offer their wares. Enjoy watching the painters, woodworkers, and potters as they hone their craft.

Hours vary by artist, so check the website for times.

The Frame Up Gallery (606-324-8565; www.theframeupgallery.com), 1436 Winchester Ave., Ashland. Open Mon.–Sat. 11–8. This funky but relaxing shop offers a mix of art, framing, and gifts.

✳ Selective Shopping

ANTIQUES Chicken Coop Art & Craft Mall (606-474-9690; chickencoop.cartercountymarket.com), 10813 KY 9, Grayson. Open Thu.–Sat. Call for hours. Sited in a former chicken house, this 7,000-square-foot shop offers the works of more than 150 local crafters. The shop is rustic, and the merchandise is fabulous. You'll find antiques, crafts, handmade furniture, and more. It's different every time you go.

Catlettsburg Antique Mall (606-739-9786; catlettsburg antiquestores.com), 2606 Louisa St., Catlettsburg. Open Wed.–Sat. 10–5, Sun. 1:30–5. A roomy store with about 10 vendors, each offering a variety of antiques, collectibles, and estate items.

Old Friends Antiques and Uniques (606-928-2181), 6118 W. US 60, Ashland. Open Mon.–Fri. 9–5. Call if you want to come on Saturday. This place is big. It's spread out over two floors of a retail store, the first floor of a house, and an entire mobile home, so be careful not to miss anything. More stuff than you can imagine, from tiny knickknacks to huge pieces of furniture and everything in between.

✳ Special Events

July: ✍ **Summer Motion** (www.summermotion.com). For more than 20 years, this festival, held in the Central Park in Ashland, has been entertaining huge crowds who come for well-known musical acts like Wynonna, Billy Ray Cyrus, Merle Haggard, Herman's Hermits, Grand Funk Railroad, Trace Adkins, and John Michael Montgomery. They also have a craft show, a petting zoo, games and carnival rides, a 10K race, and a soapbox derby.

September: ✍ **Ashland Poage Landing Days** (poagelanding days.com). Named for the first immigrants in the area, the Poage family, who settled the area in 1786, this annual festival celebrates the town's roots right in downtown Ashland. The celebration features big-name live entertainment, a 5K run, a skateboarding competition, a car and bike show, and regionally inspired arts and crafts.

December: ✍ **Christmas festivities**. The city of Ashland knows how to celebrate Christmas. If you are in the area on the Tuesday evening before Thanksgiving, head for the Christmas Parade along Winchester Avenue. This is a huge parade, with more than 200 entrants that come from three states in a 50-mile radius. Fans line the route—which is at least a mile long—to cheer for the marching bands, fire trucks, and Shriners in their little cars. This parade, which ought to be called the Macy's Parade of the South, is a perfect way to get the hometown feel of Ashland. While you're in town, drive through the town's Central Park for the **Winter Wonderland of Lights Festival**, a phenomenal display of 800,000 Christmas lights open for five weeks every year. Another fun event in Ashland is the **Festival of Trees and Trains**, held annually at the Historic Paramount Arts Center. Wander through the historic theater and enjoy the hundreds of Christmas trees, each with its own theme and decorated by community groups, schools, and area businesses. They also have a huge train display and a gingerbread house competition. Ashland at Christmastime is a treat for your senses.

MOREHEAD AND
DANIEL BOONE NATIONAL FOREST

Morehead, which is the county seat and largest city in Rowan County, is located in the mountainous region of Northeastern Kentucky. It's about halfway between Lexington and Huntington, West Virginia.

Established in the mid-1800s, Morehead and Rowan County were known for coal production and timber, but by the mid-1900s the area was committed primarily to tobacco farming. Today the county has a population of about 22,000, and its biggest employer is Morehead State University. Established as a teachers' college in 1887, MSU now offers more than 80 academic majors. The scenic campus makes the most of its mountain and forest location.

Even though they had a college, the people of Morehead faced challenges of poverty and illiteracy in the early 1900s. Cora Wilson Stewart, from the nearby community of Farmers, was elected superintendent of Rowan County Schools. She knew the key to ending poverty was education, so she established the Moonlight Schools Movement in 1911. Her plan was to open school buildings to students of all ages in the evenings so adults could learn to read and write when they finished work for the day. This movement is credited with teaching more than 1,200 people from the area to read and write. One of these school buildings still stands on East 1st Street in downtown Morehead.

The **Daniel Boone National Forest** spans Kentucky, from the Tennessee border on the south on about 150 miles or so to just north of Morehead, so most outdoor recreation in this area is linked to this precious behemoth. The forest is so massive and full of opportunities to camp, mountain bike, fish, hunt, and rock climb, you could easily stay for weeks at a time, and some people do.

GUIDANCE Morehead Tourism Commission (606-780-4342, 800-654-1944; www.moreheadtourism.com), 111 E. 1st St., Morehead. Open weekdays 8:30–4:30. Located in the Morehead Conference Center, it's easy to find, right downtown. They have maps, brochures and lots of helpful tips.

For information about the **Daniel Boone National Forest**, go to www .fs.usda.gov/dbnf or stop by the **Cumberland Ranger District**, 2375 KY 801 S., Morehead. They have maps and information about the entire forest as well as local information about Cave Run Lake and Red River Gorge.

GETTING THERE Morehead sits just south of Kentucky's east–west expressway, I-65, so it's easy to access. For air travel, the closest airport is **Lexington's Bluegrass Airport** (859-425-3114; www.bluegrassairport .com). It is located about 70 miles from Morehead, and car rentals are available.

GETTING AROUND **Federated Transportation of the Bluegrass** (888-848-0989) operates bus routes through Morehead. They run Mon.–Sat., 6 AM–8 PM; the cost to ride the bus is $1 each way. They do not have a website, so please call for routes and information.

MEDICAL EMERGENCY **St. Claire Regional Medical Center** (606-783-6500; www.st-claire.org), 222 Medical Circle, Morehead. This 119-bed hospital was practically a gift to the area from the Sisters of Notre Dame in Covington, Kentucky. Prior to its 1947 opening, residents of the region had to go to Lexington or Northern Kentucky, both more than an hour's drive, for medical care. Local doctor Claire Louise Caudill set up a practice in Morehead but spent most of her time driving to homes delivering babies. A priest from Northern Kentucky was spending some time in the area, following the plight of this country doctor. When he returned home, he asked the good sisters if they could help, and they did by sponsoring the hospital.

ALCOHOL Rowan County is a moist county, which means that alcohol is prohibited except in the city of Morehead, which allows packaged alcohol sales. Kentucky law prohibits consumption of alcohol in public places and prohibits open containers of alcohol, so don't bring it to the Daniel Boone National Forest.

✳ To See

Morehead State University (800-585-6781; www.moreheadstate.edu), 150 University Blvd., Morehead. Founded in 1887 as Morehead Normal School, they currently have an enrollment of about 9,000 students, in about 80 degree programs. Take a tour of this scenic campus, which lies on the fringes of the Daniel Boone National Forest.

♂ **Tater Knob Fire Tower** (606-784-6428), Morehead Ranger District, 2375 KY 801S, Morehead. Visit the last remaining fire tower in the Daniel Boone National Forest. Climb up into this 10-by-10-foot building that sits high above the forest and take advantage of the view. The 35-foot tower, which was once used for spotting fires, was closed in the mid-1970s. It has now been restored and is open to the public. It's open dawn to dusk, but you might want to call the ranger district for directions on how to get there.

♂ **Kentucky Folk Art Center** (606-783-2204; www.moreheadstate.edu /kfac), 150 University Blvd., Morehead. Open Mon.–Sat. 9–5. Located in the historic Union Grocery building in Morehead, and with a growing permanent collection of over 1,300 works by regional folk artists, the Folk Art Center is a unique cultural experience. You will enjoy the amazing talent that creates this traditional mountain art. Free.

♣ ♂ **Minor E. Clark Fish Hatchery** (606-784-6872), 120 Fish Hatchery Rd., Morehead. Open weekdays 7–3. Call ahead to schedule a tour. This is one of the largest state-owned warm-water fish hatcheries in the nation, with largemouth bass, striped bass, walleye, and crappie. The fish are raised to stock area lakes and streams. Beautiful grounds are also a prime spot for bird-watching. Free.

✳ To Do

BINGO Cave Run Bingo (606-356-4025), 6950 US 60W, Morehead. Have fun and make some money, too. This bingo hall has 8,000 square feet with two large areas for smokers and nonsmokers. Play in the Tropicana Room or the Vegas Room; monitors are everywhere so you'll always know what's going on. Open Fri. and Sat. at 5 PM.

GOLF Eagle Trace Golf Course (606-783-9973; www.moreheadstate. edu/eagletrace), 1275 Eagle Dr., Morehead. This semi-private 18-hole golf course covers a maximum distance of 6,902 yards and is par 72. The grounds are lush and challenging with a variety of water, sand, and topographic hazards.

Sheltowee Trail Golf Course (606-784-2582), 1200 Clearfork N., Morehead. This public 9-hole course is surrounded by beautiful Daniel Boone National Forest. It is a par-36 course and covers 3,381 yards. They offer a 15-tee driving range and a snack bar.

OUTDOOR ADVENTURE Cave Run Lake Area (606-783-7001, 606-784-9709). This giant 8,270-acre lake was created in 1969 to prevent flooding of the Licking River. It lies on the western edge of Rowan County near a small community called Farmers just outside Morehead.

The pristine lake is almost entirely within the Daniel Boone National Forest. To preserve its beauty, there has been no private development along the banks, other than campgrounds. Known as the Muskie Capital of the South, the lake is stocked full of them, but fishermen looking for small- and largemouth bass, bluegill, crappie, white bass, Kentucky bass, channel catfish, flathead catfish, and trout won't go home empty-handed, either. The area also offers boating, swimming, and hiking.

Scott Creek Marina (606-784-9666), 801 S. Morehead. This well-stocked marina offers houseboat, pontoon, fishing, and paddle-boat rentals. While you are there, grab a hearty meal at **Captain Jack's Boat House Grill** (606-784-9666). They are right on the water and offer mouthwatering desserts and glorious sunsets. Open Fri. noon–9, Sat. 7–9, and Sun. 7–6.

Cave Run Bicycle and Outdoor Adventures (606-784-1818; www.cave runbikeshop.com), 995 KY 801S, Morehead. Open Tue.–Sat. 10–6. With hundreds of miles of world-class mountain bike roads and hiking trails in the area, you need to be equipped to start your adventure. They rent canoes, kayaks, and mountain bikes and sell camping equipment, maps, and other gear.

✳ Lodging

BED & BREAKFAST
✈ **Brownwood Bed & Breakfast & Cabins** (606-784-8799), 46 Carey Cemetery Rd., Morehead. Sleep in the large two-bed suite or in the all-natural one-bedroom wood cabins. Either way you will feel warm, cozy, and right at home in the mountains. Don't miss the southern-style breakfast with jams and jellies made by local Mennonite and Amish communities. Sit on the big front porch and let nature soak in. $

CABINS ✈ **Cave Run Lodging** (606-783-1234, 888-276-8759; www.caverun.org), 1190 KY 801 S., Morehead. Offering cabins and A-frame homes minutes to Cave Run Lake or the Daniel Boone National Forest. Each cabin and

A-frame is fully furnished with a stove, refrigerator, microwave, and cooking essentials. They all have a deck with a grill, a coffeemaker, and toaster. You'll be comfortable year-round, as all models have central heat and air. $–$$

✈ **Red River Gorge Cabin Rentals** (www.redrivergorgecabin rentals.com). One-stop shopping for your cabin needs in the gorge. They have about 10 secluded cabins, which can provide a romantic respite for two; a couple of families can be housed in their four-bedroom cottage. All have homey amenities, and some even have hot tubs or fireplaces, perfect for relaxing after a day of hiking. $–$$

CAMPING Twin Knobs Campground (606-784-8816, 877-444-

6777; www.reserveusa.com), 5195 KY 801 S., Morehead. Right in the middle of Daniel Boone National Forest, this is a big but secluded campground. Reserve a lakeside site or a wooded area to camp. Some sites have electric hookup. They also have a sand beach and a boat ramp. Open Mar.–Oct. $

Zilpo Campground (606-768-2722, 877-444-6777; www.reserve usa.com), US 60 E., Salt Lick. Lots to do here, like boating and hiking. They have a paved boat ramp and a sand beach. The mostly shaded campground sits right alongside the lake. The campground store has all the things you need for your stay. Open Mar.–Oct. $

✳ Where to Eat

EATING OUT All Seasons Flowers & Gifts & Café (606-784-4933), 134 E. Main St., Morehead. Open Mon.–Fri. 9–5, Sat. 9–3. This cute florist shop started selling sandwiches, and now it's a huge part of their business. Although the café isn't even listed on their sign, word of mouth has told the locals where to go for chicken salad on giant homemade croissants, deli sandwiches, and pasta salads. They have delicious desserts, too. $

Pops Southern Style BBQ (606-784-6378), 110 Hwy. 801, Morehead. Open Tue.–Sun. 10:30–8. Closed Mon. Making the most heavenly pulled pork, served slathered in savory sauce. It's not a fancy place, but locals

know it's where to go for good pork in this part of the state. If you are not a pork fan, Pops also serves up a delish smoked turkey sandwich and some wicked chocolate cake. $–$$

Pasquale's Pizza and Pasta (606-784-9111), 182 E. Main St., Morehead. Open for lunch and dinner Mon.–Sat. From the outside it appears to be a typical college-town pizza joint, and, well, it is, but the food is unexpectedly fabulous. Menu options include your typical pizza choices and toppings, but they also have phenomenal hot Italian sandwiches. You are sure to see college kids here for the inexpensive fare, but you'll also spot Morehead alums who stop by whenever they visit their alma mater. $

SNACKS Root-a-Bakers Bakery and Cafe (606-780-4282), 313 Flemingsburg Rd., Morehead. Open Tue.–Fri. 7 AM–6 PM, Sat. 8–2. Just follow your nose to this wonderful bakery, where you'll find pastries, breads, cinnamon rolls, and sticky buns. They also have lunch items like soups, salads, and sandwiches. Don't leave without trying one of the world-famous sugar cookies. $

Ole Thyme Sweetshop and Gifts (606-784-6656), 7075 US 60 W., Farmers. Open Thu.–Sat. 10–5. Calm your sweet tooth with some homemade fudge and candy. They also have a small gift shop where you'll find all kinds of quilts and Boyd Bears. $

✳ Selective Shopping

CoffeeTree Books (606-784-8364; www.coffeetreebooks.com), 159 E. Main St., Morehead. Fantastic indie bookstore where you'll find all the books you are dying to read, as well as art for sale by local artists. They are always hosting authors and special events, so check out their website to see what's going on. Grab a cuppa at their in-house coffee shop, **Fuzzy Duck**.

Old School House Antique Mall (606-783-1800), US 60 W., Farmers. Open Mon.–Sat. 10–5. Specializing in Amish furniture and quilts, they also carry a wide range of antiques and collectibles.

Frieda's Antique Shoppe (606-784-5993), 1750 US 60 W., Morehead. Open Mon.–Sat. 10–5. Specializing in antique lamps, lamp parts, shades, and accessories, they also carry lots of small antiques and willow furniture. Frieda knows what she's doing: Her antiques shop has been around for 45 years. Stop by and see for yourself.

Claypool-Young Art Gallery (606-783-5048; www.morehead state.edu). Open Mon.–Fri. 8–4. This is the largest exhibiting space in Kentucky east of Lexington, and it's loaded with contemporary art of American as well as international artists. This gallery is located in the Claypool-Young Art Building on the Morehead State University campus.

Calico Patch (606-784-7235; www.calicopatch.net), 155 Bluebank, Morehead. Call for hours. This is quilter's paradise. This shop carries all kinds of designer quilting fabrics, notions, and gifts. They have classes, kits, and a friendly staff who never tire of talking about quilting.

✳ Special Events

September: **Morehead Arts and Eats Fest** (606-780-4342; www .moreheadtourism.com). Every year the folks of Morehead block off Main Street and hold this fun festival right in the middle of the downtown. Booths from restaurants and organizations offer both sample- and full-sized portions of their menu items. They also have an arts and crafts fair, bands playing all day, and inflatables for the kids. The Rowan County Art Center also offers kids' activities inside. The festival draws quite a crowd, so come early and bring your appetite.

Poppy Mountain Bluegrass Festival (606-784-2277; poppy mountainbluegrass.com). Featuring five full days of bluegrass music and camping nestled in the 1,000 beautiful acres of Poppy Mountain. This event draws thousands of bluegrass music fans each year.

PAINTSVILLE, PRESTONSBURG, AND PIKEVILLE

These three cities, in the heart of the Appalachian Mountains, are worth the drive to this far eastern corner of the state. Although connected by US 23, the Country Music Highway, they each have their individual personalities that you will definitely want to sample.

Named for the colorful Indian markings on the white birch trees and rocks that lined the banks of Paint Creek, the city of **Paintsville**, which was first known as Paint Lick Station or Paint Landing, established a post office in 1824. The city sits at the confluence of the Big Sandy River and Paint Creek, in the heart of the Appalachian Mountains in Eastern Kentucky.

This remote location kept the city, which is the seat of Johnson County, from expanding much in those early years. In the early part of the 20th century, John C. C. Mayo, a local teacher, realized the mountains were full of coal and proceeded to become a millionaire from the bounty inside the hills. He lobbied heavily for a railroad, which finally reached Paintsville on September 1, 1904. By 1910, thousands of tons of coal were pouring out of Eastern Kentucky. This influx of money helped Mayo to establish banks, churches, streets, and public utilities in Paintsville.

Today Paintsville is home to about 4,200 people. Visitors can tour Mayo's magnificent home, the Country Music Museum, or even the birthplace of country music legends Loretta Lynn and Crystal Gayle. For outdoor recreation, Paintsville Lake State Park will meet all of your fishing, boating, and water sport needs.

Prestonsburg, the first town in the Big Sandy Valley, was also the first county seat in all of Eastern Kentucky. It lies in a valley along the banks of the Levisa Fork of the Big Sandy River. Prestonsburg was founded in 1797 by Colonel John Preston, who also named it, coincidentally, for himself. Today it is home to about 4,000 people who live surrounded by some of Kentucky's highest mountains.

Known as Star City of Eastern Kentucky, Prestonsburg achieved this name for all the entertainment and star power that comes from the region. Country music stars including Dwight Yoakam—born just a few miles from Prestonsburg in Floyd County—Loretta Lynn, Wynonna Judd, Naomi Judd, Billy Ray Cyrus, Tom T. Hall, and other big names are all from the Big Sandy Valley.

Prestonsburg is a must-see for those looking for a real taste of Eastern Kentucky.

Pike County, Kentucky's largest in terms of land area, covers 787 square miles. **Pikeville**, the county seat, was founded in 1823 and named, like the county, for General Zebulon Pike, a U.S. Army officer and explorer who discovered Pikes Peak. The area may not be as steep as Pikes Peak, but it certainly is mountainous. It is located right in the heart of the Appalachian Mountains. Although coal was discovered in the area before the Civil War, Pikeville didn't really start mining until about 1910, when the railroad finally made it to town. Today mining is still the largest employer of Pike County's 68,000 people.

COUNTRY MUSIC HIGHWAY
www.kentuckytourism.com

These strong people know they can move mountains. And actually they did. You can see their results at the Pikeville Cut-Through. It was a huge engineering project that actually rerouted the river, the train tracks, and a highway.

Come to Pike County and see what it's all about.

GUIDANCE Call or stop by the **Paintsville/Johnson County Tourism Commission** (606-297-1469, 800-542-5790; www.paintsville .org), 120 Staves Branch, Paintsville. Open 7–4 weekdays only. They are located right beside the Country Music Museum, so you can get directions and brochures and visit the museum at the same time.

Prestonsburg Convention & Visitors Bureau (606-886-1341, 800-844-4704; www.prestonsburg

ky.org), 113 S. Central Ave., Prestonsburg. Open Mon.–Fri. 8–4. Stop by this historic U.S. Post Office building to get maps and directions. You might want to stay awhile, because they also exhibit and sell locally created arts and crafts.

In **Pikeville** they have set up shop in the lobby of the Hampton Inn (606-444-5500; www.visitpikeville.com), 831 Hambley Blvd., Pikeville. They have brochures, maps, directions, and even Pikeville souvenirs. Pike County Convention and Visitors Bureau also has a helpful website—visit www.tourpikecounty.com to keep up with what is going on throughout the county.

GETTING THERE These cities are not close to any commercial airport, so driving there is the way to go. If you fly, you can choose either **Bluegrass Airport** in Lexington or **Tri-State Airport** in Huntington, West Virginia. Either is about two hours away. Prestonsburg, known as Star City, is centrally located at the confluence of five major highways. Those highways, which seem to make up a five-point star, are US 23 N., US 23 S., KY 80, KY 3, and KY 114, also known as Mountain Parkway.

GETTING AROUND The mountainside roads offer scenic views, but you'll have to drive yourself, because there is no public transportation. The downtown areas offer free parking everywhere. If you find yourself lost, don't be afraid to ask directions—the people are super-friendly.

MEDICAL EMERGENCY Paul B. Hall Regional Medical Center (606-789-3511; www.pbhrmc.com), 625 James S. Trimble Blvd., Paintsville. This 72-bed hospital serves a population base of more than 45,000 people from five counties. Formerly known as Paintsville Hospital, they have been serving Eastern Kentucky since 1920. **Highlands Regional Medical Center** (606-886-8511; www.hrmc.org), 5000 KY 321, Prestonsburg. Serving the areas of Floyd, Johnson, Martin, and Magoffin Counties with a combined population of over 90,000 residents, this hospital was started 33 years ago by a group of concerned citizens from each of these counties. **Pikeville Medical Center** (606-218-3500; www.pikevillehospital .org), 911 Bypass Rd., Pikeville. Founded in 1924 as Pikeville Methodist Hospital, this 261-bed facility serves the counties of Eastern Kentucky.

ALCOHOL Paintsville is situated in a dry county, which prohibits alcohol everywhere. In Prestonsburg, the entire county is wet, which means alcohol sales are allowed throughout the area. If you want a drink while in Pike County, you need to get it in Pikeville, because the rest of the county is dry. Actually Pike County is considered moist, which means, in relation to alcohol sales, that the county is dry but the city of Pikeville is wet.

✴ To See

In the Paintsville area

Loretta Lynn's Birth Place—Butcher Hollow (606-789-3397), Webb's General Store, Millers Creek Rd., Butcher Hollow, Van Lear. Tour the humble four-room cabin that was the girlhood home of the Queen of Country Music, Loretta Lynn. Just stop by **Webb's General Store** and ask Loretta's brother, Herman, for a tour. The authentic, rustic country store is a treat, too.

Coal Miners' Museum (606-789-8540), 78 Miller's Creek Rd., Van Lear. Located in the former headquarters of the Miller's Creek Division of the Consolidation Coal Company, they have a unique collection of tools and artifacts associated with the mining community. It is run by volunteers, so call ahead to schedule an appointment.

Mayo Mansion (606-297-1469), 3rd St., Paintsville. Visit the 43-room mansion of Eastern Kentucky's first coal baron, John Caldwell Calhoun Mayo. The beautiful three-story mansion was built between 1905 and 1912 in Classical Revival styling. Today it is a parochial school, and tours are by appointment only. It's a beautiful site, even if you just drive by.

Mayo Church (606-789-3296), 3rd St., Paintsville. After completing his spectacular home, John Caldwell Calhoun Mayo realized he needed a

WEBB'S GENERAL STORE

Deborah Kohl Kremer

www.kentuckytourism.com

MOUNTAIN HOMEPLACE

church, too. So just across the street from his home, Mayo built a stunning Late Gothic Revival stone church. It is well known for its awe-inspiring stained-glass windows and an organ that was donated by Mayo's friend Andrew Carnegie. Tours by appointment.

🎸 **US 23 Country Music Highway Museum** (606-297-1469, 800-542-5790), 120 Staves Branch, Paintsville. Open 7–4 weekdays only. Located next to the Paintsville Information Center off the Paintsville exit of US 23, the museum honors many of the country music entertainers who consider US 23 their home.

✐ **Mountain HomePlace** (606-297-1850), on the grounds of Paintsville Lake State Park, Staffordsville. Open Apr.–Oct.; call for hours. A working 1850s-era farm made up of original structures from the area. Come and see how things used to be. Visit cabins, a schoolhouse, a church, and a blacksmith shop while encountering interpreters, in authentic period costumes, who are performing their chores. The visitors center features a movie depicting the history of the early Appalachian settlers. There is also a small museum full of 1850s-era tools, clothes, and household items.

In the Prestonsburg area

Battle of Ivy Mountain Battlefield (606-886-1341), US 23, 10 miles south of Prestonsburg at Ivel. Call the Prestonsburg Visitors Center for directions. This 14-foot-high granite obelisk marks the spot of the Civil War Battle of Ivy Mountain. The conflict, which took place November 8, 1861, was a Union victory as the Confederates were outnumbered more than 12 to 1.

✐ **East Kentucky Science Center & Planetarium** (606-889-0303; bigsandy.kctcs.edu/EKSC.aspx), 7 Bert Combs Dr., Prestonsburg. Open Tue.–Sat. 1–4:30. Not only a science museum, it also features exhibits about math and technology. The 40-foot domed planetarium offers shows with close-up views of the night skies. Check the website for showtimes.

Middle Creek National Battlefield (606-886-1312; www.middlecreek .org), KY 114, Prestonsburg. Open dawn–dusk. This battle, which took place on January 10, 1862, ended Confederate supremacy in the region. Coincidentally, it also launched the career of James A. Garfield, the 20th president of the United States. Make a visit and see the battlefield where it took place.

✔ **Ranier Racing Museum** (606-886-1341), 113 S. Central Ave., Prestonsburg. Call for hours. See memorabilia such as trophies, pictures, and uniforms of the former Floyd County coal operator Harry Ranier, who became famous in Winston Cup stock-car racing in the 1980s. Ranier Racing fielded cars that won 24 NASCAR races, including three Daytona 500s. Small fee.

Samuel May House (606-886-9608, 606-432-3528; www.mayhouse.org), 1035 N. Lake Dr., Prestonsburg. Tours of the May House can be made by appointment. Built in 1817, it is the oldest brick house in the Big Sandy Valley. Tour this childhood home of Colonel Jack May, a leading Confederate officer in the Civil War. The 5th Kentucky Infantry was organized at the May Farm, and the house was used as a Confederate recruiting post during the Civil War period. This fine home, and the grounds surrounding it, has been restored to its original grandeur.

In the Pikeville area

♿ **Big Sandy Heritage Museum** (606-218-6050; www.bigsandyheritage .org), 773 Hambley Blvd., Pikeville. Open weekdays 10–5. Located in a historic railroad station in downtown Pikeville, this museum portrays the rich history and culture of Eastern Kentucky. For a snapshot of the region, study the exhibits about coal mining, devastating floods, and the infamous Hatfield–McCoy feud. $3 adults, $2 children, $2 seniors.

✔ **Elkhorn City Railroad Museum** (606-754-8300; elkhorncityrrm .tripod.com), 100 Pine St., Elkhorn City. Open Tue.–Sat. 10–4, Sun. noon–4. Closed Jan.–Mar. Even though it's about 35 miles outside of Pikeville, this is worth the drive if you're a train enthusiast. It was founded in 1990 by retired railroad employees whose fascination with trains and pride in museum's collection is obvious. They have two cabooses, motor cars, antique uniforms, and equipment. They even have a velocipede, a one-man-propelled vehicle used by track inspectors. More than 1,000 pieces of rare railroad memorabilia are well displayed.

Historic Dils Cemetery (606-423-5063), intersection of Chloe Rd. and the Bypass, downtown Pikeville. The first integrated cemetery in Eastern Kentucky, Dils is the final resting place for local notables such as Randolph McCoy, who was credited with leading the famed Hatfield–McCoy feud. Graves of soldiers from the Revolutionary War are also on the grounds.

☞ **Pikeville Cut-Through** (606-423-5063). Residents of Pikeville were plagued with devastating floods from the Levisa Fork of the Big Sandy River for decades. The Cut-Through Project, which was the most extensive land-moving project in the Western Hemisphere after the Panama Canal, moved 18 million cubic yards of earth. By moving the mountain, and diverting the highway, the railroad, and the river itself, the area was made safe from flooding. See the whole picture for yourself at the overlook at the top of the mountain. Get directions at the visitors center.

✳ To Do

ARENA FOOTBALL The East Kentucky Drillers (www.kentucky drillers.com). Pikeville's professional arena football league, just like the major leagues without the wind and the cold! The team plays home games at the East Kentucky Exposition Center, Nov.–Mar. Check the website for kickoff times.

BOATING/FISHING Paintsville Lake State Park (606-297-8486) in Staffordsville, is 3 miles west of Paintsville. Bordered by steep cliffs and wooded coves, this 1,140-acre lake is just the right size for boating, skiing, and fishing. It's stocked with walleye, bass, trout, and crappie. They also have a full-service marina with docking and boat-launching ramps. Rent a houseboat, pontoon, or fishing boat, or just fish off the dock. Open year-round.

DRIVING TOUR The Hatfield–McCoy Feud Driving Tour (606-432-5063, 800-844-7453). Pick up an audio guide at the tourism center. Listen to the antics of the famous feud between the McCoys of Kentucky and the Hatfields of West Virginia as you drive past authentic sites from their mid-1800s interfamily battle. In 2012 Hollywood created a TV mini series, *Hatfields & McCoys*, starring Kevin Costner. The show was very well done and if you see it before you get here, you will enjoy the tour even more. A fun fact about the mini series: The producers, in their infinite wisdom, decided it would be less expensive to shoot the entire production in the country of Romania instead of using the actual hills of Kentucky. Although Romania does a nice job as a stand-in, it is no Kentucky. Come see for yourself.

GOLF Paintsville Golf Course and Country Club (606-789-4234), 2960 KY 1107, Paintsville. This 18-hole, par-70 course is very well known in the area for its beautiful surroundings. It has a cool swinging bridge that connects the back 9 to the front 9. They also have a well-stocked pro shop.

StoneCrest Championship Golf Course (606-886-1006; www.stone crestky.com), 911 Clubhouse Dr., Prestonsburg. Come for the golf, stay for the view. Built on a reclaimed strip mine high atop a mountain, this championship-caliber, links-style course offers 18 holes with phenomenal views. Golfers can see about 50 miles in any direction from nearly every spot on the course. They also have a putting green, driving range, and clubhouse.

Mountain Pub-Links (606-437-0339), 8709 Lower John's Creek Rd., Pikeville. Settled right into the mountains, this 18-hole public golf course has a serene setting. This course offers club rentals, snack bar, and practice green.

HORSE RACING Thunder Ridge Racing (606-886-7223) 701 KY 3, Prestonsburg. This track offers harness racing in April and May. Because the schedule changes often, race fans are encouraged to call to find out post times and dates.

STATE PARKS **Jenny Wiley State Resort Park** (606-886-2711, 800-325-0142; parks.ky.gov). Located in the heart of the Appalachian Mountains, this park is named in honor of a brave frontierswoman. Jenny Wiley, who was captured by Native Americans in 1789, witnessed the murder of her children, and endured months of torture herself. Jenny Wiley escaped and went on to raise more children and live a productive life in nearby Johnson County. The state park is widely known for Broadway-style shows at the Jenny Wiley Theatre. This is Kentucky's only pro-

DEWEY LAKE AT JENNY WILEY STATE PARK

www.kentuckytourism.com

fessional theater east of I-75, and the productions really are first-rate. The park also boasts many outdoor activities on the 1,100-acre Dewey Lake, which covers 18.5 miles and offers 52 miles of shoreline. Fish for large-mouth bass, catfish, and crappie. Pontoon boats are available for rent at the marina. They tend to get rented out quickly on weekends in summer, so call ahead and reserve one early. The park offers miles of scenic hiking trails, a disk golf course, and swimming in the lodge pool. Stay in one of the 48 comfy rooms or 18 rustic cottages of the **May Lodge**, which is surrounded by peaceful woods and scenic mountains and overlooks Dewey Lake. They also have a 117-site campground with utility hookups, a dump station, and a grocery store. Dining is available at the **Music Highway Grill**, open every day: breakfast 7–10, lunch 11:30–2, dinner 5–9. Sun. brunch is served 11–3. Offering bar-style appetizers like a deep-fried onion, mozzarella sticks, and potato skins, as well as entrées ranging from mahimahi to baby back ribs. The menu covers a wide range of favorites and includes locally grown meats and produce whenever possible. The restaurant, which overlooks Dewey Lake, offers a lunch buffet every day and a dinner buffet on weekends. $–$$

♨ ♿ **Breaks Interstate Park** (276-865-4413, 800-982-5122; www .breakspark.com), KY/VA 80 E., Breaks, VA. Visit this interstate park—known as the Grand Canyon of the South—and you'll see how it earned its nickname. Located right on the Kentucky–Virginia border, the massive 1,000-foot gorge is the centerpiece of a park made up of 4,500 acres of mountains, forests, and cliffs. The park, which is best known for the rugged and scenic hiking trails, offers a lodge, restaurant, and campground. The 82-room **Rhododendron Lodge**, which is open seasonally Mar.–Dec., sits right along the edge of the canyon, so all the balcony rooms have phenomenal views. They also have rustic two-bedroom cottages, which are available year-round. The cottages are tucked into the woods and fully equipped. They also have an outside pool and laundry facilities, and they allow pets. **Breaks Interstate Park Campground** is open Mar.–Oct. 31. This wooded campground features 122 sites with full hookup, electricity, water, and sewer. They do not take reservations, however, so it is first come, first camped. The **Rhododendron Restaurant** is open 7 AM–9 PM, serving all three meals. They are closed on Mondays and Tuesdays. This is where you will find fine dining right in the heart of the Grand Canyon of the South. They offer daily lunch specials as well as delicious homemade soups and deserts. $–$$

Fishtrap Lake State Park (606-437-7496; parks.ky.gov), 2204 Fishtrap Rd., Pikeville. Somewhat of an engineering marvel, Fishtrap Lake was created when the Army Corp of Engineers constructed the highest dam in Eastern Kentucky. This giant lake covers about 1,100 acres. Come for boating, fishing, and hiking and enjoy the scenery.

www.kentuckytourism.com

BREAKS INTERSTATE PARK

WALKS The Kiwanis Walking Trail (606-297-1850). Located across from the visitors center at the Mountain Home Place. Enjoy a leisurely 1.6-mile walking trail around Paintsville Lake. Take a break on one of the many benches and maybe you'll see one of the wild turkeys or deer that are abundant in the area. Open from daylight to dark.

Historic Downtown Pikeville Walking Tour. Pick up a map at the tourism center. See 53 historic buildings and homes, some of which are on the National Register of Historic Places, while enjoying a walk through the downtown area.

✳ Green Space

🎣 ♿ **Bob Amos Park** (606-437-5116). This park, which is adjacent to the famous Cut-Through Project, offers a rubberized oval walking track, horseshoe area, tennis courts, basketball courts, soccer, Little League, and baseball fields. They also have a miniature golf course, a driving range, a picnic shelter with an enclosed grill, and playground equipment. Surrounded by open woodland, a nature trail takes you to "The Overlook," which is the place to get a bird's-eye scenic view of the Cut-Through Project.

Rucker Park (606-789-8540), 78 Miller's Creek Rd., Van Lear. Open to the public during daylight hours. Just east of the Coal Miners' Museum, you'll find this cute park. It is owned and operated by the Van Lear Historical Society. The park features an old C&O Railroad caboose, perfect for climbing and exploring. Basketball and volleyball courts, playground equipment, and a picnic shelter, too.

Levisa Fork River Park (606-886-2335) Front St., Prestonsburg. Located right in downtown Prestonsburg, this park includes a boat ramp, picnic shelter, and outdoor stage.

✳ Lodging

& **The Landmark Inn** (606-432-2545, 800-831-1469; www.the-landmark-inn.com), 190 S. Mayo Trail, US 23, 460, and 11, Pikeville. Around since 1962, this 103-room inn offers huge rooms and excellent service. The decor is somewhat dated but the staff of this independently owned hotel are so happy to have you, you won't even notice. $–$$

CAMPING ☸ **Paintsville Lake State Park Campground** (606-297-8488; parks.ky.gov), 1551 Hwy. 2275, Staffordsville. This campground features 32 developed sites with utility and sewer hookups and 10 primitive sites with terraced pads for tents. All have a picnic table, a campfire ring, and a lantern post. Restrooms, showers, and laundry facilities are close to all sites. Relax and enjoy the playgrounds, a sand volleyball court, basketball court, and horseshoe pits. Open year-round. Leashed pets allowed. $

✳ Where to Eat

In Paintsville

& **Carriage House Restaurant** (606-789-4242), 624 James Trimble Blvd. Open 7–9 daily. Located inside the Ramada Inn Conference Center, this is fine dining in Paintsville. This white-tablecloth, excellent-service kind of place has flame-broiled steak, charbroiled chicken breast, and jumbo fried shrimp. They also offer a jam-packed lunch buffet. $$–$$$

Wilma's Restaurant (606-789-5911), 212 Court St. Open daily 7–7. Wilma's is a staple in Paintsville. Everyone knows one another, and if you ask for a menu, well, they know you're from out of town. Get a menu anyway so you don't miss anything. Breakfast is available all day with local-recommended choices like biscuits and gravy or home fries. For lunch or dinner, try the open-faced roast beef, mashed potatoes, pinto beans, and corn bread. Wilma also has a mean apple pie. $

Mandarin House (606-789-5313), 507 S. Mayo Trail. If you are looking for delightful choices from the Orient, this is your place. Asian dishes like spicy-hot General Tso's chicken or hot-and-sour soup are recommended by locals. Fri. and Sat. nights they offer specials on seafood, frog legs, and prime rib. $$–$$$

In Pikeville

&. **The Top of the Inn at The Landmark Inn** (606-432-2545, 800-831-1469; www.the-landmark-inn.com), 190 S. Mayo Trail, US 23, 460, and 11. Serving three meals daily. Offers fine dining on the top floor of the hotel. Menu choices range from prime rib to fried oysters to a delicious chicken potpie. $$–$$$

Chirico's Ristorante (606-432-7070), 136 Pike St. Open Mon.–Fri. 10–9, Sat. 3–10. Closed Sun. Located in the historic McCoy home, of the Hatfield and McCoy feud. You will wish the walls could talk—but since they can't, you're just going to have to sit back and enjoy the amazing food that the Chirico family, who have roots in southern Italy, will be whipping up for you. All menu items are made from scratch, using recipes that have been handed down for generations. Make sure you save room for the homemade bread. $$–$$$

ḇ **Bank 253** (606-432-6566), 253 2nd St. Mon.–Wed. 11–11, Thu.–Fri. 11 AM–1 AM, Sat. 11 AM–2:30 AM; closed Sun. Housed in a former bank downtown—thus the name and a bar made from the former tellers' counter—they serve up typical American fare and have music on the weekends. Wide range of burgers, sandwiches, and salads and excellent appetizers like ham and cheese potato skins and to-die-for homemade beer cheese. Entrées served with "bottomless" salads. Full drinks menu, too. $–$$

Mona's Creative Catering (606-437-6662), 180 Town Mountain Rd. Open 10–9; closed Sun. Try this little spot for sandwiches and salads. Mona tries to make almost everything low cal or at least healthy. Try the alfa turkado sandwich, which is a tasty combination of turkey, alfalfa sprouts, and avocado. She also makes a heavenly angel food cake from scratch daily. $

&. **Rusty Fork Café** (606-754-4494), 105 S. Patty Loveless Dr., Elkhorn City. Open daily 9–9. This is a fantastic place to go for a home-cooked meal. They serve hearty breakfasts featuring homemade buttermilk biscuits, which they used to claim were bigger than a cat's head. They also have daily lunch specials like country-fried steak or chicken 'n' dumplings. Named for the Russell Fork River—which runs through Elkhorn City and right by the café—this cute restaurant is full of antiques, crafts, and locals. Stop by and get some brown beans and corn bread. $

In Prestonsburg

Billy Ray's Restaurant (606-886-1744), 101 N. Front Ave. Open for lunch and dinner. Closed Sun. This family-style restaurant was formerly known as Playhouse Pool Hall, a somewhat seedy bar and pool room. Owner Billy Ray—not *that* Billy Ray, but Billy Ray Collins—transformed it to a family eatery that is truly a hometown favorite. Serving up

Deborah Kohl Kremer

DAIRY CHEER

home-style meals like southern fried chicken and pinto beans, they also have homemade red velvet cake and apple dumplings for dessert. Just like Mom used to make. The walls are loaded with old photos of Prestonsburg and local sports teams. $

✍ **Dairy Cheer** (606-886-8666), 1384 N. Lake Dr. Despite the name, this fast-food restaurant specializes in big sloppy cheeseburgers, like their signature Smashburger, and crispy onion rings. They also have a tempting array of ice cream, sundaes, and shakes. $

SNACKS Country at Heart & Old Town Fudge Co. (606-886-8957), 128 S. Front Ave., Prestonsburg. Closed Sun. Owner Ken Wells makes creamy mountain

fudge daily. While you're there, have a cup of gourmet coffee or tea, or wake yourself up with an espresso. The shop also carries locally made Kentucky crafts.

✍ **Sherry's Candy Kitchen** (606-433-1470), 109 Division St., Pikeville. Mon.–Fri. 10–3. You're expecting candy, which is great, but Sherry also has lunch specials that will make you want to come back every day. Amazing fudge.

✳ **Entertainment**

Historical Sipp Theatre (606-789-6487; www.cityofpaintsville .net/sipp), 330 2nd St., Paintsville. Originally built as a vaudeville house, the Sipp has hosted the stars in the entertainment world from the 1930s to the present. Today it's both the downtown movie theater and the host of a "Bluegrass at the Sipp" music series. Call to see what's showing.

In The Pines Amphitheater (606-297-1850). In The Pines Amphitheater is located on the grounds of the Mountain Home-place at Paintsville Lake. It resem-bles a Greek amphitheater and has the capacity to seat 700. Enjoy outdoor concerts under the stars. The schedule changes throughout the year, so call ahead.

&. **Billie Jean Osborne's Ken-tucky Opry** (606-886-2623, 888-622-2787; www.macarts.com), Mountain Arts Center, 50 Hal Rogers Dr., Prestonsburg. This is the answer to Saturday-night fam-ily entertainment. Kentucky Opry troupe, formed in 1990, comprises a cast of very talented individuals, all of whom call Eastern Kentucky home. They present variety-style shows covering everything from musical acts to comedy. Perform-ances are held in the Mountain Arts Center's 1,050-seat theater. Check the website for showtimes and dates.

✳ Selective Shopping

Something Old and Something New (606-789-4210), 320 Main St., Paintsville. Tue.–Fri. 10–6, Sat. 10–4; closed Sun. and Mon. This is the place to find used and vintage furniture, antiques, and dishes. They also have new quilts, candles, and crafts for your home. The shop is set up so you can see what the merchandise will look like in your home. Friendly staff, too.

Country Cottage Gifts (606-297-6520), 325 N. Mayo Trail, Paintsville. Open Mon.–Sat. 10–6; closed Sun. You can't miss this stately historic mansion just off the highway. The home features 15-inch walls, nine fireplaces, and 1800s-era woodwork. While you are there, browse inviting home interior pieces like quilts, trunks, candles, and baskets.

&. **David Appalachian Crafts** (606-886-2377; www.david appalachiancrafts.com), KY 404, about 9 miles from Prestonsburg. Call for hours. David Appalachian Crafts is a nonprofit organization aimed at preserving traditional mountain crafts. The people of this region are an extremely tal-ented bunch, and after touring this gallery, you will be convinced, too. You will find beautiful quilts, handmade baskets, woodworking, and other crafting techniques that have been handed down for gen-erations. All items are for sale, so get something for yourself and you will be helping to supplement the income of these local craftsmen.

Pike County Artisan Center (606-433-0193; www.pikeartisan center.org), Main St., Pikeville. You will enjoy their wide selection of arts and crafts by local artisans. They are a nonprofit, dedicated to promoting the works of Eastern Kentuckians. Their slogan, "Where Community Meets Cre-ativity," really is true. You'll find goods such as paintings, pottery, and jewelry, all locally made. Call ahead to check hours.

ANTIQUES Southern Hospitality Antiques (606-886-9995), 5459 KY 321, Prestonsburg. This is a first-class collection of antiques, furniture, and glassware. They also have new gift items like silk floral arrangements, dishes, linens, and candles. Stop by this renovated service station and have a look around.

GALLERIES Mountain Arts Center Gallery (606-886-2623; www.macarts.com), 50 Hal Rogers Dr., Prestonsburg. Closed Sun. Enjoy the work of many local artists at this gallery. The exhibits change monthly, so you never know what you'll get to see.

✳ Special Events

April: 🐾 ✐ ♿ **Hillbilly Days** (www .hillbillydays.com). This huge fes-

www.kentuckytourism.com
MOUNTAIN ARTS CENTER

tival, celebrating all things hillbilly, has been a Pikeville tradition since 1977 and draws more than 100,000 people each year. Visitors enjoy live down-home music, rides and carnival games, and a grand parade where you never know

DAVID APPALACHIAN CRAFTS

www.kentuckytourism.com

what you'll see—from bands playing in the back of a pickup truck to gaudy jalopies to locals in crazy hillbilly costumes. It's all in good fun and it benefits the Shriners Children's Hospital in Lexington, Kentucky.

June: 🏅 ✍ ♿ **Hatfield–McCoy Heritage Weekend**. This event, founded in 1999 by Ron and Bo McCoy, promotes the cultural heritage of the world's most famous family feud. Although in 2003 the Hatfield and McCoy families signed a truce officially putting an end to the feuding, the festival has a celebration commemorating the signing of the truce. It includes a marathon run, an apple pie and old-fashioned stack-cake bake-off, arts and crafts, and bus tours to feud sites.

October: 🏅 ✍ ♿ **Kentucky Apple Festival** (606-789-4355; www .kyapplefest.org). For more than 40 years, people have gathered in Paintsville each fall to celebrate all things apple. Purchase homemade apple cakes, pies, and muffins, and breathe in and enjoy the aroma coming from the giant iron kettle of apple butter being cooked over an open fire. This event draws more than 75,000 attendees, who come for the free music, arts and crafts, a flea market, rides, car shows, and a parade.

🏅 ✍ ♿ **Jenny Wiley Pioneer Festival** (www.jennywileyfestival .com). This weekend captures the spirit of Jenny Wiley, a local pioneer woman who survived a brutal Indian attack that took the lives of several of her children. This weeklong festival includes arts and crafts, food, and musical entertainment. They also usually have a car show, a talent show, a beauty pageant, and even a parade. It takes place at various locations around the area. Check the website for events and sites.

LONDON AND CORBIN

Geographically, both **London** and **Corbin** are situated right along the foothills of the Appalachian Mountains. This location makes you feel like you're verging on an adventure . . . and very likely you are. Both cities are adjacent to the massive Daniel Boone National Forest and feature access to huge lakes and three rivers: the Rockcastle, the Laurel, and the Cumberland. So if you are looking for an outdoorsy getaway, this might be your place.

Recreation is not your only option, though. History buffs can traipse along the Wilderness Road, the route created by Daniel Boone as he brought pioneers into Kentucky. This was also the site of Camp Wildcat, a Civil War battlefield.

If you are in the area in September, don't miss the Annual World Chicken Festival, an homage to native sons Colonel Harland Sanders of KFC, Lee Cummings of Lee's Famous Recipe, and all things chicken.

GUIDANCE London–Laurel County Tourist Information Center (606-878-6900, 800-348-0095; www.laurelkytourism.com) is located at I-75, Exit 41. The office is open Mon.–Sat. 9–5, Sun. 10–2. You can't miss this center, right off the interstate. They even have a cute little gazebo out front where you could relax. Inside you'll find maps, brochures, and a very friendly staff. **Corbin Tourism Commission** (606-528-8860; www.corbin kytourism.com), 805 S. Main St., Corbin. Open weekdays 8–4. The Tourism Reception Center, right inside Corbin City Hall, has brochures you need no matter which direction you're headed.

GETTING THERE There is a **Greyhound** bus station in London (606-864-2040; www.greyhound.com), 1938 London Shopping Center. The nearest commercial airport is 70 miles away, **Lexington's Bluegrass Airport** (859-425-3114; www.bluegrassairport.com). If you can find a better flight into Knoxville, Tennessee's, **McGhee Tyson Airport** (865-342-3000 www.tys.org), you might want to fly there. It is 85 miles from Corbin and an easy commute right up I-75.

GETTING AROUND London is located at the intersection of I-75, the Hal Rogers and Cumberland Parkways, and US 25, so it's easy to find and easy to get around by car once you arrive. There is no public transportation, but you can call **Venture Cabs** (606-526-1211) if you need a taxi.

Corbin straddles I-75 and US 25, which splits into 25E and 25W just north of Corbin. Most everything runs off these two arteries, so make sure you have a good map, and you shouldn't have any trouble getting around. There is no public transportation, but you can call **Park Taxi** (606-549-1977) based out of nearby Williamsburg if you need a ride.

MEDICAL EMERGENCY St. Joseph London (606-878-6520), 310 E. 9th St., London. Changing its name in 2008 from Marymount Medical Center, this hospital covers a population of 50,000 in Laurel, Jackson, Clay, and Whitley Counties. It was founded in 1926, and at the time, it was the most modern hospital in Southeastern Kentucky. In fact, it was the only facility between Lexington and Knoxville located in a building specifically to house a hospital. Today the 89-bed facility provides a full range of medical, surgical, and obstetric services. **Baptist Regional Medical Center** (606-528-1212; www.baptistregional.com), 1 Trillium Way, Corbin. Located in Whitley County off I-75, situated in Southeastern Kentucky's "Valley of Parks," this 200-bed facility has three specialty units: adult and pediatric, burn intensive care, and coronary care.

ALCOHOL Laurel County is a dry county, meaning that alcohol sales are prohibited, but by-the-drink sales are permitted at some London restaurants. Corbin city limits are actually in two counties, Whitley and Knox. Both counties are dry but allow by-the-drink sales in restaurants that serve more than 100 people. Call ahead and ask if a restaurant sells alcohol if you really want a beer or glass of wine with dinner.

✳ To See

Camp Wildcat Civil War Battlefield (www.campwildcatpreservation foundation.org). This site is slightly complicated to get to, so it is recommended that you grab a map at the London–Laurel County Tourist Information Center. Due to its location on a major north–south artery, the Wilderness Trail, both the North and South wanted control of Camp Wildcat. On October 21, 1861, a battle took place in which the 5,400 Union soldiers defeated 7,500 Confederates. Today you can hike the walking trail to the top of Hoosier Knob, where you can look into the trenches where fighting took place. Stop by in mid-October to see enactments of the battle.

Deborah Kohl Kremer

KENTUCKY MUSIC HALL OF FAME

&. **Kentucky Music Hall of Fame and Museum** (877-356-3263; www
.kymusichalloffame.com), 2590 Richmond Rd., Renfro Valley. Honoring
Kentucky performers, songwriters, broadcasters, and other music professionals who have contributed to the music industry in Kentucky and
around the world. The museum
includes exhibits for instruments,
artifacts, costumes, and memorabilia. Some members of the Hall
of Fame include famous Kentucky
names like Crystal Gayle, Patty
Loveless, John Michael Montgomery, Ricky Skaggs, Dwight
Yoakam, and Naomi and Wynonna
Judd. Closed Mon. and Tue.

THE ORIGINAL KFC

Deborah Kohl Kremer

&. **Colonel Harland
Sanders Cafe and Museum**
(606-528-2163; www.kfc.com),
I-75 Exit 29, US 25W. Visit the
colonel's original restaurant, which
turned out to be the "Birthplace of
Kentucky Fried Chicken." First
opened in 1940, this is the home
of the still-secret 11-herbs-and-

spices recipe used at KFC restaurants around the world today. See where it all happened and take a look at some of the historic photos and memorabilia of KFC's humble beginnings. Museum-like displays, and a working KFC, too, so stay for lunch.

Dr. Thomas Walker State Historic Site (606-546-4400; parks.ky.gov/findparks/histparks/tw), 4929 KY 459, Barbourville. A physician and surveyor, Dr. Thomas Walker led the first expedition through Cumberland Gap in 1750, beating Daniel Boone by 17 years. Dr. Walker built the first cabin in Kentucky, a replica of which stands on the site today. Free.

✳ To Do

CANOEING AND RAFTING Sheltowee Trace Outfitters (800-541-RAFT; www.ky-rafting.com), KY 90, Whitley City. Just outside Cumberland Falls State Park, you'll find this one-stop shop for water sports. In addition to all the supplies you need for a day of outdoor fun, Sheltowee arranges rafting and canoeing expeditions on the Cumberland, Laurel, and Russell Fork Rivers. Call early because these trips fill up fast in the summer months.

FISHING Lake Cumberland is the granddaddy of them all. With a shoreline covering over 1,200 miles, it extends from the Cumberland Falls area into seven counties and downstream for more than 100 miles west to

SHELTOWEE TRACE OUTFITTERS

Deborah Kohl Kremer

Wolf Creek Dam south of Russell Springs and Jamestown. Fish varieties include five species of bass, walleye, crappie, and trout. Bring your rod and reel and toss in a line.

Wood Creek Lake. Located about 6 miles northwest of London, this 900-acre lake offers terrific fishing. In fact, it's the home of the state large-mouth bass record of 13 pounds, 10 ounces. Although it's too narrow for pleasure boating, there are lots of docks and ramps available to launch your fishing boat. The lake is stocked with rainbow trout, largemouth bass, smallmouth bass, spotted bass, white crappie, channel catfish, bluegill, red ear sunfish, rock bass, long ear sunfish, and yellow bullhead. While there, stay at the **Wood Creek Lodge** (606-878-0972; www.woodcreeklodge .com), 1961 Moiah Rd., London. Six fully equipped mini cabins are located just 1,000 yards from public boat docks and only 150 feet from the water's edge.

Laurel Lake (606-864-6412), 1433 Laurel Lake Rd., London. With over 200 miles of shoreline and 5,800 acres of water, this lake is protected by the Daniel Boone National Forest. Known for rainbow trout fishing, it also offers excellent largemouth and smallmouth bass, walleye, catfish, and crappie. Laurel Lake holds the state record smallmouth, 8 pounds, 12 ounces, caught in 1998.

Laurel Lake marinas

Grove Marina (606-523-2323; www.grovemarina.com). Rent fishing, pontoon, and houseboats and stock up on camping and fishing supplies and detailed maps of the lake. The marina is open year-round. They also have a public boat ramp. Other facilities include camping sites, hiking trails, and picnic areas.

Holly Bay Marina (606-864-6542; www.hollybaymarina.com). Get all you need for a boating weekend at this marina, open year-round. You can rent all kinds of boats, stock up on supplies, and purchase your fishing license, too. They have hiking trails and campsites.

Pier 1 Rental (606-864-5196), KY 192, London. Rent boats and Jet Skis as well as tubes, skis, and knee and wake boards. Call for hours.

GOLF Crooked Creek Golf Club (606-877-1993), 781 Crooked Creek Dr., London. Golf at this semi-private club and enjoy the beautiful 18-hole, par-72 championship course. They have a driving range and a pro on site to help you with your swing.

Sweet Hollow Golf Course (606-523-1094; www.sweethollowresort .com), 424 Sweet Hollow Rd., Corbin. This 9-hole public course has 12 water hazards spread out over 125 acres. They also have a lit driving range.

Cedar Rapids Country Club (606-256-4112), 3021 New Brodhead Rd., Mount Vernon. This 9-hole, par-36 public course features 3,228 yards of golf from the longest tees.

HIKING Travel the **Sheltowee Trace National Recreation Trail** (www.sheltoweetrace.com), a 269-mile multiple-use recreation trail that traverses the length of the **Daniel Boone National Forest**. The trail is named in honor of Daniel Boone. Sheltowee (meaning "big turtle") was the name given Boone when he was adopted into the Shawnee tribe as the son of the infamous war chief Blackfish. Go to the website for maps and more information.

OFF-ROAD PARKS **Daniel Boone Motorcross Park** (606-877-1364; www.danielboonemx.net), 775 Falls City Rd., London. Enjoy extreme sports racing featuring motorcycles, ATVs, bicycle Motocross, and cross-country mountain bikes. Weekly racing runs Mar.–Nov. Check the website for schedule.

London Drag Way (606-878-8883; www.londondragway.com), 3835 White Oak Rd., London. Come watch the excitement on the regulation-sized drag strip every Sat., Apr.–Nov. Family-style entertainment. Call for a complete schedule.

CUMBERLAND FALLS

Deborah Kohl Kremer

Deborah Kohl Kremer

THE DUPONT LODGE

D&K Off-Road Park (606-598-2776). Situated about 30 minutes off I-75's Exit 41, you'll find 3,150 acres of off-road trails, muddy, rocky, and hilly. Drag races every Sat. night, Apr.–Nov.

STATE PARKS *🐾 ♿* **Cumberland Falls State Resort Park** (606-528-4121, 800-325-0063; parks.ky.gov), 7351 KY 90, Corbin. You've got to see "Niagara of the South." This beautiful 125-foot-wide waterfall drops 68 feet into the Cumberland River. If you can arrange your visit during a full moon, you can witness a moonbow, a rainbow made by the light of the moon. Catch it here because it's the only moonbow in the Western Hemisphere. This park also has 17 miles of scenic hiking trails, fishing, rafting, horseback riding, and playgrounds. Stay at the **DuPont Lodge** with its massive stone fireplaces, solid hemlock beams, and knotty-pine paneling. Enjoy views of the Cumberland River and scenic wooded valley from all rooms and cabins. They have 52 hotel-style rooms in the lodge along with Woodland Rooms, which are adjacent to the lodge but slightly larger than a lodge room. These have kitchenettes and a small porch with a grill. There are also one- and two-bedroom cottages available. They are a little more secluded and private but offer a full kitchen, cozy fireplaces, and private patio or deck. Campers will enjoy one of the 50 campsites, all with electric and water hookups, showers, grocery, and a dump station. Close to the hiking trails. The campground is closed mid-Nov.–mid-Mar. Dine at the **Riverview Restaurant**, open 7 AM–9 PM daily, while you enjoy the breathtaking view of the Cumberland River. The menu is full of dishes prepared with locally grown meats and produce. They have a buffet at each meal, or you can order sandwiches, wraps, and salads as well as their famous catfish,

MCHARGUE'S MILL AT LEVI JACKSON WILDERNESS ROAD STATE PARK

Deborah Kohl Kremer

hush puppies, or frog legs off the menu. Make sure to ask for a window seat. $–$$

❀ ♿ **Levi Jackson Wilderness Road State Park** (606-878-8000), 998 Levi Jackson Mill Rd., London. Named for one of the area's first permanent settlers, the park is a tribute to the more than 200,000 pioneers who came through the area between 1774 and 1796. Most of these pioneers followed either the Wilderness Road or Boone's Trace, both of which go through this park's 800 acres. Visit the Mountain Life Museum, a re-created pioneer settlement full of tools and home furnishings from that period. Another section of the park is right on the banks of the Little Laurel River. Here you will find McHargue's Mill, a replica of a mill, surrounded by the largest display of millstones in the country. This state park also has a 146-site campground situated in the middle of a wooded area. The campground has a large swimming pool, mini golf, and planned recreation programs.

❋ Lodging

♿ **Cumberland Inn** (800-315-0286; www.cumberlandinn.com), 649 S. 10th St., Williamsburg. Owned by the University of the Cumberlands, this inn employs students to help fund their education. This beautiful property features standard rooms as well as suites with kitchens. They also have a heated indoor pool for year-round swimming. If you are traveling with a large group, try their Hearth and Home, a six-bedroom log home with more than 3,000 square feet. It is fully furnished and perfect for relaxing in the cozy family rooms or grilling outside on the deck. $

Country Cabin Retreat (606-864-7685, 606-682-0490), 410 W. Pinehill Rd., London. Nestled into the woods on the banks of a 3-acre lake is this cute cabin retreat. Built by the owners from trees on the property, this cabin is authentic, but still has modern amenities like appliances and indoor plumbing. $

❋ Where to Eat

In London
GiGee's (606-862-1052), W. 4th St. Open Mon.–Fri. 11–2. In an old white house with black shutters, right behind the courthouse, you'll find GiGee's. Nancy, the owner, named the restaurant for the nickname her grandkids bestowed on her. And those are some lucky grandkids, if they get to eat GiGee's cooking all the time. Everything on the menu is homemade, so it's hard to know where to start. But go ahead with salad, loaded baked potato soup, or a stuffed sandwich, but save room for dessert. GiGee whips up treats like homemade pies and cakes every day, but her most-ordered item is her strawberry pretzel salad, which locals eat as a

salad or a dessert, or possibly both. $–$$

Gondolier (606-878-1222; gondolieroflondonky.com), 305 W. KY 80. Open 11–11 every day. Either come to Gondolier's hungry, or be prepared to take some home with you. Their portions are huge—and so good that you don't want to stop eating. Speaking of huge, wait until you see their menu. It is massive, offering, more than 50 choices. Something else to keep in mind, though, is that their desserts are as good as their pasta dishes, so plan ahead. In fact, you might want to take a glance at the dessert case before ordering. $

Shiloh Roadhouse (606-877-9363), 218 Russell Dyche Memo-rial Hwy. Open for lunch and dinner every day. Crack your peanuts and throw the shells on the floor. It's even better than home, because you don't have to sweep them up. This steak house is similar to the chain-style steak houses but with a hometown feel. They have lots of choices of steaks and ribs, but people just rave about the baked sweet potatoes and the homemade rolls that you can cover with their honey butter. $$

✿ ♿ **Weaver's Hot Dogs** (606-864-9937), 131 N. Main St. Open Mon.–Wed. 8–3 and then Thu.–Sat. 8–7. This is the town's oldest restaurant, and you will feel the walls can talk when you eat there. The interior is covered,

INSIDE WEAVER'S HOT DOGS

Deborah Kohl Kremer

really covered, with old photos of people and events from the area. Get a history lesson along with one of their famous dogs. Locals come for the sausage and egg breakfast platter, but the chili dogs and wiener buns are worth getting off the interstate for. $

&. **Burger Boy Restaurant** (606-864-2675), 1625 S. Main St. Open 24/7. This restaurant looks a lot like it used to be a former chain eatery, the one that has a statue of a large boy out front holding a very big burger. You know the one. Burger Boy's logo is a boy with a large head wearing plaid pants and, well, holding a burger. Copyright infringement aside, this little hole-in-the-wall serves up good burgers. They also have a daily breakfast bar with staples like eggs, sausage, French toast, and biscuits. It's a stick-to-your-ribs kind of place filled with locals every morning— that oughta tell you something. $

In the Corbin area

&. **Patriot Steakhouse** (800-315-0286; www.cumberlandinn.com), I-75 Exit 11, 649 S. 10th St., Williamsburg. Open Mon.–Sat. 7 AM–9 PM and Sun. 7–2. You will find both southern and contemporary menu choices in this white-tablecloth restaurant. Whether you want fried green tomatoes or a juicy strip steak, they have what you are in the mood for. Try their appetizers, large enough for a meal. $$–$$$

Basil's (606-523-1114), 907 Beatty Ave. Open for lunch and dinner every day. Who knew you could get such authentic Italian deep in Kentucky? Stop by and visit with Chef Rick and you will see the pride he takes in the fabulous dishes he creates. He says the stuffed shells and the pizzas are his most popular choices, but his menu covers offerings from the entire boot of Italy. $

Ⓨ **The Depot on Main** (606-523-1117; www.thedepotonmain .com), 101 N. Main St. Open daily for lunch and dinner. Closed Sun. You'll have lots of fun at this locals' favorite right in the heart of Corbin. They serve certified Angus beef as well as a selection of pastas, seafood, and sand-wiches. Try their homemade potato chips for an interesting side dish. Stop in on a weekend to hear some local live music. $–$$

Dino's Italian Restaurant and Lounge (606-877-2525 London; 606-523-0600 Corbin), 384 Lon-

THE DEPOT

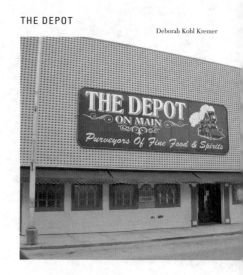

Deborah Kohl Kremer

THE DEPOT ON MAIN
Purveyors Of Fine Food & Spirits

don Shopping Center, London; 1895 Cumberland Falls Hwy., Corbin. Open for lunch and dinner every day. With locations in London and Corbin, if you are in the area, you are close to a Dino's. Although they are known for their pizzas and huge array of Italian pasta specialties, the huge menu will tempt you with Greek dishes, steaks, and the very popular fried catfish. Dino is a local resident whom everyone seems to know, so stop in and say hi. $$

Crabtree's Rootbeer Stand (606-528-4163), 129 18th St. When's the last time you had a real root beer float? Well, the folks at Crabtree's know how to make 'em, thick and creamy. They also have very good cheeseburgers and fries. Unfortunately they are only open seasonally, so call ahead to make sure it's their season, and to check hours. $

✳ Entertainment

Felt's Music Place (606-526-0606), 4676 5th St., Corbin. Open weekends. The Felt family has been offering entertainment to the people of Corbin for more than 40 years. Starting off with a barn dance venue, they transformed and moved into town in the 1980s to offer people a place to dance and hear live music. If they do not have a band booked, Felt's offers karaoke and DJ music. They do not offer alcohol, and families are welcome.

✳ Selective Shopping

✧ ♿ **Dog Patch Trading Post** (606-864-4531; www.dogpatch tradingpost.com), KY 80 and I-75, London. This family-owned business has been a part of Laurel County since the 1950s. They claim to be the largest and oldest

DOG PATCH TRADING POST

Deborah Kohl Kremer

souvenir store in Southeastern Kentucky. Stop by to get Kentucky-related treasures, joke gifts, and discounts on cigarettes.

Paula's Quilting Pantry (606-231-3543), 833 W. Hwy. 3094, East Bernstadt. What could be more charming than a quilting bee? That's what you'll find on Sit and Sew Days. Shop here to pick up all things related to quilting—fabrics, sewing notions, and ideas, too.

Flea Land Flea Market (606-864-3532; londonflealand.com), KY 229 at 192 Bypass, London. Open weekends year-round. With over 80,000 square feet of shopping and 500 vendors, if they don't have it, you probably don't need it very much anyway.

ANTIQUES Antiques and Accents (606-526-0646; www.antiques-accents.com), US 25E, Cumberland Gap Pkwy., Corbin. This shop is loaded with antiques of all kinds including furniture, quilts, and jewelry. They also have a huge selection of concrete and cast-iron benches and fountains for your yard.

On a Whim Antiques and Collectibles (606-526-7232; onawhimantique.com), 194 S. Stewart Rd., Corbin. Closed Wed. All kinds of antiques in this brightly colored fun Victorian house, but owner Nancy Chandler specializes in architectural salvage. She grabs the good stuff out of houses due for demolition, like staircases, doorknobs, and mantels. You really never know what you'll find.

✳ Special Events

August: ✿ ✿ ✿ **NIBROC Festival**. This festival, which takes its name from *Corbin* spelled backward, began in 1952. People come from all over to enjoy the four nights of free open-air concerts by world-famous performers. In addition to the music, they also have a run/walk, carnival rides and games, food, and crafts. A Closing the Streets Party starts it all off, all in downtown Corbin.

September: ✿ ✿ ✿ **Annual World Chicken Festival** (606-878-6900; www.chickenfestival.com). Held annually in downtown London, this four-day festival has been named Best Festival in the State by *Kentucky Monthly* magazine. It has received similar accolades from other noted tourism venues as well, so this is not one you want to miss. Celebrating the works of Colonel Harland Sanders, founder of Kentucky Fried Chicken, and Lee Cummings (Sanders's nephew), co-founder of Lee's Famous Recipe Chicken. Both got into the chicken restaurant business right here in Laurel County, so what better reason to have a festival? Have a fried chicken dinner, cooked in the World's Largest Skillet, which is more than 10 feet in diameter. Enter the chicken-inspired competitions, like the hot-wing-eating contest, the egg toss, or the Colonel Sanders Look-Alike contest. There is live music all weekend, as well as thrill rides and kids' activities.

HAZARD AND HINDMAN

Hazard is a coal town. This mountain community would not even be on a map had it not been for the discovery of the black gold hidden deep inside. Hazard is the seat of Perry County, which was founded in 1790. Both city and county are named for Commodore Oliver Hazard Perry, an American naval hero in the War of 1812, who had no apparent ties to the area.

This small town, which is not easy to reach, is known as the "Queen City of the Mountains." It is truly in the heart of the Appalachians. In the early years, the isolation of the mountains stunted its growth. It sometimes took more than two weeks to travel about 45 miles out of the valley and reach civilization. That changed in 1912 when the railroad finally made it to town. The area, now accessible, became more prosperous—yet even today, as home to about 6,000 people, it has its share of poverty.

The natural backdrop in the mountains makes a perfect setting for nature lovers. With the creation of Buckhorn Lake State Park and the recent increase in the elk population, tourism is on the rise.

Hazard did receive some notoriety in the early 1980s with the CBS television show *The Dukes of Hazzard*. Even though this show was based on a fictional county in Georgia, tourists began to make Hazard a destination; some of the show's stars have come for Hazard's annual Black Gold Festival.

Hindman, the seat of Knott County, is situated in a narrow valley at the fork of Troublesome Creek along KY 80. It dates back to about 1884, when the tiny berg was named for then Lieutenant Governor James P. Hindman. The town's economy has been largely dependent on coal, but tourism is quickly helping the area become a destination.

The area is rich with Appalachian culture and history as home to the Hindman Settlement School and the Kentucky Appalachian Artisan Center, two stops you must make here. Knott County, as well as its surrounding counties, is home to more than 5,000 free-ranging elk, the largest elk herd east of the Mississippi River. These massive elk were transplanted to this area in the late 1990s and now call it home. There are many opportunities to go elk-watching and see them in their natural setting.

Stop by and enjoy the slow pace of Hindman. The rugged terrain prevented the extension of rail service to the town, and its isolated mountain location kept it from growing at the quick pace of more centrally located burgs. The result is a relaxed group of residents who are happy to see visitors. Stop by the courthouse to see a statue of Hindman's best-known native son, Carl D. Perkins, who served Eastern Kentucky as a U.S. representative from 1949 until 1984. He is credited for his work to better the lives of people in the area by bringing in educational opportunities and aiding the underprivileged.

GUIDANCE Perry County Department of Tourism (606-487-1580, 888-857-5263; www.hazardperrytourism.com), 481 Main St., Hazard. They are open during the week to help you find your way around Hazard and Perry County. Lots of friendly help to plan your stay. **Knott County Tourism** (606-785-5881), 40 Center St., Hindman. Located right behind the courthouse is the tourism office. They are open weekdays 8–4 and they have maps, directions, and information about your stay in Knott County.

GETTING THERE Lexington's Bluegrass Airport (859-425-3114; www.bluegrassairport.com) is the nearest commercial airport, about 120 miles away. If you're traveling from the west, the Hal Rogers Parkway—which covers the mountainous region—turns into I-80 in Hazard. Just stay on I-80 and it will bring you right to Hindman.

GETTING AROUND The small mountain town of Hazard has some winding roads that can be difficult to navigate, especially in bad weather. But the downtown streets are marked, and there is plenty of free parking. There is no public transportation, but if you need a taxi, call **Miller Cab Company** (606-439-5161). Hindman is a small mountain town that's somewhat remote, but not terribly hard to navigate once you get there. There is no public transportation there, either, so get a good map and directions from the tourism office before you head out.

MEDICAL EMERGENCY Hazard ARH Regional Medical Center (606-439-6600; www.arh.org/Hazard), 100 Medical Center Dr., Hazard. Dedicated to rural health care, this 308-bed hospital is well respected in the area. Formerly part of the Miners Memorial Hospital Association, they operate hospitals in Harlan, Hazard, McDowell, Middlesboro, Morgan County, South Williamson, and Whitesburg, Kentucky.

ALCOHOL You cannot order a drink in Hindman or surrounding Knott County, which is dry. But in Hazard and Perry County, alcohol is available.

If you want a frosty beer with dinner and are not sure which county you're in, call the restaurant ahead of time.

✳ To See

⚳ **Bobby Davis Memorial Park & Museum** (606-439-4325), 234 Walnut St., Hazard. When local boy Bobby Davis lost his life in World War II, his parents built this museum to honor him and others who died. They have amassed a huge assortment of local memorabilia. The collection includes an outstanding photography display that traces the progress of Hazard from dirt streets at the turn of the 20th century through the turmoil of World War II. The museum houses a library and archives containing photographs, historical documents, oral history tapes, and artifact collections. Closed weekends.

Eversole Cabin (606-439-1816), Chavies. This dirt-floor log cabin was originally built around 1789 by Jacob and Mary Eversole. They added on around 1800, making it a dog trot cabin—really two separate cabins connected by a roof. The space between them was an open porch. It still stands today and is privately owned. It is one of the oldest landmarks in Kentucky. Call for directions and a private tour.

🎫 **The Mother Goose House**, KY 476, Hazard. You have to see this house to believe it. It is a stone structure made to resemble a goose, complete with a goose head on the top. It was built in 1940 by local resident George Stacy, who actually killed a goose to use its skeleton as a model. The oval-shaped base, which resembles a nest, is made of sandstone from nearby creeks. The roof is ribbed just like a goose, and the head is 15 feet high. The house is not open to the public, but take the time to drive by; you won't be disappointed.

⚳ **Kentucky Appalachian Artisan Center** (606-785-9855), 16 W. Main St., Hindman. Open weekdays 10–6, Sat. 10–4. This is a must-see while in the area. They have an overwhelming display of art exhibits and craft demonstrations of artisans from 49 counties of Eastern Kentucky. The center, which aims to help crafters and artisans make and sustain a living from their art, features works juried by the Kentucky Craft Marketing Program and the Kentucky Guild of Artists and Craftsmen. When you see the talent and dedication these artisans put into their work, you'll want to fill your home with their pieces. The building they call home is a work of art in itself. It was crafted from the sandstone of a nearby mountain around 1913.

Alice Lloyd College (606-785-5475; www.alc.edu), 100 Purpose Rd., Pippa Passes. This private liberal arts college was founded in 1923 by Alice Spencer Geddes Lloyd, a journalist from Boston who wanted to create educational opportunities for residents of Appalachia. Students are required to participate in the work-study program in janitorial, office, or food service jobs. This small college tucked in the mountains has a beautiful campus that you will want to explore.

Hindman Settlement School (606-785-5475; www.hindmansettlement .org), 71 Center St., Hindman. Open weekdays 10–4. Established in 1902, the Hindman Settlement School became the first and most successful rural social settlement school in America. Today you can tour the grounds, which include historic buildings, a museum full of Eastern Kentucky crafts, and a consignment shop loaded with unbelievable juried arts and crafts from the region. Free.

Buckhorn Lake Area Presbyterian Church Log Cathedral (606-398-7382), 300 Buckhorn Lane, Buckhorn. Dating back to 1928, this log building constructed of white oak is a sight to behold. Attend a service and enjoy the sounds of their famous Hook & Hasting pipe organ. Free tours are available by request.

✳ To Do

Saddle Up Elk Tours (606-642-3656; www.trailsrus.com/saddleuptours). Be sure to call for directions to the trailhead. Ride horseback through the rolling hills of elk country. See magnificent elk as well as other native wildlife while enjoying the scenery on one of their gentle horses. Tours last about three hours. Closed Jan. and Feb.

Knott County Sportsplex (606-785-5932; knottcountysportsplex.com), 450 Kenny Champion Loop, Leburn. Recreation is the name of the game. They have softball and soccer fields, indoor volleyball and basketball courts, an arcade, a bowling alley, a batting cage, and an indoor walking track. Fun for all ages.

Fugates Entertainment Center (606-439-4613), 197 Entertainment Dr., Hazard. Fun for everyone with bowling, skating, and, in summer, a water park with a wave pool.

Mine Made Paradise Park (knottcountyadventure.com). The address is 64 Clydean Rd., Leburn, but pay attention to the following directions because this actually takes you to a BP gas station at the intersection of Hwys. 80 and 1098. From there take Hwy. 1098 north. Go exactly 2 miles to top of mountain, turn left onto Elk View Dr., and follow the signs to the campground. It only sounds complicated, but it is worth the extra effort. What are you going to do with 43,000 acres of reclaimed coal land? Well, someone had the brilliant idea of turning it into 100 miles of looping trails for ATVs and dirt bikes. Dress for the weather and plan to get muddy.

✷ Green Space

Addington Wildlife Management Area (606-785-5881, 606-378-3474), KY 80, Knott County. From December 1997 through March 2002, free-ranging Rocky Mountain elk were released into southeast Kentucky, and this area is the perfect place to get a glimpse of them. The area is also full of wild Canada geese and wild turkeys. Open year-round dusk to dawn.

✒ **Perry County Park** (606-436-5095), 354 Perry Park Rd., Hazard. Swimming pool, tennis and basketball courts, 18-hole miniature golf course, walking track, picnic shelters, and playground equipment. Farmer's market every Wed. and Sat., May–Oct.

Battle of Leatherwood Memorial Park, KY 699S, Cornettsville. Named for the Civil War battle that took place nearby, today this is a nice park to shoot some hoops or play a few sets of tennis. There is also a walking track and a picnic shelter.

STATE PARKS ✒ ⅙ **Buckhorn Lake State Resort Park** (800-325-0058; parks.ky.gov), 4441 KY 1833, Buckhorn. Located at the northern edge of the Daniel Boone National Forest, Buckhorn Lake State Park has 856 acres of lush Kentucky mountain land for recreational enjoyment. They offer fishing and boating in the 1,230-acre Buckhorn Lake, as well as swimming in the lodge pool and disk golf. Stay at the **Buckhorn Lodge**, a warm and inviting inn featuring 36 rooms with private balconies so you can take in all the mountains have to offer. They also have executive cottages with kitchens and separate bedrooms for even more privacy. The lodge restaurant, **Bowlingtown Country Kitchen**, is open seven days a week for breakfast. Call for hours. It is named for a city that was located where Buckhorn Lake is today. This restaurant has a wonderful view. Local favorites are on the menu, but try the Bluegrass Special— country-style beans with home fries, coleslaw, and fried corn bread—if you want to get the feel for the place. $–$$

✒ ⅙ **Kingdom Come State Park** (606-589-2479; parks.ky.gov), 502 Park Rd., Cumberland. Straddling the Kentucky–Virginia border high atop Pine Mountain, you'll find Kentucky's home for the black bear. Sightings, which are not uncommon, are a huge draw to the park. Park rangers advise that most sightings occur in the summer months, and they can tell you where to go in the park if you really want to see one. But don't come just for the bears. With 1,300 acres of wilderness, forest, caves, and rock formations— including one that lurches 290 feet into the air at a 45-degree angle— there is a lot to see. There are rugged hiking trails, including the most popular, Pine Mountain Trail, as well as a lake for fishing and paddle-boating, a 225-acre nature preserve on the north face of Pine Mountain,

BLACK BEARS AT KINGDOM COME STATE PARK

and a gift shop. Most Kentucky state parks are named for their geographic location, but this one honors *The Little Shepherd of Kingdom Come*, a popular 1903 novel that was set in Civil War Kentucky and written by Appalachian author John Fox Jr.

Carr Creek Lake State Park (606-642-4050; parks.ky.gov), KY 15, Sassafras. Mostly known for excellent fishing, Carr Creek Lake also boasts the longest sand beach in Kentucky's state park system. So relax and swim or fish for large-mouth bass, crappie, and walleye. Located 15 miles southeast of Hazard, Kentucky, this lake covers 750 acres. It was created in 1976 by a 720-foot dam above the mouth of the Carr Fork River. The state park offers a marina where you can rent fishing and pontoon boats and stock up on supplies, as well as a 39-site campground and picnic areas. Keep your eyes open for wildlife. The unusual marsh environment in the area is inviting for ruffed grouse, great blue and green herons, wild turkeys, wood ducks, bobwhites, raccoons, skunks, and even red-winged blackbirds.

✳ Where to Eat

EATING OUT Frances's Diner (606-436-0090), 1315 Combs Rd., Hazard. Stop by and see Frances and she will set you up with a tasty meal. Stop in anytime, because they are open 24 hours per day. Home-cooked meals, like the meat loaf and mashed potatoes, are big sellers. Breakfast is available all day, served with biscuits that are heavenly. Look around at the photos scattered about. They are old pictures of local mines that have since shut down. If you look long enough, someone will probably come over and start telling you about them. $

Circle T Drive In (606-436-6984), 1519 Combs Rd., Hazard. Open 24/7. This family-style diner is packed on Tuesdays and weekends when the locals know they can get a chicken-and-dumplin' dinner with all the trimmings for under $5. Everything they make is from scratch, so if you're there another day, finding something good won't be a problem. Try the Kentucky silk pie for dessert. $

Kristen's Café (606-398-7250), 18543 KY 28, Buckhorn. Open daily, but hours change seasonally. Stop in for some fried chicken, and while you're there pick up some bait and maybe some camping supplies. Daily plate lunch specials. $

Holly Hills Mall Restaurant (606-785-0909), 92 Holly Hills Villa Rd., Hindman. Open Mon.–Sat. 11–8, Sun. 11–4. This cute restaurant inside the Holly Hills Shopping Center serves up home-cooked meals and has a locals-favorite lunch special. They have everything from burgers to salads but are best known for steaks and individual homemade pies. Try the butterscotch or coconut cream—or try them both, they're small. $

Five and Dine Café at the Kentucky Appalachian Artisan Center (606-785-9855; www.artisancenter.net), 16 W. Main St., Hindman. Open Mon.–Fri. 10–6, Sat. 10–4. Offering light lunches and unique menu items, the café aims to have as much variety as the artisan center itself. They offer sandwiches, soups, and salads and try to use locally grown products whenever possible. $

El Azul Grande III (606-487-0334), 124 Corporate Dr., #105, Hazard. Good service and fresh ingredients make this the kind of Mexican restaurant you will remember. Standard Tex-Mex

menu with a very casual environment. $

✳ **Entertainment**

&. **Greater Hazard Area Performing Arts Series** (606-436-5721; hazardperformingarts.com), 1 Community College Dr., Hazard. Presenting arts and entertainment events in music, drama, and dance, this organization features artists known locally and internationally. Check the website for the upcoming performance schedule.

✳ **Selective Shopping**

Buckhorn Lake Gift Shop at Buckhorn Lake State Resort Park (800-325-0058; parks.ky.gov), 4441 KY 1833, Buckhorn. Full of outstanding Kentucky Crafted products—juried craft items made by Kentuckians. You'll find beautiful pottery, handmade baskets, and scented candles. They also carry books by Kentucky authors and Kentucky Proud food items, like jellies, sauces, and candies. Grab a Buckhorn Lake T-shirt while you are there, too.

✳ **Special Events**

September: ❀ ✎ &. **Black Gold Festival** (606-439-6614; www.blackgoldfestival.com). Held in downtown Hazard, this tribute to Kentucky coal offers fun for everyone. In addition to the parade, food, arts and crafts, and live entertainment, they also have the Road Hazards Extreme Team Stunt Show, Black Diamond

Street Rod Show, and Black Gold Bike Show.

✿ ✍ ♿ **Knott County Gingerbread Festival**. Started in 1981, this festival features the world's largest gingerbread man, made from real gingerbread. He sets a new record each year. Also carnival games, a parade, free bluegrass music, a huge selection of food, and lots of arts and crafts.

October: **Fall Horse Ride** (606-785-5881). More than 6,000 people and their horses from all over the country come together each year for a weekend of horseback riding and camping. There are trails, some up to 37 miles long, over the 60,000 acres of a reclaimed mine site. Although they also have a ride in spring, the fall event seems to be more popular. Bring your own horse—but make sure you have an equine health certificate with you or you won't be allowed to participate.

PINEVILLE AND MIDDLESBORO

This area is rich in history, nature, and mineral resources. Historically, it encompassed Cumberland Gap, a natural phenomenon in the mountain range that made it possible for thousands of settlers to enter Kentucky between 1750 and the early 1800s. During the Civil War, both the North and the South recognized the value of the Cumberland Gap; it was eventually occupied by both sides during the course of the war.

According to scientists, the small city of **Middlesboro** sits in a valley that was created by an asteroid strike. Although that is an interesting fact, it is not something you would just notice when in the city limits. The small city sits right along the Wilderness Road, traveled first by pioneers but then by explorers who realized the value of land. Middlesboro is the result of the planned mining and manufacturing city, financed by Europeans. Although it never became the manufacturing giant they had envisioned (the backers were bankrupt by 1893), the area did survive on coal- and ironworks.

The city of **Pineville**, which is about 14 miles north of Middlesboro, is located where the Cumberland River cuts through Pine Mountain. It's one of the oldest settlements in Kentucky; it dates back to 1781, when it was called Cumberland Ford.

Today, with a county population of about 30,000, the area still survives on coal and tourism. Pine Mountain State Resort Park and Cumberland Gap National Historical Park are in the 361 square miles of Bell County. Hunting, hiking, and fishing are the huge attractions, and the options are limitless. Come all the way over to Bell County and see where Kentucky really started.

GUIDANCE Come for guidance and tour a local museum at the same time. The **Bell County Tourism Commission and Visitor Center** is housed inside the **Arthur Museum** (800-988-1075; www.mountain gateway.com), 2215 Cumberland Ave., Middlesboro. This museum includes the artifacts and memorabilia of Alexander A. Arthur, founder of Middlesboro. This wonderful 1890s home is on the National Historic Register. Tour the grounds and then get information and maps for the rest of your trip. Closed weekends.

GETTING THERE To get to this mountainous community by private plane, you can fly into **Middlesboro Bell County Airport** (606-242-3134), but if you need to fly commercial, your best bet is **Knoxville McGhee Tyson Airport** (865-342-3000; www.tys.org), which is just 56 miles away.

GETTING AROUND The communities of Middlesboro and Pineville are about 14 miles apart. Middlesboro is about eight times the size of Pineville, the county seat. Both have well-marked streets but neither has public transportation, so you'll have to get around by car.

MEDICAL EMERGENCY Pineville Community Hospital (606-337-3051; www.pinevillehospital.com), 850 Riverview Ave., Pineville. When it opened in 1938 with 40 beds, PCH was a leader in patient care. Today with 150 beds, this tradition continues.

ALCOHOL The county is dry, meaning alcohol sales are prohibited, but Pineville restaurants that serve more than 100 people can sell alcohol by the drink.

✳ To See

✍ **Cumberland Gap Tunnel** (606-248-2817), US 25E, Middlesboro. Experience one of the region's most ambitious construction projects by traveling through the 4,600-foot tunnel that passes under the Cumberland Gap. Seventeen years in the making, at a cost of $280 million, this tunnel was created to replace narrow and dangerous roads through the gap and restore the area to resemble the path used by the pioneers of the late 1700s. It opened in 1996.

Bell County Coal House and Coal Museum (606-248-1075), 215 N. 20th St., Middlesboro. Built in 1926 out of 42 tons of bituminous coal, this building is hard to miss. Known as the Coal House, it now houses the Middlesboro Chamber of Commerce. Get glimpses of the coal-mining life at this outdoor museum featuring a mine locomotive, a coal-cutting machine, and other mining equipment from the 1960s.

✳ To Do

FISHING Chenoa Lake (606-337-3011), KY 190, Pineville. This 37-acre lake is well stocked with largemouth bass, green sunfish, white crappie, channel catfish, bluegill, red ear sunfish, and brown bullhead. It is 15 miles west of Pineville.

Cannon Creek Lake, US 25E, Pineville. Six miles south of Pineville, you can fish for rainbow trout, largemouth bass, smallmouth bass, spotted bass, warmouth, channel catfish bluegill, and crappie on this 243-acre lake.

GOLF Wasioto Winds Golf Course at Pine Mountain State Resort Park (606-337-3066; parks.ky.gov), 1050 State Park Rd., Pineville. This course is situated in a valley between two mountains, hence the name (pronounced *wah-see-OH-tuh*), which means "valley of the deer." This championship 18-hole course has a practice range, putting greens, and an indoor-use training center.

OFF-ROADING Holler Crawlers Off-Road Club (606-499-0567; www .wildernesstrailoffroadpark.net), Hwy. 119 Trailhead, at 7526 US 119, Pineville. Bring your four-wheel vehicle and hit some of the most fun and challenging trails you'll ever find. The trails are open year-round minus Kentucky deer rifle season, which is usually the third week of November. They are open to the public and are free of charge. Covering about 9,000 acres and over 100 miles of trail, it is never the same adventure twice. Camping and fishing available, too.

✳ Green Space

Shillalah Creek Public Wildlife Area (606-248-2482), 2215 Cumberland Ave., Middlesboro. Running along Brush Mountain just north of Cumberland Gap is this 2,640-acre, old-growth forest. Turkey, deer, raccoons, squirrels, and grouse can all be found here, but you're going to need a four-wheel-drive vehicle to navigate the rugged terrain and steep, undeveloped roads. You can hunt here, too, but you'll need a permit.

STATE PARKS ✐ ♿ Cumberland Gap National Historical Park (606-248-2817; www.nps.gov), Middlesboro. This huge national park, which covers 20,000 acres in Kentucky, Virginia, and Tennessee, is the largest historical park in the nation. Known as the Doorway to the West, Cumberland Gap forms a major break in the Appalachian Mountain chain, which covers about 1,500 miles from Canada to Alabama. The gap was first used by migrating buffalo, and then by Native Americans. As pioneers headed west, they, too, used the gap instead of traveling over the 3,000-foot mountains. From 1775 to 1810, around 300,000 people passed through. Today visitors can tour one of the 24 caves and the historic Hensley Settlement, a mountain village that was used in the early 1900s. With 20,500 acres of park (with 14,000 acres of wilderness), the hiking is spec-

www.kentuckytourism.com

CUMBERLAND GAP

tacular. You'll feel like the settlers did as they walked these same trails. Hike to Pinnacle Overlook so you can see the breathtaking view that encompasses four states. There are unbelievable views in each direction, breathtaking waterfalls, and lots of trees, flowers, and wildlife. Keep your eye out for black bears.

🎣 ♿ **Pine Mountain State Resort Park** (606-337-3066; parks.ky.gov), 1050 State Park Rd., Pineville. Visit Kentucky's first state park, which sits high atop the Kentucky Ridge State Forest. This is Kentucky's second largest state forest, with 11,363 acres of unspoiled wilderness. The hiking alone is fantastic, but you'll also find mini golf, an outdoor pool, and play-grounds. In summer, they have daily recreational activities at the on-site nature center. Stay at the **Herndon J. Evans Lodge** for a real getaway. This lodge offers 30 rooms, each with a private patio or balcony to enjoy the mountain views. They also have rustic one- and two-bedroom cottages or one- and two-bedroom log cabins with stone fireplace and private deck. While you are there, try some local cuisine at the **Mountain View Restaurant**. Open 7 AM–9 PM daily. Enjoy the unforgettable mountain scenery from every seat in the dining room. The menu features a wide variety of choices, using locally raised meats and produce when available.

✳ Lodging

The Cumberland Manor Bed and Breakfast (606-248-4299; www.cumberlandmanorbedand breakfast.com), 208 Arthur Heights, Middlesboro. Surrounded by mountains in all directions, guests really feel like they've left their cares behind. Built in 1890, this huge Victorian beauty boasts a gorgeous hand-carved staircase, stained-glass windows, and intricate woodwork and flooring. They have four inviting guest rooms, but you'll want to spend some time on the great big front porch, which offers views of three states. $

✳ Where to Eat

The Flocoe (606-337-2034), 122 W. Kentucky Ave., Pineville. Open for lunch only. Closed weekends. Created as a sweets shop in the 1920s, this former drugstore is located right on the courthouse square. If you are craving a home-cooked meal, this is your place. Locals rave about their chicken and dumplings, so try some to see what they are talking about. $

Avenue Cafe & Antiques (606-248-3958), 1915 W. Cumberland Ave., Middlesboro. Open for lunch only. Closed weekends. Situated right on the main drag of Middlesboro, in a historic building, this is the place to go for a yummy chicken salad sandwich and daily hot lunch specials. Thursday is spaghetti day, really popular with local lunch crowd. $

Conley's Drive In (606-248-1721), 707 E. Lothbury Ave, Mid-dlesboro. Chain restaurants have been popping up all over the country that try to re-create the old-fashioned drive-in-style restaurant with carhop service. Well, forget about them. Conley's is the real deal. In business since 1960, they send a carhop out to your vehicle to take your order for their juicy burgers and fries or their ever-famous hot dogs. Go for the experience and the food. $

✳ Selective Shopping

Cumberland Crafts (606-242-3699), US 25E, Middlesboro. Located in the Cumberland Gap National Historical Park Visitors Center, this unique gift shop offers handmade crafts created by members of the Southern Highland Craft Guild. They have beautiful selections of pottery, woodworking, photography, paintings, and jewelry.

✳ Special Events

May: 🐾 ✍ ♿ **The Kentucky Mountain Laurel Festival** (www .kmlf.org). Started in 1931, this festival celebrates the blooming of the native mountain laurel. It also honors Dr. Thomas Walker, the first European to settle in the region. Walker's settlement was somewhere around 1750, which was 40 years before Kentucky became a state. The festival features entertainment, carnival games, a grand ball, and a street dance. The highlight is the crowning of the Mountain Laurel Queen. The festival is held on the grounds of Pine Mountain State Resort Park.

South-Central Kentucky

2

BOWLING GREEN, GLASGOW,
AND THE HORSE CAVE AREA

CAMPBELLSVILLE, GREENSBURG,
AND THE GREEN RIVER LAKE AREA

THE LAKE CUMBERLAND AREA,
INCLUDING SOMERSET, JAMESTOWN,
RUSSELL SPRINGS, AND MONTICELLO

INTRODUCTION:
SOUTH-CENTRAL KENTUCKY

This southern section of Kentucky is filled with deep lakes and
sometimes-raging rivers, which ultimately created caves and caverns, all
of which make this Kentucky's recreation mecca.

On the western edge is cave country. Anchored by Mammoth Cave, the
largest cave in the world, and surrounded by smaller and privately owned
caves, it is a spelunker's paradise. No matter which cave you choose, you'll
be sure to see stalactites, which form on the ceiling by slowly dripping
water, and stalagmites, which grow upward. If a stalactite and a stalagmite
meet, it results in a column. Although these cave decorations are a common occurrence underground, they are a marvel each time you see one.

If hiking is your passion, the heavily wooded terrain and slightly rolling
hills of Southern Kentucky could be just what you're looking for. At Mammoth Cave National Park, they have 52,000 acres of wooded trails for hikers and horseback riders. About half of the park's visitors come for the
hiking and never even go into the cave. The hiking, hunting, and nature-
watching opportunities spread eastward into the area of Green River Lake
and Lake Cumberland, which is adjacent to the Daniel Boone National
Forest. Just on the border of Tennessee is the Big South Fork National
Recreation Area, which offers 125,000 acres of gorges, sandstone bluffs,
and miles of trails that lead to waterfalls, natural arches, and other wonders of nature.

But if it's the water that's calling you, your possibilities are vast. With
rivers like the Nolin River, Green River, and Cumberland River all flowing
through the region, as well as the human-made Nolin River Lake, Green
River Lake, and Lake Cumberland, you'll be hard-pressed not to catch
some kind of fish while you're there. These lakes are stocked, so do a little
research to find the spot that has your choice of catch.

Although the fish are abundant, some people just like to boat. Come
to the lakes and rivers of Kentucky to enjoy kayaking, canoeing, and

houseboating. If you don't have a boat, all the lakes offer rentals of various sizes of boats, as well as the supplies you need for your lake outing.

Tucked in among the lakes, caves, and rivers, you'll find the small towns and bergs that make Kentucky special. Tiny towns like Jamestown and Greenville will welcome you with open arms. They offer hometown-style diners, cute specialty shops, and antiques-laden downtown districts. They also have various attractions like parks, old-time drive-in movies, and a few sprinklings of history, just to keep it interesting.

BOWLING GREEN, GLASGOW, AND THE HORSE CAVE AREA

I n the heart of downtown **Bowling Green** is the 2-acre Fountain Square Park, which is the city center and focal point for this charming town. The fountain, statues, landscape, and ages-old trees draw you in, much as the town itself does. The 19th-century buildings, nearby Western Kentucky University campus, and outlying rolling farmland make you want to get to know this area, which has so much more to offer than just the caves and Corvettes that get all the publicity.

As the fourth most populous town in Kentucky, Bowling Green has roots dating back to its incorporation in 1798. Although Kentucky was considered neutral in the Civil War, the Confederate loyalists declared the city to be the state capital in 1861. This honor didn't last long, as it was taken over by the Union army in 1862.

You can tour various aspects of Bowling Green's role in the War Between the States on the Civil War Discovery Trail. This itinerary includes visits to caves where soldiers purportedly hid out, historical markers and homes, and Riverview at Hobson Grove Historic House Museum, a home whose foundation was used as a fort.

As home to the longest cave system known in the world today, Mammoth Cave has to be seen to be believed. Plan to visit Mammoth Cave National Park and enjoy the forested park and a magnificent cave tour. With more than 70 miles of trails and 52,000 acres of secluded natural preservation available, lots of visitors never even head underground. The park has a plethora of tours and caving adventures, one to meet any and all of your needs. With several smaller, lesser-hyped cave tours in the area, novice cavers could enjoy a privately owned cave just as well. Wherever you go, you'll find stalactites, stalagmites, and formations that were created millions of years before we were born.

If boating and fishing are your calling, you are heading in the right direction. Nolin River, Green River, Barren River, and Barren River Lake

State Resort Park offer an assortment of marinas and fishing spots perfect for your catch of choice.

A stop in the area wouldn't be complete, however, without a nod to General Motors and their roadster, the Corvette. Tour the assembly plant and the museum that pays homage to the car. Or stick around for the annual Corvette Homecoming Festival in July, when thousands of loyal 'Vette owners bring their cars and their enthusiasm to Bowling Green for a weekend of fun.

GUIDANCE Pick up advice, maps, and brochures at the **Bowling Green Area Convention and Visitors Bureau** (800-326-7465; www.visitbgky .com), 352 Three Springs Rd., Bowling Green. The Cave City Convention Center and Tourism Bureau, located at the visitors center at I-65 Exit 53, is also jam-packed with maps, coupons, and brochures.

GETTING THERE Bowling Green is about two hours south of Louisville and one hour north of Nashville, Tennessee. For airline travel, check both for deals. The **Louisville International Airport** (502-368-6524; www.fly louisville.com) is located at the intersection of I-65 and I-264. **Nashville International Airport** (615-275-1675; www.flynashville.com) is an easy trip right down I-65. Car rentals are available at both airports. From Nashville, you can take the **Airport Shuttle of Bowling Green** (270-996-1227, 866-234-8705; www.anytimetransport.com). **Greyhound Bus** also serves Bowling Green (270-842-5131; www.greyhound.com); the station is located at 55 Parker Ave.

GETTING AROUND Bowling Green, with its small-town feel, has well-marked streets and is easy to navigate by car. But if you are looking for public transportation, bus service is available. **Bowling Green Public Transit** (270-782-3162; www.casoky.org/transportation) offers fixed-route bus service Mon.–Fri. beginning at 7 AM and ending at 6 PM. Check the website for schedules and routes.

MEDICAL EMERGENCY TriStar Greenview Regional Hospital (277-793-1000; www.greenviewhospital.com), 1801 Ashley Circle, Bowling Green. This hospital has 211 beds and serves Bowling Green and Warren County.

ALCOHOL Although it is the seat of Warren County—a dry county where alcohol sales are prohibited—Bowling Green does permit alcohol sales within the city limits. Barren County, home of Glasgow and Cave City, is also dry, but allows alcohol sales by the drink at restaurants in these two cities.

✴ To See

🍴 🎣 ♿ **National Corvette Museum and Plant Tour** (270-781-7973, 800-53-VETTE; www.corvettemuseum.com), 350 Corvette Dr., Bowling Green. Museum open 8–5 (Central Time), seven days a week year-round except Easter, Thanksgiving, Christmas Eve, Christmas Day, and New Year's Day. Welcome to the world of the 'Vette. This huge 68,000-square-foot showroom is an ode to the true American sports car, the Corvette. With 75 on display, you can learn about each one and see rare collections and memorabilia. While you are there, sign up to tour the assembly plant. Every Corvette driven is made at this plant, so when you see one on the road, it will remind you of Kentucky. $10 adults, $8 seniors, $5 youth (6–16), under 6 free, family (same household) $25, active military free. Plant tours, conducted just across the street from the museum, are $7 per person, free for active military. Visit the website to make the required reservations: www.bowlinggreenassemblyplant.com; 270-745-8019. Tours available Mon.–Thu. at 8:30 AM, 11:30 AM, 12:45 PM, and 2 PM. All participants must have closed-toe shoes and be older than 7. No cameras or purses allowed on tour.

🎣 ♿ **Barren River Imaginative Museum of Science** (270-843-9779; www.brimsbg.org), 1229 Center St., Bowling Green. Open Thu.–Sat. 10–3, Sun. 1–4. Enjoy more than 50 fun science exhibits like the van de Graff Electrostatic Generator, which will make your hair stand on end,

CORVETTE MUSEUM

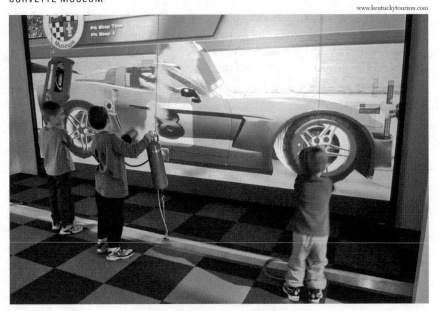

www.kentuckytourism.com

and the BRIMS Blaster where you can experience the force of a mini tornado. They have a huge model train exhibit, too. $5 adults, $4 children.

Riverview at Hobson Grove (270-843-5565; www.bgky.org/riverview), 1100 W. Main Ave., Bowling Green. Tue.–Sat. 10–4, Sun. 1–4. Closed late Dec.–Jan. and all major holidays. This late-1800s Victorian home was used for storage of Confederate munitions when the Rebel forces held Bowling Green. Tour the home and grounds now that it has been restored to its original splendor. On the National Register of Historic Places, this home lets visitors see how families and their servants lived during that time period. Admission and 45-minute tour, $7 adults, $3 students; under 6 free.

Ġ **Shaker Museum at South Union** (800-811-8379; www.shaker museum.com), 850 Shaker Museum Rd., Auburn. Open Mar. 1–Nov. 30, Tue.–Sat. 9–5 and Sun. 1–5. During winter hours (Dec. 1–Feb.), the museum is open for tours Tue.–Sat. 10–4. Closed on major holidays. This site was home to the Shakers, a communal religious sect that lived in the area from 1807 until 1922. The museum is filled with original furniture, crafts, textiles, and manuscripts of this group, named for their extremely active style of worship. Tour the buildings and see how they lived. $8 adults, $4 ages 6–12; 5 and under free.

Western Kentucky University (270-745-2497; www.wku.edu), 1906 College Heights Blvd., Bowling Green. What started out in 1906 as a teachers' college has grown to 18,000 students and 88 college majors. The campus, built high on a hill overlooking the Barren River Valley, is home to the Hilltoppers. While on campus, plan a visit to the Kentucky Library and Museum, where they collect pieces of Kentucky history. Learn more about native son Duncan Hines, a traveling salesman who became well known for his restaurant reviews in the 1930s. View their rich collection of maps, letters, furniture, toys, diaries, and even an 1800s log cabin.

✄ **Historic L&N Depot, Railpark, and Train Museum** (270-745-0090; www.historicrailpark.com), 401 Kentucky St., Bowling Green. Mon.–Sat. 9–5, Sun. 1–4. Closed Mon. during winter months. Housed inside the 1925 Classic Revival–style L&N depot, the museum has interactive exhibits and artifacts from the heyday of train travel. Take a private tour of the real, retired train cars on site like the 1953 Luxury Pullman Sleeper Car and the Chessie Class Caboose. $12 adults, $5 under 12.

🍴 ✄ Ġ **Kennys Farmhouse Cheese** (888-571-4029; www.kennys farmhousecheese.com), 2033 Thomerson Park Rd., Austin. Mon.–Fri. 9–3, Sat. 9–1, closed Sun. Kenny Mattingly has been making cheese on his 200-acre family dairy farm for about 10 years, and he invites visitors in to see the whole process. Don't leave without some Gouda, Colby, cheddar, or the variety of your choice. Kenny sells 70,000 pounds a year, so he must know what he is doing. Look for Kenny's Farmhouse Cheese on menus and where ever Kentucky Proud products are sold.

✳ Green Space

Fountain Square Park, 225 E. Main St., Bowling Green. Open dawn to dusk. Two acres of green space, right in the center of town. The land was donated in 1797 as the town was being laid out. It was originally intended for public buildings and was the site of a log cabin courthouse and jail, but today it has evolved into a lushly landscaped retreat with park benches and a gorgeous fountain.

✳ To Do

⚓ **Beech Bend Park & Splash Lagoon** (270-781-7634; www.beech bend.com), 798 Beech Bend Rd., Bowling Green. In the business of entertaining Western Kentuckians since 1898, this amusement park has everything you need for a day or two of fun. With more than 40 rides, a miniature golf course, an oval track and drag strip for racing, and a giant water park, this site has it all. Open Memorial Day–Labor Day.

Kentucky Downs (270-586-7778; www.kentuckydowns.com), 5629 Nashville Rd., Franklin. Open daily from 10 AM until the wee hours of the morning. Sitting almost on the Tennessee border is North America's only European-style horse-racing course. The all-turf course makes for exciting racing at their live September meets. Although their live racing meet is

FOUNTAIN SQUARE PARK

www.kentuckytourism.com

CAVES

The terrain of Kentucky makes it seem an unlikely place to find caves, but caves you will find. Miles and miles of them. Actually, it is probably all one giant cave system, and they are all probably connected, but there are many different caving opportunities available, so choose the one that fits your needs.

In the same class as the Grand Canyon and the giant sequoias, Mammoth Cave is a natural wonder that has been revered since prehistoric times. This is the longest recorded cave system in the world, at least three times longer than any cave known. With more than 348 miles of underground world explored and mapped, the park offers tours for all ages, ability levels, and interests.

Authorized as a national park in 1926 and established in 1941, Mammoth Cave National Park is Kentucky's number one tourist destination and the second oldest tourist attraction in the United States. The cave tours are unbelievable, but with 52,830 acres of park aboveground, there is plenty to do in the lush forested area as well, including hiking, horseback riding, cycling, fishing, and other back-to-nature activities.

Mammoth Cave National Park (270-758-2180; www.nps.gov/maca). The park is open every day of the year (except Christmas Day) 8–5. The visitors center is where you can get maps and cave tour tickets, attend seminars, and watch the informative films *Water and Stone* and *Voices of the Cave* before heading underground. The cost of cave tours varies, but admission to the park and visitors center is free. **Mammoth Cave Hotel** (270-758-2225) offers an assortment of lodging accommodations, from hotel rooms to cottages, rustic cabins, and several campgrounds. There are three restaurants on site; hours vary, so call to make sure they are open. At the **Travertine Restaurant**, you'll find a casual sit-down eatery specializing in southern cuisine. The **Crystal Lake Coffee Shop** is perfect for a light lunch, coffee, or a homemade dessert. You'll also find **TrogloBITES**, which is Mammoth Cave's answer to a fast-food restaurant, serving burgers, fries, and other typical fare.

The following caves are in the area, but are not part of Mammoth Cave National Park:

Crystal Onyx Cave (270-773-2359), I-65 Exit 53, Cave City. Closed in January. Used by Native Americans as a burial site more than 2,700 years ago, this cave is an important archaeological site as well as a formation-rich cave. The tour allows views of vertical shafts, onyx flowstones and draperies, and limestone dams. Admission charged.

Cub Run Cave (270-524-1444), I-65 Exit 65, Munfordville. Tours available Mar. 24–Oct. 31. Winter tours for groups by appointment. First discovered in 1950, the cave was then closed to the public for more than 50 years. Reopened in 2006, this cave offers a 90-minute tour that is highlighted by wooden walkways, modern electric lighting, and renovated pathways for easy maneuvering and touring. Admission charged.

Diamond Caverns (270-749-2233; www.diamondcaverns.com), 1900 Mammoth Cave Pkwy., Park City. Open year-round except for Thanksgiving, Christmas, and New Year's Day. On one of the 0.5-mile-long guided tours, you'll feel like you are in a cathedral while enjoying the intricate drapery deposits of naturally colorful calcite that cover the walls. Thanks to state-of-the-art modern lighting, you won't miss any of it. Tours are available every 30 minutes. The pathways have added handrails but the tour includes 350 stair steps, so it is not handicapped accessible. $15 adults, $8 ages 4–12.

DIAMOND CAVE

www.kentuckytourism.com

♿ **Hidden River Cave** (270-786-1466; www.cavern.org), 119 E. Main St., Horse Cave. Open daily 9–5 year-round, 9–7 Memorial Day–Labor Day. Guided cave tours leave hourly, no reservations needed. This cave, as well as the adjacent American Cave Museum, is dedicated to the exploration and preservation of groundwater as well as a reminder of the delicate balance between caves and the sunlit world above. Learn about caves and their connection to groundwater, and then tour the cave where you can see it all firsthand. Descending into the cave includes 230 stairs, but one tour is handicapped accessible and includes an elevator ride into a sinkhole. $15 adults, $10 ages 12–15, $7 ages 3–11. Museum tour (all ages) $6.

Kentucky Caverns (270-786-2634, 800-762-2869; www.kdu.com), 3700 L&N Turnpike Rd., Horse Cave. Tours available year-round. Call for times. Short cave tour included with admission to Kentucky Down Under. Guided tours offer a close-up view of the colorful onyx formations that line the cave from beginning to end. The 45-minute tour is not handicapped accessible and involves stairs and winding passages. $22 adults, $13 ages 5–14; 4 and under free.

Onyx Cave (270-773-3530; www.mammothcave.com/guntown), I-65 Exit 53, Cave City. Open Mar.–Nov. Offering 30-minute guided tours on demand, this is the cave to explore when you don't have time to wait for a schedule. Tour this cave and see walls coated with calcite crystal flowstone, which results in a shimmering, colorful show. The cave tour is not strenuous but does include steps so it is not handicapped accessible. Adjacent to Guntown Mountain. Small fee.

Lost River Cave and Valley (270-393-0077, 866-274-2283; www.lostriver cave.com), 2818 Nashville Rd., Bowling Green. Open 9–5 seven days a week, except for Thanksgiving, Christmas Day, and New Year's Day. Call for tour times. The valley itself is breathtaking, but Kentucky's only Underground Boat Tour is a trip you'll never forget. Travel the lost river in a huge cave where it is always a comfortable 57 degrees. While you are there, you can walk the wooded trails, do a little bird-watching, and enjoy the butterfly garden. Cave and boat are not handicapped accessible. $15 adults, $11 ages 4–11, $4 ages 1–3.

www.kentuckytourism.com

BEECH BEND PARK

short, about six days, the track offers year-round simulcasting, instant racing games, and bingo. They also have good food, so make a day out of it.

Ballance MotoX (270-792-RACE; www.ballancemotox.com), 13101 Louisville Rd., Oakland. The first state-of-the-art motocross facility in the Southeast features a 1.3-mile lighted track. Check the website for upcoming events. Open Mar.–Nov.

Race World (270-781-RACE), 255 Cumberland Trace, Bowling Green. Featuring two racetracks for stock-car racing and a state-of-the-art arcade, there is fun here for the whole family. Call or check the website for hours.

Paul Walker Golf Course (270-393-3821; www.bgky.org/golf/paulwalker .php), 1044 Covington Ave., Bowling Green. This 9-hole, par-36 golf course, right in the center of Bowling Green, is the place to go for a nice break from touring. The course welcomes walk-ins, and tee times are not necessary. Really convenient for those last-minute golfers.

❀ **Guntown Mountain** (270-773-3530; www.mammothcave.com/guntown), I-65 Exit 53, Cave City. Open daily 9:30–8, Memorial Day–Labor Day; weekends only, 9:30–8, the rest of the year. Visit this re-creation of a Wild West town high atop a mountain. Getting there is half the fun: You ride a chairlift that takes you up 1,360 feet from the parking lot. Watch an old-time Saloon Show, a mock gunfight, or a country-western music show all in one visit. There is also an old-time country store where you can get local products like country hams and preserves. $15 adults, $9 children.

www.kentuckytourism.com

KENTUCKY DOWN UNDER

✍ **Kentucky Down Under** (270-786-2634, 800-762-2869; www.kdu
.com), 3700 L&N Turnpike Rd., Horse Cave. Open mid-Mar.–Nov. 1;
hours change seasonally. Cavern tours offered year-round. Get up close
and personal with animals typically found in Australia, like kangaroos,
wallabies, and an emu. They also have reptiles, farm animals, an aviary
full of lorikeets, and a laughing kookaburra. And you don't have to settle for just looking at the animals in a cage; Kentucky Down Under lets
you get in the cage, too. The ticket price also includes admission to
Kentucky Caverns (see the sidebar). $22 adults, $13 ages 5–14; 4 and
under free.

STATE PARK ✍ ६ **Barren River Lake State Resort Park** (270-646-
2151, 800-325-0057; www.parks.ky.gov), 1149 State Park Rd., Lucas. Indians repeatedly burned this huge area of forest to make it easier to hunt,
creating open plains. When settlers discovered this "barren" land, they
assumed it was not fertile, but quickly found it was some of the lustiest
farmland in the state. With the damming of the Barren River, which created Barren River Lake, the state park soon followed. Created in 1965,

A LITTLE BIT ON THE QUIRKY SIDE

Kentucky, known for its fast horses, beautiful women, and aged bourbon, has a kitschy side; you just have to know where to look. A good place to start would be Barren County, which serves as the welcome mat to Mammoth Cave National Park and provides opportunities to enjoy some not-so-typical Kentucky activities.

If you take away the billboards, Barren County appears to have some classic, unmemorable exits off I-65. But with all the advanced advertising you get, whether northbound or southbound, you know you're going to find a whole lot more than just the longest cave in the world—you are entering territory with promises of dinosaurs, cowboys, and even kangaroos.

Mammoth Cave has been an attraction for this area since they started recording history. Long before there existed an expressway system and drive-through restaurants at the exits, humans have been traveling from afar to get here. And with good reason. The Mammoth Cave itself offers more than 390 miles of passageways, and once inside, visitors are treated to limestone formations called stalagmites, an underground river, and the massive Rotunda Room, which is like entering an abandoned coliseum.

And the cave isn't the only attraction at the park. Every year thousands of visitors come to hike more than 70 miles of trails that weave through the wooded countryside, fish on the lakes and tributaries, and even rock climb.

Over the years, there was always someone to capitalize on the onslaught of visitors, offering lodging, food, and attractions to encourage them to stay longer. Starting with Native Americans and spanning the times of famed outlaw Jesse James, tuberculosis victims looking for cures in the cave vapors, or the news media who descended on the region to report on poor Floyd Collins (who got stuck in the cave in 1925 and died after being trapped for 14 days), there have been people on hand to offer necessities along the way.

Such is the case with Cave City. In a town with about 2,000 residents, there are about 1,000 hotel rooms. Although this is out of proportion with other towns of similar size, it certainly did not happen by mistake. Cave City is still welcoming the 500,000 visitors that pass through its borders each year on their way to Mammoth Cave.

Although Kentucky has not been seen as the western frontier since the time of Daniel Boone, when Kentucky *was* the West, that is no reason not to expect to see some cowboys, gunslingers, and saloon dancing girls. **Guntown Mountain**, just a few minutes from the entrance to Mammoth Cave, sits high atop a hill that is accessed by a skylift. You are not going skiing, you are entering the Wild West, complete with an old-time-stagecoach kind of town, shows that boast realistic shoot-outs in the street, a cowboy stunt show, and a silly comedy routine with real live can-can girls.

While you are in the cowboy-and-Indian days, add to your adventure by sleeping in a wigwam. Yes, just like the Native Americans did. Cave City has been the home to **Wigwam Village Inn** (wigwamvillage .com) since the 1930s, when Frank A. Redford realized that travelers might want the chance to sleep in tepees like the Sioux. Although the wigwams look authentic, they are not made of animal skins and they do offer one or two double beds; each has a private bath. Realistic on the outside, homey on the inside. The wigwams look great in family photos, too.

Since you are already in this historic setting, why not go back a few million years? At **Dinosaur World** (dinoworld.net) in Cave City, you can dig for fossils and wander through the grassy plains and wooded acreage that features about 150 life-sized creatures, complete with information on each species. Spend some time at the dinosaur museum, watch a movie about dinos, give the kids a chance to let off some steam on the playground, and by the end of the day you will know the difference between a *T. rex*, a woolly mammoth, and a triceratops.

As those dinosaurs died and left us fossils, someone decided there might be tourist who wanted to buy them. Yes, Mike, of **Big Mike's Rock Shop** (bigmikesrockshop.com), knew back in 1970 that all that spelunking and dinosaur research would lead people who are interested in gems, minerals, and even rocks to his store. Not only does Mike's have the biggest and most popular rock in the area, they also invite visitors on a Mystery House Tour. It's a gravity house, with floors that slant and water that goes up, not down. Owner Vicky Fontana promises good clean fun, reminiscent of the tourist attractions of the 1950s that used to pop up along the famed Route 66. Mike's also has a gift shop full of jewelry, coffee mugs, and all sorts of gift-y items.

Although the region can't boast a Ripley's Believe It or Not Museum, they do have the **Mammoth Cave Wax Museum** to round out your serving of Americana at its finest. Featuring an assortment of U.S. presidents, including everyone's favorite Kentuckian, Abraham Lincoln, as well as likenesses of Geronimo, Daniel Boone, Dolly Parton, and Jesus, as well as a few surprises. Some visitors swear the eyes move, so stop by and see what you think.

Another unusual lodging option is the **Jellystone Park** of Mammoth Cave (www.jellystonemammothcave.com). Not your ordinary campground, Jellystone features a pool, miniature golf, a playground, an outdoor theater, and daily activities in the summer. They offer campsites as well as cabins—even bunkhouses for large groups.

"Everything at our park is family-oriented," said Emily Rudolph, recreation director. "Our visitors get to see Yogi, Boo Boo, and Cindy Bear at least three times a day, if not more."

The park hosts guests who are going to Mammoth Cave, which is just minutes down the road, as well as guests who are coming to Jellystone as their destination.

"There is so much to do here," Rudolph added. "We have something for everyone."

The Kentucky Action Park (kentuckyactionpark.com), also in Cave City, offers the thrill of an alpine slide, bumper boats, miniature golf, and a go-cart track. They also offer horseback riding at the Jesse James Riding Stable and a tour of Outlaw Cave, named for James, who reportedly used a cave in the area as his hideout after robbing banks.

Also in the area are touristy destinations like **Kentucky Down Under** (kdu.com) in nearby Horse Cave and a replica of Stonehenge in the unlikely town of Munfordville.

Kentucky Down Under brings Australia to the commonwealth by letting visitors get up close and personal with animals not typically found in American zoos. Where else can you get to know a northern blue-tongued skink, a stunning rainbow lorikeet, and a laughing kookaburra, all in one afternoon?

Continuing north on I-65 will lead you to the tiny but historic town of Munfordville. Although historians typically come to town to learn more about the 1862 Civil War Battle of Munfordville, people are flocking to the area to study the replica of Stonehenge, the prehistoric monument in England. Although the replica is built on private property, owner and builder Chester Fryer welcomes visitors to see his creation. He said it took about two months to build but almost a year to gather the materials.

"Rocks are hard to find when you need a certain shape and size," he said.

But he did find what he needed and built the monument to align with the sun. The original Stonehenge was erected before the time of Christ for reasons unknown, but historians believe it had something to do with worship and offering sacrifices.

"I didn't build mine for those reasons," said Chester with a laugh. "I just built it because I had the rocks and the space. People are more than welcome to come and take a look."

So if you find yourself headed in the direction of Mammoth Cave National Park, don't miss your chance to take a few roadside detours along the way. Although Mammoth, as well as other cave destinations in the area, are amazing and not to be missed, neither are some of these gems that make Kentucky, Kentucky.

this 2,187-acre park boasts a 10,000-acre lake with 140 miles of shoreline. The park offers boating and fishing opportunities as well as an 18-hole golf course, horseback riding, and a public sand beach. Stay at the Louis B. Nunn Lodge, in one of their 51 rooms or one of the two-bedroom cottages that offer lake or wooded views. They also have a 99-site campground with utility hookups for the outdoorsy set. **The Driftwood Restaurant** specializes Kentucky favorites like hot brown and fried chicken, but they also have salads and burgers. Open seven days a week, but call for hours. $–$$

✳ Lodging

BED & BREAKFASTS Victorian House Bed & Breakfast
(270-563-9403), 110 N. Main St., Smiths Grove. Sit on the huge wraparound porch and enjoy the period antiques that fill this 1875-era home, which is on the National Register of Historic Places. Innkeepers Sharon and Dave Dahle pamper each guest and are full of tips about the many antiques stores that are within walking distance. $$

Federal Grove Bed & Breakfast (270-542-6106; federalgrove .com), 475 E. Main St., Auburn. This historic home sits on land that is also historic: It was once owned by Jonathan Clark, the brother of William Clark of Lewis and Clark fame. This Federal-style home is loaded with antiques, most of which are for sale, so if you love that settee in your room, you might be able to buy it. Make sure you don't miss breakfast; the homemade pastries are certainly worth getting up for. $$

& Shaker Tavern Bed and Breakfast (270-542-6801, 800-929-8701; www.shakermuseum .com), US 73, South Union. Stay in one of the six guest rooms built by the South Union Shakers in 1869. It was a business venture for the Shakers, who hoped to attract "the people of the world." They used intricate brickwork, an ornate staircase, and a towering columned facade much different from the simple style of the Shak-ers. The rooms are furnished with Victorian-style furniture and equipped with modern-day necessities. $

♪ 1852 Hall Place Bed and Breakfast (270-651-3176), 313 S. Green St., Glasgow. The pampering and well-appointed antiques-filled rooms almost cause you to miss the architectural and historical wonders of this fine home. Built in 1852 by slaves, who actually created the bricks on site, the Hall family's home once hosted a young Abraham Lincoln. This mix of history (it was even a stop on the Underground Railroad), together with the 12-foot ceilings, original woodwork, and amazing library, encourages you to enjoy all four of the splendid guest rooms. $

1869 Homestead Bed and Breakfast (270-842-0510; www .1869homestead.com), 212 Mizpah Rd., Bowling Green. Situated on 55 acres of peaceful farmland, but just minutes from Bowling Green, you'll find this historic home. Offering two guest rooms and one suite, the home also has an amazing spiral staircase and original fireplaces and flooring. Innkeepers Jan and Wendell Strode treat you like family. Corvette lovers need to make note of the fact that Wendell is executive director of the nearby National Corvette Museum, so if you want to talk to someone who knows a thing or two about 'Vettes, well, you might want to book a room. $

CAMPING ♪ **Bowling Green KOA** (270-843-1919; www.bgkoa .com), 1960 Three Springs Rd., Bowling Green. This 26-acre property has full water and electric hookups, a tent area, and KOA Kamping Kabins. For fun there is an 18-hole mini golf course, hayrides, fishing derbies, paddle-boat races, and live music. Open year-round.

♪ **Yogi Bear's Jellystone Park Camp Resort** (270-773-3840, 800-523-1854; www.jellystone mammothcave.com), 1002 Mammoth Cave Rd., Cave City. Spend some time with Yogi, Boo Boo, and all the gang at this fun resort. Accommodations include log cabins, Amish cottages, four-bedroom bungalows, and even a bunkhouse that sleeps up to 22 people. They also have campsites ranging from those suitable for the largest RV to the most primitive tent site. The resort itself features a pool and 300-foot waterslide, mini golf, an arcade, a fishing pond, and planned activities like outdoor movies and a bonfire where you can roast marshmallows. Open year-round.

✳ Where to Eat

DINING OUT ♈ **440 Main Restaurant & Micki's** (270-9793-0450; www.440main.com), 440 E. Main Ave., Bowling Green. Two fabulous restaurants, one location. Overlooking Fountain Square Park in the downtown area, this restaurant, housed in a historic building, is both warm and elegant. For finer dining they offer the 440 Main Restaurant with an upscale feel, featuring a menu that includes New Orleans favorites like jambalaya, bourbon salmon, and Cajun spring rolls. In the mood for something more casual? Then head next door to Micki's, a beer and burger place, a little more laid-back but with a full menu. Live music on weekends. $–$$

♈ **Verdi** (270-781-9817; verdi .com), 410 E. Main St., Bowling Green. Open for lunch and dinner, but closed in between the two, so check the website for hours. Closed Sunday. It's the place to go for a romantic dinner or a casual Saturday-afternoon lunch. European-inspired menu with salads, sandwiches, and wraps at lunch and more refined dining at dinner. Sit outside on a sunny afternoon and enjoy the goings-on at Fountain Square Park. $–$$

♿ ♈ **Mariah's 1818** (270-842-6878; www.mariahs.com), 801 State St., Bowling Green. Open 11–9 daily. Holding the title of the oldest brick home in Bowling Green, this casual eatery is on the National Register of Historic Homes. Menu choices include steaks, salmon, and salads, but they also have the not-so-common barbecue pizza made in their wood-fired brick oven. Have the New Orleans bread pudding for dessert. $–$$

♈ **Brickyard Café** (270-843-6431), 1026 Chestnut St., Bowling Green. Open for lunch and

DINING ROOM AT MARIAH'S

www.kentuckytourism.com

dinner every day. This is truly a culturally diverse eatery: It's owned by a Bosnian and a Croatian immigrant who specialize in delicious Mediterranean food. The old building, part of an 1857 brickyard, has thick brick walls and intricate masonry from long ago. From pasta to pizza, the typical Italian menu includes four-cheese lasagna and veal Marsala, but the flavors have a slight European twist. Wide variety of pizzas, too. Make sure to try some bread, which is made from scratch daily. $–$$

EATING OUT & **Cambridge Market & Café** (270-782-9366; www.cambridgemarketandcafe .com), 830 Fairview Ave., Bowling Green. Open weekdays 9–8, Sat.

10–3. This soup-and-sandwich deli offers daily gourmet specials like roast pork loin on Monday and BBQ on corncakes on Thursday. They have awesome cheesecakes and homemade pies, too. $

Judy's Castle (270-842-8736), 1302 US 31W Bypass, Bowling Green. Open 6 AM–7:30 PM Mon.–Sat. While it's not exactly a castle, the personal service you'll get at Judy's will make you feel like royalty. They are truly happy to have you, and you'll be happy to be there when you try their down-home breakfasts, succulent barbecue, and homemade pies. $–$$

Aunt Bee's Family Restaurant (270-786-2020), I-65 (Exit 58) and KY 218, Horse Cave. Open Sun.–Thu. 6 AM–10 PM, Fri.–Sat. 6 AM–midnight. If you are looking for a stick-to-your-ribs home-cooked meal, this is the place. Whether you want breakfast, lunch, or supper, Aunt Bee's has something on the menu for you. Stop by on Friday nights for all-you-can-eat catfish. Monday is all-you-can-eat ribs night. $–$$

Big Bubba Buck's Belly Bustin' BBQ Bliss (270-524-3333; www .bubbabucksbbq.com), 1802 Main St., Munfordville. Serving Tue.–Sat. 11–8. The name of this joint isn't the only thing that's a mouthful. Bubba's got some amazing sauce that he can put on ribs, chicken, pork, just about anything, and you will be glad he did. But don't forget to pick your sides—they are as good as the main dish, including treats like fried green tomatoes, fried pickles, spicy baked beans . . . yes, you will need some extra napkins. The decor could be described as truckstop-esque, but don't let that deter you; usually those truckers know all the best restaurants. $

Teresa's Restaurant (270-782-6540; www.teresas-bg.com), 509 Gordon Ave., Bowling Green. Closed Sun. Teresa's is the kind of place where you can get a hearty southern breakfast all day, but then you might miss out on one of the daily lunch specials like country-fried steak or meat loaf served with three vegetables. Teresa's is also known for country smoked hams. Try some there or order one to go. $–$$

Big Moose's BBQ Smokehouse (270-651-1913; bigmoosebbq smokehouse.com), 525 W. Main St., Glasgow. Mon.–Wed. 10:30–2:30, Thu.–Sat. 10:30–8. This is a barbecue joint that is near and dear to the locals of Glasgow. They cook everything out back, so you can smell what's grilling when you are down the street. Everyone loves the barbecue, but a plate of side dishes isn't out of the question. With choices of mayonnaise slaw, vinegar slaw, hush puppies, and sweet potato crunch, there's hardly room left for the pork chops, chicken, or country ribs entrées. $

SNACKS ✿ ♿ **Chaney's Dairy Barn** (270-843-5567; www .chaneysdairybarn.com), 9191 Nashville Rd., Bowling Green.

Open Mon.–Sat. 11–8, Sun. noon–5. This dairy farm, in the Chaney family for generations, is a country-style place to go for some homemade ice cream, sandwiches, and desserts. Or make it your destination and take a farm tour; you can try your luck at the giant corn maze in fall. $

The Music Room at George J's, on the Square (270-651-2161), 144 E. Public Square, Glasgow. Open Mon.–Sat. 7–9, this former pharmacy with a soda fountain has been transformed into a diner, with its famous fountain still intact. You'll find one of their original milk shake machines still on the counter, serving up creamy concoctions as it has for generations. Menu favorites are the burgers, served with waffle fries or sweet potato tots, as well as the pizzas and wraps. This place is a big hangout for local politicians, but don't let that keep you away; they are part of the fun. $

Riley's Bakery (270-842-7636), 819 US 31W Bypass, Bowling Green. Open Mon.–Fri. 6:45–5, Sat. 6:45–2. Serving up made-from-scratch products for more than 60 years. All the pastries are scrumptious, but the Hungarian coffee cake and the cream horns stand out to the locals. Order a sandwich on their famous Butter Bread and get yours filled with pimiento cheese or egg salad. $

Countryside Bake Shop (270-542-8679), 525 Quarry Rd., Auburn. With everything made one batch at a time, you can taste the difference at this family-run bakery. The Schwartz family gets up about 3 AM each day to bake their signature white, wheat, and honey oatmeal breads. Buy a few loaves and pick up a Humming-bird cake, too; full of bananas, pineapples, pecans, and cinnamon, it is delightful. $

✳ Entertainment

Capitol Arts Center Galleries (270-782-2787; www.capitolarts .com), 416 E. Main St., Bowling Green. Gallery open Mon.–Fri. Originally built as a vaudeville house in the late 1890s, this theater is truly an icon in the downtown area. The historic auditorium welcomes touring acts from around the globe. Check the website to see who is appearing. There are also two galleries, the Houchens and Mezzanine, which feature revolving exhibits throughout the year.

Public Theatre of Kentucky/ Phoenix Theatre (270-781-6233; www.ptkbg.org), 545 Morris Ave., Bowling Green. A talented community theater in the historic downtown area. The lineup features plays and musicals Sept.–May each year. Check the website for shows and times.

✳ Selective Shopping

Steamboat Salvage and Company (270-796-3606), 1750 Campbell Lane, Bowling Green. This store features an unbelievable collection of one-of-a-kind nautical items, but they are also direct importers of furniture, giftware, and oil paintings. Wander around and see what you find.

Dollar Brothers Shoes (270-842-8141), 419 Park Row, Bowling Green. Open the door and smell the leather—this shop smells like a shoe store should. Located right in the town center and specializing in men's and women's shoes, it has been part of Bowling Green's downtown since 1937. Customers are treated to old-fashioned service, like using a shoehorn to glide your foot into the shoe. For people of a certain age, it will bring back memories.

Crafty Hands Yarn Shop (270-846-4865; craftyhandsyarnshop .com), 2910 Scottsville Rd., Bowling Green. Stocked full of supplies for knitting and crocheting, this darling shop has lots to look at. It is yarn galore. When you see it all, you'll just want to start making something. Friendly staff can't wait to help you. Closed Sunday.

Candle Makers on the Square (270-843-3001; candlemakersbg .com), 417 Park Row, Bowling Green. This little shop smells delightful—and it should, as they have every flavor of candle you can think of, all hand poured, using the finest ingredients. Pick some up while you are in town.

ANTIQUES Smith Grove Antique District (270-563-6444). This quaint community features several antiques shops and two historic B&Bs, just a few minutes from downtown Bowling Green. Antiques range from rare primitives to exquisite pieces.

Flea Land of Bowling Green/ Antique Mall at Flea Land (270-843-1978; www.flealand .com), 1100 Three Springs Rd., Bowling Green. Antiques mall open daily 10–5, Flea Land open Sat. and Sun. 9–6. This is a fantastic combination of flea market and fine antiques. Kentucky's largest indoor, climate-controlled flea market is more than 85,000 square feet. The antiques mall is huge, too, with 12,000 square feet of browsing space.

ART GALLERIES Rickman Pottery (270-782-8550), 1121 E. 14th Ave., Bowling Green. Closed Sun. and Mon. Watch the potter's wheel spin to create bowls, vases, and dinnerware, and then see the kiln where it is all baked to perfection. This working pottery studio is right in the heart of Bowling Green and includes a retail shop, so you can take home your finds.

Gallery 916 (270-843-5511), 601 State St., Bowling Green. Closed Sun. The coolest of art in this ever-changing gallery.

❋ **Special Events**

July: ❦ ❧ ♿ **National Corvette Homecoming** (270-791-2117; www.nationalcorvettehomecoming

.com). All Corvettes are made at the GM plant in Bowling Green, so what better location could there be for a festival of all things 'Vette? Enjoy the all-Corvette parade, which stretches for miles, a Corvette car show, a Corvette parts swap meet, and a Corvette auction. There is also live music, festival food, and an arts and crafts show. Held at the Sloan Convention Center and Grounds.

August: ❦ ❧ ♿ **Duncan Hines Festival** (www.duncanhines festival.com). Celebrating the life and times of Bowling Green native Duncan Hines. This name, synonymous with cake mixes, belonged to a man who had a storied career writing guidebooks and producing more than 250 products aimed to aid the life of a housewife. Although he sold his company to Proctor & Gamble in 1956, the company kept his iconic moniker. This festival features a dessert recipe contest, pageants, a street dance, and an art contest and auction.

September: ❦ ❧ ♿ **Bowling Green International Festival** (www.bginternationalfest.com). Celebrate cultural diversity with music, food, games, and juried art. Held annually at downtown's Fountain Square Park. Many nationalities come together to share their unique cultures.

CAMPBELLSVILLE, GREENSBURG, AND THE GREEN RIVER LAKE AREA

These tiny communities, situated just 10 miles apart on US 68, are both basking in history. The folks from the National Historic Register should consider opening a satellite office in this part of the state, with so many remnants of the past.

Once you've doused yourself in history, it's probably time for some recreation. Head in the direction of the gigantic 8,200-acre **Green River Lake**. Known as one of the clearest in the state, Green River Lake lures (pun intended) fishing enthusiasts in their quest for white, largemouth, smallmouth, and Kentucky bass, bluegill, crappie, and muskie. The sheer size of the lake and its surrounding wooded landscape makes it a favorite of houseboaters, hikers, and campers. Most of the lodging choices center on the water, so if you're staying in the area, consider a houseboat, a rustic cabin, or even a Floating Condo.

Campbellsville, the seat of Taylor County, is approximately 85 miles from Louisville, Lexington, Bowling Green, and Somerset. This central location in the middle of a heart-shaped county lets them boast that they are truly "the Heart of Kentucky."

Nearly 10,000 people live in the city, which is surrounded by beautiful countryside, perfect for the history lover who wants to traipse through the county in search of the 30 sites on the National Historic Register. From the 1830s to the 1870s, Campbellsville served as a stagecoach stop on the national mail route between Zanesville, Ohio, and Florence, Alabama. As the railroad arrived in nearby Lebanon in the 1850s, a feeder route was created to Campbellsville, allowing the area to grow. With the start of the Civil War, the city was on the invasion route for both the Yankees and the Confederates. In 1863, the Battle of Tebbs Bend was fought on the Green River. After the battle, which was considered a victory for the North, homes and churches in Campbellsville were turned into makeshift hospitals, some of which you can see today.

You'll love the southern hospitality of the residents. They're glad to have you, and it shows.

Greensburg is a tiny speck on the map, but it has deep historical roots. Visit the 200-year-old Green County Courthouse, which is the oldest courthouse west of the Alleghenies and is listed on the National Register of Historic Places. Its claim to fame is that President Andrew Jackson once practiced law here. Currently a museum, the old limestone building houses mementos and artifacts from Greensburg and Green County history.

A stationary 445-foot-long, wooden plank footbridge, constructed in 1929, connects the town square to the historic L&N Railroad Depot and the valley across the square. It's easy to picture turn-of-the-20th-century travelers disembarking the train and walking the bridge. The town square, which is full of historic buildings, still looks as it did then.

Originally established by John Glover and called Glover's Station, the town changed its name to Greensburg in 1794. In an effort to remember John, you can visit Glover's Station Antique Mall right on the town square. While you're on the square, stop in the shops and restaurants on the way. They're darling.

GUIDANCE Taylor County Tourism Commission (270-465-3786, 800-738-4719; www.campbellsvilleky.com), 107 W. Broadway, Campbellsville. Open weekdays 8–4. Nice place to stop for guidance, with a friendly staff who know the area well. **Greensburg–Green County Chamber of Commerce** (270-932-4298; www.greensburgonline.com), 110 W. Court St., Greensburg. Open Mon.–Fri. 8–4. Although this isn't really a visitors center, per se, they have brochures and welcome tourists. In fact, everyone working there is full of friendly advice.

GETTING THERE The closest commercial airport is about 75 miles away, in Louisville. The **Louisville International Airport** (502-368-6524; www.flylouisville.com) is served by most commercial airlines and has rental cars available.

GETTING AROUND Campbellsville and Greensburg are not located near an interstate highway or parkway. The main route through Taylor County is US 68, connecting Lexington and Bowling Green. Streets are well marked and easy to get around; parking in the downtown areas is free.

MEDICAL EMERGENCY Taylor Regional Hospital (270-465-3561; www.tchosp.org), 1700 Old Lebanon Rd., Campbellsville. This 90-bed hospital serves the 110,000 people who live in Campbellsville and the

regional area. **Jane Todd Crawford Memorial Hospital** (502-932-
4211), 202–206 Milby St., Greensburg. This 44-bed hospital has been
serving the needs of the community since 1962. It's named for Jane Todd
Crawford, who in 1809 became the first person to undergo abdominal surgery in Kentucky. You can visit the actual operating room in the home of
Dr. Ephraim McDowell, which is in Danville.

ALCOHOL Taylor County is a moist county with alcohol sales permitted
in a few restaurants. The surrounding counties of Adair, Casey, and Green
are all dry, with the sale of alcohol prohibited within the county borders.

✳ To See

In Campbellsville

1823 Jacob Hiestand House (270-789-4343), on KY 210. See the period
furnishings and exquisite hand-tooled masonry of this German stone
house. It is one of only 12 in the state. Open by appointment.

1840 Atkinson-Griffin Log House (270-465-4463), 544 Lake Rd. After
the Civil War Battle of Tebbs Bend, this home served as a Confederate
hospital. Open by appointment.

The Friendship Schoolhouse (270-465-5410), 300 Ingram Ave. Built
around 1918, this one-room schoolhouse taught between 8 and 40 students at a time, in grades one through eight. Open by appointment.

In Greensburg

Green County Old Courthouse (270-932-4298), downtown. One of the
oldest public buildings still standing in Kentucky, the courthouse was built
in 1802 and in use for 135 years. It is the oldest courthouse west of the
Allegheny Mountains.

Foot Bridge at Courthouse Square (270-932-4298), 110 W. Court St.
If you are not scared of heights, walk the 445-foot-long, 40-foot-high foot-
bridge, which connects the Greensburg public square to the early-1900s
L&N Railroad depot.

✳ To Do

Miller Park (270-465-7011), KY 289, Campbellsville. This 65-acre park
features an Olympic-sized swimming pool, tennis courts, a walking trail,
and flower gardens. There is a 9-hole golf course, basketball courts, and
ball fields.

✐ **Phillips Lanes Family Fun Center** (270-465-5296; www.phillips
lanes.com), 164 Bambi Lane, Campbellsville. Bowling, arcade games, and
an on-site restaurant.

❀ ✐ ♿ **Skyline Drive-In** (270-932-2817; www.skylinedrivein.com), 5600 Hodgenville Rd., Greensburg. Watch first-run movies under the stars. With room for 300 cars, the Skyline Drive-In is the place to see a double feature for less than the cost of one movie at the theater. Open during summer months. Call or check the website to see what's showing.

Crazy Horse Archery (270-789-3776), 2422 New Columbia Rd., Campbellsville. Visit this indoor 20-yard archery range to get some target practice. Open Mar.–Sept.; call for hours. They also have all kinds of bows and hunting supplies for sale.

GOLF Green County Country Club (270-932-7031; www.greencounty golf.com), 158 Golf Course Rd., Greensburg. This 9-hole course is surrounded by mature trees and rolling hills. Go when you're short on time but want to get in a quick round of golf. They also serve up all three meals at the clubhouse.

WALKING TOUR Greensburg Walking Tour. Start at the chamber of commerce (270-932-4298), 110 W. Court St., Greensburg. The best way to get acquainted with Greensburg is to take the one-hour walking tour that includes 24 historic homes, government buildings, the railroad depot, cemeteries, and other sites. Proudly demonstrates Greensburg efforts to preserve its rich and multilayered heritage.

✳ Green Space

American Legion Park (270-932-6562), 1099 Legion Park Rd., Greensburg. This park, which is adjacent to the Green River, has a ramp, perfect for canoes. They also have walking trails, a ball field, and a picnic area with grills.

✳ Green River Lake Marinas & Lodging

Emerald Isle Resort & Marina (270-465-3412, 888-815-2000; www .emeraldisleresort.com), KY 372, Campbellsville. They can meet all your marina needs with gas, groceries, supplies, and pontoon and fishing boat rentals. They also have a very casual restaurant on site, cooking up breakfast and lunch daily. After a day of roughing it on the lake, rent a luxury condominium on the shore. Try out the large sunporches on the outside or the cozy fireplaces on the inside. With two or three bedrooms, they can accommodate up to eight people. All the amenities are included to make your stay perfect, like appliances, sheets, towels, and utensils. You can even park your boat right outside; a complimentary boat slip comes with every rental.

Green River Marina State Dock (800-465-2512; www.greenriver marina.com), KY 55S, KY 1061, Campbellsville. All the things you need in a marina, like fuel, food, emergency assistance, and a gift shop with souvenirs. They have so many houseboats available for rent, you'll have a hard time choosing which one. All these houseboats feature modern necessities, like queen-sized beds, hot tubs, and slides off the back. This dock also offers Floating Cabins or, as they like to call them, Floating Condos. These homes on water were built in the hull of a houseboat. They are moored to the dock with a boat slip for you to park. Measuring about 1,100 square feet, some sleep up to 12 people.

✳ Where to Eat

EATING OUT Creek Side Restaurant (270-465-7777; www .creeksidecville.com), 1837 New Lebanon Rd., Campbellsville. Open daily for lunch and dinner. Named for a former restaurant that used to be alongside a creek, this new location isn't even near water. No matter what the name, though, this family restaurant offers a full-service menu with seafood, country ham, salads, and sandwiches, but the buffet is so good, you won't need a menu. On weekends you can get frog legs and shrimp, as well as their famous chicken tenders on the buffet. $$

Ennis' Restaurant (270-932-5972), 113 Public Square, Greensburg. Open for breakfast and lunch Mon.–Sat. Okay, although it is nothing fancy, Ennis' is Greensburg's claim to fame. Anyone familiar with the country rock band Kentucky Headhunters knows the words to "Dumas Walker," which refer to a restaurant where you can get a juicy burger and a bottle of the now-defunct local drink called Ski; well, Ennis' was the inspiration for that song. $

Los Agaves (859-299-2020), 120 N. Public Square, Greensburg. Open daily for lunch until about 10 PM. Call for exact hours. They have an excellent variety of Mexican favorites, all featuring fresh ingredients. Flavorful salsa, but their hot is hot. Have a large ice water ready. $

Anew Blend (270-932-5339), 105 N. Main St., Greensburg. Open 6 AM–3 PM Mon.–Fri. Look for the inviting red door when you're in the historic downtown area and you will be in for a real treat. They offer soups, salads, sandwiches, and specialty burgers. Get there for breakfast and stay for lunch. You are going to want to try their cinnamon rolls. The menu also has a huge array of coffee drinks. $

SNACKS A Taste Like Home Country Market (270-932-2766), 8217 Marshall Ridge, Greensburg. Closed Sun.–Mon. Stop in to get fresh-baked goods, like homemade pies and cookies. They also have a fantastic deli. $

✳ Selective Shopping

Glover's Station Antique Mall (270-932-5588), 121 S. Public Square, Greensburg. The mall is an antique itself. Built in 1900, it was formerly a department store. Have a look at the old-time manual elevator—it's no longer in use, but fun to see. They have a huge selection of antiques and collectibles.

Brenda's Flowers and Crafts (270-932-4053), 210 S. Main St., Greensburg. In addition to meeting all your floral needs, Brenda stocks a variety of locally made craft items. Nice selection of handmade birdhouses, intricate jewelry, wind chimes, and soaps. Look for the yellow house with green shutters.

Campbellsville Cherry Reproductions (270-465-6003; campbellsvillecherryreproductions .com), 3380 Saloma Rd., Campbellsville. Visit this family-run furniture-making business and learn all about the craftsmanship it takes to build their end tables, headboards, and drop-leaf tables. Each one is a work of art. They are happy to show you their shop, as well as the showroom.

James Art Glass Studio (800-653-6790; jamesartglassstudio .com), 311 E. Main St., Campbellsville. They have an amazing collection of decorative stained-glass windows in artistic and customized designs.

Pompano's Bait House (270-469-9799), 205 North Shore Dr., Campbellsville. In a community where fishing is so prevalent, you're going to need a good supplier of bait. Pompano's has all you need: worms, minnows, crickets, along with fishing supplies. They open about 6:30 AM every day of the week, so go early for the best selection.

✳ Special Events

July: 🐾 ♿ **Green River Lake Arts & Crafts Festival** (270-465-8601). Enjoy live music, clogging demonstrations, myriad food choices, and art and craft items for you to browse and buy.

September: 🐾 ✂ ♿ **Cow Days!** (270-932-4298). A salute to our bovine friends, this two-day street festival is held right in the middle of downtown Greensburg. Carnival games, live music, a talent show, a 5K run, and a pipe-smoking contest. But the real attraction is a life-sized plastic cow that kids can milk.

THE LAKE CUMBERLAND AREA, INCLUDING SOMERSET, JAMESTOWN, RUSSELL SPRINGS, AND MONTICELLO

With the creation of the gargantuan **Lake Cumberland** in the 1950s came the transformation of these sleepy rural communities to thriving towns that now surround the lake and keep the tourists well supplied. An estimated 1.7 million vacationers head to the lake each year, and these towns, which could be easily zipped through on your way to the water, cater to this crowd. In fact, most of them make their livelihood from the lake, so you can find plenty of places to stock up on supplies. Slow down as you pass through and you will find nice restaurants, shops, and even a few tastes of history.

Known as the Houseboat Capital of the World, the Lake Cumberland area has the highest number of luxury houseboats of any lake in the United States, so there is no excuse not to rent one for a few days. See the lake as it was meant to be seen, as you float around in pure comfort.

The city of **Russell Springs** became known as a health resort in the 19th century because of a nearby chalybeate spring. The iron-laden chalybeate water was said to have health-giving properties. Tourists flocked there in the 1850s, and 100 years later, with the creation of Lake Cumberland, they are still coming—not for the springs, which are gone, but for the houseboating and all things connected to the lake.

GUIDANCE **Somerset-Pulaski Convention & Visitors Bureau** (606-679-6394, 800-642-6287; www.lakecumberlandtourism.com), 522 Ogden St., Somerset. Open Mon.–Sat. 8–4. Stop in the visitors center for free and friendly information about what to do in the area. **Russell Springs Tourism** (270-866-4333; www.lakecumberlandvacation.com), 650 S. Hwy. 127 just inside the Russell Springs city limits. Stop by for maps and

Deborah Kohl Kremer

RUSSELL SPRINGS VISITORS CENTER

directions—they've got everything you need. Open 8–4 in winter and 8:30–4:30 in summer.

GETTING THERE The closest commercial airport is the **Bluegrass Airport** in Lexington, which is about 100 miles away (859-425-3114; www .bluegrassairport.com). There are car rentals available. The nearest **Greyhound** (606-864-2040) bus station is 30 miles away in London, 1938 London Shopping Center.

GETTING AROUND Although there is no formal public transportation, you can always call **Somerset's Taxi Express** (606-679-9944) if you need a ride. Otherwise, getting around by car is fairly easy. The major route through the area is the Cumberland Parkway, also known as Louie B. Nunn Parkway, and if you travel about 60 miles, east or west, you will hit major arteries I-65 and I-75.

MEDICAL EMERGENCY Lake Cumberland Regional Hospital (606-679-7441; www.lakecumberlandhospital.com), 305 Langdon St., Somerset. Serving 42 surrounding counties and more than 300,000 people, they have 227 beds.

Russell County Hospital (270-866-4141; www.russellcohospital.org), Dowell Rd., Russell Springs. This 25-bed critical access hospital offers quality health care and round-the-clock emergency services.

ALCOHOL Although alcohol sales are prohibited in Pulaski County, alcohol sales by the drink are permitted in nearby Burnside.

Russell and Wayne County are dry, so there are no alcohol sales within the county borders.

& **Mill Springs Battlefield, Cemetery, and Museum** (606-636-4045; www.millsprings.net), in the tiny burg of Nancy. Open every day 10–4 in summer; closed Monday in winter. Call to double-check. In the Union's effort to protect the Cumberland River, the Cumberland Gap, and the surrounding area, a Civil War battle broke out on this site on January 19, 1862. There were 671 total casualties, and the Union was declared the winner. The museum allows visitors to look out on the battlefield that once held the Union camps. During your visit, watch the 18-minute video and get a good overview of what took place. You can take a driving tour, which includes the cemetery where more than 100 unidentified Confederate troops are buried under one headstone. Also on the property is Brown-Lanier House, which was built in 1830. During the war it was used as both headquarters and hospital. It was originally the home of the miller who operated the adjacent gristmill. This mill has the largest operating overshot waterwheel in the country and is powered by 13 springs. $5 adults, $3 seniors and military, $2 children.

Creelsboro Arch (270-866-4333). Near the deserted town of Creelsboro, you will find the largest natural arch east of the Rockies. With a span of 104 feet, it arches Jim Creek shortly before the creek enters the Cumberland River. Although located on private land, the bridge is open to the

MILL SPRINGS BATTLEFIELD MUSEUM

Deborah Kohl Kremer

Deborah Kohl Kremer

MILL SPRINGS BATTLEFIELD CEMETERY

public. Getting there can be a bit confusing, involving unmarked gravel roads, so get a map from the tourist office or ask a local.

🦞 ✐ **Wolf Creek Dam Powerhouse and Overlook** (615-736-7161), US 27S. Enjoy the spectacular view from this mile-long construction marvel. Constructed in 1950 to generate hydroelectricity and prevent flooding, it's better known for creating Lake Cumberland, the largest human-made lake east of the Mississippi. Free.

🦞 ✐ **Wolf Creek National Fish Hatchery** (270-343-3797; www.fws.gov /wolfcreek), 50 Kendall Rd., Jamestown. Open 364 days per year, but if you want to go on Christmas Day, you are out of luck. This hatchery raises about 800,000 rainbow and brown trout for the lakes, rivers, and streams of Kentucky each year. They welcome 100,000 people annually to their visitors center, where you can tour the hatchery and do some public fishing. Free.

Hardscratch Country Store (270-384-4671; hardscratchky.com), 7694 Hwy. 55S, Columbia. Open Mon.–Sat. 5 AM–6 PM, so you oughta be able to find a few minutes to stop by. About 11 miles outside of Jamestown, you'll find this perfect nugget of history that is still chugging along doing business like they did when they opened more than 70 years ago. They serve up a stick-to-your-ribs breakfast and plate-lunch specials, but they are so nice, they'll cook up whatever you want, whatever time you want it. Locals rave about their catfish dinners. They also sell gas and guns and other life necessities. Stop by and sit a spell.

✴ To Do

Lake Cumberland Speedway (606-561-8994; lcspeedway.net), 1 Race-track Rd., Burnside. This 3/8-mile dirt oval features races for Late Models, Open Wheel Modified, Superdirt Roadhogs, Chevettes, and Frontwheel Drives. Call for race times and events.

The Links at Lily Creek (270-343- 4653; www.linksatlilycreek.com), 500 Lily Creek Resort Rd., Jamestown. This 18-hole public golf course is designed by PGA professional Dave Wilson. It also has a driving range, practice area, and fully stocked pro shop.

Kentucky Off-Track Betting (270-343-3939; kyofftrackbetting.com), 628 N. Main St., Jamestown. Place your bets without going to the track. They offer thoroughbred racing from Keeneland, Churchill Downs, Turfway Park, and other top tracks across the country.

MINIATURE GOLF ✍ **Somerset Falls Miniature Golf Course** (606-451-2000; www.somersetfalls.com), 100 Family Fun Dr., Somerset. This 18-hole mini golf course has waterfalls, streams, and natural limestone.

SCENIC TOUR ✍ **Big South Fork Scenic Railway** (606-376-5330; www.bsfsry.com), 100 Henderson St., Stearns. Open Apr.–Oct.; call for reservations. Ride the 16-mile round trip through the Daniel Boone National Forest on the 100-year-old Kentucky & Tennessee Railroad. Your rail ticket also includes admission to the McCreary County Museum, which is located in the 1907 Stearns Coal & Lumber Company headquarters. This museum exhibits artifacts of early Appalachian life. $18 adults, $17 seniors, $9 ages 3–12.

✴ Green Space

PARKS ✍ **General Burnside Island State Park** (606-561-4104; parks.ky.gov), 8801 S. US 27, Burnside. Named for Civil War general Ambrose Burnside, who patrolled the Cumberland River. He and his troops circled this 400-acre island to protect it from Confederate troops. Today the park includes a campground, a marina, a picnic area, a swimming pool, and a golf course.

✍ **Big South Fork National River and Recreation Area** (bigsouthforkpark.com). Established in 1974 by Congress to protect the free-flowing Big South Fork of the Cumberland River and its tributaries. Encompassing 125,000 acres of the Cumberland Plateau, Big South Fork National River and Recreation Area boasts miles of scenery like gorges and sandstone bluffs. It also offers a huge range of outdoor recreational activities, including hiking, horseback riding, paddling, and hunting. While you are there, take the short, 1-mile loop hiking trail to Yahoo Falls. It is Kentucky's highest waterfall, dropping 113 feet.

Pulaski County Park (606-636-6450), 1200 Hwy. 3189, Nancy. The park located in western Pulaski County offers picnic areas, grills, shelters, camping, playground, and 18-hole disk golf courses plus hiking trails.

LAKES

Dale Hollow Lake

About 50 miles southwest of Russell Springs, you'll find Dale Hollow Lake. This enormous 28,000-acre lake straddles the Kentucky–Tennessee border, and was created in 1943 by damming the Obey River. This massive dam provides flood control and power to the area. It is 1,717 feet in length and holds back Dale Hollow Lake, which is 61 miles long, offers 653 miles of shoreline, and is 120 feet deep at its deepest point. The entire lake area offers the usual outdoor activities like fishing, camping, boating, canoeing, hiking, waterskiing, and tubing; the unique crystalline waters even allow for snorkeling.

With a lake of this size, you're sure to find people casting a line. Dale Hollow Lake is stocked with white bass, bluegill, crappie, muskie, and rainbow trout. The park has a marina that rents boats of all sizes. With more than 3,398 acres of wooded forest area surrounding the lake and lodge, don't miss the 15 miles of trails that can be used for hiking, horseback riding, and mountain biking. In addition to all kinds of water sports, Dale Hollow has one of the best golf courses in the state. The 18-hole public course is situated within the lush rolling hills.

✄ ♿ **Dale Hollow Lake State Resort Park** (270-433-7431, 800-325-2282; parks.ky.gov), 6371 State Park Rd., Burkesville. Even though most of this lake is located in Tennessee, Kentucky could not pass up the opportunity to create a wonderful state resort park on the Frogue Peninsula, on the northern side of the lake. Here you'll find the 60-room **Mary Ray Oaken Lodge**, which sits high on a bluff overlooking the lake. They also have a 165-site campground, with a few sites set aside for campers who have horses. There are a few air-conditioned cabins scattered about the woods, too. Diners love the **Island View Restaurant**, which has phenomenal views of, you guessed it, the small islands that dot the lake. Serving three meals a day, seven days a week, the restaurant offers a huge variety that includes fried catfish, barbecue ribs, and chargrilled steaks. Don't forget to try the bourbon-laced bread pudding; it's the perfect ending to any meal. $–$$

Dale Hollow marinas

Hendricks Creek Resort (800-321-4000; www.hendrickscreek1.com), 945 Hendricks Creek Rd., Burkesville. One-stop shopping for your weekend on the lake. Hendricks rents houseboats that can sleep up to 12 people. They have small runabouts and pontoons, too. The marina has a well-stocked store with everything from fuel to bait. You can also rent a furnished, family-sized fishing cottage with a nice lake view.

Sulphur Creek Resort (270-433-7272; www.sulphurcreek.com), 3498 Sulphur Creek Rd., Burkesville. Nice resort where you can rent boats of all sizes, including luxury houseboats. If you would rather sleep on shore, check out their selection of furnished cabins, which are tucked into the wooded hillsides around the lake. They also have 22 lakeside campsites, each with a boat slip. **Mike's Landing**, a floating restaurant at the resort, is a fun casual place to relax after a day on the water. Open Apr.–late Oct., Mike's serves up all three meals.

Lake Cumberland

Created by the construction of Wolf Creek Dam in 1950, Lake Cumberland is a huge tourist destination for Kentuckians as well as those from neighboring states. With 1,225 miles of shoreline, it has more waterfront access than the state of Florida and is considered one of the best boating and fishing areas in the eastern United States.

✦ ♿ **Lake Cumberland State Resort Park** (270-343-3111, 800-325-1709; www.parks.ky.gov), 5465 State Park Rd., Jamestown. This Kentucky state park covers 3,000 acres and would be a nice place to vacation even without access to the adjacent 63,000-acre Lake Cumberland. They have two lodges, the 63-room **Lure Lodge** and the 13-room **Pumpkin Creek**

HOUSEBOATING ON LAKE CUMBERLAND

www.kentuckytourism.com

Lodge. Tucked back in the woods a bit are 30 two-bedroom and chalet-style cottages. You can also camp at the 146-site campground. This resort has both indoor and outdoor pools, tennis courts, miniature golf, and horseback-riding stables. The grounds are perfect for hiking, but if you would rather hike on greens and fairways, they have a 9-hole par-3 golf course. Serving three meals daily, the **Rowena Landing Restaurant** has a nice view of the lake, as well as a varied menu featuring many locally grown ingredients.

Lake Cumberland marinas

Jamestown Resort and Marina (270-343-5253; www.jamestown-marina .com), 3677 S. KY 92, Jamestown. Offering a fleet of pleasure craft like deluxe houseboats and pontoon boats, they also have an easily accessible launch ramp, if you have your own boat. The houseboats are all fully equipped with modern-day features, but if you would rather sleep on land, they have an all-suite hotel, some rustic cabins, and three deluxe log homes. This marina also has a café offering sandwiches, burgers, and a buffet on the weekends.

Lake Cumberland State Dock (270-343-6000, 888-782-8336; www .statedock.com), 6365 State Park Rd., Jamestown. This dock has all you need to get your lake vacation started. Rent a luxury houseboat, or bring your own. They have pay-at-the-pump fuel docks for your convenience. There is a store with a full line of groceries, apparel, footwear, novelty items, boating accessories, fishing licenses, and even live bait. Always looking out for your comfort, they have recently added a fitness center complete with men's and women's showers. Get your supplies at the store and stop in at the **Lakeside Grill Restaurant** for burgers before heading out to your favorite spot on the lake.

Wolf Creek Marina (270-866-3634; wolfcreekmarina.com), 782 Island Ramp Rd., Nancy. Rent pontoons or dock for the season; at Wolf Creek they can help you with whatever you need for your time on the lake. They also have nice, furnished cabins that sit about 1,000 feet from the shore-line. **Fishtales Restaurant** (270-866-3437) offers on-the-lake dining under their tiki roof; if you need a break from the outdoors, dine inside in air-conditioned comfort. Call ahead for carryout.

Alligator II Marina (270-866-6616; 877-363-9911), 2108 KY 1383, Russell Springs. Alligator II Marina was one of the original full-service marinas on Lake Cumberland, offering clothing, gas, and bait. Rent a boat—they have everything from a 16-foot fishing boat to a luxurious wide-body houseboat. If you are hungry, visit the **Gator II Grill**. You can sit on the floating deck and enjoy a big ol' country breakfast as well as burgers and sandwiches. They also have fully stocked, comfortable resort cabins that will sleep up to 12 people.

Deborah Kohl Kremer

THE HARBOR RESTAURANT AND TAVERN AT LEE'S FORD MARINA

Ÿ **Lee's Ford Marina Resort** (606-636-6426; www.leesfordmarina.com), 451 Lees Ford Dock Rd., Burnside. As the only marina on Lake Cumberland that allows alcohol sales, this is a very popular watering spot. The surrounding county is dry, but the city of Burnside allows alcohol by the drink in restaurants. The **Harbor Restaurant and Tavern** has American and Mediterranean entrées. Sit on the deck and enjoy the view. Or take your order to go and relax in one of their cottages. Available with one to four bedrooms, these spacious cottages are well equipped and sit about 300 yards from the marina, tucked in among the trees. They are quiet and private but not far from all the action of the lake. At the marina, rent a 14-foot fishing boat, a ski boat and some skis, and a houseboat, too. They have all you need to enjoy Lake Cumberland.

Woodson Bend Resort (800-872-9825; www.woodsonbendresort.com), 14 Woodson Bend, Bronston. A true full-service resort, located 300 feet above Lake Cumberland, with breathtaking views of the lake and the limestone palisades. This is the answer to getting away from it all. Wonderful condos, some with up to four bedrooms, a Lee Trevino–designed 18-hole championship golf course, and an upscale restaurant are all right on site.

Conley Bottom Resort (606-348-6351; www.conleybottom.com), 736 KY 1275N, Monticello. If you're using a GPS, call ahead and ask them what address to plug in so you will find them. With various lodging options, boat rentals, and a full-service restaurant, what more could you want? They have lake-view cabins that sleep up to 10 people, as well as lakeside campsites that can accommodate tents, campers, and boats. At the marina, rent a huge 12-person houseboat or a pontoon or ski boat. If you already have a boat, head to the marina to rent knee boards, skis, and tubes. The **Lighthouse Café** offers lake-view dining with a menu that covers everything from pancakes, to burgers, to deep-fried jumbo shrimp. Something for every appetite. Open daily 8–8. $

✳ Lodging

BED & BREAKFASTS

✐ ৬ **Acorn & Fox Inn** (606-561-7755, 888-561-4704; www.acorn andfoxinn.com), 85 Noble Oaks Dr., Bronston. A romantic upscale inn with an amazing view of Lake Cumberland. Amenities include a gourmet breakfast, king-sized beds, and antique furnishings throughout. $

✐ **Farm House Inn B&B** (606-376-7383; www.farmhouseinn bb.com), 735 Taylor Branch Rd., Parkers Lake. You'll find this wonderful B&B on a secluded farm, surrounded by the Daniel Boone National Forest with babbling brooks, rock and cave formations, miles of hiking trails, and a few fishing ponds, too. The three guest rooms are just down the road from the innkeeper's house, offering total privacy. The loft room is perfect for families, as it has a king and a double bed in one room and a full and twin bed in the adjoining room. The lush wooded grounds feature a few ponds, lots of wildlife, and even a cave and a waterfall. $

CAMPING **Russell Springs KOA Campgrounds** (270-866-5616; www.koakampgrounds.com), 1440 KY 1383, Russell Springs. This full-service campground is just a mile from the lakeshore, boat ramps, and boat rentals. They offer tennis and volleyball courts and an in-ground pool. The large recreation hall has cable TV and plenty of video games, too. $

✳ Where to Eat

DINING OUT **The Cove Restaurant** (270-866-9191), 145 W. Steve Wariner Dr., Russell Springs. Open daily. This casual, family restaurant has delicious filet mignon, seafood, and pasta dishes, and the dessert menu fills the needs of anyone's sweet tooth. Try one of these homemade desserts: New York cheesecake, chocolate lava cake, fresh apple pie, or the delicious carrot cake. They also have live entertainment on weekends. $$

✿ **Guthrie's on the Square** (270-343-6166; guthriesriverhouse.com), 310 Monument Square, Jamestown. Open for lunch and dinner Mon.–Sat. Hip but casual, this restaurant recommends their steaks, seafood, and pasta. It's known locally for serving really good food, but people just rave about the pecan-crusted chicken and the grilled rib eyes. Enjoy the incredible lake view and their full wine menu. $$

♿ **Bread of Life Café** (606-787-6110), 14 Belden Ave., Liberty. Open Mon.–Sat. 10–8. This buffet-style restaurant lets you get your fill of southern classics like fried chicken, catfish, and meat loaf. There is always a huge variety of vegetables and home-made desserts, too. The yeast rolls are worth the trip alone. This restaurant has ties to the Galilean Children's Home, a home for severely disabled children, so patronizing this restaurant is not only good for your appetite but also supports a worthy cause. $–$$.

Jamestown Cafe (270-343-5550), On the Square, Jamestown. Open daily for lunch and dinner. This is a family-style diner with home

cooking like you remember. A little dark inside, but all the better to see the big-screen TV. $

Giovanni's Pizza (270-343-5555), 628 N. Main St., Jamestown. Open daily for lunch and dinner. A locally owned, casual pizzeria, serving up tasty Italian treats. You can't go wrong with a pizza—either thick or thin crust will impress you. They also have calzones, sandwiches, and salads. $

Mammy Frog's Diner (270-866-3813), 230 Steve Wariner Dr., Russell Springs. Open Mon.–Wed., 10–8, Thu.–Sat. 10–9. Closed Sun. They don't sell frog legs, but this diner has just about everything else. Stop in for a juicy burger or crispy chicken strips. The word *homemade* goes in front of everything on the menu. Casserole and vegetable choices change daily. Excellent pies—don't think of leaving without trying their

BREAD OF LIFE CAFÉ

Deborah Kohl Kremer

oatmeal pie. Owner Lisa describes it as a pecan pie with oatmeal instead of pecans. Add a scoop of vanilla ice cream and call it a day. $

SNACKS ✒ **Amon's Sugar Shack** (606-678-4392), 523 S. US 27, Somerset. Open Mon.–Sat. 5 AM–5 PM, Sun. 6 AM–noon. Serving up hearty breakfast favorites, like eggs and country ham. Inexpensive lunch specials during the week. Good food, but the real draw is the huge variety of doughnuts; get there early for the best selection. They are also known for their coconut cake, so get a slice (or even a whole one) to take with you. $

✒ **Haney's Appledale Farm** (606-636-6148; www.haneys appledalefarm.com), 8350 W. KY 80, Nancy. Call for hours. Come out to this fifth-generation farm, where you can pick your own apples. If you don't feel like exerting yourself, just pick out an apple pie from their bakery. They grow 25 varieties of apples and 10 varieties of peaches. They turn both into pies, jellies, sauces, and dressings that are for sale in their country store. $

✳ Entertainment

The Star Theater (270-866-7827; www.startheater.org), 546 Main St., Russell Springs. You can see entertaining community theater productions throughout the year in this vintage-1950s movie house. Check the website to see what's showing.

MOVIES ✒ � **27 Twin Drive-in** (606-679-4738; www.27drivein .com), 5270 Hwy. 27S, Somerset. Not many left of this dying breed of entertainment. This drive-in has two screens; both show double features all summer. Pack up the station wagon and check the website to see what's showing. Open during summer months only.

✳ Selective Shopping

Junkyard Pottery (606-376-8959; www.junkyardpottery.com), 66 P. P. Walker Lane, Parkers Lake. Open May–Nov. Closed Mon. and Tue. Call ahead for hours. Featuring the hand-thrown pottery of Carol Howe; stop in to see her amazing pieces.

The Mantle Florist and Gifts (270-866-8833), 3213 S. US 127, Jamestown. You'll find this cute shop in midtown, which is what locals call the area halfway between Russell Springs and Jamestown. They carry all kinds of wreaths and silk flower arrangement as well as Kentucky souvenirs.

✳ Special Events

July: ❀ ✒ � **The Jamestown Lakefest Celebration** (270-343-4594). Jamestown's annual Fourth of July weekend event, this fun gathering for locals and visitors features arts and crafts, food booths, free entertainment, and traditional fireworks. Good old-fashioned fun.

Deborah Kohl Kremer

27 TWIN DRIVE-IN

🏕 ✏ ♿ **Somerset Master Musicians Festival** (www.master musiciansfestival.org). Bringing a wide variety of multicultural, multigenerational, and multiracial music to various stages, this festival has been around since 1994. It honors musicians who have devoted much of their lives and their resources to preserving their musical heritage, and whose contributions have had a significant and lasting effect in their genre. In addition to a weekend full of live music, the festival also features games, arts and crafts, and storytelling. It is held on the campus of Somerset Community College.

Lexington and the Bluegrass Region

3

BEREA AND RICHMOND

DANVILLE AND HARRODSBURG

FRANKFORT AND GEORGETOWN

THE LEXINGTON AREA

VERSAILLES, MIDWAY,
AND SURROUNDING
WOODFORD COUNTY

WINCHESTER AND PARIS

Deborah Kohl Kremer

Bluegrass Region

INTRODUCTION: LEXINGTON AND THE BLUEGRASS REGION

The Bluegrass Region is like a patchwork quilt of horse farms, tobacco farms, dairy farms, and, well, basic fruit-and-vegetable-type farms.

Its center core is Lexington, which is Kentucky's second largest city, and it offers a mix of modern downtown buildings, a scattering of museums, and a large dose of historical sites intermingled in the downtown streets. Although it is not all about horses, there is usually something horse-related on every block.

As you head out of the downtown core and into the suburbs and farming areas, you'll likely see some glimpse of the famed Kentucky bluegrass—which, by the way, is not really blue; it's green like grass should be. It got its name because sometimes it has bluish buds that can

KENTUCKY TOBACCO

Nick Kremer

be seen in the fields if the sun is just right. No matter what color it is, it thrives on the rich limestone in Kentucky's soil, and is credited for being the key ingredient to growing a fast thoroughbred.

This part of the state is also home to the state capital, Frankfort. The town is bursting with history and also has one of the most awe-inspiring domed capital buildings in the United States.

Also in the surrounding vicinity are the college towns of Berea, Danville, Georgetown, and Richmond. Each a charmer on its own, they offer opportunities for shopping, antiquing, and taking in historical sites.

Although this area is located in the Bible Belt, ironically, some of the largest industries are tobacco, bourbon, and gambling on horses. With the decrease in tobacco usage nationally, farmers exploring other cash crops. Kentucky has seen an increase in wineries (that limestone-rich soil also grows plump and juicy grapes) and the push to legalize hemp. This outlawed plant has been used to make paper, rope, food products, cosmetics, and clothing but is verboten because it is a distant relative of marijuana. Although hemp is free of the drug-related chemicals that make up its next-of-kin, it is still shunned for its bloodline.

The Bluegrass Region was the first area of Kentucky that was settled as Daniel Boone and his followers came across the state. When they got here, they stayed. After visiting this part of the state and taking part in the dining, history, and southern hospitality of the people, you'll see why.

BEREA AND RICHMOND

M adison County is home to **Richmond**, the county seat, and **Berea**, which is about 12 miles south of Richmond. The county covers more than 440 square miles and has a population of about 81,000. That population swells during the school year as the county welcomes back students to both Eastern Kentucky University as well as Berea College.

Richmond was founded in 1798 by Colonel John Miller, a Revolutionary War soldier, and named for his hometown of Richmond, Virginia. The area is dripping in history as the home to Daniel Boone, who built and resided at a nearby fort in between exploring expeditions. A reproduction fort has been built on the site, Fort Boonesborough State Park. Visitors are invited to see what fort life was like, exploring cabins with artisans demonstrating candle making and weaving, but you can also camp and enjoy the sand beach along the Kentucky River.

Berea, which got its start around 1850, is named for a biblical town, and started out as a group of citizens sympathetic to emancipation. They quickly established a church, village, and Berea College, which is still the centerpiece of this charming, artistic community.

Madison County saw a few Civil War skirmishes, and today visitors can take a driving tour of the battlefields. To get a more personal feel for that era in Kentucky's history, tour the home of the prominent emancipationist Cassius Clay. The statesman's home, which he called White Hall, is furnished as it was in the mid-1800s. You don't have to wear a hoop skirt, but you'll definitely feel like you've gone back in time.

In the early 1900s, Richmond became the home to what is now Eastern Kentucky University. Although there are industries in the vicinity, the town relies largely on the university for its livelihood. The town has some storybook antebellum homes, a walkable downtown chock-full of historic buildings, and a notable cemetery.

As Berea College grew over the years, the Appalachian artists who came to the area to hone their craft decided to stay. Today Berea bills itself as the Folk Arts and Crafts Capital of Kentucky. One visit to the city will tell you why. There are craft shops and working artists' studios scattered about, so not only can you purchase these fine items, but sometimes you can actually watch them being created.

Madison County is Kentucky at its best. Made up of rolling Kentucky farmland, and the charm of Berea and the small college-town feel of Richmond, it has all the good things you would want in a travel destination.

GUIDANCE Both Berea and Richmond have their own tourism commissions. You can contact them individually, but they work hand in hand and will both supply you with information about the other.

Berea Welcome Center (800-598-5263; www.berea.com), 201 N. Broadway, Berea. Open Mon.–Sat. 9–5, Sun. noon–5. Closed Sun. Jan.–Mar. Visit the Berea Welcome Center, which is housed in a restored 1917 L&N train station. You can't miss it, right in the middle of the Old Town Artisan Village. As you enter town, look for signs directing you to Old Town.

The Richmond Tourism Commission (800-866-3705; www.richmond kytourism.com) is located in the Irvinton House Museum, 345 Lancaster Ave., Richmond. Open Mon.–Fri. 8–4. Grab some maps and information and tour this amazing old home while you're there. They have exhibits on Richmond's past and feature a Revolutionary War uniform, one of only seven known to exist today.

GETTING THERE The closest airport is about 30 miles away, Lexington's **Bluegrass Airport** (859-425-3114; www.bluegrassairport.com). There are

BEREA WELCOME CENTER

Deborah Kohl Kremer

Deborah Kohl Kremer

RICHMOND'S VISITORS CENTER AT THE IRVINTON HOUSE MUSEUM

car rentals available at the airport. There is also a **Greyhound** bus station (859-986-5840) at 301 W. Jefferson St. in Berea.

GETTING AROUND Kentucky River Foothills (800-819-7083; www .foothillscap.org) offers public bus service Mon.–Fri. 9–5. Richmond has two buses that run on 90-minute loops. There is one bus that services Berea; it runs on a one-hour loop. Bus stops are well marked with signs, and schedules are available at each stop. Fare is $1.

Both Richmond and Berea are easy to get around by car, with not much traffic and free parking available everywhere.

MEDICAL EMERGENCY St. Joseph Hospital Berea (859-986-3151; www.bereahospital.org), 305 Estill St., Berea. Serving the residents of Madison, Jackson, Rockcastle, and Garrard Counties since 1898, Berea Hospital is a member of Catholic Health Initiatives, one of the largest Catholic health care systems in the United States. It has been continually recognized for outstanding patient care. In Richmond, the place to turn for care is **Pattie A. Clay Regional Medical Center** (859-623-3131; www.pattieaclay.org), 789 Eastern Bypass, Richmond. This short-term hospital has been serving Richmond and the surrounding community for more than 115 years. The facility has 105 beds; services range from diagnosing broken ankles to intensive care procedures.

ALCOHOL Madison County is considered a moist county. Although alcohol sales are prohibited through most of the county, the city of Richmond is wet, allowing package liquor sales and by-the-drink sales.

✳ To See

Eastern Kentucky University (859-622-1000; www.eku.edu), Richmond. "The Campus Beautiful," as it's known throughout the state, was founded in 1906 as a teachers' college. Today EKU offers over 164 degree programs in five colleges to about 15,000 students per year. Full of ivy-covered buildings and lushly landscaped grounds, the campus always offers something to see or do.

Berea College (859-985-3000; www.berea.edu), Berea. Founded in 1855 as the first interracial and coeducational college in the South, Berea charges no tuition and admits only students with limited financial resources. In addition to a full course load, all students are required to work 10 to 15 hours per week on campus. Berea offers bachelor's degrees in 28 fields, to approximately 1,500 undergraduates, 73 percent of which come from the Appalachian region and Kentucky. Take a walking tour of the handsome campus and you'll get a feel for how special it is.

DANIEL BOONE MONUMENT

Paul Kremer

Richmond Cemetery (859-623-2529), E. Main St., Richmond. This is the largest cemetery in the area. Kentucky's most famous emancipationist, Cassius M. Clay, is buried here as well as many soldiers from the Civil War Battle of Richmond. There is also a Veterans of Foreign Wars memorial. Get a map at the cemetery office.

✍ ♿ **Daniel Boone Monument** (859-622-1000, 800-465-9191; www.eku.edu), University Dr., Richmond. On EKU's campus you'll find a huge bronze statue dedicated to one of the first trailblazers of the Kentucky frontier.

Deborah Kohl Kremer

HUMMEL PLANETARIUM

Boone, who traveled around Kentucky extensively in the 1770s, was a true Kentucky statesman. Make sure you rub his well-polished boot for luck, as so many students and visitors do as they pass.

☄ **Hummel Planetarium and Space Theater** (859-622-1547, 800-465-9191; www.planetarium.eku.edu), Kit Carson Dr., EKU Campus, Richmond. This is the fourth largest planetarium of its kind—in the world, so make sure you tour the galaxy at one of their public shows. Check the website for showtimes. Small admission fee.

♿ **Kentucky Artisan Center** (859-985-5448; www.kentuckyartisancenter .ky.gov), 975 Walnut Meadow Rd., Berea. Open 9–6 every day. Right off I-75; you can't miss this 25,000-square-foot showroom where visitors can shop for authentic Kentucky products. You'll find superbly crafted glass, pottery, woodworking, metalwork, paper, jewelry, specialty foods, music, and books. They have a helpful visitors center too, loaded with brochures and information. And, if you are hungry, the café and grill is open every day from 9:30–3:30. They have daily lunch specials, burgers, a soup and salad bar, and pastries.

🌸 ☄ **Valley View Ferry** (859-258-3611; www.lexingtonky.gov), 169 E. Kentucky Ave., Richmond. Forget the interstate. Drive aboard this old-time ferry and cross the Kentucky River from Madison to Jessamine County. In business since 1785 and Kentucky's oldest continuous business, your short ride will be a memorable one, as the view from down in the valley is fantastic. The ferry is free, but call ahead, as they sometimes close in times of bad weather or high water.

Deborah Kohl Kremer

WHITE HALL, THE HOME OF CASSIUS CLAY

White Hall State Historic Site (859-623-9178; parks.ky.gov), 500 White Hall Shrine Rd., Richmond. Open Apr.–Oct. 31, Wed.–Sun. 9–4. Tours given on the hour. During winter days and times vary, so call ahead to make sure they are open. This 44-room mansion with slave quarters and outbuildings was the home to Kentucky statesman Cassius Marcellus Clay. The restored Italianate mansion was built in 1798 and remodeled in the 1860s. Costumed guides will take you on a tour where you can take in the period pieces and artifacts of White Hall and the Clay family. Adults $7.

STATE PARK ✒ ⚹ **Fort Boonesborough State Park** (859-527-3131; www.parks.ky.gov), 4375 Boonesboro Rd., Richmond. Situated right on the banks of the Kentucky River. You can enjoy a sandy beach, nature trails, mini golf, and an outdoor pool with waterslides. Tour **Fort Boonesborough**, which is open daily Apr.–Oct. 31, 9–5. Winter hours, Nov. 1–Mar. 31: Fri.–Sun. 10–4. This reconstructed fort sits on the site of Kentucky's second settlement, which Daniel Boone helped to establish more than 200 years ago. Each cabin of the fort is furnished to represent the era and features an artisan creating items that were used at the time, such as candle dipping, pottery turning, lye soap making, and welding. Also on site is the Kentucky River Museum, which is housed in the former lock operator's home right on the banks of the river. The museum has exhibits depicting the lives of those who lived on the Kentucky River in the 1900s. Admission includes entrance to both the fort and museum. $8 adults, $5 ages 6–12; 6 and under free. **Fort Boonesborough Campground** is open year-round. It offers 167 sites, most with water and electric hookups; there are some primitive sites available, too. The campground is fairly famous for their over-the-top Halloween decorating contest each fall. The campground management supplies their share of inflatable witches and ghosts, but the campers join in, too, marking their territory with pumpkins, bats, and all things scary. It's fun to see.

✳ To Do

GOLF **Gibson Bay Municipal Golf Course** (859-623-0225; www.gibson bay.com), 2000 Gibson Bay Dr., Richmond. A driving and putting range, as well as a championship 18-hole public golf course.

The Bull at Boone's Trace (859-623-4653; thebullgolf.com), 175 Glen Eagle Blvd., Richmond. This 18-hole championship golf course was created on land that used to belong to Kentucky statesman Cassius Clay. The course winds its way along the high cliffs above the Kentucky River. Legend has it that Clay, who was struggling with a rowdy bull on this site, let go of the beast, which charged away. The bull plunged over the cliff and

THE BEACH AT FORT BOONESBOROUGH

Deborah Kohl Kremer

down the 200 feet to its death. Although this cliff is on the perimeter of the property, the 120-acre course is named in honor of the wayward bull.

Berea Country Club (859-986-7141; www.bereacountryclub.com), 104 Churchill Ct., Berea. Don't let the name scare you off. On the grounds of the country club is a 9-hole, par-36, regulation-length public golf course. It's a nice course, within walking distance of Berea College.

HORSEBACK RIDING Deer Run Stable (859-527-6339; www.deerrun stable.com), 2001 River Circle Dr., Richmond. Enjoy a relaxing day of horseback riding on their farm trails. They also offer hayrides and rustic camping.

HUNTING/FISHING Central Kentucky Wildlife Management Area (800-859-1549), 638 Dreyfus Rd., Berea. Regulated hunting, fishing, and skeet and trapshooting are available on this 1,688-acre wooded preserve.

TOURS Battle of Richmond Driving Tour (859-626-8474, 800-866-3705), 345 Lancaster Ave., Richmond. A part of the National Trust Civil War Discovery Trail, this driving tour with audio guide takes approximately two hours. The battle, which took place in 1862, covered about 17 miles of Madison County. Pick up the audio at the Richmond Tourism Center.

Richmond Downtown Walking Tour of Homes (859-626-8474, 800-866-3705), 345 Lancaster Ave., the Richmond Visitor Center, Richmond. Get a real feel for Richmond on a self-guided walking tour. The route features more than 70 historical buildings, homes, and churches in the downtown area.

✳ Green Space

John B. Stephenson Memorial Forest State Nature Preserve. Get a map at the Berea Welcome Center. Although this park is located in Rockcastle County, it is easiest to find by traveling through Berea. Enjoy the 124-acre wooded gorge that boasts a huge array of natural wildflowers and the pièce de résistance, the 75-foot **Anglin Falls**. The park also offers well-marked trails for nature study, hiking, and bird-watching.

PARK Lake Reba Recreational Complex (859-623-8753; parks .richmond.ky.us), Gibson Bay Dr., Richmond. This 600-acre complex has recreation for everyone. There are baseball and soccer fields as well as basketball and volleyball courts. You can also take advantage of the walking trails, and the huge lake for fishing.

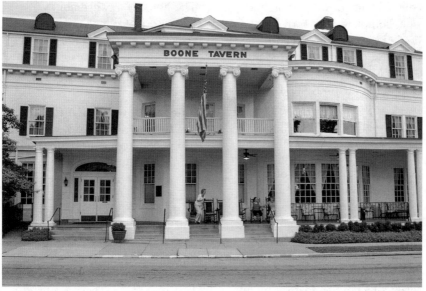

www.kentuckytourism.com

BOONE TAVERN HOTEL

✳ Lodging

&. **Boone Tavern Hotel** (859-985-9358, 800-366-9358; www
.boonetavernhotel.com), Main St.,
Berea. A true landmark in the
area, Boone Tavern Hotel was
built in 1909 as a guesthouse to
accommodate visitors to Berea
College. All 58 rooms feature
modern amenities, as well as
handcrafted cherry, oak, and pine
furniture that has been made by
Berea College student craftsmen
over the past 100 years. The hotel,
which is owned by Berea College,
is staffed by college students.
Berea College, which charges no
tuition, mandates that all students
must work at least 10 hours per
week in addition to carrying a full
course load to offset the costs of
room and board. $$

BED & BREAKFASTS The
**Bennett House Bed & Break-
fast** (859-623-7876; www.bennett
housebb.com), 419 W. Main St.,
Richmond. Listed on the National
Register of Historic Places, the

THE BENNETT HOUSE B&B

Deborah Kohl Kremer

colossal Queen Anne–style mansion, complete with turret and domed roof, has been capturing attention of passersby on Main Street in Richmond since it was completed in 1890. The home has three inviting guest rooms, all with private baths and modern conveniences like cable television and wireless Internet. The rooms are all large enough to also offer a sitting area in each. The home, which is said to have been built "three bricks thick," is an architectural gem. Architect Samuel E. Des Jardins worked a stained-glass window into the fireplace of the foyer, which was a feature he put in all his homes. Ask innkeepers Richard and Rita Smart to show you. $–$$

The Doctor's Inn Bed & Breakfast (859-986-3042; doctorsinnofbereaky.com), 617 Chestnut St., Berea. Dr. Bill Baker and his wife, Biji Baker, welcome you to their Greek Revival home located right in the heart of Berea. Guest rooms feature genuine Berea College antique furniture, Oriental rugs, and stained-glass windows. The full country breakfast specially cooked by Dr. Bill features country ham, biscuits and redeye gravy, eggs, and potatoes or grits. $$

The Great House Inn Bed & Breakfast (859-986-735), 317 Jackson St., Berea. This fully restored 1917 Arts & Crafts–style home has a scrumptious front porch with a wicker swing, rockers, and a view of the mountains.

The home is a convenient walk from Berea College Square. Pat Greathouse (hence the name), your innkeeper, serves up biscuits, gravy, country ham, and eggs each morning. $

Snug Hollow Farm and Country Inn (606-723-4786; www.snughollow.com), 790 McSwain Branch, Irvine. Situated about 20 miles east of Berea, this private inn is snuggled right in the heart of Red Lick Valley in Estill County on 300 acres of creeks, wildflowers, wildlife, and mountain views. You can stay in one of the two comfortable rooms in the farmhouse, or tuck yourself into a restored tin-roofed log cabin. Rates include breakfast, which usually consist of oatmeal pancakes with gingered bananas, crunchy oatmeal-cornmeal waffles, smoked cheddar omelets, and fresh fruit smoothies. With not many restaurants nearby, lunch and dinner are available on request. $$

CAMPING (( )) **Walnut Meadow RV Campground** (859-986-6180), KY 21, Exit 76 off I-75 in Madison County. Boasting they are city close and country quiet, they have 103 sites that can accommodate small campers to big rigs. They also have free WiFi.

OH! Kentucky Campground (859-986-1150; okcg2.homestead.com/okcg2.html), 1142 Paint Lick Rd. (KY 21W), Berea. This wooded campground offers 70 sites with water and electric hookups, tile showers, coin laundry, and two pools.

✳ Where to Eat

DINING OUT ⅋ **Boone Tavern Hotel Dining Room** (859-985-9358, 800-366-9358; www.boone tavernhotel.com), Main St., Berea. Breakfast 7–10, lunch 11–2, Sun.–Thu. dinner 5–8:30, Fri. and Sat. dinner 5–9, Sun. brunch 11–2. Known for its fine, elegant dining, this 100-year-old beauty offers traditional salads and entrées as well as southern favorites like spoonbread, a signature dish that inspired an annual three-day festival in its name. $–$$

⅋ ☿ **Acres of Land Winery and Restaurant** (859-328-3000), 2285 Barnes Mill Rd., Richmond. Standing in the middle of the vineyard in Richmond and gazing at the beautiful countryside, you get a sense of awe looking at the lush acres of land. But when owners Lowell and Katherine look at it, they feel pride. They don't see just acres of land, they see Acres of Land, because, well, it belongs to them. You see, Lowell and Katherine Land—yes, that is really their last name—put all they've got into their winery, vineyard, and restaurant. They produce award-winning wines and offer tours of the winery, on the hour, Fri.–Sun. 1–4. There is a wine tasting room and gift shop on site, where you will want to have a seat, relax, and get a generous sampling of their wines. The day wouldn't be complete, though,

unless you add a meal to it. The restaurant specializes in regional-type fare, including a delicious hot brown, but runs the gamut to include steaks, salmon, pastas, and sandwiches. The lunch menu offers soups, salads, and sandwiches. They are open for lunch and dinner, Wed.–Sun. with seating indoors or outside, overlooking the vineyard. On weekends in the summer, visitors are treated to a one- or two-piece band playing in the courtyard. The Lands will make you feel welcome, and you will see why they attribute their success to the small details that are noticeable in the wine, as well as the food. Everything on the menu is made from scratch, and the ingredients are purchased from local farmers whenever possible. The Lands go as far as putting a sign out front listing which area farms contributed to the day's menu, so customers know exactly what they are getting. $–$$$

☿ **Hanger's Restaurant** (859-353-5588; www.hangersrestaurant .com), 2187 Lexington Rd., Richmond. Open Mon.–Sat. 11–10, Sun. 11–3. At Hanger's they want you to experience fine dining without the stuffiness. So they invite you to "come as you are"— but be ready to be pampered with service and nice touches like white tablecloths and fine china. The dinner menu features everything from sea scallops, to shrimp 'n' grits, to a succulent filet mignon. They have a full wine and after-dinner drink menu, too. $$

Deborah Kohl Kremer

MAIN STREET CAFÉ

EATING OUT

♿ **Main Street Cafe** (859-986-0703; www.msc -berea.com), College Square, Berea. Mon.–Sat. 11–8:30-ish, Sun. noon–3. This is a warm cozy neighborhood restaurant where you'll feel right at home. Their menu says they probably have the best salad in town, and they are probably right. With choices like signature goat cheese salad, as well as Greek, Asian, and Caesar, they've got salads covered. They also have choices like fried green tomato ciabatta, grilled yellowfin tuna steak, and a house recipe for crabcakes. Enjoy live music on Saturday nights. $

♿ **Papaleno's Italian** (859-986-4497; www.papalenos.com), 108 Center St., College Square, Berea. Serving lunch and dinner every day. Walk in and breathe the delicious garlic-scented air. When a restaurant smells this good, you know you're in for a real treat. This Italian, family-style eatery offers favorites like pizza, pasta, and even subs on homemade bread. $

☺ **Madison Garden** (859-623-9720; www.madisongarden.net), 152 N. Madison Ave., Richmond.

PAPALENO'S ITALIAN

Ellie Kremer

Deborah Kohl Kremer

MADISON GARDEN

Tue.–Wed. 11 AM–1 AM, Thu. and Fri. 11 AM–2 AM, Sat. 10 AM–2 AM, Sun. 10 AM–9 PM. They also serve breakfast to the after-bar crowd on Thu., Fri., and Sat. nights 10 PM–2 AM. Educating EKU students about beer for 28 years, Madison Garden in Richmond, Kentucky, has about 175 kinds of beer from around the world on their menu. And you'll be glad they do, if you order up some of their legendary wings. Covered in Madison Garden's unique dry rub, the wings come in mild, medium, hot, or Xtra Hot, and you're going to need a cold beer to wash down any of them. It is a fun sports bar with lots of televisions to watch the big game. The menu also features, sandwiches, salads, burgers, bar food, and drink specials. $

Masala Indian Cuisine (859-623-8589; www.masalafinecuisine .com), 1000 Center Dr., Richmond. Open every day for lunch 11–2:30 PM and dinner 5–10. The combination of imported spices and local produce creates wonderful Indian cuisine. The owners are eager to serve you just the right level of heat, so you can order your entrée mild, medium hot, or Indian hot. Order a glass of ice water, just to be sure. Familiar entrées like chicken, goat or lamb curry top the list in popularity, but don't skip the Indian breads or tasty desserts. Not sure what to order? Go at lunchtime and enjoy everything on the buffet. $

SNACKS *&* **Stella Jane's Bakery** (859-358-6386), 809 Paint Lick Rd., Berea. Closed Sun. and Mon. They say the early bird gets the worm, which is worth noting if you are going for doughnuts. Stella Jane's rewards early risers with fabulous mouthwatering treats, but the bad news for you is: When they are gone, they are gone. The doors open at 7 and they say they are open until 1, but the earlier you go, the better. $

& **Berea Fudge Shoppe** (859-985-8799) 207 Short St., Berea. Watch 'em make it, then watch your mouth water. Delectable flavors; try some of each.

✳ Selective Shopping

In Richmond
Alley Cat Pottery (859-582-1148), 412 E. North St. Featuring traditional and funky tableware and decorative items. The pottery is hand thrown and the glazes are hand mixed from old recipes.

Big T's Gift Shop (859-623-0083), 2635 Lexington Rd. Owners Travis and Paula Timbrook invite you to look around at all their home furnishings, home decor goods, candles, jewelry, antique furniture, chimes, seasonal decorations, and decorative ornaments. Enjoy the parklike grounds and manicured landscaping, too.

Jana Kappeler Studio (859-314-4595; www.janakappelerstudio.etsy.com), 106 S. 3rd St. Jana designs stunning pieces of fused glass, creating pieces of art in the form of bowls, vases, and platters. She also offers the works of her artist friends, who create soaps, pottery, and notecards.

The Country Place Antiques (859-623-0629), 2513 Lexington Rd. Situated on a gentleman's farm on the outskirts of town, this antiques store is full of all kinds of unique items. The shop is in a former horse-breeding barn that now breeds your love of antiques.

In Berea
Berea, known as the **Folk Arts and Crafts Capital of Kentucky**, is an artisan community full of craftsmen (and -women) and the studios where they create and sell their wares. Visitors can witness glassblowing, weaving, woodworking, and myriad other talents just by poking through the shops. Berea has three main shopping areas: Old Town Artisan Village, Chestnut Street, and College Square. In each of these areas you will find unique shops, working artists' studios, and galleries.

Log House Craft Gallery (859-985-3000; www.berea.edu/studentcrafts), 200 Estill St., College Square. As one of the oldest craft galleries in Kentucky and one of the best galleries in the nation, this is the place to find genuine handcrafted art. Find pottery, woodworking, wrought iron, and handmade furniture, all created by Berea college artisans. They also have a fine collection of quilts,

LOG HOUSE CRAFT GALLERY

Deborah Kohl Kremer

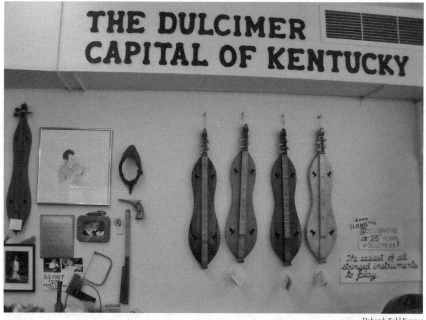

Deborah Kohl Kremer

WARREN MAY WOODWORKER

baskets, and stained-glass pieces created by some of the finest artists in America.

Promenade Gallery (859-986-1609), 205 Center St., College Square. Offering the works of Kentucky artisans, this shop features handcrafted, one-of-a-kind items like pottery, jewelry, candles, art, and ceramics.

Top Drawer Gallery (859-985-2907; www.topdrawergallery.com), 202 N. Broadway St. Featuring handcrafted items by regional artists. You will be amazed by the creations of these gifted people. They have furniture, pottery, woodworking, and even cookbooks, absolutely worth a stop.

Warren May Woodworker (859-986-9293), 110 Center St., College

Square. In business since 1977, Warren specializes in handmade furniture and Kentucky mountain dulcimers. Note the fine detail that goes into each piece.

Honeysuckle Vine Gallery and **Hot Flash Beads** (859-986-2411), Depot Circle in the Old Town Artisan Village. Two shops owned by two sisters. Stop by the gallery to see a huge assortment of pottery and handcrafted home decor items. Then pop next door and watch Jimmy Lou Jackson as she creates glass beads and jewelry using the ancient art of lampworking.

Hosfeld's Jewelry (859-985-5353; www.hosfeldsjewelry.com), 210 N. Broadway. Using precious metals and unique gemstones,

Deborah Kohl Kremer

HONEYSUCKLE VINE GALLERY AND HOT FLASH BEADS

Stephen Hosfeld creates amazing jewelry pieces.

Mitchell Tolle Studio and Gallery (859-986-1069; www .mitchelltolle.com), 633 Chestnut St. See the works of acclaimed artist Mitchell Tolle. His paintings of scenes, people, and even a Kentucky wildcat grace the walls of fans all over the world. Stop by to see where the magic happens.

Haley-Daniels (859-986-7243; www.haleydaniels.com), 119 N. Broadway. Inspired by the woodworking Shakers, but with a contemporary feel, each piece produced by Haley-Daniels is made of the finest woods and produced with the utmost dedication. They make gorgeous furniture, and you can see their sturdy

planters and flower boxes all around downtown Berea.

✳ Special Events

September: ✿ ✎ ♿ **Berea Annual Spoonbread Festival**. This festival honors Boone Tavern's famous spoonbread, a delicious warm, rich corn bread with almost a pudding feel to it, a comfort food for generations. The festival features free concerts all weekend, a balloon glow, a 5K run, a car show, and, of course, plenty of spoonbread.

✿ ✎ ♿ **Richmond's Great American Festival**. Featuring artists and potters from across the state showing their wares. They have art demonstrations, food, and a kids' play area.

DANVILLE AND HARRODSBURG

I f you need a quick infusion of history, the towns of Danville and Harrodsburg ought to satisfy your needs. Although Native Americans roamed Kentucky for generations, it was in Harrodsburg that the first permanent pioneer settlement took root. Just about 10 miles away in Danville is the location where our forefathers dotted the *i*'s and crossed the *t*'s resulting in Kentucky's statehood in 1792.

Danville, a darling college town in Boyle County, looks like the setting for a heartwarming family TV show. In fact, it has been the recipient of the Great American Main Street Award from the National Trust for Historic Preservation. It's just that picture perfect.

Along with claiming the first post office west of the Alleghenies and the first courthouse in Kentucky, Danville was also the site of the first surgery in the state. Today visitors can tour the home of Dr. Ephraim McDowell and see the actual room where this operation took place.

The town square is home to Constitution Square State Historic Site, which is the birthplace of Kentucky's statehood. Tour the centuries-old buildings and learn how Kentucky went from being a county in the western part of Virginia to becoming a state all her own.

Kentucky's oldest town, **Harrodsburg** was established in 1774 by James Harrod. Originally known as Harrod's Town or Harrodstown, it was the first permanent settlement west of the Allegheny Mountains. Today there is a full-scale replica of the original fort on the site.

Old Fort Harrod State Park, the centerpiece of town, is a formidable structure, complete with costumed craftspeople depicting the daily life of the settlers who lived here. On the grounds you'll also find a cemetery, a museum, and the Lincoln Marriage Temple, the cabin where Abraham's parents were wed. While you're there, don't miss the best climbing tree in the state. This colossal osage orange tree, which dates back to the late 1800s, is a massive tree full of low twisting branches. Usually full of kids, it's hard to resist.

Deborah Kohl Kremer

THE MASSIVE OSAGE ORANGE TREE

A stop in Harrodsburg wouldn't be complete without a visit to the Beaumont Inn. This memorable inn and restaurant oozes Kentucky ambience and southern hospitality. If you can't stay there or eat, at least stop by their gift shop and have a look around. This 1840s-era former academy for girls is situated on luxuriant grounds amid centuries-old trees.

Not only was Harrodsburg home to the original Kentuckians, it was also where the religious sect the Shakers chose to put down roots. This community arrived in nearby Pleasant Hill around 1805 and prospered for about 100 years. Today you can tour the original buildings and farmland and learn about this simple religious group whose members were known to shake, shudder, and shiver as they worshipped.

GUIDANCE Contact the **Danville-Boyle County Convention & Visitors Bureau** (859-236-7794, 800-755-0076; www.danville-ky.com) or stop in to 105 E. Walnut St., Danville. **Harrodsburg/Mercer County Tourist Commission** (800-355-9192; www.harrodsburgky.com.), 488 Price Ave., Harrodsburg. Both visitors centers are full of maps, brochures, and helpful information.

GETTING THERE If you are traveling by car, both Danville and Harrodsburg are located just a few miles apart along the 127 Corridor. By air,

Danville and Harrodsburg are both about 40 miles from Lexington's **Blue-grass Airport** (859-425-3114; www.bluegrassairport.com). There are car rentals available. **Greyhound** bus service is also available in Lexington (859-299-8804; www.greyhound.com).

GETTING AROUND Easily navigable by car, Danville and Harrodsburg offer pleasant driving with little traffic and plenty of free parking.

MEDICAL EMERGENCY The **Ephraim McDowell Regional Medical Center** (859-236-4121; www.emrmc.com), 217 S. 3rd St., Danville. Serving more than 146,000 residents from six counties in Central Kentucky, this medical center was established more than 120 years ago. This 222-bed, not-for-profit hospital is named in honor of Dr. Ephraim McDowell, a Danville doctor who performed the first surgery in Kentucky. **James B. Haggin Memorial Hospital** (606-734-5441), 464 Linden Ave., Harrodsburg. Named for Kentucky-born millionaire James Ben Ali Haggin, this 50-bed, full-service hospital serves Mercer County and more than 25,000 patients annually.

ALCOHOL Boyle County is a moist county, as they allow alcohol sales in the city of Danville, but prohibit the sales everywhere else in the county.

DANVILLE VISITORS CENTER

Deborah Kohl Kremer

Mercer County is technically a dry county, but allows alcohol on a limited basis. However, liquor is available by the drink at restaurants in Harrodsburg and Shakertown.

✳ To See

In Danville

🐾 ✐ ♿ **Constitution Square State Historic Site** (859-239-7089, 800-755-0076; www.parks.ky.gov), 134 S. 2nd St., Danville. Visit this site of the signing of Kentucky's constitution, which promoted Kentucky to statehood on June 1, 1792. Ten constitutional conventions were held in a log courthouse on this site to hammer out the basics for the constitution. The park contains a number of buildings including a tavern, built in 1785, where many heated debates took place prior to ratifying the constitution. You can also tour a Presbyterian meetinghouse, a two-room schoolhouse, and the first post office west of the Allegheny Mountains. Don't miss the bronze statue depicting two friends embracing, representing the motto "United we stand, divided we fall." Free.

✐ **McDowell House and Apothecary Shop** (859-236-2804; www.mcdowellhouse.com), 125 S. 2nd St., Danville. Mon.–Sat. 10–noon and 1–4, Sun. 2–4. Tour this home of Dr. Ephraim McDowell, the doctor who

CONSTITUTION SQUARE

Deborah Kohl Kremer

Deborah Kohl Kremer

DR. EPHRAIM MCDOWELL HOUSE

performed the first successful surgery in Kentucky, in 1809. This surgery was performed without the use of anesthesia or sterilization, which gives you a true appreciation for modern medicine. The home is filled with furniture as it must have looked between 1790 and 1830. Visit the attached apothecary and see all sorts of jars and containers full of medicine and remedies and medical devices. $7 adults, $5 seniors, $3 ages 13–20, $3 under 12.

✔ **The Great American Dollhouse Museum** (859-236-1883; www.thedollhousemuseum.com), 344 Swope Dr., Danville. Open Tue.–Sat. 11–5. Let your imagination run wild for a few hours as you peek into the world of miniature towns, fantasy lands, and even scenes from our country's history. Housed in a historic building, the museum offers plenty of room for exploring, and plenty to explore. They have a shop on site as well, where you can stock up on miniature furniture and accessories for your own dollhouse. $7 adults, $5 ages 4–12; free under age 4.

Centre College (800-423-6236; www.centre.edu), 600 W. Walnut St., Danville. First offering classes in the fall of 1820, this college was actually occupied by both Confederate and Union troops during the Civil War. Today Centre is home to about 1,300 students and offers 26 academic majors. On the 115-acre campus are 60 ivy-covered buildings, 13 of which are included on the National Register of Historic Places. Take a campus tour and see them for yourself.

Chateau du Vieux Corbeau Winery (859-236-1808; www.oldcrowinn .com), 471 Stanford Ave., Danville. They produce more than 5,000 gallons of wine each year, using berries and grapes bought from local farmers. Stop in to have a sample or two while you're there. Open Mon.–Sat. 11–6. Free.

JFC Museum (859-236-3442, 800-755-0076; www.bellsouthpwp.net/r/o /rocktown), 1369 Stanford Ave., Danville. JFC Museum is open weekends 10–6. A private collection that is now open to the public. See fossils, rocks, minerals, war memorabilia, Native American artifacts, and distinctive items from the area. Small fee.

Kentucky School for the Deaf (859-239-7017; www.ksd.k12.ky.us), 303 S. 2nd St., Danville. Call for tour info. This groundbreaking school, the first of its kind in the nation, opened in 1823. Tour the restored Italianate structure, which features a re-created 1850s student dorm and classroom.

Perryville Battlefield State Historic Site (859-332-8631; www.perryville .net), 1825 Battlefield Rd., Perryville. Check website for hours. Perryville is the site of Kentucky's largest and most brutal battle. On October 8, 1862, 22,000 Union soldiers battled nearly 17,000 Confederates. The park includes burial grounds and monuments to both armies. The on-site

PERRYVILLE REENACTMENT

Nick Kremer

Deborah Kohl Kremer

OLD FORT HARROD

museum has memorabilia from the era, and a 30-minute film that carefully describes how it all happened. Battle reenactments take place in early October. The museum charges a small fee, but you can walk the grounds for free.

William Whitley House State Historic Site (606-355-2881), 625 William Whitley Rd., Stanford. Open seasonally. Tours May 2–Dec. 14, Wed.–Sat. 9–5, Sun. noon–6. Visit the home of pioneer and statesman William Whitley. The home, called Sportsman's Hill, was the first all-brick home built in Kentucky. It was completed in 1794. The 10-acre grounds include a picnic shelter and playground. Small fee.

In Harrodsburg
✿ **Old Fort Harrod State Park** (859-734-3314; www.parks.ky.gov), 100 S. College St. A full-scale replica of the fort that was built by James Harrod in 1774 is the centerpiece of this park. Huge stockade walls made of logs enclose the cabins and blockhouses, where you'll find interpreters in period-correct clothing performing pioneer tasks such as woodworking, weaving, broom making, and blacksmithing. This park is also home to the Lincoln Marriage Temple, which protects the cabin where Abraham Lincoln's parents were married. While you are there, stop in the Mansion Museum, an 1830s Greek Revival home with artifacts from Native Americans as well as pieces of the Civil War. Look for the huge osage orange tree

right outside the fort. It dates back to the late 1800s and is unofficially the largest and oldest tree like it in the nation. It is perfect for climbing. Small admission fee.

✄ ♿ **Shaker Village of Pleasant Hill** (859-734-5411, 800-734-5611; www.shakervillageky.org), 3501 Lexington Rd. Open Apr. 1–Oct. 31, 10–5; Nov. 1–Mar. 31, 10–4:30. Visit America's largest restored Shaker community. This religious sect, named for the shaking and twitching they did while worshipping, lived in Kentucky from 1805 to 1910. The Shakers thrived through the 1800s, but alas, with their celibate lifestyle, the community eventually died out. What's left now is a village made up of 34 restored buildings, 3,000 acres of preserved farmland, and 25 miles of handcrafted rock fences. Tour the buildings and learn as skilled craftspeople demonstrate techniques commonly used by the Shakers, including broom making, woodworking, spinning, and weaving. Apr. 1–Oct. 31: $15 adults, $7 ages 12–17, $5 ages 6–11. Nov. 1–Mar. 31: $7, $4, $3.

✄ ♿ *Dixie Belle* **Riverboat at Shaker Village** (859-734-5411, 800-734-5611; www.shakervillageky.org), 3501 Lexington Rd. Late April–early Nov., rides at 2 and 4 PM daily. Call ahead to double-check times and availability. Board this authentic stern-wheeler and travel the Kentucky River through a 400-million-year-old limestone canyon. Besides the beauty of the Palisades, you will view huge cliffs, towering waterfalls, and unbelievable scenery that can only be seen from the river.

Harrodsburg Historical Society Old Mud Meeting House (859-734-5985), 220 S. Chiles St. Call ahead to arrange a tour. This original pioneer-era log meetinghouse was home to the first Dutch Reformed Church west of the Alleghenies. Built in 1800, it is constructed from oak timbers; the walls are filled with mud mixed with straw and sticks.

✳ To Do

DISK GOLF Henry Jackson Park (859-238-1233), Crosshill Dr. off Maple Ave., Danville. This 9-hole, par-30, regulation disk golf course has both amateur and professional tees. Free.

FISHING Herrington Lake (859-734-2364; www.harrodsburgky.com), KY 152E, Harrodsburg. This 3,600-acre lake was created in the 1920s by damming the Dix River. It is 32 miles long and is full of bass, bluegill, catfish, and crappie.

GOLF Old Bridge Golf Club (859-236-6051), 1 Old Bridge Rd., Danville. This course features a premier, par-72, public, 18-hole golf course and driving range adjacent to Herrington Lake.

Bright Leaf Golf Resort (859-734-5481, 800-469-6038; www.brightleaf golfresort.com), 1742 Danville Rd., Harrodsburg. Duffers will love this 36-hole championship course, with a lighted 9-hole par-3 course. They also have a driving range and a pro shop.

HORSEBACK RIDING Big Red Stables (859-734-3118), 1605 Jackson Pike, Harrodsburg. Enjoy horseback riding on this huge farm, which covers about 1,000 acres.

RACING Lightning Valley Motor Sports Park (859-854-6535, 800-755-0076; www.lightningvalley.bizland.com), 6800 US 127, Stanford. Come watch all classes of go-carts race. Check the website for race schedules.

SKATEBOARD PARK Danville-Boyle Millennium Skate Park (859-238-1233), off US 150, Perryville Rd., Danville. Skateboarders, in-line skaters, bikers, and remote-control car owners can enjoy this 10,000-square-foot skateboard park every day from dawn until dusk. Free.

✳ Green Space

Danville-Boyle Millennium Park (859-238-1233), off US 150, Perryville Rd., Danville. Created out of 124 acres of rolling pastureland, this park has all the ingredients for recreation. Spend some time on the hiking paths, baseball and soccer fields, playgrounds, concession areas, shelters, and fishing pond.

Anderson Dean Park (www.andersondeanpark.com), US 127, 3 miles north of Harrodsburg. This 213-acre recreational park was built in 1993 and has volleyball, basketball, and tennis courts, an aquatic center, playgrounds, picnic shelters, softball fields, an 18-hole disk golf course, a walking trail, and a skate park.

Central Kentucky Wildlife Refuge (www.ckwr.org), off KY 37 on Carpenter Creek Rd., near Parksville. A 500-acre preserve located 13 miles from Danville and open year-round from dawn to dusk. Visitors can walk the trails to enjoy nature in its purest form. Also a favorite of birdwatchers: Varieties of northern cardinal, blue jay, Carolina chickadee, American goldfinch, downy woodpecker, and white-breasted nuthatch, to name a few, can be seen throughout the year.

LEXINGTON AND THE BLUEGRASS REGION

✳ Lodging

In Danville

Morning Glory Manor and Cottage (859-236-1888), 244 E. Lexington Ave. This Queen Anne–style home dates back to 1895 and is positively charming. They offer two guest rooms in the upstairs of the home, which share a bath. There is also a darling, and private, one-bedroom cottage out back amid a serene garden. $

In Harrodsburg

The Beaumont Inn (859-734-3381, 800-352-3992; www.beaumontinn.com), 638 Beaumont Inn Dr. A true landmark in the area, the Beaumont Inn is the grande dame of Central Kentucky. It's the oldest family-run inn in the state, currently run by fourth- and fifth-generation members of the Dedman family. Offering hotel services with the charm of a B&B,

this stately inn has 33 guest rooms in four distinct buildings. Originally built as a school for young ladies in the 1840s, it was turned into an inn around 1919. The main inn building, a true example of Greek Revival architecture, is on the National Register of Historic Places. Rooms are full of authentic antiques like four-poster beds and marble-top dressers. Throughout the property you will find southern-inspired artwork and mementos of past residents. Walk the park-like grounds spread out over 33 acres, and enjoy the birds, fresh air, and 100-year-old trees. Check out some of books in the lobby area—they are still on the shelves from the inn's days as a girls' school. $$–$$$

& **Inn at Shaker Village of Pleasant Hill** (859-734-5411, 800-734-5611; www.shakervillageky.org), US 68E, 3501 Lexington

THE BEAUMONT INN

Deborah Kohl Kremer

Rd. Enjoy the simple, relaxing style of Shaker Village. Stay in one of the 81 rooms housed in several of the restored buildings on the property. The rooms have modern amenities, like air-conditioning and televisions, with Shaker-inspired furnishings, sparse on elaborate details but warm and homey. $$–$$$

Bright Leaf Golf Resort (859-734-5481, 800-469-6038; www .brightleafgolfresort.com), 1742 Danville Rd. Not just for golf, this resort includes a modern health club, swimming pool, and restaurant, in a casual and relaxing atmosphere. The resort offers a 65-unit motel and 40 private villas. $–$$

✎ **Aspen Hall Manor** (859-734-5050, 888-485-8870; www.aspen hallmanor.com), 558 Aspen Hall Dr. This huge 9,000-square-foot Greek Revival home, which dates back to 1840, is surrounded by lush magnolia trees. All four elegant guest rooms have king beds and fireplaces. You can walk downtown but you might not want to leave. $$–$$$

Southern Charm B&B (859-734-9340; www.southerncharm bb.com), 363 N. East St. This B&B is housed in an elegant 1831 Greek Revival home and features three spacious rooms. Enjoy modern conveniences like the in-ground pool and the big-screen TV in the family room. Delicious continental breakfast each morning and desserts by candlelight each evening. $–$$

CAMPING Chimney Rock RV Park (859-748-5252; www .chimneyrockrvpark.com), 220 Chimney Rock Rd., Harrodsburg. With huge mature trees and wonderful sites right on the edge of Herrington Lake, this campground offers a spot for everything from the smallest tent to the largest RV. They have city water, electric, and sewer hookups as well as a bathhouse, laundry facilities, and a convenience store.

✳ Where to Eat

DINING OUT ♈ **The Beaumont Inn** (859-734-3381, 800-352-3992; www.beaumontinn.com), 638 Beaumont Inn Dr., Harrodsburg. Wed.–Fri. 11:30–1:30 and 6–7:30, Sat. 6–8, Sun. 11–1:30. This dining room is so southern-inspired, it has a giant portrait of Robert E. Lee as well as an orange-lemon cake named in his honor. While hotel guests are welcomed for breakfast, the dining room is only open to the public for lunch and dinner. So if you must have their famous cheese grits, beaten biscuits, and a plate of griddle corncakes, you're going to need to book a room. But if you can hold out for lunch or dinner, you can enjoy house specialties like two-year-old Kentucky cured country ham, yellow-legged fried chicken, and their award-winning corn pudding. For dessert, have the chocolate superfecta: three mini chocolate desserts with three shots of bourbon from Buffalo Trace Distillery. $$–$$$

&. Y **Shaker Village of Pleasant Hill** (859-734-5411, 800-734-5611; www.shakervillageky.org), US 68E, 3501 Lexington Rd., Harrodsburg. Lunch, weekdays 11:30–2:30, weekends noon–3, dinner every day 5:30–8:30. Reservations mandatory. The Shakers were known for their hard work and vigorous worshipping, which involved dancing, trembling, and, well, shaking. All of this must have worked up some powerful appetites, because they left behind some awesome recipes. The salmon croquettes and fried chicken are oft-requested favorites, but they also serve soups, sandwiches, and salads. If you're going to live like a Shaker, try the Shaker Lemon Pie. The recipe uses every part of the lemon, even the rind, because Shakers never wasted anything. The dining room, which is full of Shaker-inspired furnishings, is a simple variety of elegant, but dress is more on the casual side. $$

EATING OUT Red Rooster Café (859-236-2394), 118 E. Main St., Danville. Weekdays 6 AM–8 PM, Sat. 6–3. Right in the heart of town, this is the place to go for a Mom-style home-cooked meal. Start your day with a huge country breakfast, as many locals do. Lunch and dinner choices run the gamut. They have delicious burgers, traditional hot brown, and meat loaf. They're also known for their creamy milk shakes; be sure to clean your plate so you can have one for dessert. $

Y **Mermaids Bar and Bistro** (859-236-2159), 219 S. 4th St., Danville. Open every day, 11 until about 8 PM. A darling restaurant in an old home in downtown Danville. Cute mermaid decor with an upscale feel in the dining room. The bar has cool pale blue under-lighting, which just makes you want to sit there and have a fancy drink. The menu features a mixture of dishes from seared mahimahi to Kentucky Proud steaks, veal, lamb, or chicken. Funky starters like cucumber-wrapped tuna and fried green tomatoes. The spinach artichoke dip is heavenly. Tempting, and worth it, dessert menu, too. $$

Cloud's Country Cooking (859-734-0086), 1028 N. College St., Harrodsburg. Open seven days a week, 11–8. The restaurant is smoke-free on Sunday, noon–2 PM. Get better home cooking than you can get at home. Specialties include country-fried steak and their famous dressing mound: corn bread stuffing with hidden pieces of chicken, covered in gravy. They also have a mouth-watering hash brown casserole and butterfly shrimp. $

Olde Bus Station (859-734-4202), 227 S. Greenville St., Harrodsburg. Mon. 6–2, Tue.–Fri. 6 AM–8 PM, Sat. 8–2, Sun. 11–2. Just like the name says, this hometown eatery is located in the former Greyhound bus station. You can still eat at the original soda fountain, or outside on the newly built covered deck. This is a very casual, mom-and-pop-type place with juicy cheeseburgers, plate-lunch specials, and a daily assortment of homemade pies. Owner Lori Hill treats everyone who walks in the door like family. $

&. Ⓨ **Eddie Montgomery's Steak House** (859-734-3400; eddie montgomerysteakhouse.com), 180 Lucky Man Way, Harrodsburg. Tue.–Wed. 4–9, Thu. 4–11, Fri.–Sat. 11 AM–1:30 AM, Sun. 11 AM–8 PM. Although they pride themselves on all of the national music acts they bring to stage, they also boast 22 flat screens scattered about, bringing you the games you want, when you want them. Eddie's a hometown boy who made it big in the duo of Montgomery Gentry, and now he comes back to town to share his love of music, sports, and good food, especially steaks. $$

Aunt Gravy's and Family (859-734-2151), 419 E. Office St., Harrodsburg. Open Mon.–Sat. 6:30–2; Feb.–Aug. they serve dinner Tue.–Fri. 5–8. Nothing says home cooking like the biscuits at Aunt Gravy's. These delectable bites of homemade goodness are even better slathered in gravy. In fact, aren't most things better with gravy? Locals come every day for the specials; whether it's meat loaf, spaghetti, or pork chops, it will all be good and inexpensive. Try the homemade butterscotch pie for dessert. $

SNACKS ✎ &. **Kentucky Fudge Company** (859-733-0088, 877-892-3657; www.kentuckyfudge company.com), 225 S. Main St., Harrodsburg. Tue.–Fri 10–9, Sat. 8:30–9, Sun. 11–7. Closed Mon. Starting out as Smith and

KENTUCKY FUDGE COMPANY

Deborah Kohl Kremer

BURKE'S BAKERY

Deborah Kohl Kremer

Dedman's Drug Store in the 1860s, this old-time location still dispenses all things necessary in life: gourmet coffee, homemade pastries, ice cream, and handmade fudge. Browse the high shelves, once full of medical cures, now full of interesting memorabilia. They have sandwiches and soups, too.

& **Burke's Bakery** (859-236-5661), 121 E. Main St., Danville. Mon.–Sat. 7–5. Located right across the street from Constitution Square; you can pop over during your tour. This bakery has been around since 1936, and it's a true staple in the community. They offer fresh-baked pastries, doughnuts, and cakes. They also have sandwiches at lunchtime. Yummy gingerbread men and iced apple bread. $

& (⌐) **Hub Coffee Shop and Café** (859-936-0001; www.the hubcoffeehousencafe.com), 236 W. Main, Danville. Open Mon.–Thu. 6:30 AM–9:00 PM, Fri. 6:30 AM–11 PM, Sat. 7 AM–11 PM, Sun. 8 AM–9 PM. Housed in an old department store, this cute café is warm and inviting. Stop in for a cuppa joe and some free WiFi and stay for a deli sandwich, salad, or wrap. Live music on weekends. $

✳ Entertainment

& **Pioneer Playhouse Outdoor Dinner Theater** (859-236-2747; www.pioneerplayhouse.com), 840 Stanford Rd., Danville. Founded in 1950, this theater is both rustic and inviting. It was built with a hodgepodge of building materials that all add to its character. As the oldest outdoor theater in Kentucky, the Pioneer Playhouse is credited with starting the whole outdoor theater movement in the state. Dinner is served on the adjacent patio area, and choices are limited to fried chicken or barbecued pork, served with corn pudding, green beans, salad, and a cookie. The theater itself is darling, but the shows are first-rate. The schedule includes plays, dramas, comedies, and musical performances. During summer a live performance takes place every Tue.–Sat., come rain or shine. It does move indoors in case of rain. Check the website to see what's showing.

West T. Hill Community Theatre (859-236-8607; www.west thill.com), 117 Larrimore Lane, Danville. Named for the founding member and former chairman of the Dramatic Arts Department at Centre College, West T. Hill, the group was formed in 1980. This is a very talented community theater group, producing seven or eight shows each year in their 125-seat auditorium. Check the website to see what's going on.

MOVIES **Twin Hills Drive-In Theatre** (859-734-3474, 800-734-8011; www.drive-ins.com), 1785 Louisville Rd. (US 127N), Harrodsburg. One of the few remaining drive-ins in the state, it's a fun spot to watch first-run movies all summer long. Visit the concession stand or bring your own snacks.

✳ Selective Shopping

Beehive Gifts (859-734-4403; beehivegiftsinky.net), 114 S. Main St., Harrodsburg. Pick up some gifts or a few things for yourself at this cute downtown shop. They carry popular options like Yankee Candles, Boyd Bears, Willow Tree Angels, and some Kentucky-made options that you can't find anywhere else.

My Mapletree Gallery (888-666-4331; mymapletreegallery.com), 225 W. Main St., Danville. This cute shop has items to give as gifts and keep for yourself. They are the exclusive dealer of Cranes Stationery and Pomegranate merchandise, as well as art by local artisans.

ANTIQUES **The Robin's Nest** (859-865-2282; therobinsnestky.com), 200 Main St., Salvisa. What better location for an antiques

PIONEER PLAYHOUSE

store than a home that dates back about 200 years? Just north of Harrodsburg in the tiny hamlet of Salvisa you will find an amazing piece of architecture loaded with primitives, antique home furnishings, and a country store. The Robins Nest's has something for every taste. Owners Stephen and Joann Robinson will be glad to see you and tell you about the pieces or the home itself.

Not Just Antiques in Danville (859-239-0088; notjustantiquesin danville.com), 1000 E. Lexington Ave., Suite 36, Danville. This 8,000-square-foot multidealer gallery of fine antiques, art, and decorator items also has outside display of ornamental ironwork and yard statuary.

Old Kentucky Restorations and Cairn's Antiques (859-734-6237), 122 W. Lexington St., Harrodsburg. In business for 27 years, the Cairn family knows all about the antique furniture they sell. Their main business is antique furniture restoration and repair, but call for an appointment to see their 8,000-square-foot antiques gallery.

✳ Special Events

June: ✿ ✿ ✿ **Great American Brass Band Festival**. This annual Danville event features a wide variety of brass bands, a hot-air balloon race, a parade, and live brass band concerts all weekend. Everyone loves the sound of an old-fashioned brass band.

✿ ✿ ✿ **Fort Harrod Beef Festival**. Held on the Mercer County Fair Grounds and at Old Fort Harrod State Park, this festival celebrates Kentucky's beef industry. There is a chili cook-off, a 5K run, called a stampede, juried arts and crafts, live music. There is also a beef grill-off, where teams compete to make the best brisket, steak, and burger.

September: ✿ ✿ ✿ **Constitution Square Festival**. Located right on the grounds where Kentucky's forefathers met and signed Kentucky's constitution. This festival features arts and crafts exhibitors, living history reenactments, food, music, kids' activities, and guided tours of all the historical buildings on site.

October: ✿ ✿ ✿ **Forkland Heritage Festival**. This festival is held annually at the Forkland Community Center, in southern Boyle County. Celebrating the county's heritage and rural past, the community comes together with a true folk festival including arts and crafts, games, educational displays, food, and live music.

FRANKFORT AND GEORGETOWN

These two delightful towns are just about 20 miles apart and connected by Frankfort Road, also known as US 460. The twisty country road is itself worth the trip, as you are privy to historic mansions on the Georgetown end, hand-laid stone fences and horse farms in the middle, and then the sights of Frankfort at the other end. Doesn't matter which town you start in, but both are must-sees.

Frankfort, a little storybook town on the banks of the Kentucky River, is filled with history-laden buildings and darling old Victorian homes. It also has an aura of elegance and importance, as it is the Kentucky state capital.

The town was established in 1786 as Frankfort, Virginia, and it became the capital when Kentucky became its own state in 1792. Today it boasts of approximately 28,000 permanent residents, but the daily population swells to about 50,000 based on the workforce of legislators, politicians, and state government employees who commute in each day.

Visitors can tour various state buildings, including the Kentucky State Capitol and Governor's Mansion. You'll wish the walls could talk but instead, and almost as good, you'll find knowledgeable tour guides available to fill you in on the details.

No trip to Frankfort is complete without a stop at the Frankfort Cemetery, where you can pay your respects to the grave of Daniel Boone, followed by a stop at Rebecca Ruth Candy for a free Bourbon Ball.

Frankfort is enjoyable because of its unique balance. Although it is the center of Kentucky politics, which can seem somewhat glamorous, its small-town roots allow visitors to find homey restaurants and cute antiques stores and galleries along the downtown streets.

Prior to the 1980s, when Toyota arrived, **Georgetown** was a sleepy little college town with tree-lined streets that accented 100-year-old homes, complete with turrets and porch swings.

Although the downtown looks much today as it did then, the difference is the influx of money and people that came when Toyota opened their massive plant on the outskirts of town. You can visit Georgetown without even knowing there is a 200-acre building on the other side of I-75, but try to set aside time for a tour. It really is fascinating to see these cars coming through the assembly line.

Georgetown was first settled around 1785 by the Reverend Elijah Craig and a group of Virginia Baptists. Craig, who was quite an entrepreneur, settled near the ever-flowing Royal Branch Spring, where he manufactured cloth and paper. He founded a classical school in the town, which has evolved into today's Georgetown College. This wonderful spring was vital to Georgetown's growth. Craig used it for distilling and is credited with creating a little drink that became popular throughout the state, bourbon.

Named in honor of George Washington, Georgetown is known for its antiques district in the well-preserved downtown, as well as a variety of restaurants and shops scattered about. For die-hard shoppers, there is a 20-store outlet mall right off I-75.

Today Georgetown is an easy mix of industry and farming. You'll find thoroughbred farms just beyond the downtown area in any direction. Go for a drive and enjoy the scenery of horses in their bluegrass fields, acres of hand-laid limestone fences, and rolling countryside.

GUIDANCE Frankfort Tourism (800-960-7200; www.visitfrankfort .com), 100 Capital Ave., Frankfort. Mon.–Fri. 8–5. The Frankfort Visitors Center is housed in a Victorian home with gingerbread trim and a wraparound porch that has an inviting porch swing and rocking chairs. It fits right into the neighborhood of fine homes, so look for the sign out front. In addition to maps and brochures, they have craft items from area shops, as well as a sampling of displays you will find in the area museums. They also have a computer you can use to check your email or make hotel reservations. Friendly staff make you feel like you have a friend in Frankfort. **Georgetown/Scott County Tourist Commission** (888-863-8600; www.georgetownky.com), 399 Outlet Center Dr., Georgetown. Open weekdays 9–5. Right behind the Cracker Barrel, you'll find the tourism office. They have all kinds of brochures and maps about Georgetown and other touristy areas of the state.

GETTING THERE The nearest airport is just south of Georgetown and Frankfort, in Lexington. Fly into **Lexington's Bluegrass Airport** (859-425-3114; www.bluegrassairport.com), which is about 20 miles away from each. There are car rentals available. **Greyhound** bus service is also available in Lexington (859-299-8804; www.greyhound.com).

GETTING AROUND The state capital seems to be the crossroads for every major artery in Kentucky. I-64, US 60, US 127, US 460, and US 412 all come through town, making you feel like all roads lead to Frankfort.

Streets are well marked, but a map might not be a bad idea. The downtown area has parking lots and some parking meters, but you can easily park down a nearby residential street. **Frankfort Transit** (502-875-8565; www .frankfort-ky.gov/transit-division.html) runs three routes through the city Mon.–Sat.; see the website for schedules. In Georgetown, you will find well-marked streets and friendly residents whom you can stop and ask directions from. It is easy to get around by car, with lots of free parking everywhere.

MEDICAL EMERGENCY The Frankfort area is served by **Frankfort Regional Medical Center** (502-875-5240; www.frankfortregional.com), 299 Kings Daughters Dr., Frankfort. This 173-bed hospital has been providing health care to Franklin, Anderson, Owen, Woodford, Shelby, and surrounding county residents since 1896. **Georgetown Community Hospital** (502-868-1100; georgetowncommunityhospital.com), 1140 Lexington Rd., Georgetown. This 75-bed acute care facility has won awards for its excellence in health care.

ALCOHOL Franklin County, which, by the way, is named for American statesman Benjamin Franklin, is a wet county, with alcohol sales permitted everywhere. Scott County, home to Georgetown, also allows alcohol sales, but only in restaurants.

✳ To See

In Frankfort
🍴 ✎ ♿ **Kentucky State Capitol** (502-564-3449), 300 Capital Ave. Open weekdays 8–4:30, Sat. 10–2, Sun. 1–4. The capital, which opened in 1910, houses the three branches of government. It is highly ornate and very

THE KENTUCKY STATE CAPITOL

Gene Burch

elegant. Created in the Beaux-Arts style, it includes many traditional French designs and elements of classical architecture. The first floor, or executive floor, is where you'll find the governor's office and the imposing seven-story dome and rotunda. This area is home to statues of Kentucky notables Abraham Lincoln, Jefferson Davis, Henry Clay, Alben Barkley, and Ephraim McDowell. Also on the first floor, don't miss "Kentucky's First Ladies in Miniature"—a display of dolls, one of each first lady dressed in her inaugural ball gown. The grand marble staircases take visitors to the judicial floor, where you will find Kentucky's Supreme Court. The third floor is the home of both the Kentucky House of Representatives and Senate. Stop to take in the oil-painted murals depicting Daniel Boone as he explored Kentucky. Free.

🌸 ✄ ♿ **Floral Clock** (502-564-3449), 300 Capital Ave. Adjacent to the capitol building, this working clock is 34 feet in diameter and created from a variety of colorful flowers. The minute hand alone is 21 feet long.

🌸 ✄ ♿ **Governor's Mansion** (502-564-8004; www.governorsmansion .ky.gov), 704 Capital Ave. Guided tours Tue. and Thu. mornings 9–11. Sitting on the east lawn of the capitol is the Beaux-Arts-style mansion that was modeled after Marie Antoinette's summer villa in France. It was constructed, trimmed, and finished with native stone produced from quarries in Kentucky. Although it has housed 24 governors since Governor James

GOVERNOR'S MANSION

Ellie Kremer

McCreary moved in during his 1914 term, most of the lighting fixtures, ornamental plaster, and mantels are original. Free.

♦ ✿ ᕱ Frankfort Cemetery and Daniel Boone's Grave (502-227-2403), 215 E. Main St. This historic cemetery is situated on a hill high above the state capitol grounds, offering stunning views. It is most visited for the grave site of Daniel and Rebecca Boone, but it is also the final resting place for 17 Kentucky governors. Free.

Kentucky Military History Museum (502-564-3265; www.history.ky .gov), 125 E. Main St. at Capital Ave. Open Tue.–Sat. 10–5. Located in the old state arsenal, its displays include firearms, edged weapons, and artillery and weaponry from the Revolutionary War until today. $4 adults $4, $2 ages 6–18; under 5 free.

Kentucky Vietnam Veteran's Memorial, 300 Coffee Tree Rd. One of the nation's most original and unusual memorials, it is a huge sundial made of stainless steel and granite. The names of 1,103 Kentuckians lost in the war are engraved into the plaza, including 23 missing in action. Each name is placed so that the tip of the shadow touches the name on the anniversary of death.

♦ ✿ ᕱ Rebecca Ruth Candies & Tours (502-223-7475, 800-444-3766; www.rebeccaruth.com), 112 E. 2nd St. Tours Mon.–Sat. (Jan.–Nov.) 9–noon and 1–4:30. Started by two teachers who enjoyed candy making more than instructing, Rebecca Gooch and Ruth Hanly, these ladies left their classrooms and opened a candy company in 1919. Credited with inventing the Bourbon Ball (every woman knows bourbon and chocolate go together), Rebecca Ruth offers all kinds of candy, not just those drenched with liquor. Stop in and take a tour of the factory and enjoy a free sample. No advance notice is needed. Tours $2.

REBECCA RUTH CANDIES

Deborah Kohl Kremer

Liberty Hall Historic Site (502-227-2560, 888-516-5101; www .libertyhall.org), 218 Wilkinson St. Tours Tue.–Sat. 10:30, noon, 1:30, and 3. Visit the two notable homes on the grounds. First is a Federal-style house built in 1796 by one of Kentucky's first two U.S. senators, John Brown. The second is an 1835 Greek Revival home called the Orlando Brown House (John Brown's son). These homes are filled with remarkable pieces of the past, but don't forget to stroll the lovely gardens while you are there. $4 adults, $3 seniors, $1 ages 4–18; under 4 free.

✒ ♿ **Thomas D. Clark Center for Kentucky History** (502-564-1792; www.history.ky.gov), 100 W. Broadway. Open Tue.–Sat. 10–5. Kids love the permanent $2.8 million exhibit *A Kentucky Journey*, which portrays 12,000 years of Kentucky with the help of 3,000 artifacts, hands-on activities, animatronics, and interactive exhibits. There is also a *huge* research library with rare books, maps, and manuscripts that bring Kentucky's past to life. If you have roots in Kentucky, save time to do a little genealogy research while you are here; the staff are really helpful. $4 adults, $2 ages 6–18; 5 and under free.

Vest-Lindsey House (502-564-6980), 401 Wapping St. Tours by appointment. One of Frankfort's oldest homes, dating back to the early 1800s, this Federal-style house with Victorian features was home to U.S. senator George Graham Vest. Today it serves as a state meetinghouse for Kentucky government.

♿ **Old State Capitol** (502-564-1792; history.ky.gov), 300 W. Broadway. Tours Tue.–Sat. 10–5 on the hour. Completed in 1830, this building was used as the Kentucky state capitol for about 80 years. The architectural significance of the building is that this style of Greek Revival had just been introduced into Kentucky. Another architectural marvel is in the central rotunda: an amazing self-supporting marble staircase that is held

OLD STATE CAPITOL

Ellie Kremer

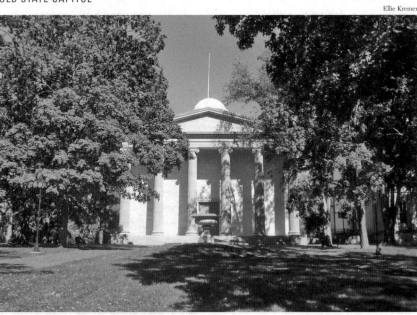

together by pressure and precision. It splits halfway up to become a double circular staircase, which is quite remarkable. Upstairs, the Senate chamber is furnished in 1830s reproduction desks and chairs. Across the hall, the House of Representatives chamber is furnished mostly in reproduction desks and chairs used prior to the Civil War through 1909. The Old Capitol building still has some original furnishings, including 1840s chandeliers and hand-blown window panes. Free.

Kentucky State Police Museum (502-875-7625; www.ksppa.com), 633 Chamberlin Ave. Open weekdays. A museum dedicated to the rich tradition and proud past of the Kentucky State Police. Memorabilia, vehicles, photographs, and weapons are displayed. Free.

Kentucky State University (502-597-6000; www.ksu.edu), E. Main St. KSU is a small, unique liberal studies university founded in 1886 right in the heart of Frankfort. Two buildings on campus, Hume and Jackson Halls, are on the National Historic Register. Jackson Hall contains a public art gallery that features exhibits by KSU students and the Center of Excellence for the Study of Kentucky African Americans. Blazer Library contains over 350,000 volumes, has a special African American collection, and is open to the public.

In Georgetown

⊛ ✿ ♿ **Toyota Motor Manufacturing Plant Tours** (502-868-3027, 800-866-4485; www.toyotageorgetown.com), 1001 Cherry Blossom Way. This tour, which lasts about an hour and a half, includes a video depicting the story of Toyota and how it came to call Kentucky home. After the intro movie, board a tram and take a tour of the 8-million-square-foot plant floor, where you can watch as cars are actually being assembled. This plant produces 500,000 Camrys, Solaras, and Avalons each year. Children

TRAM TOUR OF THE TOYOTA PLANT

Toyota Motor Manufacturing

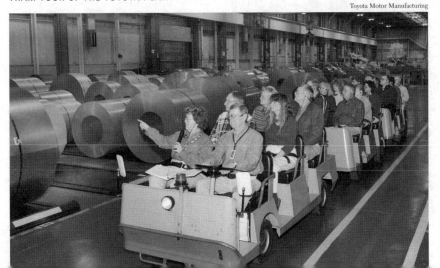

must be over eight years old, and you will need reservations for the tour. Visitors center open to the public. Free.

Georgetown College (502-863-8000; www.georgetowncollege.edu), 400 E. College St. This delightful campus, right in the middle of town, was established in 1787 and is the oldest Baptist college west of the Alleghenies. It's a small, Christian, liberal arts school home to 1,300 students. Stroll the campus and visit the Anne Wright Wilson Fine Arts building, which has one of Central Kentucky's largest art galleries.

Cardome Centre (502-863-1575; www.cardomecenter.com), 800 Cincinnati Pike. Cardome—the word is Latin for "dear home"—is a wonderful example of a public building constructed in the 1890s. It has a rich and varied past, serving as a residence for a private girls' academy. Take a tour and marvel in the colorful stained glass, intricate woodwork, and historical significance. Call to schedule a tour.

Ward Hall (502-863-2547, 888-863-8600; www.wardhall.net), US 460W. If you are interested in architecture, make Ward Hall, just a mile outside downtown Georgetown, your destination. It's said to be the largest Greek Revival house in Kentucky and referred to as the finest example of this style of architecture in the South. Built in 1853, this home is magnificent in its own right, but take time to enjoy the attractive grounds, too. Call for tour information.

Georgetown and Scott County Museum (502-863-6201), 229 E. Main St. Enjoy displays of artifacts from prominent families of the region, as well as relics from the Civil War and Indian times.

EVANS ORCHARD

Trey Zimmerman

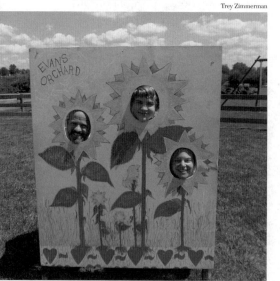

🐾 🌸 ♿ **Evans Orchard and Cider Mill** (502-863-2255; www.evansorchard.com), 180 Stone Rd. Open seasonally Tue.–Sat. 9:30–6. Enjoy a day on the farm, touring the orchards where they grow apples, peaches, and pears, plus 30 acres of vegetables. You can pick some yourself, too. They also offer a corn maze, a hay mountain with slides, and a rope maze.

TOUR 🐾 🌸 ♿ **Buffalo Gals Barn Quilt Trail** (502-863-2547; www.georgetownky.com). This driving tour through picturesque farmland is pleasant, but add the element of searching for quilt squares and it makes the ride doubly enjoyable. Quilt squares are roadside art, 8-by-4-foot squares painted to represent what is usually created with needle and thread. These works of art are painted onto the sides of barns and scattered about the area. The entire trail includes more than 100 barn quilt squares, so take a camera and "collect" them as you meander through the countryside. Contact the Georgetown tourism office for map of the trail.

✳ To Do

CANOEING Canoe Kentucky (502-227-4492, 888-226-6359; www .canoeky.com), 7323 Peaks Mill Rd., Frankfort. Offering canoe, kayak, and raft rentals year-round on Elkhorn Creek. Canoe Kentucky can set up a lazy float on the stream, a day of fishing for smallmouth bass, or a ride on the rapids. The choice is yours.

DISTILLERY TOURS Buffalo Trace Distillery (502-696-5926, 800-654-8471; www.buffalotrace.com), 1001 Wilkinson Blvd., Frankfort. Tours start on the hour, Mon.–Fri. 9–3, Sat. 10–2. This is the oldest continuously operating distillery in the United States. Tours include the fermenting room as well as the rickhouses where the bourbon barrels are stored while they age. Tastings and a free bourbon ball follow the tour. They also have a gift shop for souvenirs.

Four Roses Distillery (502-839-3436; www.fourroses.us), 1224 Bonds Mill Rd., Lawrenceburg. The 45-minute tours start on the hour, Mon.–Sat. 9–3. Closed most of the summer and major holidays. This distillery, built in a Spanish Mission style, looks like it should be in Southern California instead of on the banks of the Salt River. The beautiful building, constructed in 1911, is on the National Register of Historic Places. Guests over 21 can enjoy a small sample of this smooth and mellow bourbon.

Wild Turkey Distillery (502-839-4544), US 62E, Lawrenceburg. Offers free tours Mon.–Sat. at 9, 10:30, 12:30, and 2:30. Advance notice is requested for groups of more than 10. Closed all major holidays, the first full week of January, and the last two full weeks of July. Guests can view the process from grain delivery through barreling.

FAMILY FUN ✍ Starway Family Fun Park (502-227-1864), 3350 Louisville Rd., Frankfort. Lots of fun on the 18-hole miniature golf course complete with waterfalls and bridges. They also have a go-cart course, with rookie carts for little ones. Don't forget to bring some change for the arcade room.

GOLF Ducker's Lake Golf Course (502-695-4653; www.duckerslake golfcourse.com), 98 Buena Vista Dr., Frankfort. Nestled into the rolling hills and pastureland is an 18-hole championship public course.

THE BARN QUILT TRAIL

Most people collect something—rocks, stamps, sea shells, baseball cards—but more and more Kentuckians are collecting quilt squares: giant, 8-foot-by-8-foot quilt squares. These artistic murals adorn the sides of barns throughout the Bluegrass State. And the collector uses a camera, not a ladder and a crowbar.

The Georgetown area is home to the Buffalo Gals Barn Quilt Trail, which meanders through horse farms and back roads, encompassing more than 100 barn quilt squares. It's a pleasant drive, with the added bonus of collecting the squares.

"It's like a sightseeing trip," said Carole Landry of Stamping Ground. Landry is a member of the Buffalo Gals homemakers group in Scott County and one of the forces behind the creation of the trail. "Quilters enjoy looking for patterns they are familiar with, but to most people, it is just a huge art project."

Landry, her husband, Brad, and about eight members of the group, which is part of the Scott County Extension Service, came up with the idea in 2007. They created the guidelines and helped design, paint, create, and install about 150 of these beautiful pieces.

"There are 100 within Scott County, and about 50 more of ours are in other counties in Kentucky," said Landry. She hopes the barn quilt squares serve as an art lesson for children. "Kids see this art as their school bus passes it every day. I hope it shows them that art can come in many different forms, and you can do what you like."

The concept began in the late 1890s with ads painted on the sides of wooden barns. Yesterday's "Chew Mail Pouch Tobacco" ad evolved into today's quilt square.

As people added quilt squares to their barn, tourists traveling through the area started to take notice and wanted a list of all of them. This inspired the creation of the Barn Quilt Trail. Although you can spot these beauties all over the country, Kentucky has plenty of quilt squares along many different quilt trails. Some of the squares represent an aspect of the community's history or a design from a family quilt.

Elliott County, in eastern Kentucky, is home to about 70 barn quilt squares. Gwenda Lynn Adkins, county extension agent for family and

Nick Kremer

QUILT SQUARE IN GEORGETOWN

consumer sciences, sees people scouting for these blocks for various reasons.

"Some people make scrapbooks of their photos, and some people make the actual quilt," she said. "But usually the story of the barn is just as diverse as the story of the quilt square attached to it."

In Elliott County, the project started as a way to preserve barns. "So many old barns have been torn down, but they are part of our culture and needed to be saved," Adkins said. "Once the quilt square was in place and the barn was saved, people started cleaning up the barn itself and the sur-rounding area. It has become a source of community pride."

Hunting for these squares is not like searching for a needle in a hay-stack. County tourism agencies or county extension offices usually have maps highlighting the quilt squares, and some even list GPS coordinates. For more information, visit the following sites:

Kentucky Arts Council: www.artscouncil.ky.gov

Western Kentucky: www.kentuckyquiltline.com

Eastern Kentucky: www.kentuckyquilttrail.org

Buffalo Gals in Scott County: www.georgetownky.com

Central Kentucky: www.kyheritagequilttrail.com

Cherry Blossom Village Golf & Country Club (502-570-9849; www .cherryblossomgolf.com), 150 Clubhouse Dr., Georgetown. Voted the best public golf course in Kentucky by *Golfweek* magazine. Make sure you try this 18-hole, par 72, championship course.

Longview Country Club (502-863-2165) 3243 Frankfort Rd., Georgetown. This public, par-72 course has 18 holes, a driving range, and motorized cart and golf club rentals.

HORSEBACK RIDING Horses4U (502-223-8925; www.horses4u2.com), Frankfort. Feel the Kentucky farmland under your hooves as you ride an Appaloosa horse along the trails of this family-run farm.

Whispering Woods Riding Stables (502-570-9663; www.whispering woodstrails.com), 265 Wright Lane, Georgetown. This 250-acre farm offers wooded trails as well as pastureland for your horseback ride. They have lots of friendly horses or ponies for you to choose from, or you can bring your own

RECREATION Georgetown/Scott County Pavilion Recreation Center (502-863-7865), 140 Pavilion Dr., Georgetown. If you want to work out, head for this huge 55,000-square-foot rec center. They have a fitness center, aerobics room, gymnasium with two full-sized basketball courts, elevated walking track, eight-lane indoor lap pool, and indoor leisure pool with 108-foot slide.

✳ Green Space

🐾 ✍ ♿ **Salato Wildlife Education Center** (502-564-7863; www.kdfwr .state.ky.us/salat01.htm), 1 Game Farm Rd., Frankfort. Operated by the Kentucky Department of Fish and Wildlife Resources, this 132-acre recreational and educational complex is an enjoyable way to learn about nature. Hiking trails, boating, and fishing are available on site. The indoor education center is full of fun, interactive displays, and even a few live animals. The paved (and handicapped-accessible) walking trail treats visitors to wildlife encounters with Kentucky natives like bear, bison, elk, and a wildcat named Blue, who is the official mascot of the University of Kentucky.

Leslie Morris Park (502-696-0607), 325 Ann St., Frankfort. Right in the middle of Frankfort is 124 acres of forest, virtually untouched since the Civil War era when locals protected the city from Confederate raiders in 1864. Two of these earthwork forts remain intact. The trail into the park, which starts right behind the Capital Plaza Tower, connects to trails with interpretive markers. Be sure to look for the dry-laid stone fences while you hike.

♨ ⌀ ও **Yuko-En on the Elkhorn, the Official Kentucky–Japan Friendship Garden** (502-316-4554), 800 Cincinnati Pike, Georgetown. Wonderful Japanese-style strolling garden with walking trails, waterfalls, bridges, and a Zen rock garden. Peaceful and serene; come here to rest and recharge.

✳ Lodging

⌀ **Meek House** (502-227-2566, 866-646-7650; www.bbonline.com /ky/meek), 119 E. 3rd St., Frankfort. Located within walking distance of the state capitol, this Gothic Revival home offers comfortable rooms and a peaceful garden and pond area for you to relax. The home was built in 1869 by Benjamin F, Meek, a silversmith who helped develop the Meek and Milam Fishing Reel. $

The Meeting House (502-226-3226; www.themeetinghouse bandb.com), 519 Ann St., Frankfort. This pre–Civil War home has plenty of fascinating stories in its past, and innkeepers Gary and Rose Burke love to share them with interested guests. The home still has original fireplaces, floors, and wood moldings to help you soak it all in. The five warm guest rooms are all richly decorated. They also have a charming little café and gift shop open to all. $

⌀ **The Inn at Old Friends** (502-863-1775; www.oldfriendsequine .org), 1841 Paynes Depot Rd., Georgetown. This B&B with two guest rooms is the perfect place to get up close and personal with horses. On the grounds of Old Friends Equine, a 52-acre thoroughbred retirement farm, guests can take part in the workings of a real horse farm as well as meet some former champions in the thoroughbred industry. $$

⌀ **Pineapple Inn Bed & Breakfast** (502-868-5453; www.pineapple innbedandbreakfast.com), 645 S. Broadway, Georgetown. This bright yellow 1876 Victorian home has inviting architecture with gables, a bay window, and poplar floors. Four large private rooms are all decorated with antiques to fit the theme. The Derby Room makes you feel right at home. $

⌀ ও **Capital Plaza Hotel** (502-227-5100; www.capitalplazaky .com), 405 Wilkinson Blvd., Frankfort. Experience gracious hospitality at this 189-room hotel. Within walking distance of the downtown district and 2 miles from the capitol, you'll be close to everything. Capital Plaza has nicely furnished rooms, covered parking, interior corridors, an indoor pool, a sauna, and an exercise room. Check out the nice waterfall fountain in the lobby when you enjoy your complimentary breakfast. Ask for a room on the top floor, where you'll have an excellent view of the stunning Kentucky State Capitol. $

CAMPING Still Waters Campground, Marina & Canoe Trails (502-223-8896), 249 Strohmeier Rd., US 127N. You'll find Still Waters on the Kentucky River, at the mouth of Elkhorn Creek. Lots of RV and tent sites, with water, electric, and sewer. They also have primitive sites for those who are really gung-ho. Everything you need for outdoorsy recreation, like boat ramps, bait, canoeing, and kayaking, is available on site. They also have rugged trails for hiking.

✳ Where to Eat

In Frankfort
EATING OUT ♉ Serafini Italian Restaurant (502-875-5599), Broadway & Saint Clair St., Frankfort. Mon.–Fri. 11–2 and

5–10. Fine dining, right in the heart of the historic downtown. This open, airy restaurant offers big roomy booths, white tablecloths, and upscale menu choices. Try the Kentucky bison flank steak, the ruby-red trout, or the Memphis dry-rubbed ribs, all culinary masterpieces. $$–$$$

♉ **Capital Cellars Wine & Spirits Café** (502-352-2600; capitalcellars.net), 227 W. Broadway, Frankfort. Mon.–Thu. 10–9, Fri. and Sat. 10–10. In addition to their huge wine selection, you can order an interesting mix of salads and sandwiches. Order an assortment of stuffed olives, or try the pimiento cheese and cucumber sandwich served on ciabatta bread with a side of Chex Mix. Stop by on Thursday or Friday night for free wine tastings. $

CAPITAL CELLARS

Deborah Kohl Kremer

The Meeting House Café (502-226-3226; www.themeetinghousebandb.com), 519 Ann St., Frankfort. Call for hours. Enjoy soups, sandwiches, pastries, and gourmet coffees in this darling eatery attached to an 1840s-era home. Open for lunch only; you can eat indoors or outside in the inviting courtyard when the weather is nice. $

Y **The Terrace** (502-227-5100), 405 Wilkinson Blvd. in the Capital Plaza Hotel, Frankfort. Open for all three meals, seven days per week. This is the place to go for classic fine dining, white table-cloths, and impeccable service. The menu features steaks, seafood, and traditional dishes. They are also known for their fantastic Sunday brunch. $$

Johnny Carino's Italian Kitchen (502-223-4401), 1303 US 127S, Suite 600, Frankfort. Open 11–10 every day. This is Frankfort's answer to excellent Italian food, and don't worry, you won't leave hungry. Sumptuous menu choices include spaghetti, ravioli, salads, and sandwiches. $

♪ & **Buddy's Pizza** (502-352-2920), 212 W. Broadway, Frankfort. Open Mon.–Thu. 11–9, Fri. 11–11, Sat. noon–10. Named for a beloved dog; take a look at the wall of dog tribute photos. While you're there, enjoy the pizza, salads, and sandwiches, too. They make a traditional pizza, but their blanca pizza—which features a roasted garlic and olive oil base, covered with tomatoes, feta

cheese, and fresh basil—is outstanding. Try the Kettle Fried Wings for something different. $

Rick's White Light Diner (502-330-4262), 114 Bridge St., Frankfort. Open Tue.–Sat. 7–2. Frankfort's oldest restaurant, sometimes referred to as a hole-in-the-wall, is a favorite with locals and political types. Owner Rick Paul mans the stove and entertains customers at the same time. Enjoy the crazy signs posted all around, and try to sit at the counter so you'll be in the middle of everything. Paul serves up some southern favorites like pork barbecue, oyster po'boys, and crawfish pie, but he also has a juicy cheeseburger and fried potatoes that make an awesome meal. Save room for a bourbon ball. $$

Gibby's (502-223-4429), 212 W. Broadway, Frankfort. Open

RICK'S WHITE LIGHT DINER

Nick Kremer

Mon.–Sat. 10:30–9. Nice family restaurant with a casual feel. Menu choices rival chain restaurants, with sandwiches, pastas, and gourmet salads, but the prices are reasonable. $$

Marshall's Backstretch Diner (502-223-5006), 232 W. Main St., Frankfort. Open Mon.–Fri. 6–3, Sat. 6–1, Wed.–Fri. 6–8. When you have a hankering for country ham, homemade biscuits, gravy, and made-to-order eggs, head for Marshall's. You can sit at one of their well-worn booths or at one of the four stools at the counter. If you're there at lunchtime, they make a good burger. $

In Georgetown

& Ÿ **Galvin's** (502-863-1909), 135 E. Main St., Georgetown. Open Mon.–Thu. 11–9, Fri.–Sat. 11 AM–midnight. Billing itself as a sports bar, Galvin's has great menu choices that exceed your standard bar-food expectations. The roomy restaurant has casual family favorites like burgers, sandwiches, pizza, and calzones. The servings are big, so plan accordingly. $$

Fava's Restaurant (502-863-4383; favasofgeorgetown.com), 159 E. Main St., Georgetown. Open 6:30 AM–9 PM every day except Sun. A part of downtown Georgetown since 1910, this cute family eatery offers a huge variety—everything from snow crab legs to tuna salad sandwiches. This restaurant, which started out as an ice cream shop, still has delectable milk shakes. Enjoy the kitschy col-

lection of Disney memorabilia and coffee mugs. $

Lock and Key Café (502-867-1972; lockandkeycafe.com), 201 E. Main St., Georgetown. Located inside an old bank, this cute café has excellent sandwiches and smoothies. Save room for dessert. Every pastry, cake, and cookie is a masterpiece. Get one for now and one to take home. Really. $

Fat Kats Pizzeria and Restaurant (502-570-0773; www.fatkats pizzeria.com), 3073 Paris Pike, Georgetown. Sun.–Thu. 11–9, Fri.–Sat. 11–10. Experience homemade freshness and flavor when you eat any of their award-winning pizzas, subs, pastas, and salads. Save room for their gourmet jumbo cupcakes or homemade cinnamon rolls for dessert. $

& **Sam's Restaurant** (502-863-5872; www.samsrest.com), 1973 Lexington Rd., Georgetown. Open Mon.–Sat. 7–10, Sun. 7–2. What started out in 1952 as a truck stop diner has evolved into a family restaurant featuring Kentucky dishes like hot brown and sautéed chicken livers. Sam's has a hearty selection of burgers, salads, and sandwiches that still meet the expectations of their original trucker crowd. The cream pies are made fresh daily, and no trip to Sam's is complete without a slice. $

SNACKS Kentucky Coffeetree Café (875-3009), 235 Broadway, Frankfort. Weekdays 9:30–6, Sat. 9:30–5, Sun. 12:30–5. Inside Poor Richards Books is a cozy place to grab a bite. They have a nice selection of coffees, like the delicious Banana Bread Latte. They also serve up soups, scones, and smoothies. Check out the dog bowls outside with snacks for your four-legged friend, who can sit outside and wait for you. $

Adelia's Bakery and Café (502-227-9492), 1140 US 127, Frankfort. Mon.–Fri. 10–5, Sat. 10–3. Located in a little strip mall on the city's west side, this is where locals come for lunch. Their most popular items are the Cuban, Baja, or Italian sandwiches, which are not your run-of-the-mill deli fare. They also have a tempting array of pies and desserts whipped up from scratch. $

Granny's Goodies Bakery (502-570-0013), 143 S. Hamilton, Georgetown. Visit this cute shop located in an old home and try some of their homemade pastries or their famous sour cream pound cake. Granny also serves sandwiches; locals rave about the homemade chicken salad. $

TEAROOMS Candleberry Tea Room (502-875-0485; candleberrytearoom.com), 1502 Louisville Rd., Frankfort. Open Mon.–Sat. 11–2. This upscale treat offers homemade selections of quiche, salads, and sandwiches in a cozy inviting atmosphere. Try the bread pudding with bourbon sauce. $

✳ **Entertainment**

Country Place Jamboree (502-223-3776), 60 Old Sheep Pen Rd., Frankfort. Take the whole family out on Saturday nights for live entertainment and country music. It's down-home fun. Call or check their Facebook page to see who's in the lineup.

The Upbeat Café & Music Venue (502-863-5445; www.upbeatcafe.com), 117 N. Broadway, Georgetown. Grab a coffee, dessert, or light meal in this cute eatery, right in the heart of town. The homemade dressings and fresh croutons make the salads fabulous. Come on weekends and enjoy live music.

Georgetown Community Theater (www.gctky.com). In an effort to bring together actors in the community with Georgetown College faculty, students, and alumni, the Georgetown Community Theater was born. They produce five or six shows a year. Check the website or visit them on Facebook to see what's in store.

✳ **Selective Shopping**

Poor Richard's Books (502-223-8018; poorrichards.booksense.com), 233 W. Broadway, Frankfort. This independent bookstore, right across the street from the Old Capitol, specializes in Kentucky works but has all the popular favorites, too. Listen to Kentucky music as you browse the jam-packed aisles. Shelves are so high they have ladders on wheels that run the length of the store, just like an old shoe store. Stop and chat with owners Richard (a former poet laureate of Kentucky)

Deborah Kohl Kremer

POOR RICHARD'S BOOKS

and his wife, Lizz Taylor. They can recommend good titles and know plenty about Frankfort, too.

The Irish Sea Celtic Shop (502-223-9946; www.irishseaceltic .com), 333 W. Broadway, Frankfort. Unbelievable selection of Celtic goods from Scotland, Wales, and Ireland. It is the place to go for all things Celtic: food, china, jewelry, music, and home decor items. If you need a new pin for your plaid kilt, this is just the place.

1792 Store (502-564-1792; www .history.ky.gov), 100 W. Broadway, Frankfort. Named for the year Kentucky became a state, this is where you'll find Kentucky gifts and souvenirs. It is located inside the Thomas D. Clark Center for Kentucky History Center.

Completely Kentucky (502-223-5240, 800-457-1990; www

.completelykentucky.com), 237 W. Broadway, Frankfort. Featuring the work of more than 450 of Kentucky's best artisans, they have a huge selection of Kentucky arts, crafts, and gourmet foods.

Unique Gifts and More (502-570-9866), 149 E. Main St., Georgetown. A darling little downtown shop full of fun items to give as gifts or to keep for yourself. They carry Brighton Jewelry, as well as Caren Products and a zillion things that would look perfect in your home.

ANTIQUES Georgetown Antique Mall (502-863-1891), 124 and 132 W. Main St., Georgetown. Spread out over two buildings and four floors, you'll find 15,000 square feet of antiques shopping. In business for 33 years, this mall has everything antique.

Glover's Bookery (502-863-1275), 134 W. Main St., Georgetown. They carry all kinds of unusual items. In addition to used and rare books, you'll find African artifacts and even old maps.

Heirlooms & Gretchen's (502-863-2538; www.heirloomsand gretchens.com), 136 W. Main, Georgetown. Specializing in stained glass and supplies, they also have lots of lamps and lamp parts, dollhouse supplies, and small antiques. Chances are good you'll find something you need. Call ahead to check hours and days of operation, as they change seasonally.

ART GALLERIES Capital Gallery of Contemporary Art (502-564-2649), 314 Lewis St., Frankfort. Open Tue.–Sat. Fantastic collection of original paintings, fine art prints, crafts, and small-press books by artists from Kentucky and across the country. The gallery also includes the studio of owner-artist Ellen Glasgow.

Jessie's Art Gallery (502-227-2495; www.jessiesartandframing .com), 39 Fountain Place, Frankfort. Find signed and numbered limited-edition prints and canvases as well as collectible reproductions by America's finest artists.

Fine Art Editions Gallery (502-863-2299; www.finearteditions .net), 146 E. Main St., Georgetown. See the latest by John Hockensmith, who specializes in equine art and photography, and Rosalind Trigg, an artist specializing in sporting dogs and hounds.

OUTLET MALL Factory Stores of American Outlet Mall (502-868-0682), 401 Outlet Center Dr., Georgetown. Conveniently located just off I-75, this outlet center has more than 20 stores. So you might want to plan some time to hit the outlets.

✳ Special Events

May: ❀ ✿ ♿ **Governor's Derby Day Breakfast**. Hosted by Kentucky governors for 30 years, this annual rite of spring is held on the capitol grounds on the morning of the Kentucky Derby. All Kentuckians and their guests are invited to enjoy a free country-style breakfast of ham, sausage, scrambled eggs, cheese grits, and biscuits. After breakfast, tour the capitol and Governor's Mansion, visit Kentucky craft and food booths, or sit back and enjoy a variety of musical performances. Free.

June: ❀ ✿ ♿ **Capital Expo**. Held the first weekend in June in downtown Frankfort, this annual event features juried crafts, live music on several stages, carnival rides and games. Free.

October: ❀ ✿ ♿ **The Festival of the Horse**. This festival celebrates Georgetown's rich heritage and the role that horses have played along the way. This downtown event, which has been going on for about three decades, features horse parades, midway rides and games, live entertainment, a 5K run, and a whole weekend full of fun.

THE LEXINGTON AREA

Founded in the late 1700s, **Lexington** quickly became the state's largest town. This growth is credited to the fact that most Kentucky trails and roads passed through the city, and therefore the travelers and the peddlers did as well. Early on, Lexington was known as the Athens of the West, as it was one of the largest and wealthiest towns in what was then considered the West. Unfortunately, with the coming of the steam engine, lots of Kentucky cities were able to enjoy the payload of growth in commerce, so people started heading in other directions. Then, in the 1820s, as river traffic increased, the growth shifted to Ohio River cities like Louisville and Cincinnati.

Lexington did achieve some firsts along the way. In the days long before political correctness, the Eastern Lunatic Asylum, one of the first psychiatric hospitals in the country, opened in Lexington around 1824. Also in the 1820s, Lexington's Transylvania University became one of the most notable schools in the country, specializing in law and medicine, drawing the attention and the admissions of some very notable families.

The city has a rich past, evident by museums and historical markers. It was home to the infamous John Hunt Morgan, a Confederate soldier known for his raids in Kentucky. You can tour his home as well as those of statesman Henry

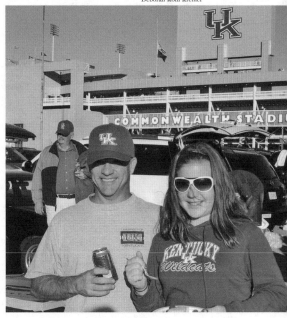

TAILGATING AT THE UK GAME
Deborah Kohl Kremer

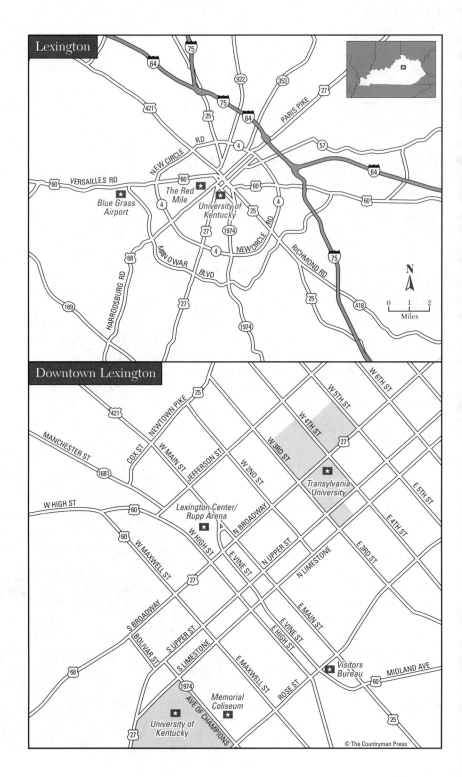

© The Countryman Press

Clay and the girlhood home of Mary Todd, who grew up to be Mrs. Abraham Lincoln.

Today's population hovers around 275,000 in the urban county area. This population fluctuates somewhat when the 26,000 students at University of Kentucky are on campus. It also increases when the beloved UK Wildcats have a home game. For basketball, it is not uncommon for 24,000 fans to migrate to downtown's Rupp Arena to see the Cats in action. At Commonwealth Stadium, where the football team plays, you can find about 70,000 fans decked out in blue and white on Saturdays in fall. These people are serious tailgaters, holding pre-game parties in parking lots, open fields, and front yards. Bring some fried chicken and make new friends on your way to the game.

If you want to spend some time with horses, Lexington's your place. It is home to the Kentucky Horse Park, Keeneland Race Track, the Red Mile Race Course, and loads of horse farms.

Lexington is the heart of Kentucky with miles of bluegrass farmland, an active urban center, amazing examples of the past, and modern-day amenities that all mix together nicely.

GUIDANCE Right in the center of town, you'll find the **Lexington Convention & Visitors Bureau** (859-233-7299, 800-845-3959; www.visitlex .com), 301 E. Vine St., Lexington. They are available to help seven days a week.

GETTING THERE If you fly into the **Bluegrass Airport** in Lexington (859-425-3114; www.bluegrassairport.com), be sure to look out the window as you come in for a landing. The airport is located very close to the famous Calumet Horse Farm and Keeneland Race Track. Seeing a bird's-eye view of these world-renowned facilities devoted to horses, just as you arrive—well, it makes a wonderful welcome mat to the Horse Capital of the World. If you travel by bus, **Greyhound** service is available in Lexington (859-299-8804; www.greyhound.com), 477 W. New Circle Rd.

GETTING AROUND Although Lexington is close to both I-64 and I-75, neither of these highways runs through the city. The downtown area is made up of roads that run from downtown to a suburban community and are named for the community—Richmond Road, Nicholasville Road, and Harrodsburg Road, for instance—so you always know where you are headed. There is also an inner beltway, New Circle Road, which connects these roads that head out of town and make up the spokes of the wheel. Sometimes rush-hour commuters refer to it as "New Circus Road," as drivers get a little nutty on their way to the suburbs.

For public bus service, **LexTran** (859-253-4636; www. lextran.com), 200 E. Vine St., Lexington, operates eight routes 5:30 AM–11:20 PM seven days a week from the Lexington Transit Center along Vine Street in downtown. Taxicab service is also available through **American Taxi Cab Company**, 859-381-1010.

MEDICAL EMERGENCY If you are going to get sick, Lexington is the place to do it. The city is served by some of the nation's most respected hospitals.

University of Kentucky Healthcare (859-257-1000; www.ukhealthcare .uky.edu), 800 Rose St., Lexington. The largest health care system in the commonwealth, with facilities that include UK Chandler Hospital, Kentucky Children's Hospital, UK HealthCare East, Kentucky Clinic, Polk-Dalton Clinic, Kentucky Clinic South, and 80 specialized clinics. They have been chosen as one of America's Best Hospitals by *U.S. News and World Report*.

Central Baptist Hospital (859-260-6100; www.centralbap.com), 1740 Nicholasville Rd., Lexington. This 371-bed major medical center is well respected for advances in cardiac research.

St. Joseph Hospital (859-313-1000; www.sjhlex.org), 1 St. Joseph Dr., Lexington. Nationally recognized for treatment in the areas of cardiology, orthopedics, and stroke, this 468-bed medical center is known as Lexington's Heart Hospital.

ALCOHOL Fayette County is a wet county, meaning alcohol sales are permitted everywhere.

✳ To See

In Lexington

✐ ᕖ **Kentucky Horse Park** (859-233-4303, 800-678-8813; www.kyhorse park.com), 4089 Iron Works Pike. Open every day, year-round, because horses are always in-season. This 1,200-acre working horse farm is the place to go to learn about horses and see them in their natural setting. The park features nearly 50 different breeds, and in the daily Parade of Breeds visitors get to see several varieties. Don't miss the award-winning 23-minute film called *Thou Shall Fly Without Wings*—a perfect introduction to the dynamic world of the horse. The park features museum exhibits, demonstrations, and shows. They also offer horseback riding for an additional fee. This is a park that you can tour at your own pace, where you can relax and just enjoy the surroundings. You'll know you're there when you see the 30 miles of white plank fencing that surrounds it. Mar. 15–Oct. 31: $15 adults, $8 ages 7–12; 6 and under free. Nov. 1–Mar. 14: $9, $6, free.

University of Kentucky (859-257-3595; www.uky.edu). What started in 1865 as a land-grant institution near downtown Lexington, UK now has a

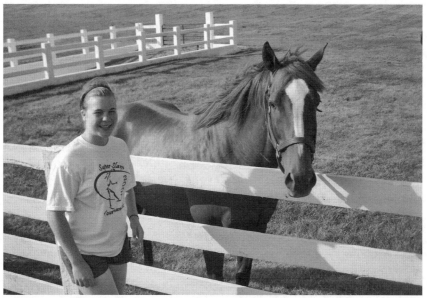

Deborah Kohl Kremer

KENTUCKY HORSE PARK

campus that covers more than 716 acres and is home to over 26,000 students. Stroll the grounds of the campus and stop by the William T. Young Library, a massive 365,000-square-foot, six-story octagonal building. If you need something to read, maybe you could find something among its 1.2 million volumes.

Transylvania University (859-233-8300; www.transy.edu), 300 N. Broadway. In 1780, when Transylvania opened, it was only the 16th college in the United States. Famous alumni include Steve Austin and Cassius Clay, as well as 50 U.S. senators, 101 U.S. representatives, and 36 governors. Today this liberal arts college, with approximately 1,100 students, has a warm, inviting campus right in the downtown area. Make an appointment to see the Monroe Moosnick Medical and Science Museum, a rare collection of anatomical models and science artifacts from the early 1800s. It will make you appreciate modern medicine. Also on campus is one of the first log cabins built

TRANSYLVANIA U

Deborah Kohl Kremer

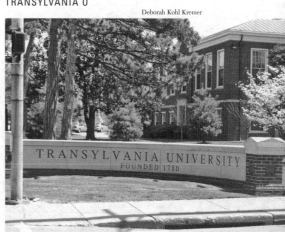

in Lexington. This home, built around 1775, belonged to Robert Patterson, one of the founding fathers of Lexington and Transylvania. Another option while you're in the area is to grab your sweetheart and steal a kiss under the famous Kissing Tree. Transy's answer to mistletoe, this 250-year-old white ash tree is said to be the most romantic place on campus.

  🖉 ♿ **Headley-Whitney Museum** (859-255-6653; www.headley-whitney .org), 4435 Old Frankfort Pike. Tue.–Fri. 10–5, Sat.–Sun. noon–5. Visit the former home of George W. Headley III, a famous designer of jewelry and unique ornate objects called bibelots. See amazing displays of gemstones, shells, and miniatures. As an affiliate of the Smithsonian Institution, the museum includes a wing added to feature revolving exhibits from Washington, DC. $10 adults, $7 ages 62 and up, $7 students; ages 5 and under free.

Ashland, The Henry Clay Estate (859-266-8581; www.henryclay.org), 120 Sycamore Rd. Open Mar.–Dec., Tue.–Sat. 10–4, Sun. 1–4. Home of the famous Kentucky statesman Henry Clay. Said to be a mentor to Abraham Lincoln, Clay lived here from 1806 until his death in 1852. This 600-acre plantation grew hemp, tobacco, and grains and was home to about 50 slaves. Clay named the property Ash Land for the huge number of massive ash trees that stood on the property. The one-hour tour includes the 18-room Italianate-style main house, outbuildings, and lush garden area. You can grab a sandwich or snack at the **Ginkgo Tree Cafe** (open mid-Apr.–mid-Oct.). $9 adults, $5 ages 6–18; 5 and under free.

Hunt Morgan House and Civil War Museum (859-233-3290; www .bluegrasstrust.org), 201 N. Mill St. Open for tours Wed.–Sun. mid-Apr.–

ASHLAND, THE HOME OF HENRY CLAY

HUNT MORGAN HOUSE

Deborah Kohl Kremer

mid-Dec. Call for hours. Built in 1814, this Federal-style home was an architectural wonder of its time. Home to John Wesley Hunt, the first millionaire of the New West, John Hunt Morgan, a radical soldier of the Confederacy, and Nobel Prize winner Thomas Hunt Morgan. This home features artwork and furnishings that once belonged to this notable family. The second floor has an extensive collection of Civil War memorabilia. $7 adults, $5 students.

✍ **Explorium of Lexington** (859-258-3253; www.explorium.com), 440 W. Short St. Tue.–Sat. 10–5, Sun. 1–5. Formerly known as the Lexington Children's Museum. Kids of all ages will enjoy the hands-on exhibits. See what it feels like to be inside a bubble, explore the human brain, or learn all about dinosaurs. $8 per person over the age of 1.

🍴 ♿ **Lexington History Museum** (859-254-0530; www.lexingtonhistory museum.org), 215 W. Main St. Call for hours and exhibits. Housed in the former Fayette County Courthouse, this museum offers rare peeks into Lexington and Kentucky history. Adults $5, children $3.

Lexington Cemetery (859-255-5522; www.lexcem.org), 833 W. Main St. Established in 1849 and encompassing 170 acres of fully landscaped gardens, this feels more like a park than a cemetery. You will be amazed by the size of the trees—they are massive. It is the final resting place of many Civil War soldiers and famous Kentuckians. Free to visit.

Mary Todd Lincoln House (859-233-9999; www.mtlhouse.org), 578 W. Main St. Open March 3–Nov. 30, Mon.–Sat. 10–4. The first museum in America to honor a first lady. Tour the girlhood home of Mary Todd, who became the

LEXINGTON HISTORY MUSEUM

Deborah Kohl Kremer

wife of Abraham Lincoln. This two-story brick Georgian home was built in 1806 and is filled with period pieces, some original to the home. The Lincolns and their children spent time in this magnificent home, and there are some artifacts from the 16th president on the third floor. $9 adults, $4 ages 6–12; under 6 free.

Waveland State Historic Site (859-272-3611; parks.ky.gov), 225 Waveland Museum Lane. Open year-round, Mon.–Fri. 9–4, Sun. 1–5. The museum and gift shop may be closed during winter months. Tour the home of the Joseph Bryan family, who followed Daniel Boone through the Cumberland Gap and became early settlers of Kentucky. The site includes the 1848 Greek Revival antebellum home, three original outbuildings, slave quarters, smokehouse, and icehouse. $7 adults, $6 seniors, $4 children.

Deborah Kohl Kremer

LEXINGTON CEMETERY

✐ **The Thoroughbred Center** (859-293-1853; www.thethoroughbred center.com), 3380 Paris Pike. Guided tours at 9 AM. Experience a day in the life of a thoroughbred in training. At this 240-acre site, you can tour the various tracks, barns, and paddocks, and talk to trainers who hope their young colts get to experience the Run for the Roses someday. Learn about the cost of training a thoroughbred, how much exercise is required, and even how they teach a horse to go into the starting gate. This tour is suitable for all ages but does involve getting on and off a bus a few times. Reservations highly recommended, especially in spring and fall. $15 adults, $8 children.

MARY TODD LINCOLN HOUSE

Nick Kremer

Deborah Kohl Kremer

THOROUGHBRED CENTER

Aviation Museum of Kentucky (859-231-1219; aviationky.org), 4316
Hanger Dr. Closed Mon. See historic aircraft in their 12,000-square-foot
indoor exhibit area as well as several outside. The museum's mission is
educating young people about aviation's career potential, but they have a
cool collection of planes and memorabilia. $7 adults

✳ To Do

In Lexington (unless otherwise noted)
GOLF Tates Creek Golf Course (859-272-3428), 1400 Gainesway Dr.
This par-72, 18-hole public course has been around since 1958 and is a
true favorite of Lexington golfers.

Meadowbrook Golf Course (859-272-3115), 370 Wilson Downing Rd.
An inexpensive 18-hole, par-55 course. Greens fees include a golf cart.

Peninsula Golf Resort (859-548-5055, 877-249-4747; www.penisula
golf.com), 200 Clubhouse Dr., Lancaster. Just south of Lexington, but
worth the drive, is this 18-hole championship course. Stay at the furnished
two-bedroom condos right alongside the course for a perfect golf-weekend
getaway.

HORSE RACING ♿ **Keeneland Race Track** (859-254-3412, 800-456-
3412; www.keeneland.com), 4201 Versailles Rd. Conducting live race
meets in Apr. and Oct. since 1936, this thoroughbred track is steeped in

KENTUCKY HORSE FARMS

Horse racing has been a part of human culture as far back in time as the ancient cave dwellers who drew hieroglyphics of such races on cavern walls. It has deep roots in Kentucky history, too.

As early as the 1775 Transylvania Convention, Daniel Boone introduced the first bill "to improve the breed of horses in the Kentucky territory." As forts transformed into cities, many Kentucky towns had a "Race Street" used for, yes, racing horses. And according to history books, the Lexington Jockey Club was formed in 1809 with famous Kentucky statesman Henry Clay as a founding member.

As home to the infamous Kentucky Derby, which first ran in 1875, the Bluegrass State became known for fast horses and beautiful women, although sometimes the adjectives are swapped if the speaker has had one too many bourbon-laced mint juleps.

The horse industry progressed in Kentucky, probably due to the rolling acres of pasture, the limestone-rooted bluegrass—or, most likely because religious reformers were shutting down tracks in the East. Lexington always had a nice track, with plenty of affluent fans ready to make a wager.

Nonetheless, thoroughbreds from Kentucky took on a pedigree status, and people came from all over the world to witness Kentucky horse racing. The tradition continues today, as Kentucky is home to famous tracks like Churchill Downs and Keeneland and more than 450 horse farms in the Bluegrass Region, with nearly 150 in Lexington's Fayette County alone.

Viewing a Kentucky horse race is something all visitors should do while in the state, but if schedules and itineraries don't match up, maybe you could take in a horse farm tour while you're in the area.

Several tour companies operate in the Lexington area. They will pick you up at your hotel and give you a great overview of horses, farms, tracks, and the area. They stop at a few farms to let you see where the horses are raised, trained, and bred.

If you are more interested in just heading straight to a farm for your own tour, that's fine, too, but you must remember to call ahead and schedule an appointment, as well as remember to tip your groom (somewhere in the $5-per-person range) when your tour is complete.

Deborah Kohl Kremer

THREE CHIMNEYS

There is much involved in the life of a thoroughbred, and in the Lexington area, you can learn about each step of a horse's life. Visit Three Chimneys Farm, where they specialize in breeding; the Thoroughbred Center, where they specialize in training; and Old Friends, a farm where they specialize in horse retirement.

At **Three Chimneys Farm** (859-873-7053; www.threechimneys.com) in Versailles, one-hour walking tours are given Tue.–Sat. at 1. These tours are by reservation only and they do fill up fast, so call well in advance of your trip. This farm, owned by Robert Clay, began as a small 100-acre site in 1972. It is the former home of infamous Seattle Slew; today Kentucky Derby winners Smarty Jones and Big Brown live comfortably there.

"When the Clays started this farm, they had the ambition of being a worldwide name, but never imagined that someday they would have more than 2,000 acres and welcome more than 25,000 visitors per year," said Ann Hays, director of tours.

The tour covers aspects of the thoroughbred business as well as breeding. "Sometimes in the spring, the visitors actually get to witness the breeding," Hays added. "Although it is very interesting, it is sometimes a little much for children."

Just as five-year-olds go to kindergarten, prospective race horses go to the **Thoroughbred Center** (859-293-1853; www.thethoroughbred center.com) in Lexington when they are about two. It is here that they live and learn to run the track, get used the starting gate, and train to race.

Taking advantage of the daily one-hour tours is a great way for visitors to see what goes into the making of a racehorse. "It is a behind-the-scenes look at racing," said Ann Wilson, who arranges the tours. "It's not a place to come to ride or pet horses, but a place to learn about the racing profession."

This 200-acre facility has two training tracks and can board and train about 1,000 horses at a time. Wilson noted that you can see the horses up close but you also get a taste for their workouts and the training involved. "Our visitors are usually just in love with horses when they come, and they have so much respect for horses when they leave."

THE RETIRED HORSE CREATOR AT OLD FRIENDS

Deborah Kohl Kremer

Paul Kremer

AT CLAIBORNE FARM

After a few years of racing, a horse usually becomes a breeder. They head back to the farm and have a pretty nice life filled with, uh, well, breeding. But that chapter, too, closes on a horse's life, and the future is retirement.

Although you won't find shuffleboard or bingo games at this retirement home, the old folks here can spend their days as they please. Based in Georgetown, **Old Friends, A Kentucky Facility for Retired Thoroughbreds** (502-863-1775; www.oldfriendsequine.org) is a welcoming place for horses to live out their golden years.

"When we bring horses here, you can just see them unwind," said Michael Blowen, president and founder. "They go from being competitive and high-strung athletes to laid-back, relaxed horses."

Specializing in stallions (because they typically require a little more care and separate paddocks), the facility is one of a kind. They welcome all retired horses here, however, and go above and beyond to keep older animals out of the slaughterhouse.

"If we hear of a stallion in Japan that has finished his breeding career, we begin fund-raising to bring him home," said Blowen. "We've brought five back to Lexington from Japan, and we are willing to bring more."

Free, hour-long tours are given daily so visitors can get to know the residents. As you hear each horse's story, you begin to feel you are in the presence of celebrities, and rightly so. Horses such as Sunshine Forever, the 1988 Turf Horse of the Year, and Williamstown, who held the 10-year record for the mile at Belmont Park, call Old Friends home.

Incorporating an aspect of the horse industry into your trip to the Bluegrass is a must. But the good news is, the opportunities are limitless. Whether you visit one of the establishments listed above or spend a day at the huge **Kentucky Horse Park** (www.kyhorsepark.com), tradition-steeped **Keeneland Race Track** (www.keeneland.com), or history-rich horse farms like **Claiborne Farm** (www.claibornefarm.com) and **Gainesway Farm** (www.gainesway.com), your trip is sure to be a winner.

tradition. The fieldstone grandstand looks as stunning when the surrounding cherry blossom trees are in bloom as it does wrapped in the dramatic colored leaves of fall. Come for the racing but stay for the scenery. You'll also find a gift shop and track eateries where you can try famous Kentucky burgoo as well as the heady bread pudding with bourbon sauce.

KEENELAND RACE TRACK

Deborah Kohl Kremer

& **Red Mile Harness Track** (859-255-0752; www.theredmile.com), 1200 Red Mile Rd. It's not just about thoroughbred racing in Kentucky. Come to the Red Mile and watch the harness racing, where horses pull two-wheeled carts called sulkies. The track, the second oldest in the country, is open year-round for simulcasting. Check the website for live racing dates.

MINOR-LEAGUE BASEBALL Lexington Legends (859-252-4487; www.lexingtonlegends.com), 207 Legends Lane. This minor-league base-ball team is an affiliate of the Houston Astros. The games are fun, so try to take one in if the Legends are in town when you are. Their home field, Whitaker Bank Ballpark, is not too far from downtown.

TOURS Blue Grass Tours (859-252-5744, 800-755-6956; bluegrasstours .com), 817 Enterprise Dr. See the sites of Lexington and the region on one of their bus tours. It's a great way to take in all the sites of Lexington in just a few hours.

Lexington Livery Horse-Drawn Carriage Tours (859-259-0000; www .lexingtonlivery.com), 171 Saunier Ave. Enjoy the clippity-clop of horse hooves as you relax for a carriage ride. Tours depart each evening from Broadway and Vine St.; both 30-minute and one-hour versions are offered.

BleuPlate Tours (www.bleuplatetours.com). Think of this as a walking tour with snacks . . . but the snacks are amazing. This three-hour walking tour includes stops at some of Lexington's finest dining establishments. The knowledgeable tour guide will fill you in on some obscure facts about the city and introduce you to three or four restaurants along the way. Tours are given on Saturday and Sunday. Reservations are mandatory.

WINERIES Equus Run Vineyards (859-846-9463; equusrunvineyards .com), 1280 Moores Mill Rd., Midway. Although this farm used to be known for their tobacco, as consumption went down, they had to find a new way to work the land. And that way is grape growing and winemak-ing. Take a guided, or self-guided, tour of the tobacco-barn-turned-winemaking-facility and the vineyard. Equus Run hosts concerts in the summer months. Check the website to see what's going on.

Jean Farris Winery and Bistro (859-263-9463; jeanfarris.com), 6825 Old Richmond Rd. Come for the wine, but stay for the food? Or vice versa? Both the wine and the food are glorious, so plan to participate in both and purchase a few bottles for home, too. Check their website for special events. They are special. The Winery & Restaurant is open for dinner Tue.–Sun. 5:30–close; brunch Sat.–Sun. 11–3; wine tasting bar Tue.–Sun. noon–close.

WoodSongs Old Time Radio Hour (859-252-8888; www.woodsongs
.com), 214 E. Main St., Lexington.

When Michael Johnathon began broadcasting a small radio show
comprising a mix of folk and bluegrass music a few years ago in his
friend's studio in Lexington, he never dreamed that he would soon have
fans from around the globe, with faithful listeners from Thailand to
Topeka.

WoodSongs Old Time Radio Hour, which is available on local radio
and the web, also airs on PBS channels nationwide. Viewers get to see
not only the artists but also the technical crew, the audience, the
incredible performances, and all the WoodSongs action from the stage
of the historic Kentucky Theatre in Lexington, Kentucky.

Johnathon and his guests hope the national broadcast of this show
does for Kentucky what *Austin City Limits* has done for Texas and
Prairie Home Companion has done for Minnesota.

Broadcasting acoustical, genre-free shows with a blues or bluegrass feel, Johnathon explains that WoodSongs is not about famous
stars. "A real artist has a passion for their art, and their goal is to bring
it to an audience," he said. "They are not interested in their pocket-
book, which is good because no one on the show earns a dime."

Not only are the performers unpaid, the entire crew are volunteers.
Luckily the show is financed through donations of listeners, the $10
ticket price, and corporate sponsors.

Each show is archived on the website (www.woodsongs.com). It
is available for downloading, so that each show can be heard in its
entirety, no matter where in the world you are. The average show
gets about 125,000 full-view streams worldwide the first five weeks it
is posted, which explains why Johnathon gets emails from people in
Australia and Asia asking questions about the show.

"Our global audience loves folk music," he said. "They care more
about the art than the marketing. They are not interested if the artist has
signed with a national recording company, which is why we say on the
show, 'Our artist don't have to be famous, they just have to be good.'"

Each Monday night the Kentucky Theater in Lexington is packed with
music fans who come to enjoy good folk music. They do not know who
they will be listening to or what instruments will be played, but the venue
sells out week after week. Johnathon explained, "Our audience trusts us

www.kentuckytourism.com

WOODSONGS OLD TIME RADIO HOUR

to supply the talent. The fact that they are unknown is what keeps them interested."

Johnathon, a songwriter, folksinger, and playwright, is the host of the show. Although he is not a native of Kentucky, he feels he is a Kentuckian by now. With a love of Appalachian music in his heart, he moved to rural Knott County, where he went around knocking on doors, going house to house, learning music and songs from people who lived there. As his talents grew, he eventually moved to Lexington, where he now lives.

Years ago Johnathon was having his banjo repaired in the basement workshop of Homer Ledford, who is known for his Appalachian dulcimers. Surrounded by all the beautiful wooden instruments, he coined the term *WoodSongs* as a better alternative to *folk music*. Sometimes *folk music* conjures up a negative image, and Johnathon did not want his warm, peaceful shows to ever conjure up anything negative. Featuring artists who specialize in everything from the cello, the mandolin, and the banjo to a laptop dulcimer, *WoodSongs* takes the audience to a wonderful place with the music.

Johnathon believes *WoodSongs* has such a large audience because folk music is what gave birth to rock and country music. "Lexington is the global crossroads of bluegrass, blues, and folk music," he said. "It is perfect that *WoodSongs* comes from Kentucky."

✳ Green Space

In Lexington

Raven Run Nature Sanctuary (859-272-6105; www.lexingtonky.gov), 5888 Jacks Creek Rd. Enjoy 11 miles of hiking trails along the Kentucky River Palisades in this 734-acre nature preserve. Raven Run is home to over 56 species of trees, 600 species of plants, 200 species of birds, and other wildlife.

University of Kentucky Arboretum (859-257-6955; www.ca.uky.edu /arboretum), 500 Alumni Dr. Spread out over 100 acres, this arboretum lets you enjoy nature at her finest. Open year-round so you can learn about native trees, grasses, and flowers, but plan your visit to coincide with the blooming of the 1,500 varieties of roses.

Legacy Trail (mylegacytrail.com). This 12-mile paved walking and biking trail meanders its way from the east side of Lexington to the Kentucky Horse Park. Bike rental is available at the nearby YMCA (859-258-YMCA). For the most up-to-date information, look them up on Facebook.

PARKS McConnell Springs (859-225-4073), 416 Rebmann Lane. You might think you're lost as you enter this industrial park, but keep going and you'll end up at McConnell Springs. Hike the 2 miles of trails that

UNIVERSITY OF KENTUCKY ARBORETUM

Nick Kremer

Deborah Kohl Kremer

THOROUGHBRED PARK

surround the natural springs on this 26-acre park. It's a combination of nature and history, as it was the original campsite for the first settlers in the Bluegrass Region.

✐ **Thoroughbred Park** (859-288-2900), E. Main St. at Midland Ave. Not really a park, more like a drive-by attraction. See seven life-sized bronze racehorses that appear to be galloping along the sidewalk to the finish line. Located right downtown.

Masterson Station Park, 3051 Leestown Rd. Open every day from dawn to dusk, year-round. Just northwest of town is the huge, 660-acre park known as Masterson Station. The park has an interesting history, as it was settled in the mid-1700s by some of Lexington's first residents. In the 1920s the land was purchased by the U.S. government and turned into a Narcotics Farm. No, they did not grow narcotics; it was used for rehabbing those addicted to the stuff. The Narcotics Farm, which encouraged patients to work the land to help their addiction, operated around from 1935 to 1974. After that, the land was transferred to local government for recreational use. Dairy barns and silos are still on the property today. Although no farming is done here now, the land is used for ball fields, a dog park, and in-line skating; there are also facilities for equestrian events.

✳ Lodging

In Lexington

&. **Gratz Park Inn** (859-231-1777, 800-752-4166; www.gratz parkinn.com), 120 W. 2nd St. This luxury boutique inn offers 42 rooms, each decorated in 19th-century antique reproductions, exquisite mahogany furniture, and local artwork. $$$

 Lyndon House Bed and Breakfast (859-420-2683; www .lyndonhouse.com), 507 N. Broadway. This fascinating home was built in 1883 and features five guest rooms. Each themed room honors a different aspect of Kentucky. $$–$$$

✳ Where to Eat

In Lexington

DINING OUT ♈ **Giuseppe's** (859-272-4053; www.giuseppes lexington.com), 4465 Nicholasville Rd. Lunch weekdays 11:30–2:30, dinner every day 5–10, Sun. brunch 11–2:30. Venture down the hidden, wooded driveway off busy Nicholasville Road to find this secluded, romantic Italian fine-dining establishment. In business since 1994, this wonderful combination of upscale dining and award-winning entrées features Italian favorites like manicotti, lasagna, and fettuccine. But in an attempt to please everyone, they offer veal, chicken, seafood, and Black Angus beef dishes, too. With more than 100 Italian wines on the list, have a glass with your tiramisu, homemade cannoli, Italian cream cake, spumoni, or gelato dessert. $$–$$$

&. ♈ **The Mansion at Griffin Gate** (859-288-6142; www .mansionrestaurant.com), 1720 Newtown Pike. Dinner Tue.–Sat. 6–10. Dine in this spectacular pillared antebellum mansion while surrounded by crystal chandeliers

THE MANSION AT GRIFFIN GATE

Deborah Kohl Kremer

and priceless antiques. French-based menu with Asian influences and plenty of familiar choices like king salmon and boneless rack of lamb. $$–$$$$

℣ **Jonathan at Gratz Park Inn** (859-231-1777, 800-752-4166; www.gratzparkinn.com), 120 W. 2nd St. Open for lunch 11–2 and dinner 5–10 every day. For an upscale dining experience in the heart of Lexington, Jonathan is the place. The menu features American fare like filets and seafood, but some dishes have a southern twist, like the sea scallop hot brown and the pimiento cheese grit fries. Sunday brunch lets you try lots of favorites like the southern eggs Benedict made with fried green tomatoes and country ham, and Kentucky burgoo. $$$

℣ **Dudley's on Short** (859-252-1010; www.dudleysrestaurant .com), 259 W. Short St., Suite 125. Lunch Mon.–Sat. 11:30–2:30; dinner Sun.–Thu. 5:30–10, Fri.–Sat. 5:30–11. Sun. brunch 11:30–2:30. Covering two floors of The Northern Bank Building, which was built in 1889, you'll find this upscale, inviting restaurant. Both the food and the ambience are unmatched. Menu options include steaks, lamb, pasta, and seafood dishes. $$–$$$

℣ **Bellini's** (859-388-9583; www .bellinis.us), 115 W. Main St. Lunch weekdays 11:30–2:30, dinner every night starting at 5. Offering fine Italian dining right in the center of downtown, this upscale eatery serves traditional dishes that are as enticing to look at as they are to eat. They have all your pasta favorites as well as steaks, chops, and seafood. $$–$$$

Natasha's Bistro (859-259-2754; www.beetnik.com), 112 Esplanade. Mon.–Sat. 11–10. This artsy restaurant has a far-reaching menu and an eclectic decor. Enjoy soups, salads, wraps, or even Hungarian goulash. The choices are vast but the ingredients are all fresh and flavorful. Live music acts range from accordions to sax solos; check the website to see who's on stage. This funky restaurant is fun every time. $$

℣ **Merrick Inn** (859-269-5417; themerrickinn.com), 1074 Merrick Dr. Serving dinner Mon.–Sat. A part of Lexington's dining scene for more than 30 years, this upscale but casual restaurant is the place to go for a nice evening out. Their southern-inspired menu features crabcakes, fried chicken,

BELLINI'S

Deborah Kohl Kremer

and the locals' favorite: pecan-crusted pork tenderloin topped with Maker's Mark apple chutney. The dining room is warm and welcoming, but eat outside on the patio if you can. It continually wins awards for the best outdoor dining in the state. $$–$$$

Y **Malone's** (859-335-6500; bluegrasshospitality.com), 3347 Tates Creek Rd. Open 11:15–11:15 every day. In business since 1998, it is the place to go for steak. They also have seafood, pork chops, and burgers, but why bother? This is a steak restaurant, and Malone's knows how to do it right. All entrées are served with Malone's bottomless Lexingtonian salad, which could be a meal on its own. $$–$$$

Y **A la Lucie** (859-252-5277; www.alalucie.com), 159 N. Limestone. Open for lunch and dinner every day. This hip place with funky decor verges on elegant but doesn't feel stuffy. They have white tablecloths and an upscale menu, but servers are relaxed so it's not so hoity-toity. A wide variety of steak and chicken dishes are available, but also unusual choices like buttermilk-fried quail. $$

EATING OUT Y **Cheapside Bar & Grill** (859-254-0046; www.cheapsidebarandgrill.com), 131 Cheapside. Open for lunch and dinner every day. This is the kind of place where you go for happy hour and end up staying for last call. The relaxed, casual atmos-

CHEAPSIDE BAR AND GRILL

Nick Kremer

phere and tropical-inspired patio usually bring in a fun crowd. Menu choices range from appetizers (they call it Social Grazing) to rare entrées like a duck enchilada, chipotle meat loaf, and a real backyard burger. $$

Ψ **Winchell's Restaurant and Bar** (859-278-9424; www.winchells restaurant.com), 348 Southland Dr. Mon.–Sat. 8 AM–1 AM, Sunday 8 AM–11 PM. A casual restaurant with a sports bar feel. They have an extensive sandwich menu that includes an open-faced beef brisket, a country-fried steak and egg, and a pulled pork barbecue topped with vinegar slaw. As if that weren't enough, their dinner entrées include country-fried steak, grilled chicken cordon bleu, blackened salmon, and Kentucky hot brown. Unbeatable variety at reasonable prices. $–$$

Stella's Kentucky Deli (859-255-3354; www.stellaskentuckydeli .com), 143 Jefferson St. Mon.–Fri. 8:30–4, Sat. (brunch buffet only) 10–2. Inside this cute yellow house is a wonderful restaurant where everything is made from scratch. Committed to using fresh, local ingredients, they can tell you how to get to the farm where the cheese was made and where the tomato on your sandwich was grown. Open for breakfast and lunch. $

Bourbon n' Toulouse (859-335-0300; www.bntlexington.com), 829 Euclid Ave. Open Mon.–Sat. 11–10. For a taste of the bayou in the heart of the Bluegrass State,

B and T, as locals call it, is the place to go. Not at all fancy, just a relaxed atmosphere and a menu loaded with all the classic Cajun choices you would expect. Try the étouffée, jambalaya, or gumbo, and heat things up with their wide selection of sauces. They also have a tasty bluegrass barbecue sandwich, if you are not in the mood for Louisiana fare. $

Windy Corner Market and Restaurant (859-294-9338; www.windycornermarket.com), 4595 Bryan Station Rd. Open Mon.–Fri. 7 AM–8:30 PM, weekends 10–8:30. Disguised as an old-time general store that you might be tempted to drive right past, this is a darling, homey restaurant. The menu will astound you

213

STELLA'S DELI

Nick Kremer

because everything sounds so good, you won't know what to order. The good news is, you really can't go wrong, whether you are going for one of their famous two-handed po'boys, a seafood or barbecue basket, or one of their nightly dinner specials. Locals rave about the Thursday-night bluegrass burritos and the giant Kentucky-style breakfast plates. The creaky wood floors made from reclaimed horse barns; the shelves loaded with Kentucky Proud products like jelly, honey, and pickles; and the abundance of local ingredients all show the owners commitment to the Bluegrass State. $–$$

& Y **The Atomic Café** (859-254-1969; atomiccafeky.com), 265 N. Limestone. Open for lunch and dinner. With the spicy smell of island cuisine mixed with the Latino music and wall and ceiling murals of beaches, waves, and palm trees, you'll wonder if you are still in the Bluegrass State. The menu features such island favorites as jerk chicken and coconut shrimp, but you can also find comfort foods like mac 'n' cheese and chicken potpie. Home-made salad dressings like green onion coconut, honey papaya vinaigrette, and orange sesame add to the island ambience. In summer, live bands play on the patio out back. $$

& Y **Joe Bologna's** (859-252-4933; www.joebolognas.com), 120 W. Maxwell St. Open every day 11–11. Eat in this restored Jewish temple, surrounded by priceless stained-glass windows and chandeliers that were original to the 1890s building. It's probably the only pizza place listed on the National Register of Historic Places. Casual dining in an energy-charged environment. Pizzas and pastas are delectable, but the reason locals keep coming back to Joe B's is the garlic bread-stick. Each entrée comes with a small loaf of bread that is served, literally, swimming in garlic butter. Put your napkin on your lap, because it will drip. $$

& & **Parkette Drive In** (859-254-8723; www.theparkette.com), 1216 E. New Circle Rd. Open every day except Sun., for lunch and dinner. You can eat inside at the '50s-inspired diner, but to get the real feel for the place, order from your car and have the carhop serve you there. That's right: This place is the real deal. Parkette is a genuine drive-in restaurant that has been part of Lexington's history since 1952. The most popular item on the menu is the poor-boy burger and fries, but the onion rings are stellar, too. $

& Y **Columbia Steak House** (859-253-3135; www.columbia steakhouse.com) 201 N. Limestone. Open for lunch and dinner. Open since 1948, Columbia is a part of Lexington dining history. The walls are lined with photos of celebs and sports stars who have come to visit over the years. The ambience has a 1960s wine-cellar feel to it with ambient lighting and high-backed booths. Columbia's is a steak house, so you know you can't go wrong by ordering one of these babies, all with a garlic butter that you won't soon forget. Not in the mood for steak? Well, how about the Kentucky hot brown, all melted, gooey, and rich? For dessert, people rave about the Kentucky Silk Pie, but Flo, the general manager who's been there forever, usually has a dessert special to temp your taste buds, too. $$

✦ ☿ **Ramseys** (859-259-2708; ramseysdiners.com), 496 E. High St. Three other locations throughout Lexington, but this is the original. Open weekdays 11–11, weekends 10–11. Don't let the creaky wood floors and mismatched tables and chairs scare you away. This highly casual restaurant is where you'll find a bonanza of comfort-food choices. Try the open-faced pot roast sandwich with a side of kale, or southern-style catfish with creamed corn and apple fritters. Portions are huge, but save room for a piece of Mile-High Meringue Pie: The flavor choices change, but the pies are legendary. $$

☿ **Two Keys Tavern** (859-254-5000; twokeystavern.com), 333 S. Limestone. Open seven days for lunch and on into the wee hours. This legendary bar, a staple for any University of Kentucky grad or fan, has been part of UK's party

JOE BOLOGNA'S

Nick Kremer

scene for as long as anyone can remember. Wildcat memorabilia creates the decor, and Wildcat fans fill the seats. Typical bar food makes up the menu, which tastes good and is inexpensive. Go for lunch when the college crowd is presumably in class, or go to watch a UK game on one of their dozens of TVs for the full experience. $

&. **Alfalfa Restaurant** (859-253-0014; www.alfafarestaurant.com), 141 E. Main St. Open every day for breakfast and lunch; dinner Wed.–Sat. only. Notable for their vegetarian choices like eggplant burritos and hoppin' john, they also have wonderful salads, soups, and country ham sandwiches. Everything on the menu is fresh; the ambience is artsy and eclectic. Check out the daily specials on the chalkboard when you come in the door. $–$$

Y **Nick Ryan's Saloon** (859-233-7900; nickryans.com), 157 Jefferson St. Serving lunch and dinner every day. The upscale, hip ambience makes you want to hang out a little longer, even after you have enjoyed your crabcake appetizer—which people rave about—or your entrée of ribs, chops, or steak. Live a little and order their hot brown or shrimp 'n' grits, two Kentucky favorites that are done correctly here. Full bar. $$

&. **Wheeler Pharmacy** (859-266-1131), 336 Romany Rd. Open for breakfast and lunch. Wheelers opened in 1958 with a full variety of pharmaceuticals, plus two

U-shaped counters and three booths where you could order a milk shake. And that's what you'll find today, except in the 1960s they added a grill so you could get a burger or bacon and eggs to go along with your ice cream. They open at 9 AM and there is usually a line of regulars waiting to get in, which tells you a lot about this homey place. $

&. Y **AP Suggins** (859-268-0709; suggins.com), 345 Romany Rd. Mon–Sat. 11 AM–10ish. Closed Sunday. Neighborhoody kind of

ALFALFA RESTAURANT

Deborah Kohl Kremer

Nick Kremer

WHEELER PHARMACY

place where you can take the family, or catch the big game with your buddies. Appetizers like cheese fries, quesadillas, and deep-fried banana peppers pair up well with their wide selection of domestic and imported beers. Dinner choices include fish, chicken, burgers, and some southern favorites like chicken livers and Suggins hot brown. Impressive wine list, too. $$

♿ † **Le Deauville** (859-246-0999; ledeauvilleresto.com), 199 N. Limestone Open for dinner Tue. through Sat. Offering fine French cuisine, you don't have to speak the language to order off the menu. Although you should be able to recognize popular favorites like steaks, chicken, and rack of lamb,

the menu does have a whole section dedicated to mussels, something you don't see every day. $$

Oasis Restaurant (859-269-6440; oasisrestaurant.net), 837 Chevy Chase Place. Open for lunch and dinner Mon.–Sat. Awesome Mediterranean food at reasonable prices. They offer salads and pitawiches stuffed with favorites like hummus, falafel, and tabouli. Check out the lunch buffet so you can try a little bit of everything. $

♿ † **Pazzo's Pizza Pub** (859-255-5125; pazzospizzapub.com), 385 S. Limestone. Mon–Wed. 11–10, Thu.–Sat. 11–11, Sun. noon–10. Just off campus, you'll find Pazzo's Pizza Pub, a staple in the diets of many UK students. They have mouthwatering pizza, subs, calzones, salads, and cheesy appetizers. If you are in a hurry, stop by for a giant pizza slice to go. It will tide you over until mealtime, but it's big enough to be the meal. Amazing drink specials and 40 beers on tap to wet your whistle. They offer patio dining and free parking around the back. Make sure you bring your receipt back with you—the parking attendant is strict! $

&⅞ ⅂ **Saul Good Pub** (859-273-4663; www.saulgoodpub.com), Fayette Mall, 3801 Mall Rd.; second location at Hamburg Center, 1808 Alysheba (859-317-9200). Open for lunch and dinner every day. Yeah, they have really good salads, sandwiches, burgers, and pizza, but why bother with all that when you can head straight for the chocolate dessert bar? You'll find favorites like chocolate fondue, chocolate popcorn, chocolate pizza, and white chocolate cheesecake. Okay, okay, eat your meal first (you'll be happy with anything you choose, it's all good), but make sure you save room. $$

Tolly-Ho (859-253-2007; tollyho .com), 606 S. Broadway. Open 24 hours, right on the edge of UK's campus, you'd think Tolly-Ho is just a college dive, but you'd be surprised at the business suits and grandmas you see for breakfast and lunch. The after-bar crowd stops in about 3 AM on their way back to their dorms, but no matter who you're dining with, you're going to love this greasy spoon. Breakfast all day, sloppy burgers,

huge, crispy onion rings, Ho's has all the favorites. $

SNACKS ✿ & **Magee's Bakery** (859-255-9481; www.magees bakery.com), 726 E. Main St. Open weekdays 6:30 AM–5:30 PM, Sat. 6:30 AM–2 PM, Sun. 8–2. Proudly meeting Lexingtonians' bakery needs for more than 50 years. The glazed doughnuts are like eating sweetened air. They are simply perfect. Have one while you choose the rest of your order. Make sure that order includes at least one transparent pie, their number one best seller. These come in traditional 9-inch and convenient 3-inch tart sizes. They are also famous for their homemade mallowbars. Yes, they are as amazing as they sound. They have a wide array of doughnuts, cakes, cookies, and pastries—and you'll find a coffee bar and a deli offering fresh sandwiches, salads, soups, or quiche. $

Ruth Hunt Candies (859-268-1559; www.ruthhuntcandy.com), 2313 Woodhill Dr. The original location is in Mount Sterling, but you don't have to drive all the way there to get this awesome candy. Although they produce about 70 varieties, Ruth Hunt is best known for Woodford Reserve bourbon balls and Kentucky pulled cream candy. Don't forget to order a Blue Monday—a candy bar made of cream candy dipped in dark chocolate. $

Sunrise Bakery (859-255-0304; www.valotta.com), 111 W. Main

Deborah Kohl Kremer

MAGEE'S BAKERY

St. Tue.–Fri. 8–2:30, Sat. 8–noon. This is a bread lover's paradise! Breads, pastries, coffees, well, they are all delish! And sandwiches served on their just-out-of-the-oven bread . . . or their bagels, or their croissants. Just doesn't get much better than this. It is all good, so don't worry about ordering the wrong thing. $

Spaulding's Bakery (859-252-3737; spaldingsbakery.com), 760 Winchester Rd. Open Wed.–Sat. 6:30–noon; they sleep in a few minutes on Sunday and open at 7. Closed Mon. and Tue. In business since 1929, the Spaulding family knows how to make a doughnut. They don't need to turn on a neon light to let customers know when their doughnuts are hot; if you get there early enough, chances are they will be. Their yeast and cake doughnuts are melt-in-your-mouth fabulous. Yes, they sell other bakery items like cakes and rolls and brownies, which are baked with the same dedication and commitment, but it's the doughnuts that have been a Lexington tradition for more than 75 years. $

✳ Entertainment

Actors Guild of Lexington (859-233-7330; www.actorsguildof lexington.org), 141 E. Main St., Lexington. Professional theater company offering a wide variety of performances featuring both local and world-renowned actors. Check the website to see a list of upcoming shows.

Studio Players Community Theater (www.studioplayers.org), with performances at the Carriage House Theatre, 154 W. Bell Court, Lexington. Established in 1953, they have been providing the Lexington community with high-quality theatrical productions ever since. Check the website to see what's on stage.

Lexington Beer Works (859-359-6747; lexingtonbeerworks), 213 N. Limestone, Lexington. Open seven days a week; check the website for hours. Beer Works is a beer lover's paradise. It's a bar catering to those who have a palate for beer, as well as just those folks who like the taste. They have a wide variety, in bottles and on tap. Rate the beers on their website. Beer Works also carries all the supplies you need to brew your own at home.

✳ Selective Shopping

In Lexington
Third Street Stuff and Coffee (859-255-5301; thirdstreetstuff .com), 257 N. Limestone. You can't walk past this shop; it looks so cool and funky on the outside, you'll want to know what's inside. So go in, order a cuppa joe from their extensive coffee menu, and maybe a sandwich or something sweet to go with it. You won't be disappointed. Then wander into their fun gift shop full of novelty gifts and hand-painted jewelry, artwork, and crafts. Even the outside electric meter is painted purple with stripes!

Kentucky Korner (859-231-8899; www.kentuckykorner online.com). Adjacent to Rupp Arena, home of the Kentucky Wildcats, this is the place to grab your UK fan wear and Kentucky souvenirs.

Artique (859-233-1774, 859-272-8802; www.artiquegallery.com). Two locations: Civic Center, 410 W. Vine St. and the Lexington Green (closed Sun.); and 161 Lexington Green Circle, open every day. Featuring the work of more than 1,000 artists, Artique is a fun, funky, colorful store. More than an arts and crafts gallery, it is the place to find distinctive works of art, intricate jewelry, hand-blown glass, and fabulous pottery.

Kentucky Proud Market (859-455-4532; kentuckyproudmarket .com). Located in the Civic Center Shops attached to Rupp Arena downtown, this is the place to go for Kentucky-made products. They have a huge assortment of Kentucky-made food items, wine, books, clothing, and art. You can be assured of the quality, too: Every maker represented in the store is a registered member of the Kentucky Proud or the Kentucky Crafted program.

Keeneland Gift Shop (859-254-3412; www.keeneland.com), 4201 Versailles Rd. Although this prestigious track only runs in April and October, the shop is open for your equestrian-themed gift needs all year round. Fabulous selection of horse-related home decor, clothing, and jewelry items. They also

Deborah Kohl Kremer

KENTUCKY PROUD MARKET

have Keeneland logo hats, shirts, and jackets.

Kennedy Book Store (859-252-0331; kennedys.com), 405 S. Limestone. This independent bookstore has been serving the needs of University of Kentucky students since 1950. Even if you are not in the market for college textbooks, Kennedy's has a fabulous selection of UK merchandise.

Fayette Cigar Store (859-252-6267), 137 E. Main St. If you are looking for a fine selection of cigars, head for the walk-in humidor in the back. Cigar aficionados know this is the place to find rare cigars and a friendly, knowledgeable staff. But there is more to this shop than cigars. You will also find a newsstand with an enormous selection of newspapers and magazines. A word of caution to those traveling with small chil-

dren: In the back corner of the store is quite a selection of X-rated magazines. Although these are discreetly displayed away from the general-interest publications, you might want to keep little eyes near the front of the store. Fayette Cigar Store also

FAYETTE CIGAR STORE

Deborah Kohl Kremer

sells candy, books, gift items, and artwork.

Peggy's Gifts and Accessories (859-255-3188; www.peggysgifts .com), 112 Clay Ave. Located in a renovated old home, Peggy's offers a full line of purses, jewelry, and baby and wedding gifts; most can be personalized. They also have an assortment of customized sorority gift items.

Black Swan Books (859-252-7255; www.blackswanbooks.net), 505 E. Maxwell St. Closed Sun. Close to the University of Kentucky's campus, you'll find Lexington's finest collection of used books. They also carry new books, but it's the stacks and stacks of used volumes that really put Black Swan on the map. In business for more than 25 years, they claim to specialize in history, horses, military, and Kentucky literature, but they really have everything.

Dandelion Bead Connection (859-335-9600; www.dandelion beads.net), 209 Rosemont Garden. Jewelry makers and bead collectors will think they've died and gone to heaven when they enter this darling shop. In business for about 20 years, owner Mark Lightfoot knows his beads. The shop is stocked with semi-precious stones, freshwater pearls, and hard-to-find glass beads as well as clasps, thread, and supplies.

Miss Priss (859-254-2110; www .missprissdowntown.com), 401 W. Main St. Even if you are not going to the junior prom or competing

PEGGY'S GIFTS

Deborah Kohl Kremer

Deborah Kohl Kremer

MISS PRISS

in a beauty pageant anytime soon, stop by this darling shop and look at all the bling! They specialize in fancy-schmancy dresses, but you just might find the perfect one for an upcoming event. They have sizzling purses and jewelry, too.

The Morris Book Shop (859-276-0494; morrisbookshop.com), 882 E. High St. At Morris, you will find about 20,000 books to peruse if you have the time. Although they would love to see you in person, their website has a pretty reliable searchable database to help you see what is in stock.

ANTIQUES Belle Maison Antiques (859-252-9030; www .bellemaisonantiques.com), 525 W. Short St. Owner Debbie Chamblin scours the famous Marché aux Puces, also known as the Paris Flea Market, and the small towns of France looking for antiques she can bring back to Lexington. Furniture and home decor items as well as lots of urns and planters for your garden.

Athens Schoolhouse Antique Show (859-255-7309; athens schoolhouse.com), 6270 Athens Walnut Hill Rd. Located 1 mile east of I-75. This antiques show, featuring 150 to 170 dealers, takes place in an old school building the second weekend of every month. Hours are Fri. 9–5, Sat. 9–5, Sun. 11–5. This place is huge, so allow yourself plenty of time to make the rounds. A snack shop on site is called **Back Door Café**. They offer soups and sandwiches if you need a break from all that antiquing. Admission $2.

ART GALLERIES Loudoun House Gallery (859-254-7024, 800-914-7990; www.lexington artleague.org), 209 Castlewood Dr. Providing exhibit and educational arts programs, this organization does all it can to support local artists. Ever-changing gallery; stop by to see what's on display.

Cross Gate Gallery (859-233-3856; www.crossgategallery.com), 509 E. Main St. Specializing in equine and sporting art, this gallery has some breathtaking pieces. They are located in a massive Greek Revival home that was

built in 1901, so enjoy the art and historic building at the same time.

✳ Special Events

April: ♦ ♿ **Rolex Kentucky Three Day Event** (www.kyhorse park.com). Held the last weekend in April at the Kentucky Horse Park, this is the premier event for equestrian riding in the United States. The event, which draws thousands of spectators from around the world, includes competitions in dressage, cross-country, and show jumping.

May: ♈ **Kentucky Wine & Vine Fest** (www.kywineandvine.com). Kentucky's list of wineries grows each year, keeping up with the plump grapes that are flourishing on the former tobacco farms

CROSS GATE GALLERY

around the state. Nicholasville (just 8 miles south of Lexington) has created a festival to celebrate all things vino. This weekend event, held in the historic downtown, includes bus tours of local vineyards and wineries, a grape stomp-off, and a winemaking competition. You can also enjoy the live Dixieland and jazz music featured all weekend. Although the weekend is lots of fun, it is, obviously, not for children.

June: ⌀ ⌂ **The Festival of the Bluegrass** (www.festivalofthe bluegrass.com). A whole weekend committed to the enjoyment of Kentucky bluegrass music. Held on the grounds of the Kentucky Horse Park, there are three stages hosting well-known acts as well as local artists.

September: ⌘ ⌀ ⌂ **Roots & Heritage Street Festival** (www .rootsandheritagefestival.com). Capturing the powerful spirit of Lexington's African American culture, this festival features live music with internationally known acts, an African marketplace, and a wide variety of exciting, culturally enriching activities.

VERSAILLES, MIDWAY, AND SURROUNDING WOODFORD COUNTY

Versailles is a darling community in the heart of thoroughbred country in Woodford County. The area is filled with rolling countryside and horse farms tucked inside familiar white plank fencing. The town is named for a city in France—but when you're here, you have to say it like a Kentuckian, and Kentuckians say *ver-SAILS* (as opposed to the French version, *ver-SIGH*).

The area has many ties to the railroad. The nearby town of **Midway** was actually built by the L&N Railroad, and the tracks run right through the shopping district. In Versailles you can visit the Bluegrass Railroad Museum, located in a former L&N railroad station, which was built in 1911.

The breezy countryside and winding back roads, sometimes lined with handmade stone fences, make it a glorious place to drive. Along the way you can shop for antiques in the Versailles downtown area, stroll around Midway College, Kentucky's only all-women's college, dine at the fabulous Holly Hill Inn, and take a tour of a horse farm or two.

GUIDANCE Woodford County Chamber of Commerce (859-873-5122; www.woodfordchamber-ky.com), 141 N. Main St., Versailles. Open weekdays 9–4:30. You'll find lots of brochures, regional information, and recommendations right in downtown Versailles.

GETTING THERE Versailles is just 14 miles from downtown Lexington, so the **Bluegrass Airport** is your best bet (859-425-3114; www.bluegrass airport.com). There are car rentals available at the airport. **Greyhound** bus service is available in Lexington (859-299-8804; www.greyhound.com), 477 W. New Circle Rd., Lexington.

www.kentuckytourism.com

DOWNTOWN MIDWAY, KENTUCKY

GETTING AROUND Located about halfway between Lexington and Frankfort, this small country town has an unhurried feel to it. Streets are well marked. Getting around by car is a pleasure.

MEDICAL EMERGENCY Bluegrass Community Hospital (859-873-3111; www.bluegrasscommunityhospital.com), 360 Amsden Ave., Versailles. This 25-bed hospital consistently ranks above the 95th percentile in national patient, employee, and physician satisfaction surveys.

ALCOHOL Woodford County is a wet county, allowing alcohol sales throughout the area.

✳ To See

🏵 **Bluegrass Scenic Railroad and Museum** (859-873-2476, 800-755-2476; www.bgrm.org), 175 Beasley Rd., Versailles. Grounds open year-round. The gift shop and ticket office hours are open 12:30–4 every Sat. and Sun. from mid-May until the end of Oct. Train rides at 2. Enjoy a one-hour train ride aboard coaches built in the 1920s and '30s. Visit the museum full of railroad memorabilia. You can even send a message with their working telegraph. Brush up on your Morse code before you get there. $10 adults, $9 ages 65 and over, $7 ages 2–12; under 2 free. Locomotive cab rides $25.

✔ Nostalgia Station Toy & Train Museum (859-873-2497), 279 Depot St., Versailles. Open Wed.–Sat. 10–5, Sun. 1–5. The train exhibits, housed in a restored 1911 L&N Railroad passenger station, include vintage toys and toy trains that date back to 1900. There is also a gift shop full of fun train-related merchandise.

Equus Run Vineyards (859-846-9463, 877-905-2675; www.equusrun vineyards.com), 1280 Moores Mill Rd., Midway. Take a guided tour of the tobacco-barn-turned-winemaking-facility, or spend time walking the vineyard area on your own. Equus Run also has a nice amphitheater where they host concerts in summer.

Jack Jouett House (859-873-7902), 255 Craigs Creek Rd., Versailles. Open Wed.–Sun., Apr.–Oct., or call for an appointment. This house was built in 1793 by Captain Jack Jouett, a prominent leader for Kentucky statehood and Revolutionary War hero. This Federal-style cottage is well preserved and furnished with period pieces. It fact, it looks much as it did when Jack and his wife, Sally Robards, were raising their 12 children here, except it's a lot less noisy.

Pisgah Presbyterian Church (859-873-4161), 710 Pisgah Rd., Versailles. Call for tour information. This church was established in 1784 as the first Presbyterian church west of the Allegheny Mountains. Originally made of logs, the current facility, built in 1812, is constructed of fieldstone. It is home to priceless stained-glass windows and an immense pipe organ. There is also a cemetery on site, in which lies the remains of seven Revolutionary War soldiers.

Woodford County Historical Society Library and Museum (859-873-6786; www.woodfordkyhistory.org), 121 Rose Hill Ave., Versailles. Open Tue.–Sat. 10–4. Housed in the restored 1819 Big Spring Church and Meeting House, the museum has artifacts, data, and genealogy information from people who have lived in the Woodford County area. Free.

Woodford Reserve (859-879-1812; www.woodfordreserve.com), 7855 McCracken Pike, Versailles. Open Tue.–Sat. 9–5, Sun. 12:30–4:30. Tour the distillery of Labrot & Graham, home of Woodford Reserve Bourbon. The limestone buildings reflect the traditions of the area and the distiller, where they still use the time-honored copper pot method to make their fine bourbon. $5 adults (18 and up); under 5 free.

✳ To Do

GOLF The Brook Golf Course (859-873-8404; www.thebrookgc.com), 2260 Lexington Pike, Versailles. This 18-hole championship public golf course is a favorite of locals and visitors due to its central location and lush setting.

RECREATION **Falling Springs Recreation Center** (859-873-5948; fallingsprings.net), 275 Beasley Dr., Versailles. Go have some fun at the indoor and outdoor pools, three-court gym, and fitness center.

✳ Green Space

Buckley Hills Wildlife Sanctuary, 1305 Germany Rd., Frankfort. Open Wed.–Sun. This 374-acre wildlife haven encompasses parts of Woodford and Franklin Counties. It is operated by the National Audubon Society and offers a 2-mile loop nature trail, bird-watching, and special events.

✳ Lodging

In Versailles
&. (((ツ))) **Castle Post Luxury Tourist Home** (859-879-1000; www.the castlepost.com), 230 Pisgah Pike. Royalty never had it so good. This Lexington landmark, which was once a private home, has been transformed into an off-the-charts upscale getaway. Complete with turret rooms, 30-foot ceilings, and 12-foot wooden doors, the massive structure is surrounded by a solid stone wall. It's not all cold and castle-like, though, and the owner describes it as a castle on the out-side and a palace on the inside. Imported chandeliers, million-dollar woodwork, and impeccable furnishings create a truly one-of-a-kind lodging experience. The guest suites include oversized bath-rooms, well-appointed sitting rooms, and extravagance at every turn. A night's stay includes a three-course gourmet dinner and breakfast the next morning. Tours are not offered. $$$$

Montgomery Inn Bed and Breakfast (859-251-4103; www .montgomeryinnbnb.com), 270

CASTLE POST

Deborah Kohl Kremer

Montgomery Ave. Offering 10 guest suites, each with a two-person Jacuzzi tub, this spectacular Victorian home dates back to 1911. Enjoy fresh-baked cookies and snacks in the evening and a hearty gourmet breakfast in the morn. $$

A Storybook Inn (859-879-9993; www.storybook-inn.com), 277 Rose Hill Ave. This 1840s home is just as darling on the outside as on the inside. Featuring three guest rooms and a private two-bedroom cottage, this cute inn has been compared to a small European luxury hotel. Small extras like fresh-squeezed orange juice and premium roasted fresh-ground coffee make the apple-cinnamon bourbon breakfast pudding that innkeeper Elise Buckley-Snoddy whips up even better. $$$

1823 Historic Rose Hill Inn (859-873-5957; www.rosehillinn.com), 233 Rose Hill Ave. There are seven guest rooms in this lovingly renovated and preserved home. Enjoy the stained-glass windows, original ash floors, and intricate woodwork. Some rooms have kitchens, some sleep families, and some have room for your dog, so you are sure to find a room to meet your needs at this large home. Breakfast, served on lace-covered tablecloths and delicate china, offers southern choices like Rose Hill grits, ham with red-eye gravy, or orange cream French toast. $$–$$$

The Woodford Inn (859-879-9466; www.woodfordinn.com), 140

Park St. Originally built as the Versailles Female College in 1876, this 10-room inn has been updated with modern amenities. They also have a nice sit-down restaurant and a tavern. $$

✳ Where to Eat

DINING OUT ᵞ Holly Hill Inn (859-846-4732; www.hollyhillinn.com), 426 N. Winter St., Midway. Dinner Wed.–Sat. beginning at 5:30. Sat. and Sun. brunch served 11–2. Owners Chris and Ouita Michel invite you to dine with them in their 1830s Greek Revival inn. The white tablecloths and impeccable service only enhance the three- or six-course meal. Chef Ouita's menu changes seasonally to maximize the local fresh ingredients. Try the corn bread soufflé or the bourbon country lamb for a real southern-style treat. $$$

The Glitz Restaurant at Irish Acres (859-873-6956; www.irishacresgallery.com), 4205 Ford's Mill Rd., Nonesuch. Their famous three-course lunch is served Tue.–Sat. Reservations required. Housed in the basement of a former school, although you'd never know it, this fine-dining experience lives up to its name as a glitzy, glamorous place to eat lunch. $$

The Woodford Inn (859-879-9466; www.woodfordinn.com), 140 Park St., Versailles. Open Tue.–Sat. Lunch 11–2, Dinner 5–9. Eat in the dining room of the main house, which was built in 1876, the four-season sunporch, or outside on the patio. Sandwiches and salads as well as steaks, pasta, and grilled salmon choices fill the menu. $$–$$$

EATING OUT Darlin' Jean's Apple Cobbler Café (859-846-9485), 137 E. Main St., Midway. Open Mon.–Sat. 11–2. Also open for dinner Wed.–Sat. 5–9. You can't miss this place with the giant silo out front. This is a family-run restaurant, and the menu reflects generations of recipes. Notable dishes are Kentucky hot brown, bagel melt sandwiches, and coconut chicken salad. Don't even think about leaving without ordering some cobbler. Although the apple kind of started it all, they have delicious peach, blackberry, chocolate, and pecan cobblers, too. $$

& Y **Heirloom Restaurant** (859-846-5565), 125 Main St., Midway. Open Tue.–Sat. 11:30–2. Also open for dinner Tue.–Sat. beginning at 5:30. Reservations strongly recommended. This is a cool restaurant with a discriminating, upscale feel to it. The lunch menu features salads with unusual ingredients like anchovies, arugula, and goat cheese. They have burgers and sandwiches, but all with a funky twist. The BLT, for example, is a fried green tomato BLT, served on toasted sourdough with lemon aioli and cracked pepper chips. For dinner, entrées run the gamut from chile-roasted tiger prawns, to seared duck breast, to seared Alaskan halibut with kumquat relish. If you are looking

for some new and exciting taste combinations, this is the place. $$–$$$

Wallace Station Country Store, Bakery and Deli (859-846-5161), 3854 Old Frankfort Pike, Versailles. Mon.–Sat. 8–5, Sun. 11–4. Mon.-night fried chicken dinners 5–8. Stop at this homey place for lunch or dinner. You'll have a hard time deciding which giant sandwich to go with, but rest assured, they are all delicious and made on the restaurant's own homemade bread. If you are there on a Monday night for the fried chicken dinner, you'll enjoy the black-eyed peas and cheesy grit side dishes as much as the main dish. $$

Quirk Café and Coffee (859-846-4688), 131 E. Main St., Midway. Serving lunch Mon.–Sat. Tucked inside Le Marche gift shop, this lunch spot has fresh scones, deli sandwiches, and weekly quiche specials. $

Melissa's Cottage Café (859-879-6204), 167 S. Main St. Versailles. Open Mon.–Fri. 11–9 and Sat. 5–9. Lunch specials and homemade desserts are what the locals recommend, but with selections like a cold meat loaf sandwich, hot brown, and chicken potpie, you know Melissa's got some stick-to-your-ribs classics.

Y **Wilson's Pool Room** (859-879-0277), 131 Lexington St., Versailles. Open Mon.–Sat. 7:30 AM–10 PM. Although they serve up eggs, bacon, and country ham for breakfast, everyone goes to Wilson's for the giant ½-pound Willy

Burger. They'll make one for you any time of day; just ask. Shoot a game of pool with the regulars while you are there.

SNACKS ♪ **Cornerstone Pharmacy** (859-873-3007), 100 Main St., Versailles. Weekdays 9–6, Sat. 9–3. Pull up a stool and enjoy some ice cream at the old-time soda fountain. They also serve lunch specials. Monday is broccoli soup day, and there is usually a crowd for it. Cornerstone has been around for about 50 years, and Versailles residents treasure it. $

✷ Entertainment

ᕯ **The Woodford County Theatrical Arts Association** (859-873-0648; www.woodford countytheater.com), 275 Beasley Dr., Versailles. Producing several Broadway-style shows and plays each season, this community theater group is big on talent and fun. Check the website to see when the curtain will rise next.

✷ Selective Shopping

Damselfly Studio and Gallery (859-494-8759), 126 E. Main St., Midway. This cute, colorful shop features lots of photography and watercolors of local artists. They also have lampwork beads and jewelry, and sometimes offer bead-making demonstrations. It's kind of a whimsical place that you'll enjoy browsing around in. Owner Mary Thoreson loves roosters, and you'll see a wide variety of these colorful creatures

reflected in the artwork and craft items.

Crittenden Fine Gentleman's Clothing (859-846-4228; crittendenclothes.com), 141 E. Main St., Midway. After working for some of the finest designers in the country for more than 50 years, Crittenden Rawlings decided he knew something about men's clothing and started to design his own. He hung out his shingle and invites to public in to see and feel his creations. Crittenden pays extreme attention to fine fabrics and the relaxed cuts of each piece and works hard to present each one at a reasonable price. Stop in and say hi—he will treat you like a prince.

♪ **Boyd Orchards Fresh Produce & Potted Plants** (859-873-3097; www.boydorchards.com), 1396 Pinckard Pike, Versailles. Enjoy farm-style fun like hayrides, apple picking, and corn mazes. Get some fresh-from-the-field produce while you are there.

Freedman's Harness and Saddlery (859-846-9674; www .freedmanharness.com), 136 E. Main St., Midway. Closed Sun. and Mon. Whether you need a saddle for your horse or a finely made purse, Freedman's can help you out. They've been making fine leather goods since 1802, so you can trust them for quality and craftsmanship.

ANTIQUES **Irish Acres Gallery of Antiques** (859-873-7235; irish acresgallery.com), 4205 Fords Mill

Rd., Nonesuch. This antique hunter's dream features 32,000 square feet of American and European furniture, antiques, and collectibles. It's housed inside an old school, so it's huge. Plan accordingly.

ART GALLERIES Heike Pickett Gallery & Sculpture Garden (859-233-1263; www.heikepickettgallery.com), 110 Morgan St., Versailles. Surrounded by century-old boxwoods, this outdoor sculpture garden is worth the trip alone, but don't miss the adjacent Carter House, built around 1792.

It is loaded with a fantastic collection of art from both new and established artists.

✳ Special Events

June: ✿ ✎ ♿ **Francisco Farm Art Festival**. Held on the campus of Midway College each year. The festival is named for the original landowner, John Francisco, who sold his 216 acres of farmland to the Lexington & Ohio Railroad in 1835. They, in turn, built the town of Midway. Award-winning fine arts and crafts festival with music, food, and juried art vendors.

WINCHESTER AND PARIS

The Winchester and Paris area is historically significant to the state of Kentucky because, as the country's first western frontier, it was the location where Daniel Boone put down roots with the creation of Fort Boonesboro in 1775. Separated by about 17 miles along KY-627, also known as Winchester Road and/or Paris Road—depending on which direction you are traveling—Winchester and Paris sit about 20 miles outside of Lexington, but are self-supporting communities all on their own. Both are family-oriented towns that cherish their histories.

Paris, Kentucky, was named for Paris, France. Sticking to their European roots, settlers named the county after an affluent French family, the Bourbons, who were instrumental in America's fight for independence from England. The name *bourbon*, today synonymous with Kentucky's signature drink, derived its name from the county, not the other way around.

In 1792 Clark County, with its seat at Winchester, was carved from Bourbon and Fayette Counties. The county is named for George Rogers Clark, an early explorer of western Virginia, which is now Kentucky. He was also the leader of the Kentucky Militia during the American Revolutionary War. The town of Winchester started out on 66 acres donated in 1793 by local frontiersman John Baker. Probably part of the donation involved naming rights, as the town is named for Baker's hometown of Winchester, Virginia.

The city of **Winchester** is still able to boast about places visited by Boone himself, as well as history-laden cemeteries, churches, homes, and a darling downtown lined with the five-globed streetlights that the city was known for in its early days. Take in the small-town feel, and don't forget to visit the Ale-8-One plant while you are there.

If you head out of Lexington on Paris Pike, you will be enchanted by one of Kentucky's most scenic byways. Lined with stone fences and glorious horse farms, the scenery is postcard-perfect. And who knows? Those stallions you see frolicking in the fields could be hometown celebrities who earned millions on the track and now earn even more by standing

Deborah Kohl Kremer

RED RIVER GORGE

stud at Paris-area farms like the gorgeous Claiborne Farm, owner of several Triple Crown trophies, and Runnymede Farm, which was established in 1867 and is the oldest continuously operated thoroughbred breeding farm in Kentucky. The area horse farms sometimes offer tours, but please check their websites or call ahead to find out if you are welcome.

GUIDANCE **Winchester–Clark County Tourism Commission** (800-298-9105; tourwinchester.com), 2 S. Maple St., Winchester.

GETTING THERE Both Paris and Winchester are about 20 miles from downtown Lexington, so the **Bluegrass Airport** is your best bet (859-425-3114; www.bluegrassairport.com). There are car rentals available at the airport. **Greyhound** bus service is available in Lexington (859-299-8804; www.greyhound.com), 477 W. New Circle Rd., Lexington.

GETTING AROUND There really is no public transportation in these small towns, but the easily walkable main street areas and free parking just invite you in. Drive there so you can enjoy the scenery along the way.

MEDICAL EMERGENCY **Clark Regional Medical Center** (859-745-3500; www.clarkregional.org), 175 Hospital Dr., Winchester. This 79-bed community hospital was established in 1917. They are able to offer a full range of medical care in their new $60 million facility. In the Paris area, head for **Bourbon Community Hospital** (859-987-3600; bourbon hospital.com), 9 Linville Dr., Paris.

ALCOHOL Both Bourbon and Clark Counties are wet, allowing alcohol sales throughout the area. What did you expect with a county named Bourbon?

✳ To See

⚗ ⌀ Ale-8-One (859-744-3484; www.ale-8-one.com), 25 Carol Rd., Winchester. Kentucky is known for another drink besides bourbon: Ale-8-One is a carbonated citrusy drink that Central Kentuckians are raised on. When locals say the name, it comes out sounding like *A Late One*, and you might not know what they are referring to. You'll catch on quickly when you pull up to any shopping center, where you'll likely see four or five Ale-8-One vending machines and just one for Coke or Pepsi. This is definitely the soft drink of choice for the region. You can take a 30-minute tour of the factory in Winchester every Friday at 10:50. Don't forget to call ahead to make a reservation. At the end of the tour you can shop their company store, where you can buy a few cases of this fizzy drink and even a T-shirt to wear home.

Hopewell Museum (859-987-7274; hopewellmuseum.org), 800 Pleasant St., Paris. Open Wed.–Sat. noon–5, Sun. 2–4, as well as appointment. Featuring pieces of art and historic memorabilia from the area. Exhibits are changed and added frequently, so check the website to see what is happening.

The Bluegrass Heritage Museum (859-745-1358; bg heritage.com), 217 S. Main St., Winchester. Open Mon.–Sat. noon–4. You know a history museum is going to be good when it is housed in a historic building that you can't wait to visit. The building, known as the Guerrant Clinic, which served as Winchester's first hospital, opened in 1887. The museum has done a fantastic job with an exhibit outlining the importance of the clinic to the region. Other permanent exhibits capture the history of Clark

Ale-8-One

County, its ties to military service and agriculture, and even a fabulous collection of quilts and telephone memorabilia.

Cane Ridge Meeting House (859-987-5350), KY 537, Paris. Built from blue ash logs in 1791, this one-room structure was the site of the establishment of the Disciples of Christ. Today the meetinghouse and museum are open Apr.–Oct., Mon.–Sat. 9–5 and Sun. 1–5. Free, but they'll take a donation if offered.

The Winchester Opera House (859-745-6622; winchesteroperahouse .com), 10 E. Lexington Ave., Winchester. This historic opera house was built in 1873 and has been restored to her glorious self. Although she no longer hosts operas, her grand ballrooms are available for rental. If you are not invited to an upcoming posh event, swing by to check out the amazing collection of art in the 2000-square-foot gallery. Call ahead to check hours.

Duncan Tavern (859-987-1788; duncantavern.com), 323 High St., Paris. Major Joseph Duncan built this tavern in 1788 and hosted such notable guests as Daniel Boone and Simon Kenton. This architectural gem now houses the Kentucky Society of the Daughters of the American Revolution and the John Fox Jr. Genealogical Library. Guided tours are available Apr.–Dec., Wed.–Sat. at 1:30 PM and by appointment.

DRIVING TOURS The tourism people have compiled several tours of the area that you can complete at your own pace. Spend an afternoon participating in a Stone Fence Driving Tour, Guided Cell Phone Tours, Barn Art and Quilt Trail tours, or the Civil War Driving Tour. They are all glorious ways to get to know the area at your own pace. Pick up a brochure or instructions at the Winchester–Clark County Tourism Commission.

GOLF Shady Brook Golf Course (859-987-1544), 444 Hutchison Rd., Paris. This independently owned 9-hole course is the perfect size when you don't have time for 18. Reserve a tee time on weekends because it is a favorite of locals.

Cassell Creek Public Golf Club and Driving Range (859-744-9959; cassellcreekgolf.com), 4199 Lexington Rd., Winchester. Tree-lined fairways on this 18-hole course. Carts available. See the website for dress code and hours.

✳ Green Space

The Winchester Cemetery Company, Inc. (859-744-6889; www .winchestercemetery.com), 625 W. Lexington Ave., Winchester. Open every day during daylight hours. Established in 1854, this beautiful 55-acre cemetery is a peaceful respite and loving memorial. Well-manicured grounds and the lure of history make it a wonderful place to walk or do research.

Lower Howard's Creek (859-744-4888; www.lowerhowardscreek.org), 1945 Athens-Boonesboro Rd., Winchester. Made up of 240 acres of unspoiled nature, this nature preserve works to protect endangered species. This deep, forested gorge is complemented with steep slopes, natural cliffs, and trickling streams, perfect for communing with nature. Because the preserve is full of precious plant life and historic cultural sites, it is only open to the public during scheduled hikes with a knowledgeable guide.

The Wallis House & Arboretum, (859-987-6158), 616 Pleasant St., Paris. This gorgeous antebellum home is the headquarters of Garden Club of Kentucky, Inc. With such a prestigious tenant, the surrounding arboretum is immaculate. Take a stroll through and enjoy all their hard work. Open during daylight hours year-round. Free.

✳ Lodging

Country Charm Historic Farmhouse Bed and Breakfast (859-988-1006), 505 Hutchison Rd., Paris. Innkeepers David and LaVonna Snell offer a warm welcome as well as a full country breakfast each morning. Three rooms, one with private bath. The Queen Room and Central Room share a bath, perfect for families. $

✳ Where to Eat

EATING OUT ⅄ **Hall's on the River** (859-527-6620; www .hallsontheriver.com), 1225

HALL'S ON THE RIVER

Deborah Kohl Kremer

GREEN SPACE MUST-SEES

About 30 miles east of Winchester, via the Mountain Parkway at the Slade exit, you will find the Red River Gorge and Natural Bridge State Park, two gems that can't be missed.

🌾 🖉 **Natural Bridge State Resort Park** (606-663-2214, 800-325-1710; parks.ky.gov/findparks/resortparks/nb), 2135 Natural Bridge Rd., Slade. One the four original Kentucky state parks, this park was established in 1926, but was about 65 million years in the making. The sandstone arch for which it's named—78 feet long, 65 feet high, 12 feet thick, and 20 feet wide—is actually the most famous of more than 70 natural arches in the area. Situated adjacent to the **Red River Gorge Geological Area** (www .redrivergorge.org), which covers about 26,000 acres of the Daniel Boone National Forest, this region was created by wind and water, resulting in stunning cliff formations, scenic vistas, and natural rock shelters. With miles and miles of hiking trails, it offers routes for all levels of exertion. But be sure to use extreme caution, as there are many steep cliffs and hair-raising drop-offs along the paths that take lives every year.

The state park encompasses approximately 2,500 acres, with more than 18 miles of hiking trails all leading to the awe-inspiring Natural Bridge. The park also includes a 4-acre pond with an island in the middle of it. Known as Hoedown Island, it is used for square dances in the summer. There is also 54-acre Mill Creek Lake, where you can rent pedal boats and hydrobikes; it's an excellent place for fishing for bass, bream, catfish, crappie, and rainbow trout. For those not interested in hiking, take the 22-minute SkyLift up to the breathtaking Natural Bridge. Stay in one of the 35 rooms at the **Hemlock Lodge**; all have private balconies to enjoy the views of the forested mountain area. They also have secluded one- and two-bedroom cottages tucked into the woods. If you would rather camp, Natural Bridge State Resort Park has two campgrounds, **Whittleton Campground** and **Middlefork Campground**. These wooded grounds provide 82 sites with utilities, as well as primitive sites for those who really want to rough it. **The Sandstone Arches Restaurant** is a good place to go relax after a day of hiking. The restaurant overlooks the lake and Hoedown Island, the clogging capital of Kentucky (and you didn't even know there was a clogging capital of Kentucky). Diners can enjoy watching squirrels steal nuts from the squirrel feeders outside. The menu offers choices like fried catfish, fried green tomatoes, and Kentucky hot brown. Although it could be hard to choose among these specialties, the restaurant also features a daily buffet at all three meals, so you won't have to.

NATURAL BRIDGE

Deborah Kohl Kremer

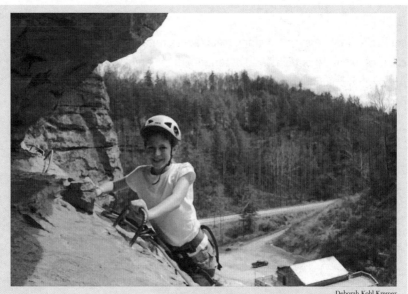

Deborah Kohl Kremer

TORRENT FALLS CLIMBING ADVENTURE

Call for hours, which change seasonally. $–$$; children under 5 eat free.

Just down the road from Natural Bridge State Park is the **Kentucky Reptile Zoo** (606-663-9160), 200 L&E Railroad, Slade. Although it is open every day in the summer, it's open on weekends only during the winter months. The center is stocked with live snakes, turtles, and other scaled creatures. Make sure you are there for the live venom extraction, which is very popular with the kids.

Those new to the climbing world might want to head for **Torrent Falls Climbing Adventure** (606-668-6613; www.torrentfalls.com), 1617 N. KY 11, Campton. Open Mar. 1–Dec. 1, 9 AM–dark. This French climbing system, the only one in the United States, is a mixture of rungs and cables connected right to the rock face to aid in climbing or rappelling. Climbers need to be age 10 or older.

While you are in the area, don't miss **Miguel's Pizza** (606-663-1975), 1891 Natural Bridge Rd., Slade. This legendary hangout for rock climbers and campers serves excellent home-style pizza. They also offer climbing supplies and overnight camping for climbers for just $2 per person. So, if you are not a climber, stop by for some tasty pizza, but if you're there for climbing, stop by for pizza and climbing camaraderie. $

Athens-Boonesboro Rd., Winchester. Serving lunch and dinner weekdays 11:30–9, weekends 11:30–10. One of the only restaurants to sit right on the edge of the picturesque Kentucky River; you can see why this has been a bar or restaurant since 1783. Known for their beer cheese appetizer, which you should order, they also have steaks, seafood, and regional favorites. If the weather is warm, eat on the deck; it's tucked into the rocky cliffs of the river valley. $$

ᵫ **Varden's** (859-987-4700; vardens.com), 509 Main St., Paris. Located inside a pharmacy that dates back to 1891, Varden's is a charming little bistro and sandwich shop. The Bistro, which is open for dinner Tue.–Sat., features Kentucky favorites like fried green tomatoes and shrimp and grits, as well as New York strip steak, rack of lamb, or just a good juicy burger. They also have a full bar. The cafe, open Mon.–Sat. 11–3, boasts deli-style sandwiches that are generous as well as delicious.

Stinky & Coco's Diner (859-744-8100; stinkyandcocos.com), 1 N. Main St., Winchester. Open Mon.–Sat. 6 AM–2 PM. Owner Don Parsons explains about a thousand times a day that the name of his restaurant comes from his cats; there's no big guy named Stinky in the back cooking up your fries. Don has gobs of experience in the restaurant business, and one visit to his diner will convince you. His

menu features familiar favorites with an occasional eclectic choice thrown in for fun. Try the shrimp 'n' grits with Cajun-seasoned cream sauce, a fried egg sandwich, or the popular Stinky burger.

JK's Café (859-744-4255) 50 S. Main St., Winchester. Serving lunch only, Mon.–Sat. 11–2. A casual little lunch spot right in the heart of town. Not only will you get a fabulous deli sandwich or salad for a reasonable price, but you'll also be served by some really nice people. Make your own deli combination, or order one of their specialty sandwiches like the Muddy Creek, a roast beef sandwich with melted provolone and bistro sauce. It's good eatin'. Plate-lunch specials, too; the tomato pie and lasagna always draw a crowd.

Paradise Café (859-987-8383), 731 Main St., Paris. Mon.–Sat. 11–9:30; Sun. 11:30–9:30. Delicious Asian menu, with Vietnamese and Chinese options. Housed in the historic 1890s Edward Shinners Building that was listed in Ripley's Believe It or Not as the tallest three-story building in the world. You don't find that just everywhere. $

Cantuckee Diner (859- 744-7377), 12 Carol Rd, Winchester. Down-home-style food served buffet-style. Fried chicken, catfish, corn bread, sweet tea—you know the drill. There is nothing at all fancy about Cantuckee, but the food is good and cheap. $

Biancke's Restaurant (859-234-3443), 102 S. Main St., Cynthiana. Mon.–Sat. 7–9, Sun. 8–2. In business for more than 100 years, Biancke's is the mom-and-pop restaurant of your dreams. Although they are located about 15 miles north of Paris, it is worth your while to head slightly off your beaten path. The decor is homey, with old graduation photos from the local high school hanging everywhere. They also have a tempting glass case full of homemade desserts right where you can see them, which is actually helpful so you can plan your meal accordingly. And although their breakfasts are huge and their meat loaf is amazing, you are going to want a slice of their chocolate cream pie. Yes, you are. $

✱ Entertainment

Leeds Center for the Arts (859-744-6437; www.leedscenter.com), 37 N. Main St. This historic downtown theater always has something artsy going on. Check the website to see current productions by their community theater group, as well as musicals and concerts.

✱ Selective Shopping

Ardery's Antiques (859-987-8180; arderysantiques.com), 627 Main St., Paris. Taking you back to the days of the dime store, this 6,000-square-foot former Newberry's store is filled to the walls with antiques. They even renovated the soda fountain area, where you can order homemade

sandwiches, soups, and pies. Closed Sun. and Mon.

Graham's Boots & Western Wear (859-744-6441; grahams-bootstore.com), 18 N. Main St., Winchester. In business for nearly 40 years, Graham's looks much as it did back then with hardwood floors and those cool ladders that are attached to the shelves on rollers. They have an amazing selection of both western and work boots as well as clothing, belts, and hats. The service is amazing in this family-run store. Stop by and pay them a visit.

Loch Lea Antiques (859-987-7070; lochleaantiques.com), 410 Main St., Paris. Owned by the Layton family, who know antiques as well as they know horses, Loch Lea has quite a collection at their cute shop right in the heart of Paris. They specialize in Kentucky antiques, like Bybee Pottery, and equine-related treasures. They also carry an assortment of art, furniture, books, and silver items.

LaGrie's Fine English Saddlery (859-987-2717; www.lagries englishsaddlery.net), 606 Main St., Paris. Catering to the dressage rider, LaGrie's is the place where you will find distinctive European brands including dressage saddles and bridles, healthy horse care products, and a unique gift line for all horse lovers. They also carry Equestrian Connoisseur clothing and matching saddle pads, personalized items, and home decor for the equestrian lifestyle. Owner Lisa Warmels will help you find exactly what you're looking for. Call ahead for hours.

Hometown Antiques and Coins (859-744-8335), 31 S. Main St., Winchester. Poke around this cute shop and see what treasures you can find. If you have rare coins, they can tell you about them, buy them, or help you find more.

Bethany Book Room (859-744-6024; bethanybook.com), 150 Redwing Dr., Winchester. Specializing in homeschool and Christian books and music.

✳ Special Events

June: ❧ ✿ ♿ **The Beer Cheese Festival**, Winchester. Witness the transformation of Main Street to Beer Cheese Boulevard. Live music and beer cheese competition at the professional and amateur level. They also have food booths, featuring beer cheese and an array of menu items, but you are at a beer cheese festival, so you might as well indulge all you can.

Northern Kentucky

4

Deborah Kohl Kremer

Northern Kentucky

© The Countryman Press

INTRODUCTION:
NORTHERN KENTUCKY

Northern Kentucky is a region of the state that is anchored to the Ohio River. Its communities all draw their history from this 981-mile-long waterway. Most of these small towns got their start as trading settlements catering to the many flatboats that made their way downriver from Pittsburgh during the westward expansion of the early 1800s.

Starting at the eastern end of the region, the town of Maysville is doused with history, as it has ties to early Kentucky frontiersmen like Daniel Boone and Simon Kenton, and later was a famous depot on the Underground Railroad. Today's Maysville and nearby Augusta are just sweetheart little towns with walkable main streets, an assortment of homegrown restaurants, shops, and fun festivals throughout the year.

The river makes its huge arc around the northernmost point of Kentucky, hugging the counties of Boone, Kenton, and Campbell, where you will find the area that locals refer to as Northern Kentucky. In most parts of the state, when you ask someone where they are from, they will answer with the name of a county. But here, "Northern Kentucky" generally covers all three counties; the suburbs blur together, making it feel like all one place.

Kentuckians sometimes refer to Northern Kentucky as simply Southern Cincinnati, but that is definitely not the case. Northern Kentucky draws the best from the large midwestern city to the north, as well as the time-honored traditions of the South, and blends them together to form a culture like nowhere else.

Although you might not always hear a southern drawl in the voice of locals, you will hear very good manners. Northern Kentuckians are notorious for using the word *Please* when they really mean *What?* So if you ask directions, and the resident misunderstands you, there is a good chance she'll look at you and say, "Please?" Translation: "What did you say?"

Another thing you will only find in this part of the state, as well as the country, is goetta. Usually served for breakfast, this sausage-like dish, with German roots, is fried up crisp and served alongside eggs at many local restaurants. It is a must-eat while you are here.

Following the river south- and westward will lead you to Carrollton and, heading inland, to the rural town of Owenton. Both offer interesting attractions and an array of dining. In nearby Sparta, you'll find the Kentucky Speedway, one of the finest motor speedways in the country. This 1.5-mile oval track hosts NASCAR events throughout the year. Even though the location is out in the country, the track is first-class.

Northern Kentucky really has it all. You will find riverfront communities, historic and vibrant downtowns, scenic farmland, multicultural dining opportunities, and a unique mix of North and South that will make anyone feel right at home, wherever you are from.

MAYSVILLE, OLD WASHINGTON, AND AUGUSTA

Huddled up alongside the Ohio River is the delightful city of Maysville. Although the area is a history lover's dream, there are attractions for all interests, including eclectic shops, phenomenal architecture, and golf and fishing opportunities.

Maysville, originally known as Limestone, was established in 1775 by frontiersman Simon Kenton. The villagers were forced out by some western battles of the American Revolution, but Kenton resettled the area in 1784. Around that same time, Daniel Boone established a trading post and tavern nearby, and the city of Maysville took root.

As a popular river trading stop, the city grew. It became known for local craftsmen who created intricate wrought iron. This ironwork can still be seen in the historic downtown and, more notably, downriver in the French Quarter of New Orleans, Louisiana. The trading of burley tobacco, once a staple to the area, also added to the growth.

Maysville's favorite daughter, Rosemary Clooney, established the Rosemary Clooney Music Festival, which is held each year just outside the historic Russell Theater downtown. The festival brings in big-name entertainers as well as folks from all over who want to enjoy the music under the stars.

This theater was close to Rosie's heart, as it was the location of the 1953 world premiere of her first film, *The Stars Are Singing*. In 2008, Hollywood came to town again as Rosie's nephew, Hollywood heartthrob and native son George Clooney, followed in her footsteps by bringing the premiere of the movie *Leatherheads*, which he starred in and directed, to the theater.

Travel just 4 miles south of Maysville proper and you will find **Old Washington**, where the original fieldstone streets and authentic log cabins make you feel like you have gone back in time. The whole village is on the National Register of Historic Places and features original 18th-century buildings where slaves lived and were sold. Several of the buildings were reputedly stops on the Underground Railroad—probably one of the slaves' final stops before crossing the nearby Ohio River into freedom.

About 20 miles downriver is picture-perfect **Augusta**. With its darling homes, adorable shops, and lovely river walk, you'll not only want to visit but might want to live here. It is so perfect that in 2005, Kentucky's most famous historian, Dr. Thomas Clark, included Augusta in his list of top 11 places to see in the state. It ranks right up there with the Cumberland Gap, Mammoth Cave, and Shaker Village. While it may seem to be some-what off the beaten path, go ahead and take that path so you can breathe the clean air, slow down, and unwind in Augusta.

GUIDANCE Stop for guidance at the **Maysville Welcome Center** (606-564-6986), 115 E. 3rd St., Maysville, next to the Simon Kenton Bridge. They are open weekdays 10–4 and Sat. 10–1. For information about Old Washington, head for the **Old Washington Visitors Center** (606-759-7411; www.oldwashington.com), 2215 Old Main St. Their address is in Maysville, but the center is in the Washington Historic District. Open Mon.–Sat. 10–4:30 and Sun. noon–4; the office is closed Dec.–Mar. The **Augusta Welcome Center** is located inside the red caboose parked on the corner of Main St. and Riverside Dr., Augusta. Open during the summer months only, Thu.–Sun. 11–4, it is stocked with all the informa-tion you'll need for a good, neighborly visit. During the rest of the year, stop by the tourism office in **Augusta City Hall** (606-756-2183; www .augustaky.com), 219 Main St., Augusta. They are open weekdays 8:30–5 and are well stocked with brochures, maps, and advice.

GETTING THERE The nearest airport is about an hour from Augusta: the **Cincinnati/Northern Kentucky International Airport** (859-767-3151; www.cvgairport.com). Car rentals are available at the airport, and you will need a car. Augusta is approximately a one-hour drive. The river cities of Augusta and Maysville are about 22 miles apart. They are con-nected by the direct AA Highway, which is also known as KY 9. They are also linked by the more scenic KY 8, which hugs the river between the two.

GETTING AROUND It is easy to get around the Maysville and Old Washington area by car, with well-marked streets and ample off-street parking available everywhere.

MEDICAL EMERGENCY In the heart of Mason County is **Meadow-view Regional Medical Center** (606-759-5311; www.meadowview regional.com), 989 Medical Park Dr., Maysville.

ALCOHOL Both Mason County, home of Maysville, and Bracken County, home of Augusta, are wet, which means alcohol is available in restaurants and stores throughout the area.

✴ To See

In Maysville (unless otherwise noted)

✎ ♿ **Kentucky Gateway Museum Center** (606-564-5865; www.kygmc .org), 215 Sutton St. Tue.–Fri. 10–5, Sat. 10–4, Sun. 1–4. With three distinct collections housed under one roof, the center has something for everyone. Whether you are interested in genealogy and research, regional history, or a 1/12-scale miniatures collection, you can see it all and take in the pioneer graveyard next door at the same time. The collection of miniatures (calling them dollhouses does not seem to do justice) is amazing. See these teeny-tiny homes, apartments, and shops filled with even teenier and tinier furniture and household items. The whole museum is well done, but the miniatures collection is a must-see. $10 adults, $2 students.

Maysville Floodwall Murals (606-564-9419; www.cityofmaysville.com), 25 E. McDonald Pkwy. Nine murals depict the history of Maysville along the city's floodwall. They illustrate the four centuries of the city and Maysville's connection to the Ohio River.

✎ **Magee's Bakery** (606-759-4882; www.mageesbakeryfarm.com), 8188 Orangeburg Rd. This bakery, a Maysville landmark in business since 1941, is best known for transparent pudding and transparent pie. Also known as poor man's pie in the South, this is a treat you can make—as owners Judy and Ron Dickson explain—with limited ingredients, just eggs, milk, and butter. And if you have some flour, you can make a crust, too. If you are there in the summer months, tour the home (it dates back to 1790) and take a hayride around the working farm. Stay for lunch and you can help make it. Don an apron and hat and make some country ham sandwiches, corn pudding, and scalloped cabbage. A wide variety of from-scratch bakery items is available, too.

National Underground Railroad Museum (606-564-9419; www.cityof maysville.com), 115 E. 3rd St. Call for appointment. This river city played a key component in the operation of the Underground Railroad, as it is located right on the border between slavery and the free state of Ohio. See slavery artifacts, documents, and memorabilia, and learn how abolitionist helped enslaved people reach freedom.

✎ **Hickory Hill Plantation and Nursery** (606-742-2596; www.bramels hickoryhillnursery.com), 6037 Mill Creek Pike, Mays Lick. Tours by appointment only. Tucked away in the Mason County countryside is the authentic 1861 Greek Revival plantation home, which was once a part of

American statesman John Marshall's estate. Tour the family home, carriage and icehouse, and combination dairy-smokehouse. Don't forget to walk through the lovely nursery and grounds.

In Old Washington

Carriage Museum (606-759-7305), Old Main St. Call for hours. This museum portrays the history of transportation prior to the car. Their time frame starts with a basic farmer's wagon and moves forward to an elegant four-seat carriage. They also have interesting exhibits and memorabilia relating to carriage travel.

Harriet Beecher Stowe Slavery to Freedom Museum (606-759-4860), 2124 Old Main St. Call for hours. This early antebellum home once hosted Harriet Beecher Stowe. While visiting in 1833, she witnessed a slave auction. That event touched her so deeply, and made such an impression, that she included a description of it in her 1850s classic *Uncle Tom's Cabin*, a book that details the horrors of slavery. It has been reported that when Mrs. Stowe was introduced to President Abraham Lincoln in 1862, he made the comment, "So you're the little woman who wrote the book that made this great war." Stop by this museum to see where it all happened.

Mefford's Fort (606-759-7411; www.washingtonkentucky.com), Old Main St. Call for hours. Get a real feel for history as you tour this rustic 1787 log cabin. Although no one had heard the term *recycling* then, it was an era when nothing went to waste. Mr. Mefford, with the help of his 13 children, transformed a flatboat into a home. After traveling down the Ohio River from Pittsburgh. they arrived in Washington, disassembled the boat, and used the planks to build their log cabin.

Paxton Inn (606-759-7411; www.washingtonkentucky.com), 2030 Old Main. Call for hours. The circa-1810 inn, a popular early-19th-century hangout for local lawyers and citizens, has a secret stairway between the first and second floors where runaway slaves could be hidden as they traveled along the Underground Railroad.

In Augusta (unless otherwise noted)

Rosemary Clooney House (866-898-8091; rosemaryclooney.org), 106 E. Riverside Dr. Open Tue.–Sat. noon–3. You can't miss this bright yellow riverfront house where Rosemary Clooney lived for more than 20 years. The home, owned by former lieutenant governor Steve Henry and his wife, former Miss America Heather French Henry, is loaded with the largest known private collection of memorabilia from the 1954 holiday movie classic *White Christmas*. There are also exhibits dedicated to

ROSEMARY CLOONEY HOUSE

Augusta's other famous residents George Clooney, Nick Clooney, and Heather French Henry. A $5 donation is requested.

Augusta River Walk (606-756-2183; www.augustaky.com), Riverside Dr. Stroll along the Ohio River and past many of Augusta's historic homes. The river is very calm through this area, so pull up a park bench, rest your legs, and watch the water glide by.

Augusta's Historic Jail (606-756-2183), City Park, W. 2nd St. Open by appointment only. Contact Bracken County Historical Society at 606-735-3337 to make tour arrangements. Built in 1811 and used until the 1960s, this is the oldest jail in Kentucky that still sits on its original foundation. See the first-floor prisoner's quarters and the second-floor living quarters of the jailer.

Lavender Hills of Kentucky (606-735-3355; www.lavenderhillsof kentucky.com), 229 Conrad Ridge Rd., Brooksville. Breathe in the sweet scent as you tour the first commercial lavender farm in Kentucky. Covering 100 acres of farmland, you can see (and smell!) more than 600 lavender plants. They have 15 different varieties in pink, white, yellow, and all shades of purple. Peak bloom time is in mid-June, but the family offers tours and workshops year-round. Call ahead to reserve a tour. There's a nice gift shop on the farm where you can find soaps, sachets, cleaning products, and recipes.

✳ **To Do**

BOATING Augusta Boat Dock and Marina (606-756-2183; www
.augustaky.com), River and E. 2nd Sts., Augusta. If you are boating on
the Ohio, this is a convenient place to stop for gas, snacks, and supplies.
They do not rent boats, but if you bring your own, they have rental slips
available.

GOLF Laurel Oaks Golf Course (606-759-5011), 808 US 62, Maysville.
Visit this 18-hole, par-72 public course with generous fairways and greens.
The course was designed to make the best use of the gently rolling terrain.

Wells Creek Golf Course (606-759-5604), Old Main St., Maysville. You
can enjoy 9 holes on this picture-perfect course located at the
Maysville–Mason County Recreation Park.

RACING Earlywine Racing Inc. (606-883-3098; www.earlywineracing
.com), 4248 Walton Pike, Maysville. Here at the nation's largest permanent indoor motocross racing facility, visitors can race ATVs, dirt bikes,
and remote-control trucks. Check the website for schedules.

Big Rock Off Road Park (606-759-9106; www.bigrockoffroadpark.com),
8157 Stonelick Rd., Maysville. This 2,000-acre ATV and dirt bike park is
slightly off the beaten path, but for fans it is worth the drive. Ride through
miles of wooded trails, some tough, some not so tough—it's up to you.
They also have paintball and laser tag, or try out their new zipline course.
Campsites available, too.

WALKING TOURS Downtown Maysville Walking Tour (606-564-
9419; www.cityofmaysville.com), 216 Bridge St., Maysville. Tour the historic downtown area on this 1½-hour excursion in which you will explore
the floodwall murals, St. Patrick's Church, Russell Theater, Mason County
Courthouse, First Presbyterian Church, Museum Center, and Pioneer
Graveyard. Call the visitors center to reserve your spot.

Old Washington Walking Tour (606-564-9419; www.washington
kentucky.com), 2215 Old Main St. in Old Washington. Tours originate
from the visitors center. The village was established in 1786 and is home
to several authentic log cabins as well as early-1800s buildings. This is a
real gem for history enthusiasts; there aren't many places left where you
can take in so many genuinely historic structures on one tour.

Augusta Walking Tour (www.augustaky.com/tourism/tours). Go online
(most of Augusta is WiFi, you know) and print out a walking tour
brochure to get started. This is the perfect way to see all that Augusta has
to offer. The tour map has some interesting facts about the historic homes,
some dating back as far as 1790. The tour also points out examples of

Colonial, Italianate, and Victorian architecture that are prevalent through-out the town.

WINERY Baker Bird Winery (859-620-4965), 4465 Augusta/Chatham Rd. (also called KY 19), Augusta. Sat.–Sun. 1–5. Visit this historic farm to tour the vineyards and taste the excellent vino. Their signature varieties include Ruby Hawk Rose, Chardonelle, and a sparkling wine served in the southern way, over ice.

✳ Lodging

✍ ♿ **French Quarter Inn** (606-564-8000; www.frenchquarterinn .com), 25 E. McDonald Pkwy., Maysville. Get a taste of New Orleans along with Kentucky hospitality at this 63-room inn. Guests compare it to a large B&B due to the warm, homey feel. The New Orleans–inspired decor features lots of wrought iron, verdigris accents, molding, and even a bronze statue right in the middle of the lobby fountain. Ask for a room overlooking the river for an unforgettable view. $

♿ **The Parkview Country Inn** (606-756-2603; www.parkview countryinn.com), 103 W. 2nd St., Augusta. This inn features several cozy guest rooms, outfitted with a mix of antiques and modern-day amenities. Built in the early 1800s, the home is on the National Historic Register. Stay in the original historic inn with several room options, or the rustic log cabin, or the darling one bedroom cottage adjacent to the inn. Enjoy your home-cooked country breakfast in the on-site Parkview Country Inn Restaurant. $

White Rose Bed and Breakfast (606-756-2787), 210 Riverside Dr., Augusta. Lie in bed and watch the beautiful Ohio River roll by in this historic home that dates back to the early 1800s. Three rooms are available; two have antique double beds and one has a queen. And just like you were staying at Grandma's, there is a shared bath down the hall. Owners Mr. and Mrs. Kelsch serve a hearty eggs and ham breakfast each morning, and do all they can to welcome you to their lovely home. $

Asbury Meadow B&B (606-756-2100; www.asburymeadow.com), 3737 Asbury Rd., Augusta. This stately antebellum home features southern details like majestic columns and a widow's walk. Inside you'll find two guest rooms, one with a Murphy bed that tucks up into the wall. Out in the backyard, you can stay in the cottage, which was formerly the slave quarters of the plantation. The cottage has come a long way since those early days: It now boasts a Victorian soaking tub, a wood ceiling, and a kitchenette. $

✳ Where to Eat

DINING OUT ♿ 🍸 **Caproni's** (606-564-4321), 320 Rosemary

Clooney St., Maysville. Open Mon.–Thu. 11–9, Fri. 11–10, Sat. 3–10, Sunday 11–3. Enjoy an upscale but casual Italian meal with a glorious view of the Ohio River. Meals are complemented with homemade garlic bread and pies, cakes, and cheesecakes. The signature dish is Chicken Caproni made with linguine, but American fare like steaks, chops, and seafood is also on the menu. $$–$$$

Y **Chandler's On Market** (606-564-6385), 212 Market St., Maysville. Open Tue.–Sat. for lunch and dinner. Tucked into the historic district of downtown Maysville is a local favorite. This sit-down, upscale restaurant is known for their tomato soup, as well as their steaks and chops. Owner Chan Warner has filled his restaurant with antiques and an inviting warm decor so that everyone feels welcome. $$

Y **Chandlers at the Beehive** (606-756-3003), 101 W Riverside Dr., Augusta. Open Fri.–Sun. for lunch and dinner. The Beehive Tavern was a staple along the riverbank in Augusta for 25 years. Locals, as well as patrons who traveled far and wide to eat there, mourned the loss when it closed in 2011. But in 2012 the owners of Chandler's in Maysville reopened the cozy old eatery, much to the delight of Beehive regulars. The menu is upscale, but the ambience is relaxed; you'll feel like you're eating at a neighbor's house. When the weather is nice, sit out-

side and enjoy the dreamy view of the Ohio River. $$

EATING OUT & **Parkview Country Inn Restaurant** (606-756-2667; www.parkviewcountry inn.com), 103 W. 2nd St., Augusta. Open daily for lunch and dinner. Enjoy the comfortable surroundings of this inn, built in the early 1800s, while dining on a big country meal. They have a popular buffet available at every meal, so you can get your fill of tasty fried chicken, smoked country ham, and maybe even some spiced catfish. Don't forget to order some potato soup; that seems to be everyone's favorite. $–$$

The Augusta General Store (606-756-2525), 109 Main St., Augusta. Open daily 6–9. This is a countrified version of those chain restaurants you see just off the interstate with rocking chairs on their porch. It looks like an old-fashioned general store, complete with gift shop in the front and good eats in the back. The menu features hearty breakfasts, juicy burgers, and toasted sub sandwiches. Save room for dessert; the assorted homemade pies, cobblers, and cookies are the best. $

Bravo Café (606-756-2727), 121 Main St., Augusta. Before learning all about the wonderful fresh selections you can get at Bravo, check your calendar and make sure it is not winter. You see, Bravo closes for winter, so if you are not sure if it is winter, give them a call to see if they have opened their doors for the season. If they have, you are in luck because you are going to find some of the most delicious tomato basil soup to team up with scrumptious salads and sandwiches. And you are going to need to save some room for their southern bread pudding with caramel raisin sauce, that is for sure. Just make sure it's not winter. $

Carota's Pizza (606-756-2343), 115 Main St., Augusta. Open daily for lunch and dinner. This is *the* place to get pizza in Augusta, and luckily the Carota family has been making fantastic pizza for generations now. They have salads and hoagies, too, but the pizza will make you ask for more. $–$$

Delites (606-564-7047), 222 Market St., Maysville. Open Mon.– Sat. 8–5. Nothing fancy, mind you, just the best burgers in Maysville. Run by John and Erato Kambelos, a darling couple who make everyone feel welcome. The menu features mostly classic diner food, but it is sprinkled with options like gyros from the Kambeloses' home country of Greece. Cash only. $

Margie's Southern Café (606-563-9424), 130 Market St., Maysville. Open Mon.–Thu. 5 AM–9 PM, Fri. and Sat. 5 AM–2 AM. Margie's is where you'll find a home-cooked meal just like Mom used to make. Owner Margie Zimmer, who is originally from New Orleans, adds a hint of Cajun spice to some of her hometown favorites. Enjoy the photos of both celebrities and ordinary folks that line the walls.

This Maysville staple has been around for more than a decade. $

SNACKS Hutchison's Grocery (606-564-3797), 1201 E. 2nd St., Maysville. Open weekdays 9–5, Sat. 9–4. A visit to Maysville isn't complete until you stop at this little grocery that has been in business for more than 150 years. Yes, Micajah Hutchison hung out his shingle in 1850, and they've been going strong ever since. Not much to look at on the outside, or the inside for that matter, but go in and try one of their legendary Kentucky ham sandwiches and maybe an order of onion rings. They have a full menu of burgers, sandwiches, and even pork tenderloin, but you'll have to order it to go, as they don't have any tables. Still worth a stop. $

✱ Entertainment

The Maysville Players (606-564-3666; www.maysvilleplayers.com), at the Washington Opera House, 116 W. 2nd St., Maysville. The oldest theater group in Kentucky, the Maysville Players present such Broadway classics as *Once Upon a Mattress*, *Our Town*, and *Nunsense*. Check the website for this year's shows.

✱ Selective Shopping

In Maysville
Steve White Art Gallery (606-564-4887; www.stevewhitefineart .com), 225 Market St., features the watercolor and oil paintings of world-renowned artist Steve

White. An award-winning landscape and portrait painter, Steve had one of his paintings featured as the cover for Rosemary Clooney's CD *Still on the Road*.

The EAT (Exquisite Art Treasures) Gallery (606-564-5578; www.eatgallery.com), 46 W. 2nd St. Specializing in art created from nature, this gallery has an amazing collection of amethysts, geodes, crystals, and wood carvings. The selection is remarkable.

Tierney's Antiques (606-564-4104), 51 W. 2nd St. Stop by and visit with Jim and Martha Tierney in their shop that specializes in Depression glass and traditional and primitive furniture. It's housed in a building that dates back to the early 1800s and still has the original tin ceiling. Open Mon.–Sat. but they close for lunch noon–1, so plan accordingly.

In Old Washington
Keepsake Treasures (606-759-0505), 2116 Old Main St. Find the perfect antique, collectible, or gift at this little shop in a historic 1900s home.

Phyllis' Antique Lamp Shop (606-759-7423; phyllisantiques .com), 2112 Old Main St. In business 40 years, these people know lamps. Specializing in antique lighting and restoration, Phyllis' is the place to go for lamp parts, specialty shades, and antique lusters. They also stock dollhouse supplies, Blue Bird china, and collectibles. Call ahead for hours.

The Strawberry Patch Country Store (606-759-7001), 2109 Old Main St. Wander through this old country store and find antiques, teddy bears, wreaths, and collectibles.

The Irongate (606-759-7074), 2103 Old Main St. Pottery lovers will be thrilled to find such a nice selection of Bybee and Hadley Pottery under one roof. They have rare books, silver, and collectibles, too.

In Augusta
Nina's (606-756-3715), 208 Main St. Call for hours. Nina's cute little shop downtown is loaded with antiques and both music and movie memorabilia.

Barbara's Art Studio and Gallery (606-756-2787), 210 Riverside Dr. Features the working studio and gallery of artist Barbara Kelsch in historic early-1800s digs. The gallery, located in the family home of Kelsch's husband, is situated on the banks of the Ohio. Sumptuous landscapes, dynamic abstracts, and richly detailed portraits are some of the subjects of her works in oils, watercolors, charcoals, and pastels.

Small Town Gift Shop (606-756-2200), 321 W. Riverside Dr. This appropriately named shop is a perfect addition to Main Street. It is the kind of place where locals pop by regularly to see what's new. They feature crafty items like comforters, throw pillows, china, homemade toys, and floral arrangements, but the merchandise changes frequently so you never know what you'll find. Everything in this darling shop was created in or near Augusta, so it is all homegrown.

✳ Special Events

In Maysville
June: ♿ **Maysville Uncorked**. This is a *really* festive festival featuring Kentucky wine. The event includes wine tastings, music, art, and locally made products for sale.

September: ♿ **Rosemary Clooney Music Festival**. Maysville's premier annual event is held at the Russell Theater where Rosie spent her childhood looking up at the big screen and later returned to for the premiere of her first major movie, *The Stars Are Singing*. Guests are treated to a night of music including Grammy Award–winning performers. Past years have featured Linda Ronstadt, Michael Feinstein, and Smokey Robinson.

In Old Washington
April: �... ♿ **Chocolate Festival**. Chocolatiers from all over the region gather to offer all things chocolate, including fudge, ice cream, funnel cakes, and even

♪ ♿ **Blue Licks State Resort Park** (859-289-5507, 800-443-7008; parks.ky .gov), US 68, Mount Olivet. Kentucky history, which is inundated with Civil War references, sites, and memorials, actually has one state park dedicated to preserving the memory of the Revolutionary War: Blue Licks State Resort Park, found 25 miles south of Maysville. On the site of the Battle of Blue Licks—sometimes referred to as the Last Battle of the American Revolution—stands a memorial to all who perished in a terrible battle among American Indians, Kentucky settlers, and the British that took place on August 19, 1782. The park features a museum full of Indian artifacts, dinosaur bones, and exhibits that depict the history of the Blue Licks area. Several short historic walking trails offer sights of buffalo paths as well as the location of Daniel Boone's capture by Shawnee Indians. **The Lodge**, which sits right on the Licking River, has 32 hotel rooms, two modern executive cottages, which have two bedrooms, and 51 campsites with utility hookups. For fine dining at the resort, **Hidden Waters Restaurant** is open seven days a week for breakfast 7–10, lunch 11:30–2, and dinner 5–9. While the spot is known for Kentucky country ham dinners and fried catfish, all menu items feature locally grown products whenever possible. $–$$

chocolate-covered cream candy and bourbon balls. Chocoholics get to enjoy live entertainment, games, and rides while they nosh.

September: ❀ ⌕ ♿ **Simon Kenton Festival**. See historical reenactments and demonstrations of frontier life. It is also a family reunion of sorts for the descendants of the famous frontiersman who fought off Indians, once saved Daniel Boone's life, and helped found the cities of Washington and Maysville.

December: ❀ ⌕ ♿ **Frontier Christmas in Old Washington**. The historic log cabins of Old Washington are decked out in fresh greenery, nuts, and fruits as the village celebrates the holidays. This festival has been an annual event for more than 40 years. It's a wonderful tradition.

In Augusta
June: ❀ ⌕ ♿ **Art in the Garden**. Spend an enjoyable day browsing the work of local and regional artists while you stroll along picturesque Riverside Drive. More than 3,000 people attend this juried art show each year

July: ❀ ⌕ ♿ **The Augusta Riverfest Regatta**. A true celebration of the river, Augusta welcomes stern-wheelers, paddle-wheelers, and all types of boats to the riverfront. Not just about boats, the festival offers juried arts and crafts, live entertainment, a beauty pageant, a 5K run, and kids' games.

❀ ⌕ ♿ **The Germantown Fair**. This regional fair, held at the Germantown Fairgrounds, Hwy. 10 in Maysville, includes Mason, Bracken, Robertson, Pendleton, Harrison, Nicholas, Fleming, and Lewis Counties and is the longest-running fair in the state. They have all the typical events of a county fair, like livestock competitions, food contests, beauty pageants, and horse shows.

September: ❀ ⌕ ♿ **Heritage Days**. This annual Labor Day weekend festival is held downtown on West 2nd and Parkview. Enjoy live music, a huge flea market, festival food, crafters, and a car show.

December: ❀ ⌕ ♿ **Rivertown White Christmas**. Come see all the shops of Augusta dressed up for Christmas. The event is usually held the first weekend in December; shops feature extended hours and holiday sales. Stick around for the lighting of the Augusta Christmas tree.

COVINGTON, NEWPORT, AND SURROUNDING SUBURBS

The Northern Kentucky region that encompasses Covington, Newport, and surrounding suburbs is a unique part of the state. Due to its close proximity to Cincinnati, Ohio, it is mainly an area made up of urban and suburban neighborhoods, but visitors are minutes away from rural Kentucky, just on the fringes of town.

It is in **Covington** and **Newport** where you will find the historical remnants of the German and Italian immigrants who flooded to the area during the early 1900s. These markings are evident in neighborhoods with names like Mutter Gottes in Covington and Spaghetti Nob in South Newport. You will find evidence in the architecture and churches in these communities as well. Traipse through a few old cemeteries; the family names will clearly show which motherland these residents hailed from.

The two cities border the Ohio River on the north and then are divided by the Licking River, which breaks off from the Ohio River and delves another 330 miles south through Kentucky. Covington, which is Kentucky's fifth largest city, sits on the western corner of the Licking. On the eastern shore of the Licking is Newport. Both Covington and Newport have attractions on their own, but together with the nearby cities such as Bellevue, Fort Mitchell, Highland Heights, Crestview Hills, and Florence they make up the regional area known as Northern Kentucky.

The city of Newport, which was once known as Sin City due to the number of seedy businesses with ties to gambling, prostitution, and organized crime, has seen an about-face in the last 30 years. Today it is home to a growing downtown, Newport on the Levee, an all-ages entertainment complex, and the state's multimillion-dollar aquarium.

Over in Covington, the Main Strasse Village is an area comprising restaurants, bars, and shops, most with a German flavor. This little neighborhood is located near the Goose Girl Fountain and Carroll Bell Chimes, two landmarks reminiscent of the Old Country.

As you head out of the urban core, you'll enter newer suburban communities where you can find excellent shopping and dining opportunities. Although there are plenty of the big-box chains and mall stores you'll find anywhere, don't miss the opportunity to explore the mom-and-pop places that give Northern Kentucky a personality you won't find anywhere else in the state.

GUIDANCE Northern Kentucky Convention and Visitors Bureau (800-STAY-NKY; www.staynky.com), 50 E. River Center Blvd., Suite 200, Covington. Open weekdays 9–5. They have racks of brochures and maps for attractions in Northern Kentucky and beyond.

GETTING THERE The area is served by the **Cincinnati/Northern Kentucky International Airport** (859-767-3151; www.cvgairport.com). Car rentals are available at the airport. Yes, the Cincinnati, Ohio, airport is in the Bluegrass State and is credited for the phenomenal growth and prosperity in the area. If you are on a plane landing at this airport, watch the faces of your fellow travelers as the flight attendant announces "Welcome to Kentucky." These travelers, who thought they were on their way to Ohio and have no idea about geography, get a panicked look as they momentarily think they are on the wrong plane.

For bus and rail service, the nearest stations are across the river in Cincinnati. **Greyhound Bus** (513-352-6012; www.greyhound.com) is located at 1005 Gilbert Ave., Cincinnati. The **Amtrak** station (800-872-7245; www.amtrak.com) is located at 1301 Western Ave., in Union Terminal, Cincinnati.

GETTING AROUND Transit Authority of Northern Kentucky (859-331-TANK; www.tankbus.org). With 27 routes through Boone, Kenton, and Campbell Counties, TANK buses operate 365 days a year. **Southbank Shuttle** (859-578-6943; www.tankbus.org). Watch for these well-marked buses and trams, which follow a loop encompassing the attractions and entertainment districts of Newport, Covington, and downtown Cincinnati. The shuttles appear about every 10 minutes and cost a small fee. Check the website for exact route information.

MEDICAL EMERGENCY Northern Kentucky is served by the highly respected **St. Elizabeth Medical Center** (859-301-2000; www.stelizabeth .com). With five locations—Covington, Edgewood, Fort Thomas, Florence, and Grant County—fine medical help is always nearby.

ALCOHOL The three main counties of Northern Kentucky—Boone, Kenton, and Campbell—are all wet, which means alcohol is available at restaurants, bars, and liquor stores.

✳ To See

✐ � **Newport Aquarium** (859-261-5888, 800-406-3474; www.newport aquarium.com), 1 Aquarium Way, Newport. Open 365 days per year. Located at Newport on the Levee, this aquarium features 200 feet of seamless acrylic tunnels where you can walk under and through the massive tanks holding killer sharks, fish, stingrays, and sea turtles. Get up close and personal with American alligators, playful penguins, a relaxing jellyfish exhibit, and thousands of other varieties of sea creatures from around the world. $19 adults, $12 ages 2–12; under 2 free.

✤ **St. Mary's Cathedral Basilica of the Assumption** (859-431-2060; www.covcathedral.com), 1140 Madison Ave., Covington. Open daily 10–4. After 21 years of construction, this immense Roman Catholic cathedral was completed in 1915. Recognized as a French-Gothic replica of Notre Dame in Paris, France, it is home to the world's largest church stained-glass window as well as 26 gargoyles that were hand carved in Italy. Fascinating arched ceilings and fluted columns are architectural marvels

FLORENCE Y'ALL

As people travel to and through Northern Kentucky along Interstate I-75 for the first time, those approaching Florence can't help but notice one of the country's most famous water towers. The red-and-white-striped tower is hard to miss anyway, but the southern greeting atop it, FLORENCE Y'ALL, usually brings a smile to their faces. People tend to wonder if it is simply signage for the nearby Florence Mall, or if everyone speaks with the stereotypical twang that Kentuckians are known for. Well, it seems neither is the real story.

The tale goes that back in the 1970s, two years prior to the opening of the mall, the developers made a deal with the city of Florence: They donated enough land for the city to build a much-needed water tower adjacent to the mall property. The deal included the stipulation that the name FLORENCE MALL would be painted prominently on top, so everyone on I-71/75 would see it. C. M. "Hop" Ewing, who was mayor at the time, was notified shortly after the completion of the paint job that it was illegal to advertise for a business not yet in existence. So a quick fix was needed. Ewing—who passed away in 2006—has been quoted as saying that the city was short on funds but he was tall on imagination. So he came up with the plan of simply changing the M in MALL into a Y with an apostrophe—and so FLORENCE Y'ALL was born. When the mall finally did open, the by-then-beloved greeting was left in place.

FLORENCE Y'ALL

Deborah Kohl Kremer

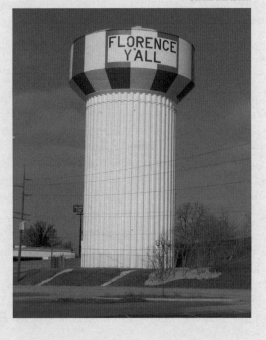

protecting more than 80 stained-glass windows, murals by famed Covington artist Frank Duveneck, sculptures by Clement J. Barnhorn, and a massive Aultz-Kersting pipe organ. Self-guided tours are free; call for an appointment for a docent-guided tour.

🦐 ✍ ♿ **World Peace Bell** (859-581-2971; www.verdin.com), 4th and York Sts., Newport. The world's largest free-swinging bell rings every day at noon. The 66,000-pound bell was built in France and brought to Newport to celebrate the new millennium. It is huge; you can't miss it.

♿ **James A. Ramage Civil War Museum** (859-344-1145; www.fortwright .com), 1402 Highland Ave., Fort Wright. Open Fri. and Sat. 10–5, Sun. noon–5. This museum, which is housed in a former residence, has interesting artifacts and memorabilia from the Civil War. It sits high atop a hill in Northern Kentucky, which was known as Battery Hooper during the Civil War. The location was a pristine spot for the Union army to be on the lookout for any Confederates who were planning to attack Northern Kentucky and Cincinnati.

✍ ♿ **Creation Museum** (859-727-2222, 800-778-3390; www.creation museum.org), 2800 Bullittsburg Church Rd., Petersburg. Mon.–Thu. 10–6, Fri. 10–9, Sat. 9–6, Sun. noon–6. This 70,000-square-foot museum

WORLD PEACE BELL

Nick Kremer

brings the pages of the Bible to life. It was designed by a former Universal Studios exhibit director, and visitors experience animatronics, murals, and computer-generated special effects that explain the origins of the universe according to the Book of Genesis. They have a lush garden area, restaurant, and gift shop, too. $22 adults (ages 13–59), $17 seniors (over 60), $12 ages 5–12; 4 and under free.

✆ **Vent Haven Museum** (859-341-0461; www.venthaven.com), 33 W. Maple, Fort Mitchell. Open May–Sept. Tours by appointment only. As the world's only museum dedicated to the art of ventriloquism, this is the one place to see more than 700 ventriloquial figures and memorabilia under one roof. The collection is amazing to see, but do not call them dummies, or you might look like one. Admission $5.

♣ ✆ ⟁ **Covington Floodwall Murals** (859-655-4159). Along the river, at the foot of Madison Ave., Covington. Learn about Northern Kentucky history by viewing the 40-by-25-foot murals painted on the concrete floodwall in Covington. Each depicts a different historical event from the area. These hand-painted murals, the work of nationally renowned artist Robert Dafford, cover 700 feet of floodwall. Individually they are gems, and as a group they're stunning. Viewers feel like they are observing snippets of history as they gaze at John Roebling, builder of the Roebling Suspension Bridge, conferring with Amos Shinkle, Covington banker, about construc-

COVINGTON FLOODWALL MURALS

Deborah Kohl Kremer

Nick Kremer

MONTE CASINO CHAPEL

tion plans. Another mural invites us to watch as escaped slave Margaret Garner struggles to cross the frozen Ohio River with her children. Take time to view all 18 panels, each one a chapter in Northern Kentucky's past.

🐾 🐾 ♿ **Carroll Chimes Bell Tower** (859-655-4159), W. 6th St. at Philadelphia St. in Covington. This 100-foot bell tower, a replica of an authentic German glockenspiel, contains a 43-bell carillon that chimes on the quarter hour. At the top of each hour, watch as automated puppetlike figures carry out a performance of the Pied Piper of Hamelin, a German folktale.

🐾 **Monte Casino Chapel** (859-341-5800), 333 Thomas More Pkwy., Crestview Hills. This tiny fieldstone chapel is just 6 by 9 feet. It was built by Benedictine monks in 1878 on the grounds of a nearby monastery. The monks left town and the property was sold, but the owner donated the tiny chapel to Thomas More College. In 1965, locals spearheaded a campaign to restore and move the wee chapel 6 miles to the campus. In 1922, Ripley's Believe It or Not named it the "Smallest Church in the World." You can't go inside, but you can look in the windows and admire it from the surrounding patio. Free.

Fort Thomas Military and Community Museum (859-815-8481), 940 Cochran Ave., Fort Thomas. Open Wed.–Sun. noon–4. Call ahead to double-check the hours. The tiny community of Fort Thomas sits high

✒ ♿ **Behringer-Crawford Museum** (859-491-4003; www.bcmuseum.org), 1600 Montague Rd., Covington. Open Tue.–Fri. 10–5, Sat.–Sun. 1–5. $7 adults, $6 seniors, $4 ages 3–18.

The Behringer-Crawford Museum, once known as an oddities museum, tells the story of Northern Kentucky history. The museum, which is located in Covington's picturesque Devou Park, uses the theme "History in Motion: Rivers, Roads, Rails and Runways." It is dedicated to relating the tales of Northern Kentucky's settlement and development through the unique lens of transportation. Not the modes of transportation, per se, but instead how these modes played a part making Northern Kentucky what it is today.

What would Northern Kentucky be without the mighty Ohio River? In the Rivers section, guests are treated to a re-creation of the famous Roebling Suspension Bridge that has spanned the river between Covington and Cincinnati since 1866, as well as a huge interactive packet boat. As immigrants from Germany, Ireland, and Italy disembarked in Cincinnati, some crossed the river into Northern Kentucky and found it to be just like home. They sent word back to the Old Country, and future immigrants made Covington and Newport, Kentucky, their destination.

In a tribute to roads, the museum invites guests to sit in a 1959 Buick Electra that has been reformatted to simulate a trip to the drive-in movies. A doctored rendition of a '50s-era movie, *Radar Men from the Moon*, is playing on the big screen. Visitors can choose to watch a video, *Today's America*, which is narrated by Northern Kentucky's own Nick Clooney.

The growth of Northern Kentucky would never be complete if the Greater Cincinnati/Northern Kentucky International Airport was not included. In the Runways section, guests can learn more about the humble beginnings of an airstrip in

DRIVE-IN MOVIE AT THE BEHRINGER-CRAWFORD MUSEUM

Deborah Kohl Kremer

Deborah Kohl Kremer

ROEBLING SUSPENSION BRIDGE

Boone County that eventually became a world-class airport. One of the gems on display is the actual telegraph sent from Senator Alben Barkley to the city of Covington alerting them that funding for the airport had been approved.

Train tracks and streetcar lines play the starring role in the Rails section of the museum. The Greenline streetcar system is credited with populating the suburbs. The centerpiece is an actual street car, The Kentucky, sitting on actual tracks, right as you enter the museum. In keeping with the rail theme, a beautiful train display, complete with scale-sized local landmarks, allows visitors to go under the tracks and come up in the middle of the exhibit for a 360-degree view. There are also several toy train sets, perfect for little hands, available for play.

"We made this as interactive as possible," said Laurie Risch, executive director. "Small kids will enjoy all the hands-on features, and adults can take in all the historical memorabilia on the walls."

So the Behringer-Crawford has grown up as a museum, but even grown-ups need to have some fun. The famous oddities, the beloved two-headed calf, the big hairball, and the shrunken head, are still there. "Those are our beginnings," said Risch. "We will always have a place for them, too."

atop a hill in Campbell County. In the late 1800s it was chosen as the replacement site for the flood-prone Newport Barracks, a military post on the banks of the Ohio River. A military installation was built, complete with a stone water tower that is still there today. The U.S. Army used the area as a training ground, beginning with the Spanish-American War and continuing right through World War II. Today the area of the fort is a city park, and a darling historic home on the grounds serves as a museum for all this military memorabilia. Another part of the museum captures memories of the community with a large area dedicated to the Beverly Hills Supper Club, a premier entertainment complex that drew Hollywood stars to Northern Kentucky from the 1950s until the late 1970s. A tragic fire in 1977 ended this glamorous destination and took the lives of more than 160 people. The museum features articles from the nightclub's heyday, as well as items salvaged from that fateful night. Small fee.

✳ To Do

BOATING BB Riverboats (859-261-8500, 800-261-8586; www.bbriver boats.com), 1 Riverboat Way, Newport. The area's oldest and largest riverboat company. Cruise the Ohio River on an authentic paddle-wheeler and enjoy a delicious meal while enjoying your excursion. Various dinner and themed cruises are available year-round, but the schedule is cut back a bit Nov.–Apr.

Thaxton's Canoe Rental (859-472-2000; gopaddling.com), 33 Hornbeek Rd., Butler. Open Wed.–Mon. Located about 30 minutes south of Newport, Thaxton's offers kayaking and canoeing on the beautiful Licking River. Bring your own or rent one of theirs. Guided trips available, too.

GOLF Devou Park Golf Course (859-431-8030; www.golffusion.com /devoupark), 1344 Audubon Rd., Covington. This 18-hole public course is open year-round, with postcard-style hilltop views high above Covington and Cincinnati.

Twin Oaks Golf & Plantation Club (859-581-2410; www.golfattwin oaks.com), 450 E. 43rd St., Covington. Built in 1927, this is a serene public course with massive mature trees right along the Licking River. They have a full-service pro shop and a somewhat upscale bar and grill.

World of Sports (859-371-8255), 7400 Woodspoint Dr., Florence. Open weekdays 8–11 and weekends 7–11. They have an 18-hole, par-72 golf course. Easy to find, right off I-75, in the middle of a shopping mecca, it's the place to go if you want to get in a quick game. This course is right on the flight path of the nearby Greater Cincinnati International Airport, so you might feel like you have to duck your head as the overseas flights come in for a landing. They also have a lighted and covered driving range, a full-service pro shop, and a fun miniature golf course that is lighted so you can play at night.

The Golf Courses of Kenton County (331-371-3200; www.kenton county.org), 3908 Richardson Rd., Independence. With three courses at one location, golfers have a chance to try out all 54 holes. The rolling hills and tree-lined fairways offer challenges for all levels of golfers.

Meadowood Golf Club (859-586-0422), 1911 Golf Club Dr., Burlington. This 9-hole, par-35 public course is fairly flat and easy to walk. Although most holes are par 3, locals claim several of them are fairly difficult.

HORSE RACING Turfway Park Race Course (859-371-0200, 800-733-0200; www.turfway.com), 7500 Turfway Rd., Florence. Home to the Derby prep race known as the Lanes End Stakes in spring and, in fall, the Breeder's Cup prep race called the Kentucky Cup. Turfway Park is a well-respected track in the thoroughbred world. Catch a live race or bet on a race at a faraway track through the beauty of simulcasting. Turfway hosts three live meets per year, the Fall Meet, the Holiday Meet, and the Winter/Spring Meet. Lucky for you, the entire grandstand is indoors, so you can enjoy racing year-round. When the weather is nice, go outside and stand right at the track's edge where you can feel the wind as the horses charge past. Call for exact dates and times. The track is dark on Monday and Tuesday, which is horse-talk for "not open." Free admission and free parking year-round, except on the days of the big prep races mentioned above.

MINOR-LEAGUE BASEBALL Florence Freedom (859-594-4487; www.florencefreedom.com), 7950 Freedom Way, Florence. Good old-fashioned baseball games, without the major-league salaries or ticket prices. The Freedom plays in the independent Frontier League and is not affiliated with the pros. They usually play about 50 home games each summer, packing each one with exciting baseball mixed with silly promotions, giveaways, and contests.

RACEWAY Florence Speedway (859-485-7591; www.florencespeedway .com), 12234 US 42, Walton. Built in the 1950s, this 0.5-mile high-banked clay oval is one of the premiere Dirt Late Model tracks in Kentucky. Open on Saturdays Mar.–Oct., this track is the place to go for a regular racing program of Late Models, Modifieds, Super Dirt Stocks, and Pure Stocks.

TOUR ✒ Ride the Ducks (859-815-1439; newportducks.com), 1 Aquarium Way, Newport. Open 9–9 daily during summer. See the area aboard a reproduction World War II–era amphibious motor vehicle. Operating on land and sea, or in this case river, the vehicle is part bus, part boat. Tours last about an hour, taking in all the hot spots on both sides of the river. Then, just in case they missed anything, the vehicle drives right into the river for a floating tour of the skylines. The tour guides are funny, and everyone on board gets a Wacky Quacker, a sort of kazoo shaped like a duck's bill. Passengers can make lots of quacking noises and grab the attention of passersby, as if cruising the streets in a giant boat weren't enough. Visit the website for prices and tours.

WALKS Riverside Drive–Licking River Historic Area & Riverwalk Statue Tour (859-655-4159), Riverside Dr., Covington. Located at the confluence of the Ohio and Licking Rivers, Riverside Drive is home to Civil War–era homes, carriage houses, and serene gardens. Take a self-guided tour and admire the J. A. Roebling Bridge, a true Covington landmark, and visit with the seven lifelike bronze statues of prominent Northern Kentucky historical figures: Simon Kenton, Mary B. Greene, James Bradley, Chief Little Turtle, John Roebling, John James Audubon, and Daniel Carter Beard.

✳ Green Space

PARKS Devou Park (859-292-2151), Western Ave., Covington. The grande dame of Covington parks, this 550-acre recreation area was a gift to the city from the Devou family in 1910. Full of rolling hills, wooded trails, and scenic vistas, it is perfect for year-round fun. It features an 18-hole golf course, playgrounds, a fishing lake, walking, hiking, and biking trails, and a breathtaking overlook of the Covington, Newport, and Cincinnati riverfronts. A historic amphitheater is home to the summer series of the Northern Kentucky Symphony Orchestra and other outdoor productions. It is also home to the Behringer-Crawford Museum, where you can learn millions of years' worth of information about the history of Northern Kentucky.

🎣 ✍ ♿ **Big Bone Lick State Park** (859-384-3522; www.parks.ky.gov), 3380 Beaver Rd., Union. About 15,000 years ago, this area was populated by mammoths, mastodons, ground sloths, and bison that were attracted by the warm salt springs. They lived and died here, making the grounds a smorgasbord of paleontology fossils. The 546-acre park includes a museum that exhibits some of these fossils as well as a life-sized diorama that shows how some of the animals died while in the marsh bog. There are also walking and hiking trails, playgrounds, bass and bluegill fishing, and a herd of live bison.

Split Rock Conservation Park (859-689-9999; www.splitrockpark.org), 4503 Belleview Rd., Petersburg. This outdoor education facility offers programs on ecology, archaeology, geology, and the history of the local area. Named for the glacial formations created on the site during the ice

Nick Kremer

BIG BONE LICK STATE PARK

ages thousands of years ago, Split Rock Park is an educational experience for both young and old. Call or check the website for tours and events.

✳ Lodging

BED & BREAKFASTS

🖋 **Christopher's B&B** (859-491-9354, 888-585-7085), 604 Poplar St., Bellevue. Named for the patron saint of travel. You'll love spending the night in this former church built in 1891. Once the home of the Bellevue Christian Church, the building still looks pretty much the same on the outside, but the 8,100-square-foot building is missing a steeple that came down back in the '70s. The two guest rooms and one suite are designed with comfort and privacy in mind. Guests have a private entrance, as well as spacious rooms with Jacuzzi tubs. All rooms are decorated around the breathtaking stained-glass windows. The Governor's Suite features a huge stained-glass window situated right above the two-person Jacuzzi tub, and his-and-her half-baths. Innkeeper Brenda Guidugli tells her guests the B&B is like heaven on earth. $$–$$$

🖋 🐾 **First Farm Inn** (859-586-0199; www.firstfarminn.com), 2510 Stevens Rd., Idlewild. Get away from it all without going very far. This 1870s farmhouse is surrounded by 200-year-old trees and 21 acres of farmland, but really only about 20 minutes from Florence or Cincinnati. Owner Jen Warner invites her guests to go horseback riding, soak in an outdoor hot tub, or simply sit on the porch swing and breathe in the clean air. If you are traveling with your horse, they have overnight stalls available. $$

Gateway House Bed and Breakfast (859-581-6447; www .gatewaybb.com), 326 E. 6th St., Newport. This Italianate town house, which dates back to 1878, is located right in the heart of Newport's East Row Historic District. It has been restored to its original grandeur with intricate woodwork and plaster moldings, but modern-day conveniences like private baths have been added. Innkeepers Ken and Sandy Clift have filled it with Victorian-era antiques, musical instruments, and artwork. The home has three guest rooms, all with queen-sized bed, private bath, and a fireplace. $

Willis Graves Bed and Breakfast (859-689-5096; www.burligrave .com), 5825 N. Jefferson St., Burlington. You'll feel like you are so far out in the country, but really you're only minutes from the hustle and bustle. Rooms and suites are available in both the 1850s William Rouse log cabin and the 1830s Willis Graves Federal brick homestead. All the rooms are wonderfully appointed with authentic antiques and accessories to make you feel right at home. Even though the surroundings are old and authentic, you might not want to get out of the modern steam showers found in each room. Innkeepers Nancy and Bob

Swartzel know how to make everyone feel welcome. Their attention to detail will amaze you. Don't miss the gourmet breakfast of crème brûlée French toast. $$

✔ ☙ **Weller Haus Bed and Breakfast** (859-431-6829; www .wellerhaus.com), 319 Poplar St., Bellevue. Just a stone's throw from the attractions of Newport, this B&B is actually two side-by-side Victorian Gothic homes. There are five guest rooms, all with private bath, and three with two-person Jacuzzi tub. Guests choose when breakfast is served and order off a menu. If you are stumped, try the banana walnut French toast. $$

Wallace House Bed and Breakfast (859-261-2717; www.wallace housebb.com), 120 Wallace Ave., Covington. This 1900s Colonial Revival home is tucked right in the heart of Covington's historic Wallace Woods neighborhood. Surrounded by Victorian mansions, Queen Anne–style homes, and huge Tudors with Palladian-inspired gable windows, fish-scale shingles, gingerbread accents, and stained-glass windows and transoms, it is an architectural dream. Each of the three guest rooms has a queen-sized bed, private bath, cable television, and high-speed Internet access. Enjoy a gourmet breakfast by candlelight; the main attraction is innkeeper Jenni Woodruff's maple croissant soufflé. $$

✳ **Where to Eat**

DINING OUT ⟵ ⟳ **Greyhound Tavern** (859-331-3767; www

.greyhoundtavern.com), 2500 Dixie Hwy., Fort Mitchell. Open every day for lunch and dinner; Sun. brunch 10–2. This landmark eatery is the upscale yet casual place to eat delicious food and see old friends. Northern Kentucky's oldest continuous operating restaurant has been serving up signature dishes like Kentucky hot slaw and huge, really huge, onion rings since 1921. You have your choice of dining in the Williamsburg Room, with a colonial decor, the Knotty Pine Room with a rustic, comfortable atmosphere, or even outside on the front porch. Crowd pleasers are the fried chicken dinners and the Kentucky hot brown. $$–$$$

& Y **The Argentine Bistro** (859-426-1042; www.argentinebistro.com), 2875 Town Center Blvd., Crestview Hills. Open daily for lunch and dinner. Tucked into a corner of an upscale shopping center is a gem of a restaurant. It feels like a coffeehouse, with a comfy couch, bistro-style tables, antiques scattered about, and fun Argentine music playing. The tapas-style menu features small entrées made for sharing and noshing. Order a few so you can try the various choices like skirt steak with chimichurri, pepper-crusted tuna, or a panzanella salad. It's all fresh and delicious. Live music on weekends. $–$$

& Y **Riverview 360** (859-491-5300; www.threesixtydining.com), 668 W. 5th St., Covington. Open Tue.–Sat. 5–10, Sun. brunch 10–2.

Get an amazing bird's-eye view of Covington, the Ohio River, and the Cincinnati skyline while eating dinner. Yes, it's an ever-changing view, as the dining room, full of floor-to-ceiling windows, slowly revolves. Located high atop the Radisson Hotel, the view is unmatched, and it is quite romantic. The upscale menu features steaks, seafood, and seasonal specials. $$–$$$

& Y **Grandview Tavern and Grill** (859-341-8439; www.grandviewtaverngrille.com), 2220 Grandview Drive, Fort Mitchell. Open Mon.–Sat. from lunch until about 1 AM. Although it's a white-tablecloth kind of place, the menu features not-so-stuffy options like burgers, meat loaf, and fancy pizzas. Appetizers like baked Brie or bruschetta go nicely with a glass of wine. Locals pack the bar on weekends, especially when they have live music. Pleasant patio dining and bar in the summer months. $$–$$$

& Y **Behle Street Café** (859-291-4100; www.behlestreetcafe.com), 50 E. RiverCenter Blvd., Covington. Open every day 11 AM–2 AM. The menu covers all the bases, with comfort food like meat loaf and shepherd's pie along with fajitas and the very popular Capellini Behle Street, a garlic-enhanced sautéed pasta dish. Salads are big and served with a wide variety of dressings. The menu also offers stuffed-full sandwiches, homemade soups, and wonderful appetizers. $$

♈ **Vito's** (859-442-9444; www.vitos cafe.com), 654 Highland Ave., Fort Thomas. Serving dinner at 5 every day. Enjoy upscale dining, authentic Italian recipes, warm and cozy ambience, all while being serenaded by singing waiters. Feast on a wheel of Parmigiano while enjoying an aria from a classic opera like *Carmen*. Owners Vito and Mary Ciepiel don't want you to stop by on your way out for the evening; they want Vito's to be your evening. $$–$$$

♈ **Dee Felice Café** (859-261-2365; www.deefelice.com), 529 Main St., Covington. Open daily with dinner served at 5; Sun. brunch 10:30–3. Nestled in the heart of Covington's German Main Strasse Village, you will find Dee Felice Café, a restaurant known not for sausage and strudel, but for Cajun and Creole specialties. This New Orleans–inspired eatery is elegant but relaxed and fun. Their most popular entrée is Dee's Filet—a blackened filet served on shrimp cream sauce and surrounded by shrimp. Ease into your Sunday morning with an omelet-of-the-day or gourmet French toast. To add to the ambience, diners get to enjoy live jazz or Dixieland music every night. $$–$$$

♈ **Tousey House Tavern** (859-586-9900; www.touseyhouse.com), 5963 N. Jefferson St., Burlington. Serving lunch and dinner Tue.–Sun. Reservations suggested. Dine in the extraordinary home Erastus Tousey built for his family in 1825.

TOUSEY HOUSE

The restaurant is full of period pieces, like antique furnishings and handmade cross-stitch samplers that enhance the original woodwork, mantels, and staircases in this home. This upscale dining establishment offers varied menu options like limestone Bibb salad, Tousey hot brown, and glazed pork chops. $$–$$$

♈ **John Phillips Restaurant and Bar**, (859-344-0444; www.drink eatenjoy.com), 2809 Dixie Hwy., Crestview Hills. This white-tablecloth kind of place makes you feel like your meal is a special occasion, even if it isn't. You don't have to be dressed up to go, but on weekends you might want to spruce yourself up a bit. Lunch choices include salads and wraps, and dinner choices range from lobster tail, to apricot-crusted pork chops, to surf and turf. They have an early-bird special 4–6 PM, but wait until you see the crowd that lines up for the sushi, which is half price after 9 every night. It is fabulous, whether you wait until 9 or not. $$–$$$

Ψ **Chez Nora Restaurant and Roof Top Jazz Club** (859-491-8027; cheznora.com), 530 Main St., Covington. Open daily 11 AM–1 AM; Sun. brunch 10–2. Located in the historic Main Strasse district, Chez Nora is in a fabulous old building with interesting interior brickwork. You can't miss the 100-year-old bar when you walk in the door, but if you make it past that stop by their rooftop terrace for a drink and an impressive view of the Cincinnati skyline. The menu is full of interesting choices, from sandwiches to steaks and a whole lot in between. Dress up or don't; owners Jimmy and Pati Gilliece will make you feel like you are eating at their house, no matter what you are wearing.

Ψ **Indigo Casual Gourmet Cafe** (859-331-4339; www.myindigo grill.com), 2053 Dixie Hwy., Fort Mitchell. Open daily 11–10. Eclectic menu features salads, pasta dishes, sandwiches, and pizzas, all with fresh and not-so-common ingredients like hummus, artichokes, shiitake mushrooms, and Asiago cheese. Try the Indigo Idaho appetizer—much like traditional potato skins, with bacon and sharp cheddar on a pizza crust. If the weather is cooperating, dine outside on their front patio. $$

Ψ **Knotty Pine on the Bayou** (859-791-2200), 6302 Licking Pike, Cold Spring. Serving dinner seven days per week. This isn't Louisiana, but you might think you've died and gone to Cajun Heaven when you arrived at this out-of-the-way gem. The menu features include garlicky frog legs, crispy crabcakes, extraordinary gumbo, and fried oysters; on Thursday nights, they even have a crawfish boil. $$–$$$

Ψ **Virgil's Café** (859-491-3287; virgilscafe.com), 710 Fairfield Ave., Bellevue. Serving lunch and dinner; closed Tue. Sun. brunch 11–2. Although you might be lured to Virgil's for their legendary shrimp Creole with cheddar cheese grits, or étouffée with garlic bread—which are both good choices—they have these cheddar jalapeño hush puppies that you just have to order. You'll think about them for days, they're so good. Although the menu doesn't offer as many choices as you might be accustomed to, just keep in mind that it is all amazing. The other thing you will remember is the outstanding service you'll receive. The owners and the servers are so glad you are there, you will feel it.

Ψ **Oriental Wok** (859-331-3000; www.orientalwok.com), Buttermilk Pike, Fort Mitchell. Open Sun.–Thu. 11–9:30, Fri. 11–10:30, Sat. 4–10:30. Mike and Helen Wong immigrated to the United States from Hong Kong in the 1970s and opened their upscale Chinese restaurant in 1977, counting on the American Dream to be their reality. Today the Oriental Wok is Northern Kentucky's answer for where to go for an elegant evening of fine dining and impeccable service. Fountains, waterfalls, and

Ŷ **Hofbräuhaus Newport** (859-491-7200; www.hofbrauhausnewport.com), 3rd and Saratoga at the Levee, Newport. Open 11–9 daily. $$–$$$

Northern Kentucky's German roots run deep. So when you are hungry for some authentic German beer and some Wiener schnitzel, well, just grab your lederhosen and head for the Hofbräuhaus in Newport. The giant dining hall and brewery is a re-creation of the famous haus in Munich.

The beer made on site is not some fancy new brew designed to compete with microbreweries. The Hofbräu brand was created in 1589 when Duke William V of Bavaria wanted to provide beer to his royal family. It's brewed on site according to the German Purity Law using water, hops, malt, and yeast only. In keeping with tradition, Newport has a Brew Master on site to supervise the production of the Hofbräuhaus beer. You can also supervise production yourself: The brewing area is surrounded by windows, and for a closer view you can ask for a tour.

Hofbräu beers are a little more potent than typical American brews, so consider yourself warned. Some good ones to sample are the Hofbräu Premium Lager and Hofbräu Maibock, which is 7.2 percent alcohol. Munich's favorite, the Original Hofbräu Dunkel, is still directly imported from Munich.

The Hofbräuhaus produces seasonal brews as well. The spring beer, Maiboch, is tied to the German tradition of Maifest. In November and December, they brew Winterfestbier, to coincide with the chilly weather.

The company wanted its U.S. version to have the same feel as the original in Munich, so the Beer Hall has imported benches, chairs, and even a stream with goldfish running through the spacious and warm dining room make the experience incomparable. $$–$$$

Ŷ **Pompilios** (859-581-3065), 6th and Washington Ave., Newport. Open for lunch and dinner every day. Pompilios, which has been a local favorite for nearly 70 years, is famous for two things: traditional Italian food and the toothpick scene from the movie *Rain Man*. Yes, Dustin Hoffman and Tom Cruise filmed that scene right there in the corner of the bar area. When you get past that star-crossed moment, grab a menu. Italian food makes up 98 percent of their offerings, and once you taste their handmade tables, as well as woodwork and brewing artifacts. It's certainly not fancy, but the giant hall is festive and feels like you're attending a party.

With seating for about 720, chances are good you'll find a table. You can dine in the rowdy Bier Hall and listen to the "Haus band" play old-fashioned oompah-pah; or in the Bier Stubbe, a quiet dining area for families and those who would like a more relaxing meal. The Bier Garden is out back and attracts a large after-work crowd in summer.

Although the brew is straight from the Old Country, the menu is straight from a German kitchen, with a few American favorites thrown in as well. The most popular menu item is the Pretzels and Bier Cheese. The pretzels are imported from Germany, but the Bier Cheese is created locally. Other German items that are imported are the red cabbage and sauerkraut. Not everything comes from Germany; they import Holtzhofenbrot, a nutty rye bread for Reuben sandwiches, from Canada.

Menu options like Sauerbraten, Fritierte Gurken (fried pickles), and Hofbräuhaus Gulaschsuppe (a type of beef stew with Hungarian paprika) all add to the German ambience. How about some Leberkäse—Bavarian meat loaf served with German potato wedges and topped with a fried egg? Certainly not your run-of-the-mill menu items.

Don't skimp on dessert. What's a traditional German meal without Apfelstrud'l (apple strudel) or Windbeutel (a traditional Bavarian creampuff)?

For those not so daring, the menu also features New York strip, chicken tenders, and glazed salmon. Looks like whatever you choose, it will be wunderbar!

meat and cheese ravioli, or their linguine cacciatore, you will know why. Start your meal with the homemade minestrone soup and wrap it up with the homemade cannoli for dessert. Don't forget to order a Coca-Cola. It's served in little 8-ounce bottles like you used to get when you were a kid. $$

EATING OUT 🍴 🍷 **Anchor Grill** (859-431-9498), 438 W. Pike St., Covington. The neon sign in the window proudly proclaims, WE MAY DOZE, BUT NEVER CLOSE, and that's how regulars remember the Anchor Grill's hours. Some may call this a greasy spoon, but to locals, that's quite an insult. The compliment is that chain restaurants try to copy this hometown diner feel, but you just can't re-create 60 years of history. The food, simple meals like pork chops, meat loaf, and burgers (order yours deluxe if you want lettuce and tomato), is always good. Round-the-clock breakfast items, like eggs, goetta, hash browns, and fried egg sandwiches, are always in high demand, especially on weekends around 2 AM when it's hard to find a table. While you're here, don't miss the band in the back room. Whenever a song is played on the jukebox (Don Ho's "Tiny Bubbles" is a popular favorite), the disco ball spins and a 2-foot-tall enclosed stage in the corner lights up. A curtain opens and a small band made up of mechanical figures "plays." One of the band members malfunctioned years ago, so now a Barbie doll fills in. $

& ⴲ **Barleycorns** (859-331-6633 lakeside location; 859-442-3400 Cold Spring location; www .barleycorns.com), 2642 Dixie Hwy., Lakeside Park, and 1073 Industrial Rd., Cold Spring. Open for lunch and dinner every day. There is always something fun going on at Barleycorns. This neighborhood sports bar and restaurant is the perfect place to bring a family or to come watch the big game on one of the many TVs scattered about. They are known for their bar food, like wings, skins, and nachos. But go for lunch or dinner and enjoy

entrées like grilled salmon, Kentucky hot brown, and grilled rib eyes. The Lakeside Park location is housed in a former tollgate along Dixie Highway, with creaky hardwood floors, walls loaded with memorabilia, and even a few stuffed wild animals. The Cold Spring location, loaded with sports paraphernalia, is the place to be when the Kentucky Wildcats are on TV. Both sites have fantastic outdoor patios, complete with umbrella tables. $$–$$$

& ⴲ **Montoya's Mexican Restaurant** (859-341-0707), 2507 Chelsea Dr., Fort Mitchell. Open for lunch and dinner every day. Stop in for authentic, casual, Mexican dining at reasonable prices. Owner Socorio Ramirez moved to the United States from Mexico more than 30 years ago, bringing with her the recipes and the know-how of a Mexican kitchen. Her most popular entrées are the enchilada plate and Montoya's Plato, which is made of bite-sized pieces of seasoned pork tenderloin. Entrées are delicious and generous in size, but locals know it is the homemade salsa that makes their mouths water. $

ⴲ **Hebron Brew Haus** (859-534-5600; hebronbrewhaus.com), 2030 Northside Dr., Hebron. Open Mon.–Sat. 11 AM–2:30 PM, Sunday 11–midnight. Not only does their menu offer a wide selection of pizzas, wings, wraps, salads, and hoagies, the haus itself is a fun place to be. $–$$

Dixie Chili (859-291-5337; dixie chili.com), 733 Monmouth St., Newport, and 3716 Dixie Hwy., Erlanger. Open every day from 9 AM until the wee hours of the morning. In the Greater Cincinnati area, you will find several chili parlor chains competing for your business. Although all are delicious, it was Dixie Chili that got its start in Northern Kentucky. Nicholas Sarakatsannis, a Greek immigrant who perfected his own version of Cincinnati chili in the late 1920s, knew he wanted to do business in Kentucky, also known as Dixieland, hence the name. He sold 9 gallons on his first day of business in the 8-by-30-foot room where the business is still located, although they have expanded it over the years. Today his sons run three locations and prepare 150 gallons each day. The Sarakatsannis brothers still use the best-quality ingredients to serve a chili that is delicious but not hard on your digestive system. Newbies should order a three-way, which is spaghetti, chili, and cheese. Once you are convinced, you can move on to a coney or even a Greek salad. You can't have a name like Sarakatsannis without knowing how to make a good Greek salad. $

&. **LaRosa's Pizza** (859-347-1111; www.larosas.com), nine locations in Northern Kentucky. Serving up authentic Italian pizza for more than 50 years, LaRosa's is the best. Their pizza, calzones, wings, and hoagies make the national chains pale in comparison. Try the Philly cheese steak calzone or the baked Buddy hoagy, named for founder Buddy LaRosa. It's a delectable combination of capicola ham, pepperoni, salami, and provolone, baked and covered in pizza sauce, onions, and pickles. Before you go, you might want to buy some LaRosa's Italian salad dressing or spaghetti sauce to take with you. Everybody does. This is the perfect place to bring a family, but they also deliver more than 40 menu items in a timely fashion. $–$$

Y **Keystone Bar and Grill** (859-261-6777; keystonebar.com), 313 Greenup St., Covington. Open every day from about 11 AM until 2:30 in the morning. They are located in the shadow of the Roebling Suspension Bridge in an old, rehabbed building. Ambience is casual but hip. The menu offers juicy burgers, not-so-common sandwiches, and a to-die-for black bean burrito. But what seems to be their biggest draw, in addition to 75 craft beers, is their mac 'n' cheese. Each cheesy variety is named for a music legend. Try the Buffalo Springfield or maybe the Gordon Lightfoot. Or come on Monday when the whole mac 'n' cheese menu is half price and you can try several.

&. **Colonial Cottage** (859-341-4498), 3140 Dixie Hwy., Erlanger. Open daily 7 AM–9 PM. If you haven't had your mandatory-while-in-Northern-Kentucky serving of goetta yet, head for the Cottage and get yourself some. They serve breakfast all day long in their warm and inviting dining room. The centerpiece is a huge fieldstone fireplace, which makes you feel like you are in someone's living room. Owner Matt Grimes and his waitresses, some of whom have worked at the Cottage for more than 20 years, are glad to have you and will probably remember your name next time you're there. In addition to their loosen-your-belt-a-notch break-fasts, they features southern favorites like hand-breaded cat-fish, cottage ham, and fried chicken. They also offer five hot vegetables each day and unbeliev-able meringue pies. $–$$

Kremer's Market (859-341-1067; www.kremersmarket.com), 755 Buttermilk Pike, Crescent Springs. In business since 1913, the Kre-mer family was known locally for their homegrown vegetables like hothouse tomatoes, sweet Silver Queen corn, and crispy Bibb let-tuce, all grown on their farm in nearby Villa Hills. The business has come a long way since then. Now run by fourth-generation Kremers, they still offer seasonal homegrown vegetables but also have a full-service deli, garden center, and unique gift items. There's no room for seating, so you'll have to get yours to go. Stop by the giant side-by-side red barns and try some famous chicken salad, homemade breads, chicken and wild rice soup, and butter cream fudge. $–$$

♈ **Otto's** (859-491-6678; www .ottosonmain.com), 521 Main St.,

Covington. Lunch Mon.–Sat. 11:30–2:30, Dinner Tue.–Sat. 5–10, Sun. 5–9; Sun. brunch 10–2. Owner Paul Weckman has gone above and beyond to make his artsy, funky bistro, artsy and funky. The decor is hip, yet it feels slightly upscale. The menu features big sandwiches and salads at lunch and some southern-inspired options at dinner like shrimp and grits and brown sugared pork. Local, fresh ingredients are abun-dant. $$

Green Derby Restaurant (859-431-8740), 846 York St., Newport. Serving three meals a day, every day. A local favorite for home-cooked meals, the Green Derby has been making people feel at home for more than 50 years. Because the spot has been repeat-edly voted Best Fish Sandwich in the Tristate, you may feel obli-gated to try the wonderful fried halibut sandwich—but you'll be equally satisfied with a burger and fries or some pork chops. They are also known for their Derby salad: shredded iceberg lettuce served like hot slaw. For dessert, don't miss their homemade pies—apple, coconut cream, lemon meringue, among others. $–$$

♈ **Stringtown Restaurant** (859-371-8222), 255 Main St., Florence. Open Mon.–Sat. 8–8, Sun. 9–2. Housed in a building that dates back to 1869, String-town used to be a stagecoach stop for weary travelers on their way between Lexington and Cincin-nati. Today it is a casual stop for locals looking for homemade food at reasonable prices. World-renowned chef Rick Potter keeps favorites like sandwiches, meat loaf, and liver and onions on the menu but introduces more exotic dinner specials to show off his culinary dexterity. $$

Ⓨ **York Street Café** (859-261-9675), 801 York St., Newport. Open for lunch and dinner every day except Sunday. On the National Historic Register, this building—which once housed a pharmacy—dates back to the 1880s. In the first-floor dining area you'll be drawn in by the floor-to ceiling cabinetry that once held elixirs and tonics, now jam-packed with funky collectibles for your enjoyment. The warm wood-work, some stained glass, and mis-matched light fixtures all add to the show. It is a mix of restaurant, art gallery, and lounge. Enjoy an entrée or a homemade dessert or settle into a comfy couch and order a conversation platter like the Mediterranean board, a sam-pling of Greek favorites including hummus, tabouli, Greek salad, and spanakopita, created for shar-ing. $$

Ⓨ **Herb and Thelma's** (859-491-6984), 718 Pike St., Covington. Mon.–Sat. 11–11, Sun. 1–7. This is a neighborhood bar with cheap, as well as excellent, cheeseburg-ers. It's an everybody-knows-your-name kind of place, so if you come alone, you are sure to make friends. The tavern has been in business since the 1930s and

hasn't changed much over the years, which is quite an asset. Watch your step as you open the door: The concrete stoop has started to wear away, evidence of the 80 years of foot traffic going in and out. $

Ⓨ **Mokka and the Sunset Bar Grill** (859-581-3700; mokka sunset.com), 500 Monmouth St., Newport. Kitchen open every day from 9 AM until about 10 PM. This cool space, in an old building right on the corner of a busy intersec-tion downtown, is always packed, which tells you something. They serve yummy breakfast treats like pancakes and frittatas every day until 3. They also have an interest-ing selection of burgers, sand-wiches, and great big salads. Live music on weekends.

Spare Time Grill (859-635-5542), 7807 Alexandria Pike, Alexandria. Open Mon.–Sat. 6 AM–2 PM, Sun. 8–2. This is one of those landmark places sometimes referred to as a "dive." This 50-plus-year-old diner has just two tables and 15 stools at the counter . . . but what it lacks in luxury, it makes up for in charm. There is usually a lively conversation going on with the regulars to the tune of bacon, eggs, burgers, and potatoes siz-zling on the grill. $

Bellevue Bistro (859-581-5600), 313 Fairfield Ave., Bellevue. Open for breakfast and lunch daily, which means, with so many mouthwatering choices for each meal, you are going to have to try it in the morning and again around noon. Taking traditional eggs Benedict in a whole new direction, the Bistro smothers theirs in sauces and flavors that you weren't expecting so early in the morning. Try yours with chicken and chili cream sauce or grained honey mustard. But take a look at that lunch menu; with fresh sandwiches and salads, it might take a few minutes to decide. The owners are well known for supporting local businesses and farmers. They know they can't do it all alone, so they head to their favorite farmers and bakers to enhance their menu and serve you the best food they can find. $

Strong's Brick Oven Pizzeria (859-291-6836; www.strongsbrick ovenpizza.com), 336 Monmouth St., Newport. Closed Mon. Using the most wonderful sauces and hand-tossed dough, topping it with extra-virgin olive oil and a selection of fresh cheeses and toppings, *and* baking it an Old World–style Italian brick oven— well, how could this go wrong? What comes out of that oven is pure heaven. Order one of their signature pizzas, or create your own. Don't leave without ordering one of their dessert pizzas, covered with either apples and cinnamon or chocolate and raspberries. You can't go wrong with either one. $–$$

Jane's Saddlebag (859-384-6617), 13989 Ryle Rd., Union. Closed Mon. and Tue. Located on the edge of Big Bone Lick State Park,

Jane's is a little diner and gift shop that combines the history of the area with a little current southern charm. The menu features Woolly Mammoth Burgers, Mastodon Brats, Ice Age Pie, and specials like the Best Damn Bean Soup in Boone County. Jane's also has a petting zoo, so come when you have time to walk around a bit. $

⚐ **Rima's Diner** (859-331-6444), 2520 Hazelwood St., Crescent Springs. Serving lunch and dinner every day. If you can walk past the dessert case without stopping to ogle the giant servings of cakes and pies that are slowly spinning their tempting way, well, you've made it farther than most people. Seems most customers know what they are ordering for dessert before they even get their menu. But take time to read the menu. Rima's has southern-influenced offerings like fried chicken, pinto beans, and lots of side dishes covered in gravy. Sandwiches, salads, and lunch specials are all good options. This family-style diner features old-time movie posters and memorabilia. $–$$

⚐ **Newport Pizza Company** (859-261-4900; newportpizza company.com), 601 Monmouth St., Newport. Open everyday at 11–11, but make that 1 AM on Fri. and Sat. Neighborhood pizzeria serving up specialty pizzas like the Cincinnatius, covered in Cincinnati-style chili, and the Highland Country Club—it's like a club sandwich on a crust. Cheap prices and friendly service. $–$$

☿ **Molly Malone's Irish Pub and Restaurant** (859-491-6699; www.mollymalonesirishpub.com), 112 E. 4th St., Covington. Open for lunch and dinner every day. A true Irish pub and eatery right in the heart of downtown Covington. The rich wood decor and huge authentic bar make the restaurant warm and inviting. The bar serves up Irish brews, and the menu features favorites like bangers and mash, fish-and-chips, and traditional lamb stew straight from the Emerald Isle. $–$$

SNACKS ☙ **Graeter's** (859-341-3005, 859-261-3160; www.graeters.com), 301 Buttermilk Pike, Fort Mitchell, and 1409 N. Grand Ave., Newport. Open daily. A Cincinnati favorite with two locations in Northern Kentucky. This is what ice cream is all about. Following a family recipe that dates back to 1870, Graeter's ice cream is so dense and creamy, it can only be made 2 gallons at a time. Of course they have vanilla and butter pecan, but do yourself a favor and order a flavor with chips, like black raspberry chip or chocolate chip. Calling it a chip is sort of a misnomer: Hidden inside the ice cream are gigantic chunks of deep dark solid chocolate. It's like finding a prize in every bite. $

Cookie Jar Bakery (859-261-3345), 919 Monmouth St., Newport. They open most days in the wee hours of the morning, 1 AM or 3 AM, depending on the day, and close shop in the late afternoon.

There isn't much better than the smell of hot coffee and warm doughnuts, and that is a smell you can't miss as you open up the creaky door that takes you back to the bakeries of your youth. With 85 years in the same family and same location, Cookie Jar knows a thing or two about baking. Coffee cake, breads, cookies . . . yeah, you get the picture. The Cookie Jar Roll is their signature pastry; it has an almond crumb filling that you will dream about afterward. $

Mrs. Potts Tea Room (859-491-2731; mrspotts.com), 339 Fairfield Ave., Bellevue. Tue.–Sat. 10–4. Walk-ins welcome, but reservations suggested. It's not just for ladies, but Mrs. Potts does seem like a girlie kind of place. They are known for their high tea, which includes a salad, tea breads, finger sandwiches, and, of course, a pot of tea and a sinful dessert. If it is not high tea time, stop in for a scoop of their homemade chicken salad and the tea of your choice. $

Twisted Sisters (859-781-6569), 411 Fairfield Ave., Bellevue. Tue.–Sat. 11–3. This little place whips up some mighty big, doughy, and heavenly gourmet soft pretzels. Perfect for dipping or for holding a sandwich together, these are some good pretzels. $

Schneider's Sweet Shop (859-431-3545; schneiderscandies.com), 420 Fairfield Ave., Bellevue. Most days aren't complete until you've had your dose of chocolate, so pop on into Schneider's and order a piece or two of their famous Opera Cream Candy. This is a little piece of rich, creamy, delectable heaven, dunked in milk or dark chocolate. You can only find them in this area, so try one of each. Then pick up a box to take home with you. They also have mouthwatering caramels, truffles, and chocolates, all made by hand. In business since 1939, these people know what they are doing. $

✸ Entertainment

Bobby Mackey's (859-431-5588; bobbymackey.com), 44 Licking Pike, Wilder. This legendary honky-tonk, owned by country singer Bobby Mackey, is as famous for its owner and the mechanical bull inside as it is for its paranormal past. Put your boots on and stop by to listen to Bobby and his Big Mac band, who play almost every weekend. You will love his music; and the fact that this joint hasn't changed a lick since he bought it back in 1978—well, that should tell you something, too. If the bull ride isn't scary enough, take a tour of the basement, a place that ghost hunters swear is haunted. Check the website for tour times.

&. **Monmouth Theatre** (859-655-9140; www.monmouththeatre .com), 636 Monmouth St., Newport. This truly eclectic entertainment venue in downtown Newport features a huge variety of live performances. Check the website to see what's showing; expect anything from live theater

to jazz shows and everything in between.

Southgate House Revival (www .southgatehouse.com), 111 E. 6th Street, Newport. Housed in an amazing old church = built in 1848, the Southgate features up-and-coming musical acts, as well as familiar classics. Three stages under one roof, so you can enjoy a different musical genre at each one. Check the website and Facebook page to see who's taking the stages.

The Thompson House (859-261-SHOW; www.thompsonhouse newport.com), 24 E. 3rd St. Newport. Built in 1814, this historic mansion, which is said to be haunted, has had many notable owners and visitors. One such resident was Brigadier General John Taliaferro Thompson, the inventor of the Thompson machine gun, better known as a Tommy gun, who was born here on December 31, 1860. Today it is a nationally recognized music venue featuring a different act on each of its four cozy floors. They are hugely supportive of the local music scene; check the website for a list of bands, acts, and performances.

Elements Create It Studio (859-647-2738), 5900 Centennial Circle, Florence. This open art studio lets you paint pottery, make fused glass designs, or paint a blank canvas. You can be as artsy as you want; just choose your passion and go. Talented staff can help you get started, or will leave you alone to create your masterpiece.

✳ Selective Shopping

Kentucky Haus (859-261-4287; www.kentuckyhaus.com), 411 E. 10th St., Newport. Call ahead to check hours. Find the finest works of Kentucky artisans in this unique shop. They have a huge collection of Louisville Stoneware and various Kentucky foods, baskets, candles, and books. Stop by and see sisters Bev and Peggy, who are always there and always have samples of fine coffees and teas for you to sip on.

Donna Salyers' Fabulous Furs (859-291-3300, 800-848-4650; fabulousfurs.com), 25 W. Robbins St., Covington. You've probably seen these impeccable wraps, throws, and fake-fur coats on stars and models, but you assumed they were real. They certainly look like they just came off a mink, fox, or rabbit, but they are actually made of the finest acrylic you can find. Visit the showroom and wrap yourself in the lap of luxury, without the guilt. Donna invites you to feel everything in the store. You won't believe it's faux.

Rabbit Hash General Store (859-586-7744; www.rabbithash .com), 10021 Lower River Rd., Rabbit Hash. Step back in time when you enter the doors of this authentic general store that has been in operation since 1831. Located right in the heart of the historic river town of Rabbit Hash, it is the centerpiece for the whole

ELEMENTS CREATE IT STUDIO

Deborah Kohl Kremer

town. Stop in and shoot the breeze with some locals while you browse an assortment of antiques, handcrafted goods, collectible pottery, and organic products. Stick around for the barn dances and impromptu concerts usually held on weekends. You might even get to meet the town mayor, Lucy Lou, a Border collie, who beat out her competition with the slogan "A bitch you can count on."

❧ **The Blue Marble Children's Bookstore** (859-781-0602; www.bluemarblebooks.com), 1356 S. Fort Thomas Ave., Fort Thomas. What little one hasn't wondered what it would be like to go into the great green room from the book *Good Night Moon*? Well, at the Blue Marble, you'll see a reproduced great green room so authentic, it even has a bowl full of mush. This independent bookseller has been around since 1979, and they are the authority on children's books. The staff are amazingly helpful and seem to know something about all 30,000 titles they have in stock.

❧ **Comic Book World** (859-371-9562; comicbookworld.com), 7130 Turfway Road, Florence. This family-owned business has been around for more than 30 years. It is the place to go whether you need a vintage copy of *Superman* or the latest issue of *The Walking Dead*. They also carry supplies for role-playing, trading card, and board games.

❧ **Bellevue Beadery** (859-292-0800; bellevuebeadery.com), 341 Fairfield Ave., Bellevue. Feeling crafty? The Beadery carries thousands of beads from all over the world. You can take a jewelry-making class or just stock up on beads for your own creation.

Phil's Music and Memories (859-441-2514; www.philsrecords .com), 3914 Winston Ave., Latonia. Phil's has been in business for more than 30 years, so whether you are looking for vintage vinyl, CDs, or DVDs, this is the place to go.

The Village Gallerie (859-331-5965), 1870 Ashwood Circle, Fort Wright. Specializing in the works of local and regional artists, this gallery has a fine collection of equestrian art and Cincinnati and Northern Kentucky scenes. They also do excellent framing.

ANTIQUES **Florence Antique Mall** (859-371-0600; www.florence antiquemall.com), 8145 Mall Rd., Florence. This is an antiques collector's dream: a one-level, air-conditioned 50,000-square-foot showroom with the finest wares of more than 300 quality dealers. They have a wonderful selection of fine antiques, collectibles, furniture, and art.

SHOPPING DISTRICTS **Newport on the Levee** (859-291-0550, 866-538-3359; www.newport onthelevee.com), 1 Levee Way, Newport. Sitting high atop the floodwall, or Levee, you'll find this hip entertainment destination. Full of trendy nightclubs, mall stores, and a variety of restaurants, the complex is anchored by the Newport Aquarium, GameWorks, and a 20-screen movie theater.

✳ Special Events

April–October: **Burlington Antique Show**. Held on the third Sunday of the month at the Boone County Fairgrounds, this show usually draws about 250 vendors from around the region. The show officially begins at 8 AM, but the early birds start bargaining about 5 AM. Get there early, wear comfortable shoes, and dress for the weather, because the show goes on regardless of rain, shine, frost, or scorching heat.

May: 🍴 ♿ **Maifest at Main Strasse**. Modeled after the German tradition that welcomes spring, Maifest is held annually on the streets of Main Strasse, the German-inspired neighborhood of Covington. There are plenty of libations to quench a thirst, as well as a huge variety of foods. Try a German egg roll—just like its Asian counterpart, except this one is filled with goetta. This festival brings together unique arts and crafts booths and a variety of musical entertainment, from oom-pah-pah German bands to Kentucky bluegrass.

June: 🍴 ♿ **Newport Italianfest**. Held alongside the Ohio River, adjacent to Newport on the Levee. Celebrating Newport's Italian heritage, this weekend festival draws thousands to enjoy authentic Italian food, music, and even a pizza-eating contest.

August: 🍴 ♿ **Goettafest**. The celebration of all things goetta, which is Northern Kentucky's answer to breakfast sausage. This German concoction of pork, beef, steel-cut or pinhead oats, and seasonings is fried up to crispy perfection and has been enjoyed for generations. This festival, held annually on Newport's riverfront, brings together food vendors who must provide a few goetta choices, a non-goetta choice, and a dessert. Since no two vendors can offer the same dish, you'll find some pretty creative uses of goetta. If you are new to the dish, try it plain. If you are a connoisseur, try the goetta pizza or goetta Reuben. Goettafest features rides, music, and fun goetta games, too.

September: 🍴 ♿ **Octoberfest at Main Strasse**. Held the weekend after Labor Day, this festival is comparable to the annual celebration in Munich. Grab a mug of German beer and a Limburger cheese sandwich and watch men in lederhosen do a polka. There are rides for the kids, live music, and unique crafts at this annual fall festival.

CARROLLTON

Situated almost halfway between Cincinnati and Louisville is the river city of **Carrollton**. Although today's visitors may find it a convenient stopping point for gas and snacks when commuting between the two cities, it was this location that put it on the map back in the late 1700s. Located right at the mouth of the Kentucky River, where it connects to the Ohio, Carrollton became a stopping point, almost an exit ramp, in those early years as river travelers decided which route to take.

Named in honor of Charles Carroll, whose signature you will find on the Declaration of Independence, Carrollton is a perfect example of small-town America. The historic downtown offers a few antiques shops, hometown eateries, and excellent views of the Ohio River. High on a hill overlooking the town, you'll find General Butler State Resort Park, offering a combination of recreation with a splash of history mixed in for good measure.

Although it's hard to call Carrollton a destination city, it is definitely worth a stop as you commute down I-71. Or, if you happen to be traveling by keelboat, there are plenty of docks available, too.

GUIDANCE Carrollton/Carroll County Tourism and Convention Commission (502-732-7036, 800-325-4290; www.carrolltontourism.com), 515 Highland Ave., Carrollton. Open weekdays 9–4:30. The welcome center here is fully stocked with brochures and maps. The helpful staff can also assist with advice and historical questions.

GETTING THERE As Carrollton is located about halfway between Louisville and Northern Kentucky, the area is served by both the **Cincinnati/Northern Kentucky International Airport** (859-767-3151; www.cvgairport.com) and the **Louisville International Airport** (502-368-6524; www.flylouisville.com), which is located at the intersection of I-65 and I-264. Check both to compare airfares. Car rentals are available at both airports.

GETTING AROUND Carrollton has no public transportation, so you will need a car. It is easy to get around the area, as streets are well marked and parking is free.

MEDICAL EMERGENCY Carroll County Hospital (502-732-4321), 309 11th St., Carrollton, is a 25-bed critical care facility. About 17 miles away across the river in Madison, Indiana, is the larger **King's Daughters Hospital** (812-265-5211; www.kingsdaughtershospital.org), 1 King's Daughters' Dr., Madison. This 115-bed hospital includes a full range of services.

ALCOHOL You can get a drink in the area, depending on which area you're in. Carroll County and Gallatin County are wet, meaning you can purchase alcohol most anywhere. Neighboring Owen County is dry, meaning no alcohol sales, except for the Elk Creek Winery (see the sidebar). And farther east, Grant County is moist, which means no liquor sales except in restaurants in the cities of Corinth and Williamstown. Call ahead if you want a drink with dinner and see what the law is there.

✳ To See

Butler-Turpin State Historic House is located inside General Butler State Resort Park (502-732-4384; www.parks.ky.gov), KY 227, Carrollton. Tours of the home and the outdoor summer kitchen are available. Tours Wed.–Sat. on the hour 9–4 (except for noon–1, when the house is closed for lunch). Originally owned by Phillip Turpin and his wife, Mary Ellen

THE BUTLER-TURPIN STATE HISTORIC HOUSE

Deborah Kohl Kremer

Butler Turpin, this Greek Revival home served this politically connected family well through the mid-1800s. The house is loaded with original family pieces and has been restored to its original splendor. Don't miss the pianoforte (which has never been removed from the home) or the drop-leaf table in the parlor, which still bears the claw marks of the family cat. $5 adults, $3 children; under 6 free.

The Masterson House (502-732-7036, 800-325-4290; www.carrollton tourism.com), Highland Ave., Carrollton. Call for tour hours. Visit what is thought to be the first two-story brick house built between Louisville and Cincinnati. An engineering marvel of its time, it was constructed by slaves around 1790 with bricks that were created on site.

The Old Stone Jail (502-732-7036, 800-325-4290; www.carrolltontourism .com), Highland Ave. and Court St., Carrollton. You won't believe that this primitive jail was still in use as late as 1969, but it was. The two-story stone structure was built in 1880, with just a few barbaric-looking cells, a potbellied stove for warmth, and small, glassless windows for light. Contact the tourism office for a tour.

🎣 ✒ **Markland Locks and Dam**, located 3 miles south of Warsaw. This concrete dam also serves as a bridge over the Ohio River. An observation tower high above lets you watch as boats and barges make their way through the locks.

STATE PARK ✒ ♿ **General Butler State Resort Park** (502-732-4384; www.parks.ky.gov), KY 227, Carrollton. Named for General William Orlando Butler, who was a recognized army general, a congressman, and a vice presidential candidate in 1848. Although he owned slaves, he was staunchly in favor of the preservation of the Union and the gradual emancipation of slaves. Today the park in his name offers a welcoming lodge with 53 guest rooms and 24 cottages, some with up to three bedrooms. The lodge's wood-paneled common area has a cozy fieldstone fireplace, and soaring windows that take in the view high above the Ohio River Valley. Dine at **Two Rivers Restaurant**, a nod to the lodge's location at the confluence of the Kentucky and Ohio Rivers. The dining room is decorated with fun and interesting fishing paraphernalia like rods, reels, driftwood, and old tackle boxes. They serve three meals a day, including a lunch buffet so popular, it brings in people from downtown Carrollton. Sandwiches, burgers, and salads are always on the menu, but entrée choices include Kentucky hot brown, fried catfish, and southern pecan chicken, which is dripping with a sauce that is sweet and sour at the same time. For recreation, the park has a 9-hole, par-35 golf course located high along the ridges of the mountaintops. The 30-acre lake is perfect for fishing for crappie, catfish, bass, and bluegill. The boat dock rents canoes and pedal boats in the summer. They also have miniature golf, tennis and basketball courts, and playgrounds. The Park Overlook, which is the highest point on the property, offers a breathtaking view of both rivers and the tiny town of Carrollton down below.

✷ To Do

GOLF Sugar Bay Golf Course (859-567-2601), 957 Dry Creek Rd., Warsaw. This 18-hole par-71 public golf course has 13 lakes that come into play on 6 holes.

Perry Park Country Club (502-484-2159), 595 Springport Ferry Rd., Perry Park. Open to the public, this club offers a 27-hole, par-72 championship course.

RACING Kentucky Speedway (888-652-RACE; www.kentuckyspeedway .com), I-71 Exit 57, Sparta. NASCAR lovers can get their fill of the industry's hottest races at the Kentucky Speedway. This enormous track seats more than 66,000 fans. Races are scheduled throughout the year and draw some big-name drivers. The website will keep you up to date.

Richard Petty Driving Experience (859-743-5745; www.1800bepetty .com), Kentucky Speedway, I-71 Exit 57, Sparta. Whether you want to ride shotgun at speeds up to 165 mph—or actually do the driving yourself—this is the ultimate experience for race fans.

KENTUCKY SPEEDWAY

www.kentuckytourism.com

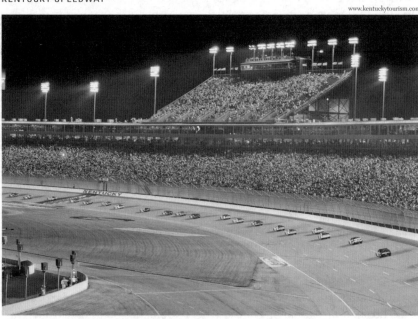

.com). Pick up a map and begin at the welcome center at 515 Highland
Ave., Carrollton. Take in all the sites, including historic and stately Carroll
County Courthouse, proud Victorian homes, and the cute storefronts of
Carrollton and the surrounding area.

✳ Green Space

Point Park (502-732-7060), 1st and Main Sts. in downtown Carrollton.
This 15-acre park sits right at the convergence of the Ohio and Kentucky
Rivers. Throughout the year it is used for city and county festivals, but on
a daily basis it has a nice playground for kids, a boat ramp for easy access
to the rivers, and relaxing places to just sit and enjoy the waterways.

Kleber Wildlife Management Area (502-535-6335), 5005 Cedar Creek
Rd., Owenton. Kleber is a 2,575-acre preserve and trail system about
halfway between Frankfort and Owenton off US 127. Trail maps are available on site. Hike these rugged trails through woods and grasslands, which
often result in wildlife encounters. Kleber is home to plenty of deer, raccoons, and squirrels, but it is also a favorite place for bird-watchers.

✳ Lodging

BED & BREAKFASTS

**The Poet's House Bed &
Breakfast** (502-347-0135; www
.bbonline.com/ky/poetshouse), 501
Main St., Ghent. Sleep in one of
the two inviting guest rooms, or
for a little more privacy book the
next-door River Dance Cottage,
which sleeps four. The Federal-
style brick home was built in 1863
and is listed on the National Historic Register. Innkeepers David
Hendren and Rick Whitfill invite
guests to eat their delicious breakfast in the formal dining room or
outdoors on a deck overlooking
the beautiful Ohio River. $$

Highland House B&B (502-732-
5559; www.bbonline.com/ky
/highland), 1705 Highland Ave.,
Carrollton. This beautiful home,

once part of an 800-acre farm, is
listed on the National Register of
Historic Places. It was built in the
early 1920s in an architectural
style called Creative Eclectic. The
three guest rooms, all furnished
with king-sized beds, are spacious
and overlook the Ohio River. The
home is surrounded by 5 acres of
lush gardens complete with walk-
ing paths and blossoming land-
scape. $$

**Riverside Inn Bed and Break-
fast** (877-313-7298; river-
sideinnbb.com), 85 US 42E,
Warsaw. Directly on the Ohio
River, this magnificent home has
phenomenal views. Plus, it was
built in 1869 but received a $1 mil-
lion renovation just last year, so it
absolutely combines the best of the

past and the present. Let innkeepers Fred and Kay Fisk spoil you, or let them leave you completely alone. The choice is yours—but you will love your surroundings either way. $$

✳ Where to Eat

Welch's Riverside Restaurant (502-732-9118), 505 Main St., Carrollton. Open Mon.–Sat. 5–8, Sun. 6–3. This is Carrollton's only restaurant offering dining with a river view, so grab a good table and enjoy the Ohio River. This is the kind of restaurant that serves breakfast all day and has a little bit of everything on the menu. The dining room consists of several different building additions, and the decor has been created out of a mishmash of booths, old photos of customers, and hotel-going-out-of-business chairs. There is *not* a nonsmoking section, but the locals swear by this place. Sandwiches like country ham, BLTs, and grilled cheese are in just as much demand as the daily specials, which include meat with side dishes like stewed tomatoes and pinto beans. $

Cooper's Restaurant (502-732-4990), 1420 Gillock Ave., Carrollton. Open daily 10–10. Stop in if you're in a hurry. It's like a fast-food restaurant, without all the bells and whistles of a national chain. The menu features choices like burgers, fries, fried chicken, and cod sandwiches. Order at the counter and they'll bring it to your table. They call everyone "honey," so relax and enjoy it. $

✳ Selective Shopping

Cornerstone Floral and Gift (502-732-9912), 519 Highland Ave., Carrollton. With the heady collection of fresh flowers and scented candles, you'll want to just stand in the doorway and breathe, but do go in and look around. It's a cute shop with country and folk art home decor items, as well as hard-to-find collectibles from Boyd Bears and Willow Tree.

The Classy Boutique (502-732-0826), 103 Parkland Shopping Center, Carrollton. Open Mon.–Fri. 10–8, Sat. 10–5. This is a consignment shop and craft boutique, full of one-of-a-kind items, collectibles, and handmade art.

ANTIQUES/FLEA MARKETS

Betty's Family Collectables (no phone), 109 5th St., Carrollton. This store is packed with all kinds of antiques: large pieces of furniture, handmade model ships, Civil War memorabilia, and lots of old pictures, bottles, and knickknack items.

Traderbakers Flea Market & Antique Mall (502-732-4173), KY 227, Carrollton. A hodgepodge of antiques and flea-market merchandise makes this the perfect place to spend some time poking around.

OUTLET MALLS **Butler Outlet Mall** (502-732-6666), KY 227, Carrollton. Open daily. Shops include the VF (Vanity Fair) Outlet, Banister Shoes, Bon Worth, Dress Barn, Van Heusen, and

Wang's Jewelry. Get factory discounts on clothes and shoes for the whole family.

✳ Special Events

June: 🎭 🎣 ♿ **Carroll County Fair** (502-732-8005, 502-732-7036). This all-American County Fair is held on the Carroll County Fairgrounds each year. They have all the fixings of a traditional fair, like rides, games, demolition derbies, lots of 4-H exhibits, and plenty of food and music. You'll enjoy this good, old-fashioned county fair.

ELK CREEK

Located about an hour from Northern Kentucky, Louisville, and Lexington, in the tiny town of Owenton, you'll find Elk Creek. Home to a resort, winery, art gallery, and hunt club, this off-the-beaten-path locale makes for a perfect respite while traveling, but is actually a destination on its own.

Elk Creek Vineyards (502-484-0005; www.elkcreekvineyards.com), 150 KY 330. During the summer months, you can tour the fields where the grapes are growing, then come inside and learn about the ages-old process of winemaking. Wine-tasting packages are available. Summer also brings live entertainment, sometimes national acts, to the outdoor amphitheater here, so check the website to see if anyone interesting is appearing. This is Kentucky's largest winery, so if you can only stop at one, Elk Creek is your place.

Elk Creek Resort (502-484-4569, 502-484-0005; www.elkcreekvineyards .com), 150 KY 330. Don't let the rustic log cabin appearance fool you. This is a new resort, which actually feels elegant inside. The high beamed ceilings, giant fieldstone fireplace, and large, welcoming guest rooms are enchanting. Book one of the four queen-sized bedrooms, or bring a group and rent the whole house. $$

Elk Creek Hunt Club and Sporting Clays (502-484-4569; www.elkcreek huntclub.com), 1860 Georgetown Rd. Open year-round Tue.–Sun. 9 AM–dark. Throwing more than 1.5 million sporting clays per year, Elk Creek is one of the top-ranked clubs in the country. The three separate courses cover 2,500 acres of rolling woods and meadows of prime hunting land.

July: ✿ ✎ ⬥ **Bluegrass Festival** (502-732-8516). Held on the grounds of General Butler State Park, this festival offers a weekend of down-home bluegrass music, food, and fun.

September: ✿ ✎ ⬥ **Bands and BBQ at the Point** (502-732-7036). Held at the confluence of the Ohio and Kentucky Rivers, at Carrollton's Point Park. Offering two days full of music and BBQ.

October: ✿ ✎ ⬥ **Carroll County Tobacco Festival** (502-732-7036; carrolltontourism.com). Enjoy some small-town fun at downtown Carrollton's Courthouse Square. The festival always has an assortment of rides and games, flea market finds, arts and crafts, and plenty of food and fun.

Louisville and the Derby Region

5

BARDSTOWN, LEBANON,
AND SPRINGFIELD

ELIZABETHTOWN, HODGENVILLE,
RADCLIFF, AND FORT KNOX

THE GREATER LOUISVILLE AREA

SHELBYVILLE, LAGRANGE,
AND THE SURROUNDING AREA

Derby Region

INTRODUCTION:
THE DERBY REGION

Blend the urban sophistication of Louisville, Kentucky's largest city, with small, hometown-y places like Bardstown and LaGrange, and you come up with the Derby Region. Travelers can get a taste for thoroughbreds, bourbon, and tobacco farms while enjoying the artsy magnetism of a major metropolitan area.

The whole region claims ties to bourbon distilleries, and with good reason. As you drive through the area, you'll see the rickhouses, full of aging barrels of bourbon, that dot the countryside. This ages-old process is a well-respected craft, and Kentuckians claim bourbon as our own. Whiskey can be made anywhere, but bourbon comes from the Bluegrass State. If your trip brings you to this region, a distillery tour is a must. Even if you don't imbibe personally, the painstaking process is interesting to see. And if bourbon is your drink of choice, remember the saying "When in Rome . . ."

Just as Kentuckians are proud of their bourbon, we are equally proud that Abraham Lincoln was born here. In this Land of Lincoln you'll find his birthplace, as well as his boyhood home. There are also cabins, monuments, tributes, and ties to our 16th president throughout the state. Lincoln is quoted as saying that his earliest memories are of Kentucky, a fact that Kentuckians relish.

The Louisville metropolitan area is a perfect mix of historic and hip. The Bardstown Road and Frankfort Avenue corridors are an eclectic combination of cool shops and happening restaurants. You'll see bumper stickers and T-shirts proclaiming KEEP LOUISVILLE WEIRD, all that funky culture oozing out. The vibrant downtown has modern office buildings, a museum district, recreation-filled waterfront parks, and cute eateries and antiques shops.

You can't mention Louisville without a nod to the first Saturday in May, the biggest day in the region . . . yes, the Kentucky Derby. It's the day the world's eyes are on Louisville, at least for two minutes, as this year's top thoroughbreds break out of the starting gate and seem to fly around the historic oval track. On the top floor of the grandstand is Millionaires' Row, a Who's Who of horse people, corporate bigwigs, and the occasional Hollywood star. Down in the infield, you'll find rowdy college kids acting like they're on spring break, along with normal folks who couldn't get grandstand seats. And those lucky enough to have seats are a wonderful mix of fancy-hat-wearing women, families, and just about everyone in between. Besides the thrill of the bets and the race, Churchill Downs is a people-watcher's dream.

The Louisville region is the place to go for a colorful snapshot of Kentucky: an urban core surrounded by suburbs, which are infused with farms, lakes, and nature. Although betting on a horse race and drinking a shot of bourbon seems like a stereotypical thing to do, it's just a small part of all the offerings of Kentucky's Derby Region.

BARDSTOWN, LEBANON, AND SPRINGFIELD

H ead south, and slightly east, away from Louisville, and latch on to the Bourbon Trail, an imaginary path that connects all things bourbon to the rest of the state. Although Lebanon and Springfield aren't quite as saturated in the firewater as Bardstown, they are appealing communities with their own share of restaurants, shops, and historical attractions.

Breathe deep and if the wind is blowing in the right direction, you might get a whiff of the official drink of the Bluegrass State, bourbon. **Bardstown** is the Bourbon Capital of the World, and it is here that you will find several distilleries and even a museum dedicated to these fine spirits.

There's a lot to do in Bardstown besides drink bourbon, which is recommended but not mandatory. Kentucky's second oldest city, home to about 10,000 people, is also swimming in history. My Old Kentucky Home State Park, where Stephen Foster got the idea for the state song, a ballad that brings a tear to most Kentuckians' eyes, depicts life in the commonwealth during the era of plantations and hoop-skirted ladies. On the not-to-be-missed list is Old Talbotts Tavern, which has been serving weary travelers since the late 1700s. Join the ranks of famous historical figures who have stopped here for a good meal and a sampling of southern hospitality. There are several historical museums, streets lined with antebellum-style homes, and even a monastery where you can learn about the life of the Trappist monks who have dedicated their lives to serving God. To get the most out of your visit, it is advised that you tour first, drink bourbon second.

Situated right smack-dab in the middle of the state is **Lebanon**, the seat of Marion County. It was incorporated in 1815 and was once considered as the site of the state capital. Alas, Frankfort won out. That didn't stop Lebanon from growing, however, while still maintaining its small-town way of life and peaceful rural qualities. True rolling bluegrass, historic landmarks, and quaint villages like Gravel Switch make Lebanon a destination that is certainly worth the trip.

Lebanon served as a Union stronghold during the Civil War and was a major recruiting center for newly freed slaves. More than 2,000 men were recruited and joined the Union army here.

The notorious Confederate general John Hunt Morgan came through Lebanon with his Raiders on three occasions. In 1863, he burned down 20 of Lebanon's buildings in retribution for the death of his brother, but Lebanon carried on and today the downtown historic district is on the National Register of Historic Places. This city played many important roles during the Civil War, and you can follow several trails that transverse it. The tourist commission has maps guiding you to the actual sites, buildings, and travel routes that help tell the story.

Lebanon is home to about 6,000 residents, all very proud of their past and even more proud of the city they have become. The unique shops and restaurants will remind you that you really are in the heart of Kentucky.

Springfield, a small town of about 3,000, boasts a darling downtown with antiques shops and a couple of mom-and-pop restaurants right along main street.

GUIDANCE Bardstown/Nelson County Tourist Commission (502-348-4877, 800-638-4877; www.visitbardstown.com), 1 Court Square, Bardstown. Open weekdays 8–5, Sat. 9–5, and Sun. 11–3. This charming building, which is situated along a roundabout right in the center of town, is hard to miss. It has a tall steeple, complete with bell. Stop in for some excellent advice and tips. **Lebanon Tourist & Convention Commission** (270-692-0021; www.visitlebanonky.com.), 239 N. Spalding Ave., Suite 200, Lebanon. Located in an old school in the downtown Centre Square. You'll find friendly advice, maps, and brochures. Lebanon loves to have company.

GETTING THERE Bardstown and Lebanon are located less than an hour's drive from Louisville and Lexington, easily accessible from I-65 or the Bluegrass Parkway. The area is serviced by both the **Louisville International Airport** (502-368-6524; www.flylouisville.com), and **Lexington's Bluegrass Airport** (859-425-3114; www.bluegrassairport.com). Car rentals are available at the airport. **Greyhound** bus service is available in Louisville, Lexington, and Elizabethtown (www.greyhound.com).

GETTING AROUND Neither Bardstown nor Lebanon has public transportation, but both are easily navigated by car, with free parking everywhere.

The Heaven Hill Distilleries Trolley (800-638-4877; www.visit bardstown.com), 1 Courthouse Square, Bardstown. Tue.–Sat. 10, 1:30, 3;

Sun. noon, 1:30, 3. Tours last approximately an hour and 20 minutes. This is an easy way to see Bardstown if you are short on time. Hop aboard this bourbon-colored trolley for a narrated tour of downtown Bardstown as well as a tour of Heaven Hill's Bourbon Heritage Center. Get your ticket at the Bardstown visitors center. $7 per person.

MEDICAL EMERGENCY With a modern, state-of-the art facility, **Flaget Memorial Hospital** (502-350-5000; www.flaget.com), 4305 New Shepherd Villa Rd., Bardstown, is available for any medical need. If you need medical help in Lebanon, turn to **Spring View Hospital** (270-692-3161; www.springviewhospital.com), 320 Loretto Rd., Lebanon.

ALCOHOL Since Bardstown is the Bourbon Capital of the World, it only seems fitting that Nelson County is a wet county, where alcohol sales are permitted everywhere. Lebanon is located in Marion County, also wet. Springfield is sopping up alcohol in the moist county of Washington, where the county is dry but they allow alcohol sales in the downtown area and at wineries.

✸ To See

In Bardstown (unless otherwise noted)
✐ ⅄ **My Old Kentucky Home State Park** (502-348-3502; www.parks .ky.gov), 501 E. Stephen Foster Ave. Tours are given 9–5, June–Aug.; open daily 9–4:45 the rest of the year. Visit the Bardstown mansion, called Federal Hill, that was the inspiration for Stephen Foster's song "My Old

OLD KENTUCKY HOME

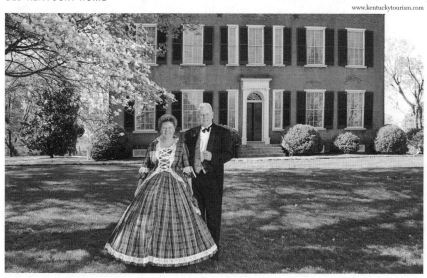

www.kentuckytourism.com

THE BOURBON DISTILLERIES

One of Kentucky's fastest-growing tourist activities is to travel around the state in pursuit of a visit to all of the bourbon distillers. As the maker of 95 percent of the entire world's supply of bourbon, Kentucky is proud to show you how it all happens. See for yourself how pure limestone water, an abundance of sweet corn, charred oak barrels, and an aging process that makes the most of the commonwealth's cold winters and hot summers can produce the silky lightning blend that the world knows as Kentucky bourbon.

The following distilleries are in the Bardstown area:

🏅 ✐ ♿ **Heaven Hill Distilleries Bourbon Heritage Center** (502-337-1000; www.bourbonheritagecenter.com), 1311 Gilkey Run Rd., Bardstown Open year round. Tue.–Sat. 10–5, Sun. noon–4; closed Sun. in Jan. and Feb. Learn all about the history of bourbon as well as the history of Heaven Hill in this state-of-the-art center. The tour includes entrance to a working rickhouse and a sample tasting. Free.

🏅 ✐ ♿ **Jim Beam's American Outpost** (502-543-9877; www.jimbeam.com), KY 245 in Clermont. Open year-round. Mon.–Sat. 9–4:30, Sun. 1–4. Closed

HEAVEN HILL DISTILLERIES BOURBON HERITAGE CENTER

www.kentuckytourism.com

www.kentuckytourism.com

MAKER'S MARK DISTILLERY

Sun. Nov.–Mar. Offers up-close views of the distilling process. The tour includes a short film about the Beam family and how their brand grew to become the world's top-selling bourbon. See the Jeremiah Beam home that traces the family's heritage back to 1775 and founder Jacob Beam's first barrel of "Old Jake Beam Sour Mash." Sample a selection of their small-batch bourbons. Free.

🦀 ✐ ♿ **Maker's Mark Distillery** (270-865-2099; www.makersmark.com), 3350 Burks Spring Rd., Loretto. Open year-round. Tours hourly on the half hour, Mon.–Sat. 10:30–3:30, Sun. 1:30–3:30. Closed Sun. in Jan. and Feb. Although it's slightly off the beaten path, getting there is half the fun. Enjoy the Kentucky countryside along the way and watch for Maker's Mark signs letting you know you're on the right track. Maker's Mark is the only distillery operating in America that has been designated a National Historic Landmark. The historic buildings on the grounds really tell a story of aging and traditions. If you purchase a bottle of Maker's while you're there, you get to dip it yourself in the famous red wax. Free.

Historic Tom Moore Distillery (502-348-3774; www.1792bourbon.com), 300 Barton Rd., Bardstown. Free tours 9:30 and 1:30, Mon.–Fri. Bardstown's newest tour comes from one of its oldest distilleries. Tom Moore founded the distillery in 1879 and produces 1792 Ridgemont Reserve, a premium brand named for the year Kentucky became a state. They also make Kentucky Tavern and Very Old Barton brands. Tom Moore founded the distillery in 1879 and produces 1792 Ridgemont Reserve, a premium brand named for the year Kentucky became a state. They also make Kentucky Tavern and Very Old Barton brands. They offer a two-hour tour covering all parts of the distilling process. Must be 21 and able to walk stairs. Reservations required one day in advance.

The following distilleries are near Frankfort:

🍴 ✐ ♿ **Buffalo Trace Distillery** (502-696-5926, 800-654-8471; www .buffalotrace.com), 1001 Wilkinson Blvd., Frankfort. Tours start on the hour, Mon.–Fri. 9–3, Sat. 10–2. This is the oldest continuously operating distillery in the United States. Tours include the fermenting room as well as the rickhouses where the bourbon barrels are stored while they age. Tastings and a free bourbon ball follow the tour. They also have a gift shop for souvenirs.

✐ ♿ **Woodford Reserve** (859-879-1812; www.woodfordreserve.com), 7855 McCracken Pike, Versailles. Tue.–Sat. 9–5, Sun. 12:30–4:30. Tour the distillery of Labrot & Graham, home of Woodford Reserve Bourbon. The limestone buildings reflect the traditions of the area and the distiller, where they still use the time-honored copper pot method to make their fine bourbon. $5 adults (18 and up); under 5 free.

Four Roses Distillery (502-839-3436; www.fourroses.us), 1224 Bonds Mill Rd., Lawrenceburg. The 45-minute tours start on the hour, Mon.–Sat. 9–3. Closed most of the summer and major holidays. This distillery, built in a Spanish Mission style, looks like it should be in Southern California instead of on the banks of the Salt River. The beautiful building, constructed in 1911, is on the National Register of Historic Places.

www.kentuckytourism.com

FOUR ROSES DISTILLERY

Guests over 21 can enjoy a small sample of this smooth and mellow bourbon.

Wild Turkey Distillery (502-839-4544) US 62E, Lawrenceburg. Offers free tours Mon.–Sat. at 9, 10:30, 12:30, and 2:30. Advance notice is requested for groups of more than 10. Closed all major holidays, the first full week of January, and the last two full weeks of July. View the process from grain delivery through barreling.

The newest distillery in Kentucky is in Lexington:

Town Branch Bourbon, 420 Cross St., Lexington. Tours available Mon.–Sat. 10 and on the hour and Sun. 1–4. The new kid on the block, opening in the fall of 2012, is part of Lyons Spirits, which produces Pearse Lyons Reserve, Town Branch, and Bluegrass Sundown.

Kentucky Home." The home, a former plantation, dates back to the late 1700s. The stately brick Georgian-style mansion has 13 rooms full of family heirlooms and authentic furniture. Your guided tour of the home will be led by a genuine southern belle complete with hoop skirt. $6 adults, $5 seniors, $4 ages 6–12; under 6 free.

Abbey of Gethsemani (502-549-4406; www.monks.org), 3642 Monks Rd., Trappist. The welcome center is open Mon.–Sat., 9–5. Home to America's oldest order of Cistercian monks. The order, which arrived in 1848 from France, settled into these hills of Central Kentucky and made it their home. Visitors can walk the grounds, attend a church service, and enjoy the peaceful chanting of the monks. Stop in to the welcome center to view a film on the order, go through the archives, and shop. The monks support themselves by selling cheese, fruitcake, and bourbon fudge, all of which are recommended purchases.

🍴 ♿ **Basilica of St. Joseph Proto-Cathedral** (502-348-3126; www.stjoe church.com), 310 W. Stephen Foster Ave. Weekdays 9–5, Sat. 9–3, Sun. 1–5. This cathedral was home to the first Catholic diocese west of the Allegheny Mountains. This church opened its doors in 1819, before advances in modern construction. Bricks were baked on the grounds, and solid tree trunks cut from the wilderness were lathed in a circular pattern to form the stately columns supporting the building. Stop in for a tour and see this architectural marvel.

🎣 ♿ **Civil War Museum/Old Bardstown Village/Natural History Museum/Women of the Civil War Museum** (502-349-0291; www .civil-war-museum.org), 310 E. Broadway St. Open Mar. 1–Dec. 15, daily 10–5. The state's largest collection of artifacts focusing on the war's Western Theater. It is the fourth largest Civil War museum in the United States. See genuine military items used during the war, including uniforms, weapons, and other personal belongings. Old Bardstown Village is an authentic village of nine log cabins from the county that date from 1776 to 1820. Each one has a different theme. Also on the property is the Wildlife/Natural History Museum, which features an extensive collection of North American animals in natural habitats, along with fossils and minerals from around the world. Don't miss the Women of the Civil War Museum while you are there. They have a fascinating collection of documents, photos, and original clothing of the women who stayed home to protect the property, nurse the injured soldiers, spy on the enemy, and, in some cases, disguise themselves as young men to fight with the soldiers. $6 adults, $5 ages 7–12; under 7 free. Packages are available if you are visiting more than one attraction.

Oscar Getz Museum of Whiskey History (502-348-2999; www.whiskey museum.com), 114 N. 5th St. Open Mon.–Fri. 10–5 (May–Oct.); Tue.–Fri. 10–4 (Nov.–Apr.); Sat. 10–4, Sun. noon–4 (year-round). If these walls could talk, oh the stories they could tell. This museum is housed in a building that was used as a hospital during the Civil War. But have a look around at all the whiskey-related memorabilia, including antique bottles, Abraham Lincoln's liquor license, and even a moonshine still. It's free to look around, but they would appreciate a donation.

Wickland (502-348-4877, 800-638-4877), 550 Bloomfield Rd. Open May–Labor Day, Fri.–Sun. 10–2. This Federal-style house, built between 1825 and 1828, features antique furniture of the period, and examples of fabulous Georgian architecture. Throughout history Wickland was home to three of Kentucky's governors and contains exhibits about each one, as well as local Civil War and African American history. Wickland is open for self-guided tours. $4 adults, $3 seniors, $2 ages 6–14; under 6 free.

In Lebanon (unless otherwise noted)
✔ **Historic Penn's Store** (859-332-7706, 859-332-7716; www.pennsstore .com), 257 Penn Store Rd., Gravel Switch. Open Fri. and Sat. 11–4, Sun. 1–4. Call to double-check if they are open. Visit this oldest country store in America, which has been run by the Penn family since 1845. This is not a restored landmark—it's authentic, and it looks about the way it did when they opened. The store still sells groceries, sandwiches, and dry goods as it always has, but features gifts and handmade crafts. Don't miss the annual Great Outhouse Blowout, a celebration in honor of the privy. Held the second week of September, the festival features drag races with outhouses on wheels, live music, and food.

Kentucky Cooperage (270-692-4518; independentstavecompany.com), 712 E. Main St., Lebanon, is one of the largest oak wine and bourbon barrel manufacturers in the country. This family business has been making barrels since 1912. Weekday tours at 9:30 and 1. No cameras and no open-toe shoes. Call for reservations.

Lebanon National Cemetery (270-692-3390), KY 208. Open daily sunrise–sunset. Closed federal holidays except Memorial Day and Veterans Day. Designated a national cemetery in 1867. The first to be buried here were the Union soldiers who perished in the Battle of Perryville. There were 865 total original interments, including 281 unknowns. The cemetery, which is on the National Register of Historic Places, still holds military funerals today.

Sisters of Loretto Motherhouse (270-865-5811; www.nerinxhs.org), 515 Nerinx Rd., Nerinx. The Sisters of Loretto Motherhouse is home to one of the oldest religious communities of women in the United States. The sisters put down roots in the area in 1824, dedicating their lives to God and the education of poor children of the area. Today you can visit this working farm situated in a parklike setting. It is the residence of active and retired members, but visitors are welcomed daily. Please call ahead.

Holy Cross Catholic Church (270-865-2521; www.sf-hc.org), 3540 N. St. Francis Rd., Loretto. Church open Sun. at 8 AM for Mass only. Vestibule open daily 24 hours a day. Glass doors allow for viewing into the church. This is the site of the first Catholic Mass and Catholic church west of the Allegheny Mountains. Originally it was a log cabin, completed in 1792. But the current building was completed in 1823, which almost makes it seem modern.

Scott's Ridge Lookout (270-692-0799). Get a map at the Lebanon Tourist Commission. On a clear day, visitors can see more than 100 square miles from this mountaintop. Enjoy the peaceful drive along the way.

✳ To Do

CARRIAGE TOURS Around the Town Carriage (502-348-0331; www .visitbardstown.com/tourism), 223 N. 3rd St., Bardstown. Open daily, 9 AM–10 PM. Enjoy this narrated tour through historic Bardstown aboard a carriage, buggy, or stagecoach.

FISHING Fagan Branch Reservoir (270-692-2491). Located in Calvary, just 10 minutes from Lebanon. A fisherman's dream, stocked with large- and smallmouth bass, bluegill, and catfish. They have a boat ramp, but only nonmotorized boats are allowed on the lake. And although you can't hunt there, you are sure to see plenty of wildlife.

Marion County Sportsman's Lake (800-858-1549), 328 S. Proctor Knott Ave., Lebanon. Created by the Kentucky Department of Fish and Wildlife, this old lake was drained and reconstructed to improve fish habitat, making the fish population swell. Hunting is permitted on the grounds; look for squirrel, deer, and waterfowl.

GOLF Kenny Rapier Golf Course at My Old Kentucky Home State Park (502-349-6542, 800-323-7803), 668 Loretto Rd., Bardstown. Golf in the shadow of My Old Kentucky Home on this par-71, 18-hole course. They have a pro shop with a snack bar, rental clubs, pull carts, and riding carts.

Rosewood Golf and Country Club (270-692-0506; rosewoodgolfcourse .com/clubhouse/restaurant), 520 Fairway Dr., Lebanon. Carved out of rolling pastureland, this 18-hole golf course has mature trees, streams, lakes, and wooded areas.

HISTORIC TRAILS Civil War Historical Trail (270-692-0021). The National Turnpike runs from Maysville to Nashville. The Lebanon portion is full of historical sites, including homes and buildings that date back to the 1800s. Get more information at the Lebanon Tourism office.

William Clark Quantrill Trail (270-337-3796, 270-692-6507), 202 W. Main St., Bradfordsville. Relive the route taken by one of the most vicious renegades of all time, William Clark Quantrill. During the Civil War, Quantrill, a Confederate soldier, took it upon himself to attack Union camps and pro-Union sympathizers in brutal and barbaric ways. By 1862 he had more than 100 followers, including outlaws Frank and Jesse James. He and his band of raiders wreaked havoc through the Central Kentucky area, burning buildings and murdering civilians. Follow the trail of devastation from New Market, near Lebanon, to Hustonville, near Danville.

John Hunt Morgan Trail (270-692-0021). The infamous Confederate Raider visited town in all three of his raids into Kentucky, and he once burned 20 buildings here in his effort to devastate the Union troops. The tour includes Myrtledene. Now a bed & breakfast, the site was once taken over by Morgan for his headquarters; here, in his grief over the death of his brother, he rode his horse right through the front door and started up the stairs.

✳ Green Space

Bernheim Arboretum and Research Forest (502-955-8512; www .bernheim.org), Clermont. Open dawn–dusk daily except Christmas and New Year's Day. Successful bourbon distiller Isaac W. Bernheim established Bernheim Arboretum and Research Forest in 1929 and gave it to the people of Kentucky as a gift and a thank-you for his business triumphs. The 14,000 lush acres are available for hiking, biking, geocaching, picnicking, or just relaxing in its beauty. Free admission weekdays. $5 per vehicle on weekends and holidays.

PARKS Graham Memorial Park (270-692-9358), 525 Graham Memorial Park Dr., Lebanon. Open Mon.–Fri. 5:30–8, Sun. 1–6. Walk the 3.5-mile blacktopped track; it's well lit, so you can walk at dusk. The park also offers tennis and basketball courts, baseball and football fields, and a disk golf course. They even have a model airplane runway. The adjacent **Lebanon Aquatic Center** has a heated indoor pool with lap lanes and an open area for splashing around.

Cecil L. Gorley Trail (270-692-2491), 120 S. Proctor Knott Ave., Lebanon. This 3.2-mile walking trail surrounds Fagan Branch Reservoir.

Lebanon Civil War Park (270-692-6272), corner of Spalding and Walnut, Lebanon. A depiction of Major General George H. Thomas, also known as the Rock of Chickamauga, who, in 1862, led Union forces from Lebanon to Mill Springs in the first major battle in Kentucky.

✳ Lodging

BED & BREAKFASTS

❧ The Jailer's Inn Bed & Breakfast (800-948-5551; www .jailersinn.com), 111 W. Stephen Foster Ave., Bardstown. Although this jail, which was in operation from 1797 until 1987, probably didn't seem all that inviting to the rowdy bunch of prisoners who stayed here, today it is a delightful mix of history and kitsch. Five of the now elegant rooms are in located in the former warden's home, and are rich in luxury and antiques. But if you go, try to book the Jail Cell Room, an actual cell complete with bunks and a waterbed. Breakfast is served outside in the courtyard when weather permits. $–$$

❧ ❀ The Historic Maple Hill Manor (800-886-7546; www .maplehillmanor.com), 2941 Perryville Rd., Springfield. This beautiful Greek Revival plantation home, built in the mid-1800s, is one of Kentucky's

THE HISTORIC MAPLE HILL MANOR
Maple Hill Manor

best-preserved antebellum homes. Surrounded by farmland, the home, with its 14-foot ceilings and massive 12-foot doors, also boasts a stunning cherry staircase that seems to be floating. The seven large guest rooms are full of antiques, some with fireplace and/or Jacuzzi tub. $$

Myrtledene Bed & Breakfast (270-692-2223; www.myrtledene .com), 370 N. Spalding Ave., Lebanon. This home has a wild history: It was once used by Confederate general John Hunt Morgan as headquarters during his raids on Lebanon. Luckily, Myrtledene is much calmer now. The historic house is just dripping in antiques. The four guest rooms all offer modern amenities, and the large yard with gardens, fishpond, and swings is a wonderful retreat. The Kentucky Heritage Committee has designated Myrtledene a Kentucky Landmark. $

Historic Eagle Hill Manor (502-252-7111; historiceaglehill manorbb.com), 118 Springfield Rd., Bloomfield. This southern Victorian mansion built in 1899 is on the National Register of Historic Places. From the wraparound porches, to the authentic woodwork, to the birds chirping in the distance, you are not going to want to leave. They have three bedrooms and a cottage, so you can find just the sleeping arrangements you need. $

❧ Rosemark Haven Inn (502-348-8218; www.rosemarkhaven .com), 714 N. 3rd St., Bardstown.

A magnificent spiral staircase draws you into this historic 1830s home. They offer seven cozy rooms in the mansion, all with king-sized bed, some with fireplace and whirlpool tub. They also have accommodations in the adjacent Federal House, which offers two bedrooms and a gathering room. The inn is a restaurant, too, so even though breakfast is included with the price of your room, you might want to arrive early and have dinner in their stately dining room. The menu is primarily Italian, but they have regional, bourbon-infused favorites as well. $$

RV PARK Country View RV Park (270-692-0408), 690 E. Main St., Lebanon. Located just three blocks from the heart of downtown Lebanon, so it's easy to find. It's a nice park, with about 14 sites that can accommodate big rigs as well as small tents. They have separate electric and water for each space. They have a well-stocked convenience store right on the property.

✳ Where to Eat

DINING OUT ⅄ **My Old Kentucky Dinner Train** (502-348-7300; www.kydinnertrain.com), 602 N. 3rd St., Bardstown. Call for schedule. When the conductor yells "All aboard" and you take your seat on the vintage-1940s train, your mouth may start to water. The luxurious accommodations include fine dining while you

enjoy the ever-changing scenery of Kentucky for the two- to three-hour excursion. In addition to the delicious meal, passengers are privy to the 1860s-era depot and the remarkable Jackson Hollow Trestle made completely of timber. By reservation only, and it fills up fast—call early. Lunch $$$, dinner $$$$

⅄ **Old Talbott Tavern** (800-482-8376; www.talbotts.com), 107 W. Stephen Foster Ave., Bardstown. Open for lunch and dinner every day. This famous tavern and inn, which dates back to 1797, was once a stagecoach stop in Kentucky's wilderness. The list of historical figures that have slept here looks like a Who's Who of Kentucky's past. The likes of Daniel Boone, a young Abe Lincoln, and George Rogers Clark have all sought shelter here. Today there is still a reminder of Jesse James, who, after possibly partaking of too much Bardstown bourbon, mistakenly thought there was an intruder in his guest room. So he whipped out his gun and shot right through the beautiful hand-painted murals that are still in the room today. Ask to see the bullet holes. Today Old Talbott Tavern offers five elegant guest rooms, but is better known for their restaurant. The menu features Kentucky comfort food, like hot brown and fried chicken, in a slightly upscale dining room with creaky wood floors. The tavern room is also the perfect place for a nightcap. Order a shot of bourbon; you're in the Bourbon Capital of the World, for goodness' sake. Rooms $, entrées $$–$$$

⅋ **The Stillhouse** (270-692-1550; stillhouserestaurantky.com), 202 W. Main St., Lebanon. Open for lunch Mon.–Fri. 11–2, and dinner Tue.–Sat. 4–midnight. Located in a historic building right in the heart of town. Bourbon-accented menu choices in a slightly upscale setting. Excellent lunch buffet. $$

⅋ **McB's Bar and Grill** (270-692-3970; mcbsbargrill.webs.com), 212 W. Main St., Lebanon. Serving breakfast, lunch, and dinner, but call ahead for hours. They are known for their scrumptious steaks. Don't miss the live music and karaoke on weekends. $$

⅋ **Mordecai's On Main** (859-336-3500) 105 W. Main St., Springfield. Open Tue.–Sat. 11 AM–midnight, Sunday for brunch. Housed in a historic building in the middle of town. The warm decor is on the upscale side and extremely inviting. Mordecai's menu runs the gamut from salads and homemade soups to frog legs, bourbon-marinated pork chops, and New York strip steak dinners. On Friday and Saturday nights, they feature a loaded buffet where you can sample all the menu favorites. $–$$

EATING OUT Los Mariachis (270-692-9746), 119 W. Main St., Springfield. Open every day 11–10. Authentic Mexican food prepared fresh each day. Los Mariachis' specials include fajitas, steak Mexicano, and enchilada rancheras. $

Mammy's Kitchen (502-350-1097), 114 N. 3rd St., Bardstown. Mon.–Tue. 6:30 AM–3 PM, Wed.–Sat. 6:30 AM–9:30 PM. This tiny diner offers down-home southern cooking served amid an assortment of signs and knickknacks that create a kind of homey decor. The food is just good and cheap, which is why you'll find a cast of regulars here every time you come in. Mammy's claims to have the "best grilled cheese in the world"—a pretty heady claim, so you might want to give it a try. Enjoy with a side of tater tots. $

Kreso's Family Restaurant & Mozart Café (502-348-9594; www.kresosweb.com), 218 N. 3rd St., Bardstown. Whether you want to catch a UK game or settle down for a sophisticated meal, Kreso has a place for you. Owners Dzevad and Merima Kreso, natives of Bosnia, have created a beautiful restaurant with a decor and menu that offer a taste of their homeland. Order anything from a burger and fries to goulash, Wiener schnitzel, or Chilean sea bass. Wide range of choices to match your mood. $

⅋ **Kurtz Restaurant** (502-348-8964), 418 E. Stephen Foster Ave., Bardstown. Serving lunch and dinner Tue.–Sat.; there's a fantastic Sunday brunch, too. A part of Bardstown since 1937, this family-owned restaurant sits just across the street from My Old Kentucky Home. The menu features stick-to-your-ribs entrées like casseroles, fried chicken, and homemade cobbler. For a "spirited" treat try the biscuit pudding, which is soaked in bourbon sauce. $

Cecconi's Restaurant (859-336-5136), 117 W. Main St., Springfield. Open for lunch and dinner. Right in the middle of town is this cute family-owned restaurant. They have thick burgers, juice Rueben sandwiches, and some tasty pies for dessert. The staff is friendly and attentive, atmosphere is very casual. $

SNACKS ✒ **Adams Pharmacy** (270-692-9115), 125 W. Main St., Lebanon. Open weekdays 8:30–4, Sat. 8:30–noon This is a real old-fashioned soda fountain where you can sit on a stool and enjoy a cherry Coke. Browse the store's cute gift items, too. $

Java Joint Café (www.thejava jointcafe.net), 126 N. 3rd St., Bardstown. Serving up mochas and more, Mon.–Sat. 7:30–5:30, and Sun. brunch 9:30–2:30. This warm and inviting café is the perfect place to stop to rejuvenate and enjoy a delicious soup, salad, quiche, or sandwich. Filled with funky Kentucky artwork and knickknacks; you'll want to stay awhile and relax. $

Hadorn's Bakery (502-348-4407), 118½ W. Flaget Ave., Bardstown. Although this full-service bakery offers cakes, pies, and breads, locals swear Hadorn's doughnuts are the best there is. Comparable to a famous southern doughnut

chain, these little beauties are best when warm, but delicious anytime you can get one. Go early because when they run out, they run out. $

✒ **Hurst Drug Store Soda Fountain** (502-348-9261), 102 N. 3rd St., Bardstown. Pull up a stool and order a chicken salad sandwich, a glass of sweet tea, and a hot fudge sundae for dessert, and they'll swear you must be a regular. Hurst's also has burgers, chili dogs, and salads, but get an old-fashioned ice cream, like a brown cow—also known as a root beer float—a butterscotch milk shake, or a big ol' banana split. $

✳ **Entertainment**

✒ ♿ **The Stephen Foster Musical** (502-348-5971, 800-626-1563; www.stephenfoster.com), My Old Kentucky Home State Park, 501 E. Stephen Foster Ave., Bardstown. Productions during summer months only. Enjoy live theater under the stars, in this charming amphitheater. This musical, which is perfect for all ages, has been continuously running for more than 50 years. It focuses on the life of Stephen Foster, composer of famous American tunes like "Oh! Susanna," "Camptown Races," and "Jeannie with the Light Brown Hair." But it was the song "My Old Kentucky Home" that forever endeared him to the commonwealth, as this became the state song. Sing along to the tunes everyone knows by heart and enjoy the dazzling costumes that reflect life in the 1850s.

✳ Selective Shopping

In Bardstown

Bardstown Booksellers (502-348-1256), 129 N. 3rd St. This shop is simply packed with books, magazines, and music. It is so inviting, you just want to curl up with a book and stay all afternoon. They have a wide variety of Kentucky gifts, too.

Mary's Art and Antiques (502-350-9009; www.atmarys.com), 214 N. 3rd St. Seems like everything in this store is happy and fun. You will find bright-colored home decor items, eclectic accessories, as well as art, antiques, and floral arrangements.

Bardstown Art Gallery (502-348-6488), 214 W. Stephen Foster Ave. In business since 1971, Bardstown Art Gallery is the oldest art gallery in the town. They represent a whole line of artists and mediums, so pay them a visit to see the variety. Hours vary, but the owners live in the building, so if you give them a call, they'll usually open up for you.

Mackin Antique Mall (502-348-9070), 213 W. Stephen Foster Ave. Giant selection of antiques, furniture, and gifts, spread out over two floors.

In Lebanon

Goodin View Farm Country Store (270-692-0165), 569 KY 208. Get a taste of the country, where they offer fresh produce and hard-to-find farm-raised shrimp, catfish, and hybrid striped bass. They also have an enormous selection of baskets and candy. Stop by in fall and try to conquer the giant corn maze shaped like Kentucky.

✳ Special Events

January: ♣ ✎ ✦ **Lebanon's Blue Grass Music Kick Off** (270-692-0021). Bands from across Kentucky compete in the Battle of the Bluegrass Bands. Workshops for banjo, fiddle, dobro, mandolin, vocals, and guitar are held, and there are areas designated just for jamming.

July: ♣ ✎ ✦ **Jets Over Kentucky**. Lebanon's annual competition among and demonstrations of remote-controlled airplanes are really a sight to see. Cast your eyes to the sky and watch these daredevils. It is called the thoroughbred of radio-controlled jet shows.

September: ♣ ✎ ✦ **Marion County Country Ham Days** (270-692-9594). Just like a good old-fashioned country fair, Ham Days features a parade, a 5K run, a car and truck show, a juried arts and crafts show, games for adults and kids, and live entertainment.

✦ **Bardstown's Kentucky Bourbon Festival** (www.kybourbon festival.com). Paying homage to the spirit as well as the fine distillers who helped Bardstown become the Bourbon Capital of the World, this annual five-day event features fun for all ages. Hotels in the area fill up months in advance, so if you will be in attendance, make your reservations early.

ELIZABETHTOWN, HODGENVILLE, RADCLIFF, AND FORT KNOX

South of Louisville and heading into Western Kentucky, visitors will find themselves in the communities of Elizabethtown, Hodgenville, Radcliff, and Fort Knox.

In the Elizabethtown area, you can immerse yourself in Abraham Lincoln history by visiting his birthplace and boyhood home. Although Lincoln spent most of his life in Illinois, he still loved Kentucky and had many ties to the commonwealth. During the Civil War, he was quoted as saying, "I hope to have God on my side, but I must have Kentucky."

Just up US 31W, you will find the military base Fort Knox and its suburb, Radcliff. Fort Knox is famous as the home of the US Bullion Depository, the keeper of all the gold. They don't give tours, ever. So set your sights on touring the fort and the community surrounding it and keep all those visions of gold in your dreams.

With pioneers in the area as early as 1779, settlement consisted of small forts used as stockades for defense against Native Americans. One of these early settlers was Andrew Hynes, who in 1797 had his 30 acres of land surveyed and marked off into lots and streets to establish **Elizabethtown**, which he named in honor of his wife.

E-town, as it's known to locals, is located 35 miles south of Louisville on I-65 at the crossroads of the Western Kentucky Parkway and the Bluegrass Parkway. Because Elizabethtown is so conveniently and centrally located, tourists do not have to travel far to see attractions in surrounding cities. The warm, country feel of the town welcomes you back after a day of easy sightseeing.

But Elizabethtown is a star in its own right. In 2005, Hollywood came calling, filming a major motion picture titled *Elizabethtown* right in the downtown area. The movie, directed by Cameron Crowe and starring

Orlando Bloom and Kirsten Dunst, makes E-town look as darling on film as it does in person.

Learn about Elizabethtown by taking the Downtown Walking Tour, which is available in summer months. Follow the map and you may just bump into some historical figures (or costumed actors portraying them) who are scattered about town, full of stories about the buildings and the people who lived and worked there.

A perfect marriage of nature and history is available at Freeman Lake Park. You can hike, fish, canoe, and picnic on the picture-perfect grounds, as well as take in Lincoln-era log cabins and buildings right in the park.

Come to Elizabethtown to relax and wind down. You'll feel like a local as soon as you arrive.

A true military community, the **Radcliff and Fort Knox** area comprises Fort Knox, Fort Duffield (which overlooks the town of West Point), and Radcliff.

Dating back to the Civil War, both Fort Knox and Fort Duffield saw action as the Union and Confederate armies occupied the area. Around the time of World War I, the US military established a field artillery training center, which was named for Major General Henry Knox, chief of artillery for the Continental army during the American Revolution and later the nation's first secretary of war.

In the 1930s Fort Knox became known for the mechanized cavalry—otherwise known as the use of tanks in battle. One of the first American soldiers to distinguish himself in this revolutionary form of warfare was a 33-year-old cavalry captain named George S. Patton.

In his honor, the General George Patton Museum of Leadership is located on Fort Knox. The museum contains personal artifacts of the fine general, and exhibits related military leadership.

Fort Knox is also home to the US Bullion Depository. The Gold Vault opened in January 1937. Inside you would find $100 billion worth of gold bullion, if you could go in. Access is so restricted a presidential order is required to get in. In fact, only two presidents have ever seen the place: Franklin Roosevelt and Harry S. Truman.

During World War II, Fort Knox trained thousands of new recruits and served as home base to military families. Today it encompasses 109,000 acres in three Kentucky counties. This respected military base has a population of over 23,000 soldiers, family members, and civilians.

As the army expanded the size of Fort Knox in the 1930s and '40s, by purchasing surrounding land, residents who were displaced moved to Radcliff. This small burg became home to civilians who worked on the base and a second home to thousands of soldiers who spent their leisure hours at the USO there.

Today Radcliff is a city of approximately 22,000 citizens. They play host to hundreds of military reunions every year and pride themselves on their military roots. Several festivals are held annually as a tribute to our men and women in service.

It's not all military, all the time, though. Kentucky's terrain has given way to biking, hiking, and walking trails as well as historical landmarks to round out your visit.

GUIDANCE **Elizabethtown Tourism & Convention Bureau** (270-765-2175, 800-437-0092; www.touretown.com), 1030 N. Mulberry St., Elizabethtown. The office is open Mon.–Fri. 8–6, Sat. 10–2, Apr.–Sept.; Mon.–Fri. 8–5 Oct.–Mar. Visitors looking for guidance should look for the giant mulberry-colored arch on the top of this building, which sits right on Mulberry Street. The staff just can't wait to share E-town with you. In addition to maps and brochures, there is also a small gift shop full of Kentucky crafts and souvenirs. **Radcliff/Fort Knox Tourism & Convention Commission** (270-352-1204, 800-334-7540; www.radclifftourism.com), 562 A1 N. Dixie, Radcliff. Open weekdays 8:30–4:30. Look for this little tourism office, right downtown, right next to Stithton Baptist Church and directly across the street from a BP station. It's full of information on both local and regional attractions, and they even have free postcards of the area.

GETTING THERE Elizabethtown is located 35 miles south of Louisville, just off I-65 at the crossroads of the Western Kentucky Parkway and the Bluegrass Parkway. The **Louisville International Airport** (502-368-6524; www.flylouisville .com) is the closest airport; it's located at the intersection of I-65 and I-264. Car rentals are available at the airport. **Greyhound Bus** also serves Elizabethtown and Radcliff (270-765-4777; www .greyhound.com). The station is located at 2022 N. Mulberry St. in E-town.

GETTING AROUND Elizabethtown is easy to navigate by car. Off-street parking is available everywhere. You'll need a car to get around the Radcliff/Fort Knox area, but there is plenty of parking available.

ELIZABETHTOWN VISITORS CENTER
Deborah Kohl Kremer

MEDICAL EMERGENCY Hardin Memorial Hospital (270-737-1212; www.hmh.net), 913 N. Dixie Ave., Elizabethtown. A 300-bed hospital providing care to citizens in Hardin and 10 surrounding counties. Ireland Army Hospital is located on Fort Knox but is only open to the military. There is also a **Carefirst Urgent Care Center** (270-351-1150) on Rogersville Rd. in Radcliff.

ALCOHOL Elizabethtown is the seat of Hardin County, a moist county. This means that alcohol sales are prohibited in the county, but they allow by-the-drink sales in E-town and Radcliff restaurants that seat more than 100 people.

✳ To See

Fort Knox Bullion Depository, Bullion Blvd. and Gold Vault Rd. Housing most of the U.S. gold reserves, the Fort Knox Bullion Depository is locked up tight and you're not invited. You can drive by, but this place is doesn't let anybody in. The building was completed in 1936 and is made of concrete, granite, and reinforced steel. The vault door alone weighs more than 20 tons. This place is so secure, during World War II, it housed the English crown jewels and the Magna Carta for safekeeping. It holds about 4,603 tons of gold, mostly in the form of gold bricks. Drive by and dream about the riches inside.

The Brown-Pusey House (270-765-2515; brownpuseyhouse.org), 128 N. Main St., Elizabethtown. Open Tue.–Sat. 10–4. Tour the Georgian mansion, which was built in 1825, and view artifacts and memorabilia from the residents' history. Free.

Black History Gallery (270-769-5204), 602 Gallery Place, Elizabethtown. Open weekends noon–5, or call for an appointment. A museum dedicated to the historical and cultural heritage of black Americans. Displays include many untold stories, pictures, articles, biographies, and prints from magazines. Free.

The Cannonball (800-437-0092), corner of Public Square and W. Dixie Ave., Elizabethtown. Not a lot to see, but there is an actual cannonball embedded in the side of a building. During the Civil War, 3,900 Confederates attacked 652 members of the Union army right in downtown E-town. Many cannonballs struck homes and businesses nearby. This one had been stuck in the side of the Depp Building and was retrieved from the rubble when that building burned down in 1887. When the current building was under construction, the ball was placed back in the wall, close to its original location.

✐ Kentucky Railway Museum (502-549-5470, 800-272-0152; www.ky rail.org), 136 S. Main St., New Haven. Mon.–Sat. 10–5, Sun. noon–5.

Train rides Tue.–Fri. at 2, Sat. 11 and 2, Sun. 1 and 3:30. Closed Sun. and Mon. in Jan.–Mar. Enjoy a 22-mile ride through the historic Rolling Fork River Valley on a restored passenger train. The museum houses all kinds of railroad memorabilia and equipment, a 3,000-square-foot model train display, and a museum of railroad memorabilia. Museum: $5 adults and $2 ages 2–12; if you purchase a train ride, the museum admission is included. Train rides: $15 adults, $10 ages 2–12; under 2 free.

Hardin County History Museum (270-763-8338; www.hardinkyhistory .org), 201 W. Dixie Ave., Elizabethtown. Guided tours by appointment only. The history of Hardin County from its early Indian inhabitants to modern times is portrayed in easy-to-follow exhibits.

✐ & **Swope's Cars of Yesteryear Museum** (270-765-2181; www.swope museum.com), 1100 N. Dixie Ave., Elizabethtown. Open Mon.–Sat. 10–5. See a 1910 Brush Runabout, a 1928 Packard Sedan, and about 50 other antique and classic cars. Free.

🏛 ✐ & **Abraham Lincoln Birthplace National Historic Site** (502-358-3137), Hodgenville. Open daily. An early-19th-century cabin is preserved in a memorial building in honor of our 16th president's humble beginnings. It is on 116 acres of the original Sinking Springs Farm and includes a visitors center with lots of information about Honest Abe. Free.

🏛 ✐ & **Abraham Lincoln Boyhood Home** (270-358-3137; www.nps .gov), US 31E, Hodgenville. Open daily Apr.–Oct. Visit this re-created cabin on the land where the Lincolns lived from the time Abe was two until about he was about eight years old. Free.

Fort Duffield (502-922-4574). Located at US 31W (Dixie Hwy.) at Salt River Dr. in West Point. Open dawn to dusk daily. General William Tecumseh Sherman ordered this earthen fortification built in 1861 to protect the Union supply route to Louisville. It still stands, and is probably Kentucky's best-preserved blockade, now listed on the National Register of Historic Places. Take a short hike from the parking lot to see the actual fort. Although reenactments are held on Memorial Day weekend, the park is open year-round. They have 10 miles of mountain bike and hiking trails, a nice garden area, and Memorial Hill Cemetery, which is a tribute to the 61 soldiers who died building the fort.

🏛 ✐ & **General George Patton Museum of Leadership** (502-624-3812; www.generalpatton.org), 4554 Fayette Ave., Fort Knox. Open 9–4:30; holidays and weekends, 10–5. Closed Thanksgiving, Dec. 24 and 25, and Dec. 31 and Jan. 1. Named for the infamous general George S. Patton Jr., who led American troops through World War II. This museum exhibits personal artifacts as well as memorabilia and vehicles relating to great leaders of the U.S. Army. Free.

www.kentuckytourism.com

PATTON MUSEUM

✳ To Do

DRIVING TOUR Self-Guided Elizabethtown Driving Tour (270-765-2175; www.touretown.com), See historic homes, churches and even the Elizabethtown City cemetery where there is a panoramic view of the city, without leaving your car.

GOLF American Legion Park (270-765-4030), 801 N. Miles St., Elizabethtown. A 9-hole, par-3 public golf course with tennis courts, playground, and clubhouse.

Pine Valley Golf Resort (270-737-8300, 800-844-1904; www.pinevalley golfandresort.com), 850 Pine Valley Dr., Elizabethtown. This 18-hole, par-4 golf course offers a driving range, two bars, a pro shop, and a restaurant. They also have several two-bedroom condos, making it a perfect place for a golf getaway weekend.

Lindsey Golf Course (502-624-4218, 502-943-9929 tee times; www .knoxmwr.com/Rec/golf.asp), 4024 Bullion Blvd., Fort Knox. This challenging course features a par-5 18th hole—something to keep in mind as you wind your way through the fairways. Open daily.

SHOOTING RANGE **Knob Creek Gun Range** (502-922-4457; www
.machinegunshoot.com), 690 Ritchey Lane, West Point. Offers recreational shooting, as well as full line of guns and gun-related supplies and
equipment.

TRAILS **Bridges to the Past** (270-352-1204), at the road junction of the
old L&N Turnpike and old Dixie Hwy. Pick up a brochure and map at the
visitors center. Travel along the original route of the L&N Turnpike on
this walking tour, which takes about an hour. Cross stone bridges and
enjoy the babbling brooks as you wander through a historic wooded area.
You can even pretend to travel back in time, as you won't see any electric
lines or signs of progress along the way. A peaceful way to commune with
nature.

Tioga Falls Hiking Trail (270-352-1204), 8 miles north of Fort Knox off
US 31W. Open at designated times, as it crosses into Fort Knox and is
sometimes used for training. But when it is open to the public, it's worth
your time to try out this trail. Allow yourself about two hours so you can
take your time and see the 33 points of interest, like the hand-laid stone
walls, fossil formations, and 130-foot Tioga Waterfall. Parts of this trail are
nearly 200 years old; while it's very well preserved, it is rugged, and in
some places the terrain is rough. Make sure all your hikers are up to it.

WALKS **Elizabethtown Greenbelt** (270-765-6121). More than 18 miles
of walking trails surrounding Freeman Lake, Buffalo Lake, and Fisherman's Lake make up this scenic walk. Maps are available at the Elizabethtown Tourism Bureau.

Self-Guided Downtown Elizabethtown Walking Tour (270-765-6121).
Enjoy a leisurely stroll past 25 historic sites and buildings varying in age
and architectural style. Pick up your map at the tourism bureau.

✳ Green Space

Elizabethtown Nature Park (270-765-6121), 1916 Ring Rd. E., Elizabethtown. Created as a passive park, so the only action you will find is
nature at her finest. Visitors can enjoy the 104 acres of gently rolling terrain and beauty.

Saunders Spring Nature Preserve (270-351-1875), located between US
31W and Fort Knox (entrance off N. Wilson Rd.). Open dawn–dusk year-
round. This nature preserve offers scenic hiking trails through 26 forested
acres that show examples of the many sinkholes, caves, and natural springs
that are abundant in this region. They also have a handicapped-accessible
trail that winds through the woods and past a few waterfalls.

A TASTE OF LOCAL HISTORY

A side trip to **Freeman Lake Park** (270-769-3916), 140 Freeman Lake Park Rd., Elizabethtown, will whet your appetite with authentic log cabins and a state-of-the-art recreation area. This giant lake could be the attraction on its own, but tucked over on the side of the lake are three historic buildings that have ties to the area. The park is open year-round, but the historic buildings are only open June 1–Oct. 1, Tue.–Sun. 10–5.

Sarah Bush Johnston Lincoln Cabin. This tiny, one-room log cabin is a replica of the 1819 home of Sarah Bush Johnston Lincoln, before she became the second wife of Thomas Lincoln and stepmother to Abraham Lincoln.

One Room Schoolhouse. See the schoolhouse that opened in 1892 and taught local children for 50 years. The white frame building housed about 100 children when it opened, all in one room.

The Lincoln Heritage House. This is the former home of Hardin County resident Thomas Lincoln, father of our 16th president, Abraham. Made up of two log cabins, one built in 1789 and a second, larger home built in

SARAH BUSH JOHNSTON LINCOLN CABIN

Deborah Kohl Kremer

Deborah Kohl Kremer

ONE ROOM SCHOOLHOUSE

1805. The second cabin is the home that Thomas and Nancy Lincoln lived in when Abe's sister Sarah was born in 1807. See actual woodwork, mantels, and staircases built by the elder Lincoln.

Bring a picnic lunch and spend some time at this huge park. They have 7 miles of walking trails, an 18-hole disk golf course, volleyball courts, paddle boats, playgrounds, a 170-acre lake, and 93 acres of nature. It's a nice way to spend an afternoon.

LINCOLN HERITAGE HOUSE

Deborah Kohl Kremer

✴ Lodging

✱ & **Homegate Inn** (270-769-1301), 905 N. Mulberry St., Elizabethtown. Similar to big chain motels, this 36-room, locally owned inn is less expensive than competitors and offers warm, friendly service. Complimentary continental breakfast available daily. $

✱ & **Gold Vault Inn** (800-266-2104; www.goldvaultinn.net), 1225 N. Dixie Blvd., Radcliff. Radcliff's largest hotel features 94 rooms, a continental breakfast, and an indoor pool. Special rates available for military personnel. $

✱ ✻ & **Fort Knox Inn** (270-351-3199, 800-852-6164; www.fortknox inn.com), 1400 Dixie Blvd., Radcliff. Located about a mile from Fort Knox, this clean, 40-room hotel is perfect for extended stays—they offer free guest laundry, as well as microwaves and refrigerators in the rooms. $

✱ & **Radcliff Inn** (270-351-8211, 800-421-2030; www.radcliffinn .com), 438 S. Dixie Blvd., Radcliff. Specializing in serving both military and civilians, they have 83 rooms, some with Jacuzzi tub. They also have a nice outdoor pool, fitness center, and game room. $

✴ Where to Eat

DINING OUT ♈ **Stone Hearth** (270-765-4898; www.stonehearth etown.com), 1001 N. Mulberry, Elizabethtown. Lunch Sun.–Fri. 11–2, dinner Mon.–Sat. 5–9. For an elegant gourmet meal or just a light lunch, locals have been going to Stone Hearth for more than 30 years. Dinner menu ranges from Mediterranean shrimp, to crab-crusted salmon, to slow-roasted prime rib. Save room for the house specialty pie, which tastes like a thick, warm chocolate chip pecan cookie, piled high with whipped cream. $$–$$$

Back Home Restaurant (270-769-2800; www.backhome restaurant.com), 251 W. Dixie, Elizabethtown. Sun.–Mon. 11–3, Tue.–Sat. 11–9. You'll feel like you are back home when you order a pimiento cheese sandwich, fried green tomatoes, or a chicken-fried chicken dinner. Try these country meals and enjoy the comforts of this historic home, which dates back to 1872. $$

Uncle Franks German Food (270-352-4444), 821 N. Dixie Blvd., Radcliff. Open weekdays 11–2 and 5–9, Sat. noon–9:30. Closed Sun. The menu is so authentic, Uncle Franks has become a favorite for members of the military who have been stationed in Germany. Regulars order the Jaegerschnitzel, a breaded pork chop with mushroom gravy, that tastes like it was prepared in Munich. $$

EATING OUT Cobbler Café (270-982-2233; www.cobblers cafe.com), 125 E. Dixie Ave., Elizabethtown. Weekdays 7–3:30, Sat. 10–2. Housed in a historic downtown building that was once home to a shoe repair shop, this cute café now serves pastries, wraps, and sandwiches. There's a warm, inviting interior—and nice patio dining is available, too. $

Laha's Red Castle Hamburgers (270- 358-9201), 21 Lincoln Square, Hodgenville. Open 9–4 every day but Sunday. This restaurant's history spans several generations of the LaHa family (pronounced *Lay-Hay*). And even though they have a limited menu of burgers and cheeseburgers, who really cares? That is all anyone wants to order anyway. These burgers are freshly made and fried up on a bed of onions. The delicious smell wafts through Hodgenville, reminding you where to go for lunch. Sit at the counter so you can get a feel for the place. $

Ÿ **Back Stage Café** (270-234-1686), 109 N. Mulberry, Elizabethtown. Tue.–Thu. 11–4, Fri. 11–11, Sat. 11–4. Stop in for deli-style lunches during the week and local music on the weekends. Enjoy the very artsy atmosphere. $

Asian Buffet of Golden House (270-351-6888), 1225 N. Dixie Blvd., Radcliff. Open for lunch and dinner every day. With a 75-item buffet, you know you will find something you like. Locals swear by this place for great Asian specialties. $

Ruthie's Lincoln Freeze (270-358-4987), 700 S Lincoln Blvd., Hodgenville. In a town like Hodgenville, it's surprising that everything doesn't have Lincoln in its name. But Ruthie's is one of the few that does and it uses it well. It's a hometown favorite, serving up home-cooked lunch and dinner with ice cream for dessert. Nothing fancy or overrated, just a locals' diner where you can get a good basic meal. $

Los Nopales Mexican Restaurant (270 -352-2230), 440 S. Dixie Blvd., Radcliff. Mon.–Thu. 11–10, Fri. 11–10:30, Sat. noon–10:30, Sun. noon–9:30. Tex-Mex fare using authentic Mexican recipes. Try the fajitas, quesadillas, and popular combo meals. $

✳ Entertainment

Historic State Theatre Complex (270-234-8258; www.historic statetheater.org), 209 W. Dixie Ave., Elizabethtown. An art-deco-inspired movie theater that opened in 1942 and kept Elizabethtown entertained for 40 years, this regal facility has been restored and completely resurrected. Patrons can now enjoy live music, art displays, and drama and comedy shows. Check the website for a list of performances.

Hardin County Playhouse (www .hardincountyplayhouse.com). Located in the Historic State Theatre's Plum Alley (see above), this community theater stages an ambitious lineup of productions that has included *The Wizard of Oz*, *Steel Magnolias*, *A USO Christmas*, and other shows. Shows change seasonally, so check the website to see what's showing.

Hardin County Schools Performing Arts Center (www.the
pac.net), W. A. Jenkins Rd., Elizabethtown. Presenting a variety
of programming, including live
theater, gallery showings, and
curriculum-based teaching units
tied to the arts. The center was
designed and is operated by theater professionals but owned by
the public school system. Check
the website for featured shows.

✳ Selective Shopping

Cottage Charm (270-765-7084;
www.cottagecharm.biz), 232 W.
Dixie Ave., Elizabethtown. With
a wide variety of Vera Bradley
purses, Waterford crystal, and
everything in between, you'll find
something for everyone on your
gift list here.

The Red Brick Cottage (270-
351-1224; www.theredbrick
cottage.com), 776 S. Dixie Blvd.,
Radcliff. A nice little shop specializing in Kentucky gift baskets.
You'll also find a wonderful selection of items like candles, soaps,
purses, and gourmet food items.

The US Cavalry Store (800-777-
7172; www.uscav.com), 2855
Centennial Ave., Radcliff. Not an
army surplus store, but a store that
focuses on outfitting individual soldiers. Complete line of military,
law enforcement, and homeland
security equipment.

**Blueball Mountain Spindle
and Needlework Shop** (270-
360-9959; blueballmountain
spindleandneedleworks.com), 114

W. Dixie Ave., Elizabethtown.
This cute shop is absolute heaven
for knitters, crocheters, felters,
spinners, and weavers. They have
everything crafty and artsy folks
need to get down to business.

ANTIQUES Buried Treasurer
(270-982-4404), 516 N. Main St.,
Elizabethtown. Open Wed.–Sat.
10–4. They have a large selection
of all kinds of antiques.

Goldnamers (270-766-1994), 210
N. Main St., Elizabethtown. Open
weekdays by chance and appointment. Antiques and other treasures are available in this cute
house in the heart of E-town.

Touch of the Past (270-765-
2579), 9 Houchens Plaza on
Sycamore St., Elizabethtown.
Open Wed.–Sat. 11–4. They carry
all kinds of antiques, collectibles,
jewelry, and quilts. Stop in this
cute shop to see what's new.

**Somewhere in Time Antique
Mall** (270-352-0055), 332 N.
Dixie Blvd., Radcliff. Spend an
afternoon browsing around the
thousands of antiques and collectibles.

SHOPPING DISTRICT
Historic Glendale (270-369-
6188; www.historicglendale.com).
Located about 10 miles south of
Elizabethtown is another lovely
little burg to visit. Glendale is a
true old-fashioned railroad country town. It boasts more than a
dozen antiques and gift shops and
unique dining all within two

blocks. Most notable is the **Whistle Stop Restaurant** (270-369-8586), where you will find scrumptious fried green tomatoes, homemade soups, and their legendary fried corn bread. If you need a place to stay, the **Petticoat Junction Bed & Breakfast** (270-369-8604) is just a darling B&B, drenched in antiques but with all the modern amenities that you need.

✳ Special Events
In Radcliff
May: 🏵 ✎ ⴟ **Hooray for Heroes!** (www.radcliffchamber.org). This festival shows appreciation for members of the military, both past and present. It features live band music, games for children, clowns, and prizes.

🏵 ✎ ⴟ **Civil War Days at Fort Duffield**. This annual event held on Memorial Day weekend pays homage to those who fought in the Civil War. Union and Confederate reenactors make you feel like you were there.

September: 🏵 ✎ ⴟ **Golden Armor Festival**. This weeklong event pays tribute to the Armored Force and Fort Knox personnel with a parade through town. They also have country-fair-type offerings like horseshoe-pitching contests, food competitions, and reunions.

In Elizabethtown
Wednesday before Thanksgiving–January 1: 🏵 ✎ ⴟ **Christmas in the Park** (270-737-6568), Freeman Lake Park. Open 6–11 PM. With over a million lights, on more than 100 holiday displays, spread out over a mile of illuminated park roads, you'll be in the holiday spirit before you leave. Free.

THE GREATER LOUISVILLE AREA

Souvenir T-shirts are available all around the city, proclaiming:

LOO EY VILLE
LOO A VUL
LOU IS VIL
LUH VUL

Making you wonder, how many ways can you say Louisville? Apparently several, and after spending some time there, hearing the different dialects, you'll understand the shirts. So choose your favorite pronunciation, they all work, but use *lou-is-vil* if you want everyone to know you are from out of town.

Kentucky's largest city, home to more than a million people in the metro area, was founded in 1778 by George Rogers Clark. He promptly named it in honor of King Louis XVI of France who was, at that time, sending troops to help American hold back the British during the Revolutionary War.

This river city credits its development to the Falls of the Ohio, a 2-mile stretch of rapids and shallow water that made boat navigation nearly impossible. It was the only such obstruction between Pennsylvania and the mighty Mississippi. On the Ohio River, boaters had to remove their loads onto the shore and pull the vessel carefully through the rough stretch of water, then load back up on the other side. All this loading and unloading created a powerful thirst, so taverns, inns, and restaurants started springing up to meet the demand. Next thing you know, Louisville was a bona fide city. The Falls of the Ohio was a legitimate landmark, noted in the writings of Clark, Daniel Boone, and Native Americans who used it as a reference point. With the completion of a canal system, and later locks and dams, the falls are no longer a problem for river travelers.

Louisville offers some swanky lodging options. From the glam of downtown's Seelbach or Brown Hotel to the opulent 100-year-old mansions-turned-B&Bs that line the neighborhood of Old Louisville, you will be

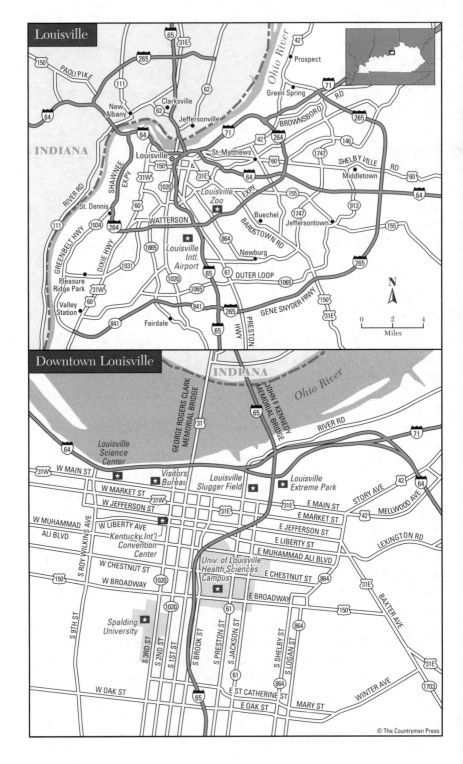

Louisville

Downtown Louisville

© The Countryman Press

living the high life. If you will be staying during Derby Week, plan ahead. Way ahead. With so many people descending on the city, the rooms fill up fast. They are not impossible to get, but the closer it gets to Derby Week, the farther out of town you will be staying.

As for dining, Louisville, quite an artsy city, has a wide array of, well, artsy restaurants. You'll find not only traditional southern cuisine but also a smattering of international favorites like Greek, Italian, and even Brazilian, which well represent the city's melting pot of cultures. Speaking of melting, Louisville is the home to the famous Kentucky hot brown, an open-faced turkey-and-bacon sandwich oozing with creamy warm cheddar cheese sauce. This sandwich, which was obviously invented before cholesterol tests, was first introduced in 1926 at The Brown Hotel, hence the name. Visitors will find this dish on menus all over the state, but if you want the authentic recipe, head for The Brown.

Louisville, which is sometimes referred to as the northernmost city of the South, or the southernmost city of the North, draws the best features of both regions and presents itself as a world-class city, no matter how you pronounce it.

GUIDANCE For information, contact the **Louisville Convention & Visitors Bureau** (502-584-2121, 800-626-5646; www.gotolouisville.com), 301 S. 4th St., Louisville. Right downtown, you'll find this helpful visitors center. They have exhibits honoring Colonel Harland Sanders and a little restaurant he started called Kentucky Fried Chicken. Another exhibit showcases the Bourbon Trail, where you can learn about all the nearby distilleries and where to find them. They have brochures for any direction you are headed. If you need Louisville T-shirts and souvenirs, they have all shapes and sizes. Architecture and history buffs may want to set aside time to tour Old Louisville, a spectacular 50-block area of the city. You can also get information at the **Visitors Center in Historic Old Louisville** (502-637-2922), 218 W. Oak St., Louisville. This center is open Tue.–Sat 10–5. Although they have information about the whole city, this center specializes in helping visitors to see the architectural gems of the Old Louisville neighborhood.

GETTING THERE The area is served by the **Louisville International Airport** (502-367-4636; www.flylouisville.com). Car rentals are available at the airport. **Greyhound Bus** (502) 561-2805; www.greyhound.com) is located at 720 W. Muhammad Ali Blvd., Louisville. The **Amtrak** station (800-872-7245; www.amtrak.com) is also located at 720 W. Muhammad Ali Blvd.

GETTING AROUND Public transportation is run by the **Transit Authority of River City**, also known as TARC (502-585-1234; www.ridetarc.org).

The city buses serve all parts of downtown Louisville and Jefferson County, as well as Kentucky suburbs in Oldham and Bullitt Counties. For quick transportation within the downtown hotel and shopping districts, try the motorized trolleys, which run about every 20 minutes.

MEDICAL EMERGENCY Norton Healthcare (www.nortonhealth care.com) is Kentucky's largest health care system, with four hospitals in Louisville, including Kosair Children's Hospital, Kentucky's only free-standing full-service children's hospital.

ALCOHOL Jefferson County is a wet county, so alcohol sales are permitted everywhere.

✳ To See

In Louisville

✐ ♿ **Kentucky Derby Museum** (502-992-5905; www.derbymuseum .org), 704 Central Ave. Mon.–Sat. 8–5, Sun. 11–5. Tours given at various times throughout the day. Even though the Derby is called the greatest two minutes in sports, you can spend the whole day learning about its history and traditions. Watch film footage of Derbies dating back to 1919. View historic memorabilia, including hats worn on Millionaires' Row and silks worn by jockeys. Speaking of jockeys, capture a whole new appreciation for the sport when you mount a simulated horse and try to stay in the jockey's stance for the two minutes it takes to run the 1.25-mile Derby

KENTUCKY DERBY MUSEUM

Deborah Kohl Kremer

route. Don't leave without attending the film *The Greatest Race*, a 360-degree multimedia presentation that uses 96 projectors to tell the story of the Kentucky Derby. If you have time, sign up for a walking tour or back-side tour of Churchill Downs. Café and gift shop on site, too. $14 adults, $13 seniors (55-plus), $11 ages 13–18, $6 ages 5–12; under 5 free.

✐ ♿ **Glassworks** (502-584-4510, 800-795-9429; www.louisvilleglassworks .com), 815 W. Market St. Guided tours Sat. 10, 11, 1, and 3. Self-guided tours weekdays 10–4. Learn about the art of glassblowing in this one-of-a-kind gallery. Watch glassblowers pull molten glass from a 2,200-degree furnace and transform it into stunning works of art. Attend a glassblowing workshop or just mosey into their walk-in studio, where you can make awesome suncatchers and other glass pieces. Before you leave, don't forget to go to the on-site gallery where you can purchase some of the professionally made, breathtaking (no pun intended) art. Guided tour $6.

Kentucky Museum of Art and Craft (502-589-0102; www.kentucky arts.org), 715 W. Main St. Mon.–Fri. 10–5, Sat. 11–5. Featuring the work of more than 200 artists, the museum offers art in all media, folk art to furniture. There is also a galley shop so you can bring some of these treasures home with you.

✐ ♿ **Louisville Slugger Museum & Factory** (502-585-5226, 877-775-8443; www.slugger museum.org), 800 W. Main St. Hours vary slightly through the year. Typically open Mon.–Sat. 9–5, Sun. noon–5. There is no bat production on Sunday. Please call or check the website for exact times. Since 1884, Louisville Slugger has been practicing the craft of baseball-bat making. They make the Official Bat of Major League Baseball, and you can watch. Take a tour through the factory and learn how they do it. In the museum, enjoy a short movie called *The Heart of the Game* featuring some of baseball's greatest hits, and view bats used by baseball greats such as Ty Cobb, Babe

GLASSWORKS

Deborah Kohl Kremer

Ruth, Pete Rose, Hank Aaron, and Jackie Robinson. Lots of memorabilia and interactive features about America's favorite pastime as well as the bats that make it happen. Not sure if you're at the right place? Just look for the World's Biggest Bat, a six-story bat (it weighs 68,000 pounds!) propped up against the building. $9 adults (ages 13–59), $8 seniors (60-plus), $4 ages 6–12; 5 and under free.

✑ ♿ **Louisville Science Center and IMAX Theater** (502-561-6100; www.louisvillescience.org), 727 W. Main St. Mon.–Thu. 9:30–5, Fri. and Sat. 9:30–9, Sun. noon–6. Visit Kentucky's largest hands-on science center, with more than 120 exhibits covering all areas of science in a fun, exciting kid-friendly way. Don't miss the IMAX theater with a screen that is four stories tall. Call to find out what's showing. Prices range $6–15.

✑ ♿ **Muhammad Ali Center** (502-584-9254; www.alicenter.org), 144 N. 6th St. Mon.–Sat. 9:30–5, Sun. noon–5. This six-story, 96,750-square-foot museum is devoted to the life and values of Louisville's native son

LOUISVILLE SLUGGER MUSEUM & FACTORY

Deborah Kohl Kremer

Muhammad Ali. See all his boxing memorabilia, a film about his life, and a full-sized boxing ring where a large projector shows Ali in his signature fight. $9 adults (ages 13–59), $8 seniors (65-plus), $4 military, $4 ages 6–12; 5 and under free.

✑ ♿ **Frazier International History Museum** (502-753-5663; www.fraziermuseum.org), 829 W. Main St. Mon.–Sat. 9–5, Sun. noon–5. Cover 1,000 years of history, with a focus on military artifacts like armor and weaponry. The entire third floor is an actual branch of the United Kingdom National Museum. Don't miss the Royal Armories, a collection of British arms, armor, and artillery dating from antiquity to the present day. Artifacts from American history, such as the Daniel Boone family Bible and Geronimo's bow, are also on display. On weekends you might just run into characters from history, like a former slave or a suffragette campaigning for

Deborah Kohl Kremer

FRAZIER MUSEUM

women's right to vote as they mill about the museum. $9 adults, $8 military, $7 seniors, $6 under 14; under 5 free.

University of Louisville (502-852-5555, 800-334-UofL [8635]; www.louisville.edu). Just 3 miles from downtown, you'll find the 287-acre campus of U of L. Home to more than 20,000 students, the campus is steeped in history and tradition. Tour the campus to see one of the original castings of Rodin's *The Thinker* on the front steps of Grawemeyer Hall. If you are there in the fall, deck yourself in red and white and attend a football game at Papa John's Cardinal Stadium with 42,000 of your closest friends. On game day, everyone is a Cards fan.

Speed Art Museum (502-634-2700; www.speedmuseum.org), 2035 S. 3rd St. Tue., Wed., and Fri. 10:30–4, Thu. 10:30–8, Sat. 10:30–5, Sun. noon–5. Impressive, to say the least, this is the oldest and largest art museum in Kentucky. See more than 12,000 pieces in the permanent

UNIVERSITY OF LOUISVILLE, *THE THINKER*

THE *BELLE OF LOUISVILLE*

exhibit that spans 6,000 years, ranging from ancient Egypt to the modern day. Free admission, although a donation of $4 is recommended.

Spirit of Jefferson/Belle of Louisville (502-574-2355; www.belleof louisville.org), 609 W. Jefferson St. Call for cruise times and reservations. Take a lunch, dinner, or sightseeing cruise aboard a National Historic Landmark, the *Belle of Louisville,* or her sister paddle-wheeler, the *Spirit of Jefferson.*

Museum of the American Printing House for the Blind (502-895-2405; www.aph.org), 1839 Frankfort Ave. Open weekdays 8:30–4:30, Sat. 10–3. This printing house published its first raised-letter embossed book, *Fables and Tales for Children,* in 1866 and has been bringing the written word to blind and visually impaired people ever since. Visit the museum where you can try out a mechanical Braille writer and use your sense of touch to read Braille and raised-letter books. You will have a whole new appreciation for the services this printing house has given to the blind community. Free.

Louisville Zoo (502-459-2181; www.louisvillezoo.org), 1100 Trevilian Way. Open daily Sept.–Feb. 10–4, Mar.–Labor Day 10–5. Open evenings in summer months. Check the website for exact hours. Visit with 1,300 animals, living in their natural habitats. Don't miss the 4-acre

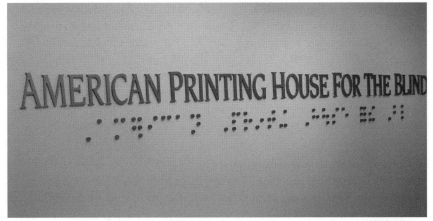

Deborah Kohl Kremer

Gorilla Forest Exhibit, where you can get really close to the gorillas and watch them play. Crowd favorites are Scotty, the zoo's youngest elephant, and King Louie, a rare white alligator. They also have a splash park for an additional fee. $12 adults (ages 13–59), $9 seniors (60-plus), $9 ages 3–11; 2 and under free.

Farmington (502-452-9920; historichomes.org), 3033 Bardstown Rd. Tour this home, which was completed in 1816 from plans designed by Thomas Jefferson. The home, owned by John and Lucy Speed, was part of their hemp plantation and built by slaves. The Speeds' son Joshua invited his friend Abraham Lincoln to come visit from his home in Springfield, Illinois, and ol' Abe ended up staying for three weeks back in 1841. Open Tue.–Sat.; call for hours. $9 adults, $8 seniors (60+), $4 children (6–18), free for children under 5.

LOUISVILLE ZOO

Ellie Kremer

✄ ⬥ **Louisville Mega Cavern** (502-855-6342, 877-614-6342; www .louisvillemegacavern.com), 1841 Taylor Ave. Open seven days a week 9–5. Tour this former limestone quarry hidden under the Louisville Zoo. Covering 100 acres with 17 miles of roads, all underground, this massive cavern is a sight to see. The 70-minute tram tour covers areas of interest, including the geological aspects of the cavern, the green initiatives of building underground, and the fact that in 1962 it was designated an official bunker for the Cuban Missile Crisis. $14 adults, $12 seniors, $8 ages 3–11.

✄ **Louisville Stoneware Factory Tour** (502-582-1900, 800-626-1800; www.louisvillestoneware.com), 731 Brent St. Mon.–Sat. 10–6. Tour one of the oldest and best-known pottery-manufacturing sites in the country. Watch the potters hand make and then hand paint each piece. There is also a museum, a paint-your-own pottery shop, and a factory retail store. $5 per person.

The Portland Museum (502-776-7678; goportland.org), 2308 Portland Ave. Tue.–Thu. 10–4:30, Fri. by appointment. This museum captures Louisville's historic beginnings through photos, architecture, and exhibits. Portland—once a town just south of the Falls of the Ohio—is the predecessor of Louisville. Go to the website to see what is happening. $7 adults, $6 seniors, $5 students; children (5 and under) free.

Waverly Hills Sanatorium (502-933-2142; therealwaverlyhills.com), 4400 Paralee Lane. Waverly originally opened as a tuberculosis hospital in 1910 high atop a hill where the air was clean for the patients. The current building opened on October 17, 1926, and functioned as a tuberculosis hospital until 1961 and a geriatrics/nursing home until the 1980s. Today the entire area is a well-known stomping ground for ghost hunters. They have evidence of all kinds of paranormal activities and offer tours, some overnight, for those who are really brave. If you go, don't miss the Death Chute, a tunnel the staff would use to get all the dead bodies down the hill to the undertakers. Call for hours and tour availability.

Cave Hill Cemetery (502-451-5630; cavehillcemetery.com), 701 Baxter Ave. Cave Hill is the final resting place for Colonel Harlan Sanders, the goateed, white-suited gentleman who started Kentucky Fried Chicken, and George Rogers Clark, one of the founding fathers of Kentucky. You can also see the grave sites of many famous names in Kentucky history, as well as Civil War soldiers from both sides. Absolutely beautiful grounds. Take a guided tour or wander around on your own.

Locust Grove (502-897-9845; locustgrove.org), 561 Blankenbaker Lane. Visit this fine Georgian mansion, which dates back to the 1790s, and see how it has been lovingly restored to its antebellum roots. It is the original home to William and Lucy Clark Croghan, who built the home with slave labor. The Croghans were very politically connected and hosted President James Monroe and General Andrew Jackson on separate occasions. Lucy Clark Croghan's brother, George Rogers Clark, founder of Louisville, also resided with the Croghans for the last few years of his life. Tours include aspects of farm life in the late 1700s. $8 adults, $7 for seniors, $4 ages 6–12. Mon.–Sat. 10–4:30, Sun. 1–4:30. Last tour at 3:15. Call to double-check the hours.

Farnsley-Moremen House (502-935-6809; riverside-landing.org), 7410 Moorman Rd. Tour the Farnsley-Moremen House—built in 1837—or stroll the 300-acre historic park. They have ongoing archaeological digs and educational programs throughout the year. Check the website for events. Tue.–Sat. 10–4:30, Sun. 1–4:30. Tours begin at 10:30 and continue every hour on the half hour. Last tour 3:30 PM.

The Louisville Clock, near 4th St. and Broadway, at Theater Square. This Louisville landmark is a must-see. It is a giant freestanding sculpture in the shape of a racetrack. A few times per hour, the sculpture comes to life introducing the contestants: small statues of famous people from Louisville's past, like Thomas Jefferson, Daniel Boone, and Henry Watterson. Some may think it is hokey, but they are wrong.

TOURS Old Louisville Tours (502-637-2922; www.oldlouisville .net/vc), the Visitors Center in Historic Old Louisville, 218 W. Oak St. Open Tue.–Sat. 10–5. This 50-square-block section of the city is home to 1,400 structures built between 1885 and 1905 and includes practically every style of architecture prevalent during the Victorian era. It is a virtual open-air museum for lovers of architecture and old homes. As one of the largest National Register Historic Districts in the country, it is also one of the largest contiguous collections of Victorian mansions you'll ever see. A guided tour is

OLD LOUISVILLE

www.kentuckytourism.com

worth your time. Both walking and motorcoach tours are available and are led by guides who are knowledgeable and passionate about Old Louisville. Tours last approximately 90 minutes. Ghost tours offered every Fri. night. Tours range $15–25 per person. Reservations required.

✷ To Do

FAMILY ENTERTAINMENT ✐ **Kart Kountry** (502-543-9588; www .gokartkountry.com), Paroquet Springs Dr., Shepherdsville. Home of the world's longest go-cart track, this 1.5-mile course is fun for the whole family. They have five sizes of carts so everyone can take a spin. While you are there, take in 18 holes on their miniature golf course, ride the bumper boats, or take a few swings in the batting cage.

✐ **Gheens Science Hall and Rauch Planetarium** (502-852-6664; Louisville.edu/planetarium). On the Belknap campus of the University of Louisville is a world-class planetarium with laser, educational, and just plain stellar shows. Check the website for shows and times.

✐ **Kentucky State Fair** (502-367-5180; kystatefair.org), 937 Phillips Lane, Louisville. The fair dates back to 1816, but was officially recognized as the Kentucky State Fair beginning in 1902. Tradition runs deep here, and one of the best-loved traditions is the 18-foot-tall Freddy Farm Bureau, who has been sitting at the entrance since the 1950s. Held at the Kentucky Exposition Center, the fair typically draws 600,000 people to the competitions in art, photography cake decoration, aquarium design, vegetable growing, and everything in between. See all kinds of farm animals looking their finest, as well as the prestigious World Championship Horse Show, which draws horses and their owners from all over the world. And, as with any state fair, Kentucky has plenty of thrill rides, concerts, and deep-fried food choices.

GOLF Nevel Meade Golf Course (502-228- 9522; www.nevelmeade .com), 3123 Nevel Meade Dr., Prospect. A well-known, privately owned 18-hole golf course with a pro shop, clubhouse, and snack bar.

Quail Chase Golf Course (502-239-2110; www.quailchase.com), 7000 Cooper Chapel Rd., Louisville. With 27 holes, this public course has achieved a four-star rating from *Golf Digest* magazine.

HORSE RACING Churchill Downs Race Course (502-636-4400; www .churchilldowns.com), 700 Central Ave., Louisville. Historic Churchill Downs, home to the Kentucky Derby, with its famous twin spires situated high above the grandstand, is a place legends are made. Although it is best known for the Derby, on a daily basis it's a thoroughbred racetrack featuring live racing and simulcasting. The **Fall Meet** runs from the end of

✍ ♿ *The Kentucky Show!* (502-562-7800; www.kentuckyshow.com), 501 W. Main St., Louisville.

Now appearing at the Kentucky Center for the Performing Arts is a one-of-a-kind tribute to the commonwealth of Kentucky. Called *The Kentucky Show!*, this fast-paced, 30-minute film, shown on a gigantic screen, takes you to all corners of Kentucky. With a combination of fantastic photography, compelling music, and the sheer size and pace of the show, that exclamation point is there for a reason.

Encompassing the state's history, people, culture, traditions, and economy, *The Kentucky Show!* melds together 75 hours of video and 125 hours of interviews that took 18 months to produce. The result is phenomenal.

Narration is by Ashley Judd; viewers also hear from famous and not-so-famous Kentuckians while taking in landscape, panoramic, and action shots of the wonderland that makes up the Bluegrass State.

"It doesn't seem to make a difference if you are in third grade or you are 93 years old, there is something in this for everyone," said Tim King, director of marketing and sales for *The Kentucky Show!* "As soon as the show starts, you do not hear a peep from the crowd for the next 32 minutes."

Since its debut on September 12, 2008, more than 25,000 people have enjoyed the show from the specially designed 100-seat theater.

The show was created by Donna Lawrence, of Donna Lawrence Productions of Louisville. No stranger to the field of multimedia, Lawrence has also created awe-inspiring videos for the Kentucky Derby Museum, the College Football Hall of Fame, and the U.S. Capitol Visitors Center.

Every Kentuckian, as well as every visitor to the state, should see this magnificent show. For visitors it could reshape their trip and lead them to some of the greatest places in the state. For residents, well, seeing the Bluegrass State looking her finest on that big screen will inspire pride and possibly a lump in your throat.

Check the website for show times. Closed Monday. Admission $7; seniors and students $6.

October to the end of November. The **Spring Meet** runs from the end of April through early July. The track is usually dark—track-talk for "not running"—on Mon. and Tue. Call for exact dates and times.

MINOR-LEAGUE BASEBALL The Louisville Bats (502-212-2287; louisville.bats.milb.com), Louisville Slugger Field, 401 E. Main St., Louisville. The Louisville Bats are the Triple-A affiliate of the Cincinnati Reds. Modern Louisville Slugger Field can hold about 13,000 fans and is about a block from the river, right downtown.

✴ Green Space

Olmsted Parks (502-456-8125; www.louisvilleky.gov/MetroParks). Created by famed landscape designer Frederick Law Olmsted, who also created Central Park in New York City, this system of parks, including 3 flagship parks and 15 smaller ones, is a true gem in the layout of the city of Louisville. Olmsted began working with Louisville in 1891, and his concept of creating a system of parks connected to tree-lined parkways was instrumental in the expansion of the city and the protected green space within it. This park system is one of only five nationwide designed by Olmsted. The flagship parks, Cherokee, Iroquois, and Shawnee, include charming vistas, rolling open plains, mature trees, and thousands of varieties of plants and wildlife. **Cherokee Park**, 745 Cochran Hill Rd., open dawn to dusk. The main feature is the 2.4-mile scenic drive, with separate lanes for cars and recreational users. The park also has a spray pool, an off-leash dog park, ball fields, and playgrounds. **Iroquois Park**, 5216 New Cut Rd., open dawn to dusk. Known for its scenic beauty, as well as an outdoor amphitheater that draws big-name acts in the summers, the 725-acre park has walking and biking trails leading to scenic views. Nice golf course for duffers, plus a playground and a splash play area that is a favorite of little ones. **Shawnee Park**, 4501 W. Broadway. Originally created as a public gathering spot, this 285-acre park does just that. They have a really nice golf course and terrific ball fields, for football, baseball and soccer. There are also basketball and tennis courts available. The park sits right along the Ohio River, so there is a scenic river walk that you really don't want to miss.

Jefferson Memorial Forest (502-368-5404), 11311 Mitchell Hill Rd., Fairdale. Preserved since the 1940s, this beautiful 6,191 acres of forest offers 35 miles of hiking trails, both tough and easy. The forest is also a favorite of fisherman and bird-watchers. Primitive campsites are available and there are horseback riding trails, but you have to bring your own horse. Dawn to dusk.

Louisville Waterfront Park (louisvillewaterfront.com). Surrounded by the banks of the Ohio on one side and the skyscrapers of downtown, this

85-acre park is a breath of fresh air. It offers a grand view of the river, space for concerts and festivals, and green space for kids to run and families to picnic. There are walking trails and a playground; a water park is open in the summer months. Bike rental available, too. Open 6 AM–11 PM.

McNeely Lake Park, 10500 Cedar Creek Rd. One of Louisville's largest parks, it offers 746 acres of recreation including a 46-acre fishing lake and boat dock. They also have ball fields, tennis courts, and a memorial dedicated to the Korean War. Open dawn to dusk.

✳ Lodging

In Louisville (unless otherwise noted)

HOTELS ⅃ **The Brown Hotel** (502-324-1389; www.brownhotel .com), 335 W. Broadway. On the National Register of Historic Places, The Brown Hotel has been providing upscale accommodations to visitors for almost 100 years. The 293 guest rooms boast 5-inch pillow-top featherbeds with 310-thread-count Egyptian cotton linens and European white goose-down comforters for superior comfort. Just walk through the lobby and take note of the ornate hand-painted plaster relief ceilings, intricately carved railings, decorative crown moldings, and other classic architectural details of this grand English Renaissance hotel. $$$–$$$$

🐾 ⅃ **Galt House Hotel & Suites** (502-589-5200, 800-843-4258; www.galthouse.com), 140 N. 4th St. The city's only riverfront hotel; fabulous views are available from some of the 1,291 guest rooms. Full of history, the Galt House originally opened in 1835 and over the years offered shelter to notable visitors, such as presidents, politicians, and celebrities. During the Civil War, Generals Grant and Sherman met here to plan the capture of Atlanta. Although the original building no longer exists, today's visitors can enjoy modern conveniences, six restaurants, a rooftop fitness center, and 2,500 covered parking spaces. $$$–$$$$

⅃ **The Seelbach Hilton Louisville** (502-585-3200; www.seelbach hilton.com), 500 4th St. A Kentucky tradition since 1905, The Seelbach is one of Louisville's premier hotels. Having played host to nine U.S. presidents in its first 100 years, it's a glorious combination of glamour and southern hospitality. The 300 guest rooms have an understated elegance. Many notable characters have ties to this grande dame. Gangster Al Capone stayed here so frequently that he had access to secret passages where he could hide in case of a raid. He once donated a large mirror that still hangs in an alcove of the Oakroom dining room. It wasn't just a generous gift; the mobster used it to watch his back during card games. Another claim to fame is the mention of The Seelbach in *The Great Gatsby*, a 1925 novel by F. Scott Fitzgerald, who was known to frequent the hotel. $$$–$$$$

&. **21C Museum Hotel** (502-217-6300, 877-217-6400; www.21 cmuseum.org), 700 W. Main St. Ironically, you will find this contemporary hotel located right in the heart of the historic Museum Row on Main in the downtown area. Stay in one of the 91 modern rooms and enjoy the surrounding art and luxurious amenities. $$$–$$$$

DUPONT MANSION

Nick Kremer

BED & BREAKFASTS DuPont Mansion (502-638-0045; www .dupontmansion.com), 1317 S. 4th St. Built in 1879, the mansion reflects the Victorian-era Italianate Renaissance Revival style that is prominent in this Old Louisville neighborhood. With soaring 10-foot doors and windows, marble fireplaces, and crystal chandeliers, the architecture is something to behold. Each of the eight perfectly appointed guest rooms comes complete with fireplace and whirlpool tub, making the DuPont a fabulous place to unwind. Innkeeper Mary Pat acts as a personal concierge ready to help their guests with any need. $$–$$$$

Inn at the Park (502-638-0045; www.innatpark.com), 1332 S. 4th St. Located right in the heart of Old Louisville, this massive 7,400-square-foot mansion originally was home to Russell Houston, president of the Louisville & Nashville Railroad. Built in 1884, this Richardsonian Romanesque mansion features a stunning staircase. The eight guest rooms with original hardwood floors, intricate woodwork, and fine furnishings are simply the icing on the cake of this spectacular home. $$–$$$$

✨ **The Columbine Bed and Breakfast** (502-635-5000, 800-635-5010; www.thecolumbine .com), 1707 S. 3rd St. Unique Greek Revival architecture in the heart of historic Louisville. The Columbine's white columns and portico make it truly memorable.

Unwind in one of the six guest rooms. Filled with antiques and reproductions, the rooms also feature in-room fireplaces, 12-foot ceilings, and original hardwood floors. Breakfasts range from omelets to caramelized apple French toast. $$

Inn at Woodhaven (888-895-1011; www.innatwoodhaven.com), 401 S. Hubbards Lane. This historical Gothic Revival mansion, which was built in 1853, features eight guest rooms. Listed on the National Register because of its architectural wonders, the home still boasts diamond windowpanes with trefoil decorations, delicate plasterwork on the ceilings, interior shutters, and 14-foot arched Gothic doors. Enjoy your breakfast with fresh flowers, flickering candlelight, soft music, white tablecloths, and fine china. $$–$$$

1888 Historic Rocking Horse Manor B&B (502-583-0408; www.rockinghorse-bb.com), 1022 S. 3rd St. Built in 1888 out of stone, this mansion still features glorious architectural treats such as stained-glass windows, clawfoot soaking tubs, and original woodwork. The six guest rooms are decorated in period furnishings but have all the modern amenities that today's travelers expect. Enjoy your gourmet breakfast in the fabulous dining room surrounded by lace tablecloths, crystal, and massive chandeliers. $$–$$$

Pinecrest Cottage and Gardens (502-454-3800; www.bbonline.com /ky/pinecrest), 2806 Newburg Rd. This one-bedroom guest house provides complete privacy. Guests will enjoy a fully stocked kitchen, a living room with a pullout couch, and a bedroom with a king-sized bed. The cottage sits on 6½ luscious acres of carefully tended perennial beds and 100-year-old trees. There is also a pool and tennis court on the property. $$

CAMPING Louisville South KOA (502-543-2041; louisville southkoa.com), 2433 Hwy. 44E, Shepherdsville. About 20 miles south of Louisville proper, this resort-style campground offers tent camping, cabin rentals, and RV hookups.

✳ Where to Eat

In Louisville (unless otherwise noted)

DINING OUT ⍦ **The English Grill at The Brown Hotel** (502-736-2996), 4th and Broadway. Dinner Mon.–Sat. 6–10. Immerse yourself in fine elegance by dining at this landmark restaurant. The decor looks as it must have when they opened in the 1920s, with dark wood paneling, stately upholstered armchairs, and china- and crystal-covered tables. This sophisticated restaurant is tailored to diners with discriminating tastes. You won't find chicken nuggets on the menu, but a blend of choices like roasted venison, New York strip steak, and fresh grouper with leeks and Dungeness crab. The service is impeccable, complete with palate cleansers between courses and never-ending home-baked breads to accompany your meal. Leave the kids at home and enjoy this grown-up indulgence. $$$–$$$$

Ⴟ **Oakroom at The Seelbach Hilton** (502-807-3463; www .seelbachhilton.com), 500 4th Ave. Tue.–Sat. 5:30–10, Sun. brunch 10–2. Arguably the finest dining experience you can have in Kentucky. This glamorous restaurant has been awarded the prestigious Five Diamond Award from AAA for more than 10 years. It's Kentucky's only Five Diamond restaurant, so make reservations and enjoy the fabulous cuisine and flawless service. Their wine list, if you can call 1,200 choices a list, is the most expansive in the state. $$$–$$$$

Ⴟ **August Moon Chinese Bistro** (502-456-6569; www.augustmoon bistro.com), 2269 Lexington Rd. Open for lunch and dinner every day. Chef Peng Looi serves up a menu right from the Orient, mixing together flavors and countries, with Malaysian, Indonesian, and Chinese dishes all promising a delicious meal in a cool contemporary dining room. $$

Ⴟ **Buck's in the Mayflower** (502-637-5284; www.bucks restaurantandbar.com), 425 W. Ormsby. Lunch Mon.–Fri. 11–3, dinner Mon.–Thu. 5–10, Fri.–Sat. 5–11. Right in the heart of Old Louisville, Buck's offers upscale, romantic dining with a full array of menu choices. The dim lights,

fresh flowers, and Victorian accents show the elegance, but the chic mishmash of china and utensils reveals Buck's eclectic side. $$–$$$

Ⴟ **Lilly's: A Kentucky Bistro** (502-451-0447; lillyslapeche.com), 1147 Bardstown Rd. Open for lunch and dinner Tue.–Sat. They say they are locally inspired, internationally influenced, and that is a great way to sum up their menu. They work with local farmers and even grow some of the organic produce in their own garden. You'll also see Kentucky names like Weisenberger Grits, Broadbent bacon, and Newsome's Hams offered alongside their homemade linguine and locally raised honey. Although they have steaks, burgers, pork, and chicken dishes, the chef prepares each in a way that is original, as well as delicious. Menu changes with the seasons, so check the website to see what's cooking. $$–$$$

& Ⴟ **Jack Fry's** (502-452-9244; www.jackfrys.com), 1007 Bardstown Rd. Serving lunch Mon.– Fri. 11–2:30; dinner Mon.–Thu. 5:30–11, Fri.–Sat. 5:30–midnight, and Sun. 5:30–10. For nearly 40 years, beginning in the 1930s, Jack Fry's restaurant was a staple in the Louisville scene. Jack was a bit of a character; he loved amateur boxing and visiting the track, and he brought in quite a following of people who visited his back room for his bookie and bootlegging business. The restaurant closed in the 1970s, but was resurrected in the late 1980s and has been in business ever since. Although the crowd has gone from roustabouts and gamblers to fine diners and cloth-napkin users, you'll still find pictures scattered about of Jack and his cronies. Now known as one of Louisville's finest establishments, the menu features upscale choices like steaks, lamb chops, and short ribs. Folks rave about the appetizers like garlicky escargots, foie gras with caramelized apples, and their southern favorite, shrimp 'n' grits. They have an equally enticing dessert menu. Turtle cheesecake, anyone? $$–$$$

Y **De La Torres Spanish Restaurant** (502-456-4955; www.delatorres.com), 1606 Bardstown Rd. Open for dinner Tue.–Sat. Classic Spanish menu and Madrid accents make you think you're in Spain. This is fine dining with dishes like paella, marinated meats, and chorizo (traditional Spanish sausage) on the menu. $$

Y **Limestone Restaurant** (502-426-7477; www.limestone restaurant.com), 10001 Forest Green Blvd. Lunch weekdays 11:30–2, dinner Mon.–Sat. 5–10, Sun. 10–2. The menu is a true taste of southern-style cooking. With appetizers like fried chicken livers and shrimp 'n' grits, and entrées of beef short rib on braised collard greens, or white beans and country ham, you'll know you're in the South. So try it while you're here. $$

Y **Mayan Café** (502-566-0651; themayancafe.com), 813 E. Mar-ket St. Lunch weekdays 11:30–2:30, dinner Mon.–Thu. 5–10, Fri. and Sat. 5–10:30. Each dish looks like a work of art, and the not-so-common ingredients combine to make a one-of-a-kind meal. Mayan recipes are very flavorful; try the Veracruz duck mole—sautéed duck with chocolate sauce—or the smoked salmon crêpe topped with light pumpkin seed cream sauce. $$

Y **Napa River Grill** (502-893-0141; www.napariverlouisville.com), 1211 Herr Lane, Westport Village. Lunch weekdays 11–2, dinner every night beginning at 5. Upscale casual dining featuring Northern California–inspired dishes as well as a few Pacific Rim menu choices. Weather permitting, you can eat outside on the fieldstone, vine-trellised patio near the oakwood grill. This cool bistro has plenty of drink choices, too. Check out the custom-built wine rack with more than 1,000 bottles to choose from. $$–$$$

Y **Z's Oyster Bar & Steakhouse** (502-855-8000; zsfusion.com). Two Louisville locations: 115 S. 4th St. and 101 Whittington Pkwy. Serving lunch Mon.–Fri. 11:30–2:30; dinner Mon.–Thu. 5–10, Fri. and Sat. 5–11. Closed Sun. With more than 50 unique Kentucky bourbons available every day, maybe they should add *bourbon bar* to their name. But aside from their amazing collection of Kentucky spirits—and wine, too, by the way—Z's will make you a steak that you might not forget. And seafood? Their chef goes to the airport every day to pick it up as it is flown in. Talk about fresh. Instead of a nightcap after dinner, try their Woodford Reserve Float: It's like a root beer float, but with bourbon. Yep. $$

℟ **Palermo Viejo** (502-456-6461; www.palermoviejo.info), 1359 Bardstown Rd. Open for dinner Mon.–Sat. at 5. The owners, the Elbl brothers, chose the name for a vibrant neighborhood in Buenos Aires that is an eclectic mix of quirky shops, restaurants, and Tango Houses; Louisville's version is Bardstown Road, minus the Tango Houses. The menu is country cooking, just from another country. Most entrées have Spanish or Italian roots. Several are served on small hibachi-style grills that are brought right to the table. Don't miss the extensive list of Argentine wines. Never had Argentine food? Try a beef dish. All of them are marinated and served with chimichurri sauce, a blend of oil, vinegar, and herbs. The Elbl brothers claim this sauce is so good, diners have suggested they turn it into a drink. $$–$$$

℟ **Saffron's Restaurant** (502-584-7800; www.saffronsrestaurant .com), 131 W. Market St. Lunch weekdays 11:30–2:30, dinner Mon.–Thu. 5:30–9:30, Fri.–Sat. 5–10. Serving authentic Persian cuisine in a relaxed but upscale atmosphere, this restaurant is very inviting. Since Persian recipes are not always familiar, the staff work extra hard to make sure you know

what you will like, the personal service is unmatched. For dessert, order some Persian ice cream, with hints of saffron, pistachio, and rose water. $$

℟ **Vincenzos** (502-580-1350; www .vincenzositalianrestaurant.com), 150 S. 5th St. Lunch every day beginning at 11:30, dinner every day beginning at 5:30. Reservations recommended. Owned by brothers Agostino and Vincenzo Gabriele, who grew up in Palermo, Sicily, their menu reflects European specialty dishes in an elegant yet relaxed setting. In addition to traditional pasta dishes, Vincenzos also has a nice variety of seafood, lamb, beef, and chicken dishes. Try the pesce spada con capperi e olive schiacciate—swordfish with capers. $$–$$$

EATING OUT ℟ **Café Lou Lou** (502-893-7776; www.cafeloulou .com), 106 Sears Ave.; second location, 2216 Dundee Rd. Open Sun.–Thu. 11–10, Fri.–Sat. 11–11. They have an amazing variety of calzones, pizzas, pastas, and sandwiches. The Cajun fries are so hot, they seem to numb your taste buds. The chef has ties to New Orleans—hence the name, for Lou(iville) and Lou(isiana). Most menu items have Cajun, Greek, or Italian influences. The bright, funky walls and artwork seem to make this hip place buzz. $–$$

℟ **J. Graham's Café at The Brown Hotel** (502-736-2996; www.brownhotel.com), 4th and Broadway. Open weekdays 6:30–3, weekends 7–3. Home of the legendary Kentucky hot brown, a sandwich that has been a favorite since it first appeared on the menu in the 1920s. This open-faced combination of turkey, bacon, cheese sauce, and toast points is worth the indulgence. The casual café also features a daily breakfast and lunch buffet that draw crowds. $–$$

Ŷ **Marker's Mark Bourbon House and Lounge** (502-568-9009; makerslounge.com), 446 S. 4th St. Open for lunch and dinner every day. Feels upscale and hip with contemporary furnishings and cool lighting. Broad menu includes salads and sandwiches at lunch, steaks and pork chops for dinner. They actually have a menu for all the bourbon they serve, so take your time and make an informed selection. If you're in doubt about which to choose, stick with a winner and remember the name of the restaurant. $$

Ŷ **Captain's Quarters Riverside Grille** (502-228-1651; www.cq riverside.com), 5700 Captain's Quarters Rd., Harrods Creek. Open for lunch and dinner every day, Sun. brunch 10:30–2:30. Just north of Louisville, you'll find a welcoming place for outdoor dining right on the Ohio. The menu offers everything from appetizers to steaks, chops, and chicken favorites. They have sandwich and pizza selections, too. This casual restaurant has an upscale feel to it. If you can't eat outside, curl up next to the giant stone fireplace and enjoy the river view out the window. $–$$$

Ŷ **Cunningham's Restaurant** (502-587-0526), 630 S. 4th St. Open for lunch and dinner every day. Part of Louisville's history for more than 100 years, with photos on the walls to prove it. Everyone seems to know that this is the place for turtle soup and a generous-sized fried fish sandwich. Although those are the hometown favorites, Cunningham's also serves up burgers, hot brown, and even pan-fried oysters. It's a casual place with very reasonable prices. $–$$

Ŷ **Garage Bar** (502-749-7100; garageonmarket.com), 700 E. Market. Serving dinner beginning at 5 PM on weeknights; opening at 11 AM on Sat. and Sun., when they serve brunch until 4. Most nights the kitchen is open until about 10, but the bar is open later. This is one of those hip, happening places that make you feel like you are at the right place at the right time. Housed in a former service station—hence the name—the Garage serves up hand-tossed pizzas baked in an authentic Italian wood-fired Ferrara oven. They also have a ham bar, which serves up samples of regionally known ham. You can try one or you can try them all. Recommendation: Try them all. And given the word *bar* in their name, count on them for a huge selection of craft beers and Kentucky bourbons.

Ramsi's Café on the World (502-451-0700; ramsiscafe.com),

1293 Bardstown Rd. Serving Mon–Thu. 11 AM–1 AM, Fri–Sat. 11 AM–2 AM; Sun. brunch 10 AM–2 PM, dinner till 11 PM. Stop in and visit with Ramsi; he'll tell you about his native Jerusalem or the special of the day, whatever you are interested in. The menu is all over the map—Jamaican, Greek, Mexican, Chinese. Whatever cuisine you are looking for, Ramsi probably has it. $$

Ⴗ **Come Back Inn** (502-627-1777; www.comebackinn.net), 909 Swan St. Open for dinner Tue.–Sat. A favorite of locals, this is a cozy place to relax with tasty food and a full bar at very reasonable prices. The menu features Italian American food like Chicago-style Italian roast beef sandwiches and tortellini with prosciutto in a garlic cream sauce. Don't forget the pizza; it's award winning. $$

Ⴗ **Bodega at Felice** (502-569-4100), 829 E. Market St. Open Mon–Thu. 7–7, Fri. 7 AM–11 PM, Sat. 9 AM–4 PM. Closed Sunday. It's a market, deli, wine shop, and coffee bar, so what else do you really need? Scrumptious sandwiches, hard-to-find gourmet items, and the perfect cuppa joe to wake up in the morning. $

Ⴗ **Baxter Station Bar and Grill** (502-584-1635; www.baxterstation.com), 1201 Payne St. Mon. 11:30–2, Tue.–Thu. 11:30–10, Fri. 11:30–11, Sat. 4:30–11. Closed Sun. This fun, casual restaurant has an international and regional American menu. From the crab-cakes to the warm goat cheese salad to the fajita burritos and salmon croquettes, there really is something for everyone. Large selection of import and specialty beers on tap, too. Eat outdoors year-round and don't miss the adorable train that runs around the restaurant—it's up near the ceiling. $$

Ⴗ **Against the Grain Brewery and Smokehouse** (502-515-0174; atgbrewery.com), 401 E. Main St. Open Mon.–Sat. 11 AM–midnight. Visit this three-story brewery located adjacent to Slugger Field. They brew all kinds of beer and offer pub-style fare. $$

Ⴗ **Tony BoomBozz Pizza** (www .tonyboombozz.com). Open every day. With four locations around Louisville, you're always close to one of the city's favorite pizza places. Pizza maker Tony Palombino named his restaurant Boom-Bozz because it is Italian slang for "wild, crazy, and fun." So stop in for some gourmet pizza and have some *boombozz* while you're there. $–$$

Mark's Feed Store (502-458-1570; marksfeedstore.com), 1514 Bardstown Rd. Mark's is your go-to place if you are looking for southern Bar-B-Q whether you are looking for pork, beef, or chicken. Their tangy sauce is available by the bottle, so you might want to get some to take home. They also have spicy fries, hot wings, and a dessert menu you are going to wish you had saved room for. Four locations in the Louis-ville area. Open every day from

Nick Kremer

BAXTER STATION BAR AND GRILL

11 AM until at least 9 PM, later on weekends. $–$$

Grape Leaf Restaurant (502-897-1774), 2217 Frankfort Ave. Mon.–Thu. 11:30–9, Fri.–Sat. 11:30–9:30, Sun. 12:30–8:30. Recommended by vegetarians and fans of Mediterranean- and Middle Eastern–style cuisine, this is Louisville's answer to where to go for gyros, falafel, and hummus. $–$$

Molly Malones (502-473-1222; mollymalonesirishpub.com), 933 Baxter Ave. A darling Irish pub with two Louisville locations. Both have are so welcoming, you'll expect St. Patrick himself to be stopping by. Traditional favorites include corned beef hash and soda bread, Irish mussels, shepherd's pie, and bangers and mash—but you'll also find a variety of not-so-typical Irish fare like black bean

burgers, soups and salads, and even fried pickles. There's a huge assortment of beers, both on tap and by the bottle—it is an Irish pub, you know. Open seven days a week for lunch and dinner. The second location (502-882-2222) is at 3900 Shelbyville Rd., Saint Matthews. $$

&. ((y)) **Nancy's Bagel Grounds** (502-895-8323; nancysbagels .com), 2101 Frankfort Ave. Mon.–Fri. 6:30–5:30, Sat. and Sun. 7:30–3. Nancy's serves up soups, wraps, and yummy sandwiches, but go for the bagels and coffee drinks . . . that *is* what it's called, you know. She usually has about 12 varieties of crispy-chewy bagels each morning that you can top of with an equal amount of dreamy cream cheese, which means you can go about three months before you have to start repeating the combinations.

City Café (502-459-5600; city-cafelunch.com), 1250 Bardstown Rd. Although they pride themselves on lunch, the Bardstown Road location is open right into the dinner hours. Just what you need, sandwiches, soups, and salads, all are fresh and homemade. They feature daily lunch specials—one is always meatless—that are filling to your belly and do not empty your wallet. The atmosphere is fun at all three locations. At Bardstown Road they're open Mon.–Thu. 11–9, Fri.–Sat. 11–10, Sun. 11–8. At 505 W. Broadway (502-589-1797), they're open Mon.–Fri. 10:30–3. At 500 S. Preston (502-852-5739), hours are Mon.–Fri. 7:30–3. $

Mike Linnig's Place (502-937-9888; www.mikelinnigsrestaurant .com), 9308 Cane Run Rd. Tue.–Thu. 11–10, Fri. and Sat. 11–11, Sun. noon–10. Around since 1925, the Linnig family continues to dish up fish sandwiches and seafood plates the way they have since they started serving food at their small roadside market. In addition to crawfish, alligator, and swordfish steaks, Linnig's has juicy burgers, turtle soup, and onion rings. Even the homemade tartar sauce is worth coming back for. This casual place is a local favorite, and their back-to-basics menu has something for everyone. Eat outside at a picnic table alongside the Ohio River, or eat in the front room where you are sur-rounded by mounted animals who have made a trip to the taxidermist. $–$$

& **Toast on Market** (502-569-4099; www.toastonmarket.com), 736 E. Market St. Open Mon.–Sat. 7–3. This cool place to eat breakfast and lunch is housed in a former theater downtown. Check out the huge stained-glass window on the front of the building with the word EMPIRE in the middle. No one seems to know what it means, but it looks really hip. You know the food is really good when you find that you have to wait for a table, no matter what time you go. They have hearty breakfast specials, as well as huge sandwiches and salads. Smells like homemade bread as soon as you open the door. Try a grilled cheese sandwich; they have four varieties to choose from. $–$$

& **Smoketown USA** (502-409-9180; smoketownusa.com), 1153 Logan St. Open Tue.–Thu. 11–9, Fri.–Sat. 11–10; closed Sun. We'll get to the food in a minute. This funky eatery is also a giant yard sale in progress. Yep, you like the table, it's for sale. How about that art on the wall? Yes sir, it's going home with you. Everything in the place is up for purchase. How cool is that? But now for the real reason to come: The food is awesome. Known for their tasty ribs and pulled pork sandwiches, Smoketown isn't just a BBQ joint. They have burgers, salmon, and a nice selection of salads, too. Order the corn bread. $–$$

🖌 🍸 **Lynn's Paradise Café** (502-583-3447; www.lynnsparadisecafe.com), 984 Barret Ave., Louisville. Mon.–Fri. 7–10, Sat.–Sun. 8–10. $–$$

If you look up *eclectic* in the dictionary, there ought to be picture of Lynn's Paradise Café there. This is a nutty restaurant with a giant coffeepot and a huge moose that looks like a zebra in the parking lot, a life-sized metal bear dressed like Elvis to greet you, and a dining room full of wacky, kitschy things to look at while you eat. The menu is equally entertaining. Breakfast is available all day, so you might want to try the French toast or two massive chocolate chip pancakes, but the dinner menu's meat loaf and Paradise hot brown are good choices, too. Stop in Lynn's attached gift shop, the World of Swirl, for hip gift items that you've never seen before. Bring a donation for the Ugly Lamp contest that Lynn's Paradise sponsors at the Kentucky State Fair each year. Look around the restaurant for this year's nominees.

LYNN'S PARADISE CAFÉ

Paul Kremer

&. Ÿ **Havana Rumba** (502-897-1959; www.havanarumbaonline.com), 4115 Oechsli Ave. or 12003 Shelbyville, Rd. Open Mon.–Thu. 11–9:30, Fri. 11–10, Sat. noon–10, Sun. noon–8:30. Owner Marco Lorenzo arrived in America back in 2000, and although he had been a civil engineer back in Cuba, he quickly realized Louisville's need for some Havana-inspired cuisine. Apparently, the people of Louisville have noticed, too, because the place is always hopping. Sandwiches are made of thin Cuban breads topped with equally thin-sliced meats, and entrées of beef, chicken, and pork dishes are served with a side of sweet plantains. Save room for an after-dinner Cuban coffee and their signature dessert, Havana Bananas, drenched in dark Cuban rum and served over ice cream. $–$$

✐ **WW Cousins Restaurant** (502-897-9684), 900 Dupont Rd. Open every day for lunch and dinner. Locals swear this is the place to go for the best burger in Louisville. The buns are homemade, and they have a huge fixin's bar where you can dress up your burger just the way you want it. This is a casual, family-style restaurant where everyone can find what they want. In addition to making buns every day, they also make some iced cookies that are simply wonderful. $

Ÿ **Wick's Pizza** (www.wickspizza.com). Open every day. Several locations around town. Michael and Meredith Wickliffe are the proud owners of four Louisville locations, all offering comfortable dining, their well-known pizza, and more than 60 foreign and domestic beers and 75 blends of liquor. Sure, the pizza is awesome, but so are the aptly named Stuffed Breadwick and the Hot Sicilian Sandwick. $

Wagner's Pharmacy (502-375-3800), 3113 S. 4th St. Open Mon.–Sat. 8–3. Given the prime location, just across the street from Churchill Downs, you'll be eating with authentic horse people. It's a favorite of jockeys and trainers who know you don't need fancy accommodations to get a good fried egg sandwich or burger. In business for about 100 years, Wagner's is a staple in the community. Listen up, you might just hear a tip about an upcoming race. $

SNACKS Homemade Ice Cream and Pie Kitchen (www.homemadeicecreamand piekitchen.com). Open Mon.–Thu. 10–10, Fri.–Sat. 11–11, Sunday noon–10. They are easy to find because they have nine locations around Louisville. What started out as a lunch counter that served pie turned into a pie restaurant that served homemade ice cream. They claim that the Caramel Iced Dutch Apple is their signature pie, but with flavors like Key Lime, Sweet Potato, and Red Raspberry Cream, who could choose? Make sure you order your pie à la mode—the fresh-churned ice cream is made of 14 percent butterfat and tastes like your mom just made it. People come from miles around when the pumpkin ice cream is in season. $

Blue Dog Bakery and Café (502-899-9800; bluedogbakery andcafe.com), 2868 Frankfort Ave. Open Tue.–Sat. 7–4. The Blue Dog's artisan breads are in so much demand, the owners have to put their baking schedule on their website, so people know what days which loaves are available. These delightful pieces of art are also available in some of Louisville's finest restaurants, though a restaurant might not tell you so. But swing by this popular eatery in the Crescent Hill neighborhood for brunch (starting at 9 AM) or lunch (starting at 10:30) and you will get much more than delectable bread. Their selection of soups, salads, and sandwiches is unmatched. Each is made with the freshest of ingredients in delightful pairings that you won't find just anywhere. Try the bacon sandwich with cheese curds, cider vinegar onions, and spice mayo. You might never forget it. Sit by the window so you can watch all the happy people leave with their bread purchases. $–$$

✒ **Muth's Candies** (800-55MUTHS; www.shop.muths candy.com), 630 E. Market St. Closed Sun. In business since 1921, Muth's has been treating locals to fine candy for generations. The confectionary has a huge selection of sweets like bourbons, creams, and jellies, but they are known for the Modjeska. This caramel marshmallow wonder, as it is referred to, is a heavenly combination of soft marshmallow dipped in chewy caramel. It was named for a famous Polish actress, Helena Modjeska, who appeared in Louisville several times during the late 1800s and was quite fond of the city. Maybe she liked caramel, too. $

Cake Flour Bakery (502-719-0172; cakeflouronmarket.com), 909 E. Market St. Open Mon. 7–2, Tue.–Fri. 7–6, weekends 8–2. Yep, you are getting the real deal at Cake Flour. Nothing fake,

MUTH'S CANDIES, HOME OF THE MODJESKA

Deborah Kohl Kremer

nothing artificial, just real good food. Their flour and sugar are certified organic and unbleached; they use free-range eggs, European chocolate and butter, local berries, even organic paint on the walls. Baker and owner Claudia M. DeLatorre has one simple goal: to offer quality, natural alternatives to processed "fake" food so people can experience the difference. Go there and you will. $

&. ((ᵖ)) **Heine Bros. Coffee** (heine broscoffee.com). With multiple locations around town, you are always close to a Heine Brothers. Open Mon.–Thu. 6:30 AM–9 PM, Fri.–Sat. 6:30 AM–11 PM, Sun. 7 AM–9 PM. They have an excellent assortment of coffee and tea drinks and an equally excellent assortment of sweets to go along with them. All locations are cool and hip. As founding members of Cooperative Coffees, they are committed to partnering with farmer co-ops in growing countries. $

The Bakery at Sullivan University (502-452-1210; sullivan.edu /bakery), 3100 Bardstown Rd. At Louisville's Sullivan University, students can major in culinary arts. What a better way to practice than by selling their wares at a real live bakery? They have a decadent selection of breads, Danish rolls, cookies, and truffles. And wait until you see their cakes. Well, they are art on a plate. In the back room you can see all the bakers-in-the-making, having hands-on classes. Fun to watch. More fun to sample! $

✳ Entertainment

In Louisville

Ⓨ **4th Street Live** (502-584-7170; www.4thstlive.com), 420 W. Liberty St. This entertainment district, covering more than a block of the downtown, is chock-full of bars, restaurants, live entertainment, a comedy club, and even a high-tech bowling alley. You'll find all the major clubs, a few retail chains, and cool eateries. During summer months they have free outdoor concerts featuring big-name county entertainment. Kick off your shoes and dance in the street; everyone else does.

Louisville Palace Theater (502-583-4555; www.louisvillepalace .com), 625 S. 4th St. A true palace in the heart of downtown, this magnificent showplace was rumored to cost more than $2 million when it opened in 1928. Today you can see rock concerts, comedians, and Broadway shows in this Spanish Baroque–inspired 2,700-seat theater. Even if you aren't there to see a show, poke your head into the lobby and admire this gorgeous Louisville treasure.

Actors Theater (502-584-1265; actorstheatre.org), 316 W Main St. Founded in 1964, Actors Theater has won an array of awards and worldwide recognition for excellence. Their goal is to be a major force in revitalizing American playwriting, and over 300 Actors-debuted scripts are now in publication. Check the website for showtimes.

Jodi Karem

4TH STREET LIVE

Louisville Ballet (502-583-2623; louisvilleballet.org), 501 W. Main St. Since its founding in 1952, the Louisville Ballet has been bringing fine ballet to the city. They are the only regional company with which Mikhail Baryshnikov has performed in repertoire productions. Louisville Ballet reaches nearly 50,000 people each year because of their national reputation as one of the country's leading regional ballet companies.

The Louisville Orchestra (502-587-8681; www.louisvilleorchestra .org), 323 W. Broadway, Suite 700. Founded in 1937, this professional 71-member ensemble performs for the Louisville Ballet and the Kentucky Opera. They also offer classical and pops performances.

✳ Selective Shopping

In Louisville (unless otherwise noted)

Nitty Gritty (502-583-3377; nittygrittyvintage.com), 996 Barret Ave. Now, this is a cool vintage store! Clothes from the '70s and before. Fur-collared wool coats like your grandma used to wear, leisure suits with silky shirts and white belts, housedresses from the '50s. You could stay all day. Perfect when you need an accent piece or a whole ensemble for a theme party or if you just want to make a fashion statement.

Dot Fox (502-452-9191; www .dotfoxclothingculture.com), 1701 Bardstown Rd. You'll find a wide selection of progressive and independent lines of men's and women's clothing, shoes, and accessories.

A Taste of Kentucky (atasteofky .com). Get your taste at one of their three shops in Louisville: 400 W. Market, The Mall at St. Matthews at Shelbyville Rd. at I-264, or Village Square at Middletown, which is at 11800 Shelbyville Rd. All are filled with some of the finest Kentucky items; you will be certain to find something for everyone on your gift list, including yourself. Derby items, Kentucky Proud food items, stoneware and art pieces, they have it all.

Regalo Unique Gifts (502-583-1798; regaloart.com), 982 Barret

Ave. Oozing with coolness, this gift shop has all kinds of merchandise that you'll want to own. Hip jewelry, interesting art, Louisville-inspired home decor and clothing. You're going to want to take this stuff home. Sun.–Mon. 10–4, Tue.–Sat. 10–6. They have a second location (502-561-4024) inside the Galt House, 140 N. 4th St.

Scout (502-584-8989; www .scoutonmarket.com), 742 E. Market St. An eclectic mix of home accessories, giftware, artwork, and jewelry located in the downtown East Market Street Business District.

WHY Louisville (502-456-5400; whylouisville.com), 1583 Bards-town Rd., Books, funny T's, and all the hippest Louisville souvenirs you could ever want. Cool shop. Worth your stop. Mon.–Fri. 11–8, Sat. 10–8, Sun. noon–6. A second location at 806 E. Market St. in the neighborhood known as NuLu carries the same types of items but is more of an art gallery, with monthly shows featuring the works of local artists.

Carmichael Bookstore (502-456-6950; carmichaelsbookstore .com), 1295 Bardstown Rd. Sun.–Thu. 8 AM–10 PM, Fri.–Sat. 8 AM–11 PM. This is Louisville's oldest independent bookstore, and after one visit you'll know how they've lasted for more than 30 years. They have the coolest, hippest books—plus Carmichael is the neighborhood hangout, because they always have something going on.

Caufield's Novelty (800-777-5653; caufields.com), 1006 W. Main St.; second location (502-896-6950) 2720 Frankfort Ave. Caufield's is the kind of place where you should expect the unexpected. In business since 1920, the place is jammed with party decorations and supplies, as well as every costumes you might want. They have everything you need for a big Derby party—where else can you find a jockey costume *and* this year's edition of Derby glasses? But Halloween is quickly becoming their specialty. You'll find everything from a pair of false buck teeth, complete with cavity, to a pair of bloody zombie thigh-highs.

Margaret's Consignment (502-896-4706; margaretsconsignment .com), 2700 Frankfort Ave. In business since 1982, Margaret can fix you up whether you want to make a few bucks or save a few. Huge, really huge, selection, which Margaret divides up by color. Looking for a black sweater? Head for the Black Room.

A Reader's Corner Bookstore (502-897-5578; www.areaders corner.com), 2044 Frankfort Ave. With about 50,000 books in stock, this indy bookstore has been selling new, used, rare, and out-of-print books since 1997.

Hadley Pottery (502-584-2171; hadleypottery.com), 1570 Story Ave. Hadley Pottery, known throughout the world, has been a Louisville mainstay since around 1940. You can see the entire col-

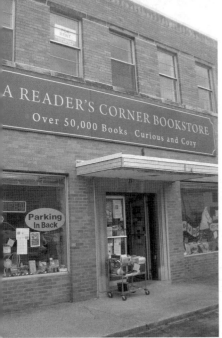

Deborah Kohl Kremer

A READER'S CORNER BOOKSTORE

615 E. Market St. Located in an 1890s schoolhouse downtown, this well-known antiques store has been a Louisville attraction for more than 35 years. Not just knickknacks and dainty items, at Joe's you'll find architectural pieces like old gas pumps, hundreds of mantels, and an impressive assortment of carousel horses. They have china, books, toys from your (and your grandmother's) childhood, and more than 5,000 doors for that house you've been restoring on the weekends. You just never know.

GALLERIES Mellwood Arts and Entertainment Center (502-895-3650; www.mellwood artcenter.com), 1860 Mellwood Ave. This huge old warehouse—a former meatpacking plant—is now

JOE LEY ANTIQUES

Deborah Kohl Kremer

lection and get a deal on a piece of Mary Alice Hadley's fine pottery at this warehouse store. The somewhat whimsical pieces, which are all hand painted, each features Mary Alice's logo M. A. HADLEY written on the back.

Zappos Shoe Outlet (502-921-4949; www.zappos.com), 376 Zappos.Com Blvd., Shepherdsville. If you've ever shopped this mega online retailer, you might want to head 20 miles south of Louisville and see what you can find at their outlet. The prices are not rock-bottom as you might expect with the word *outlet* in the name, but the selection is huge and the prices are lower than you'll find online. So swing in—it's right off I-65—and see what they have.

ANTIQUES Joe Ley Antiques (502-583-4014; www.joeley.com), home to more than 200 artists and entrepreneurs who use the space for studio and storefront. Watch the artists at work and browse their wares as you wander through the amazing collection of talent all under one roof.

Zephyr Gallery (502-585-5646; www.zephyrgallery.org), 610 E. Market St. As the oldest cooperative, contemporary, fine art gallery in the region, Zephyr's 20-plus years of experience shows. It is owned and operated by the members, which allows visitors direct contact with the artists.

Pottery Rowe (502-896-0877; potteryrowe.com), 2048 Frankfort Ave. Potter Melvin Rowe has been selling his gorgeous creations

since 1971. Melvin doesn't use molds so you know that each piece is formed by hand on his potter's wheel, making it truly one-of-a-kind. His unique glaze patterns make each piece an exceptional work of art. Stop by his gallery to see it all. Mon.–Sat. 10–5.

Pyro Gallery (502-587-0106; pyrogallery.com), 624 W. Main St. Featuring contemporary art meant to ignite, excite, and inspire, this cooperative gallery includes a visual feast for the eyes with the works of many artists on display at one time. The artists, whose media vary as much as the artists themselves, join together to run the gallery, pay the bills, and keep it open. They share the burden of

MELLWOOD ARTS CENTER

Nick Kremer

Deborah Kohl Kremer

ROWE POTTERY

being gallery owners, but they enjoy the perks of personally selecting the pieces they want to display. Changing exhibits feature works from recent additions to the co-op, as well as a once-a-year exhibit that displays at least one piece of work from every artist involved. Thu. 11–3, Fri. 11–5, Sat. 11–5, Sun. 11–3.

The Higgins Maxwell Gallery (502-584-7001; www.higgins maxwell.com), 1200 Payne St. Featuring fine examples of vintage American and European art. Knowledgeable staff are on hand to help you with anything you need.

Swanson Reed Contemporary (502-589-5466; swansonreed gallery.com), 638 E. Market. Featuring works that have never been shown before, but the body of work you see in Swanson Reed has never been on display anywhere else. New show every four or five weeks, covering everything from paintings, sculpture, and photography to video, installation, and performance art. Wed.– Sat. 11–6.

✳ Special Events

Spring: **Humana Festival of New American Plays** (www .actorstheatre.org). Rub shoulders with actors, producers, playwrights, directors, journalists, critics, and theater lovers from around the world, who gather each year for a sampling of the newest American plays. For more than 30 years, the Actors Theater of Louisville has hosted this festival, which presents more than 500 performances of both classical and contemporary plays. It also encompasses meet-the-cast parties, discussion panels, and social events.

July: **Lebowski Fest** (www .lebowskifest.com). A celebration of all things Lebowski, a tribute to the Coen brothers' 1998 film and cult classic, *The Big Lebowski*. It's kind of like a *Star Trek* convention for bowlers. True fans gather for unlimited bowling, trivia contests, and the overuse of movie quotes like "Not on the rug, man," and "The Dude is not in." Some of the actors from the movie have shown up from time to time. Lots of music, too.

September: ♪ **Pee Wee Over Louisville—Louisville's Big Adventure** (peeweeoverlouisville .com). From the creator of Lebowski Fest comes a festival dedicated to all things Pee Wee. Held at Tyler Park, the daylong event features carnival games and a bike parade; costumes are encouraged. Rated G, it's a family fun event.

October: ♿ **St. James Court Art Show** (www.stjamescourtartshow .com). One of the largest juried art shows in the country, the St. James draws 700 artists and a quarter of a million people to the open-air show held in historic Old Louisville. Surrounded by 100-year-old trees and Victorian homes, art lovers can stroll the historic neighborhood and browse paintings, drawings, prints, watercolors, ceramics, pottery, and hand-decorated porcelain. There is also jewelry, floral arrangements, metalwork, woodwork, furniture, toys, crafts, stained glass and art glass, windows, clothing, needlework, quilts, leather goods, and enamel work, just to name a few.

MAY: THE DERBY AND ITS FESTIVAL

Okay, so the race lasts two minutes. Still, preparations for the Kentucky Derby are years in the making. After all, these young thoroughbreds have been groomed and trained for this event since their birth, three years prior. Just a few minutes in town will clue you in to the fact that the city of Louisville does not take this event lightly. And for this reason, you will find over-the-top galas, star-studded formal balls, an open-to-the-public Governor's Breakfast (please see *Special Events* in the Frankfort chapter), and Derby Festival events that usually start to kick in two weeks prior to these sacred two minutes.

Produced annually since 1956, the **Derby Festival** entertains 1.5 million people during the 70 special events held each year in the lead-up to the most prestigious horse race in America and the first jewel of the Triple Crown. The events, which are scattered around town, are fun to enjoy on their own, but add to the excitement of the two weeks before the derby. Don't forget to pick up a Pegasus Pin, a cute little lapel pin that serves as your ticket into most of the big events. It is available all over town, costs $3, and instantly becomes a collector's item. A few of the notable events are:

The **Pegasus Parade** is held the Thursday before Derby day. This parade has been a tradition since 1956. One of the largest parades in the United States, it's full of floats, inflatables, marching bands, equestrian acts, and celebrities. The route is downtown on Broadway. Bleacher seats require tickets, but free viewing is available along the route, too.

Thunder Over Louisville is a huge fireworks display, one of the largest around. The fireworks are launched from barges right on the Ohio River. Phenomenal viewing sites are all around the Louisville area.

Watch as more than 35 hot-air balloons chase the lead, or hare, balloon at the **Great Balloon Glow and Race.**

The annual **Great Steamboat Race** on the Ohio River takes place between the *Belle of Louisville* and the *Belle of Cincinnati*. Stand along the shore and listen to the calliope play as the two paddle-wheelers race—well, they don't really go very fast—to the finish line.

Kicking off two weeks prior to the Derby and running right up through the big day, the **Fest-a-Ville on the Waterfront** features music, socializing, and gobs of food. It is also known as the Chow Wagon, and you'll know why when you see all the food vendors.

Be sure to check the **Kentucky Derby Festival** website (www.kdf.org) for dates, times, and further information.

MINT JULEPS

Deborah Kohl Kremer

SHELBYVILLE, LAGRANGE, AND THE SURROUNDING AREA

J ust north, and slightly east, of Louisville city limits is a lesser-known area of Kentucky. **Shelbyville**, **LaGrange**, Eminence, and Crestwood are examples of small towns that are misleadingly known as bedroom communities. Although quite a few of their residents do commute into the big city each day, the fact is they return each night to darling hometowns that offer cute shops, restaurants, and attractions that make this the kind of place where you want to live. So veer off the main expressway routes and take the back roads for a change. You will find scenic byways, farming communities, and out-of-the-ordinary eateries that will make you want to stay awhile.

GUIDANCE These towns are fairly small, so tourism isn't their main focus. For helpful advice you can always turn to www.kytourism.com, which offers regional information and a searchable database broken down by city. The city of LaGrange does have a website (502-269-0126; www .discoverlagrange.org) that will help you plan your day in the downtown area. In surrounding Oldham County, contact Kim Buckler at the **Oldham County Tourism Commission** (800-813-9953; www.touroldham county.com). She can direct you to all the hot spots, and if your group is larger than four people, she'll even create a whole itinerary for you.

GETTING THERE The area is served by the **Louisville International Airport** (502-367-4636; www.flylouisville.com). Car rentals are available at the airport. **Greyhound Bus** (502-561-2805; www.greyhound.com) is located at 720 W. Muhammad Ali Blvd., Louisville. The **Amtrak** station (800-872-7245; www.amtrak.com) is also located at 720 W. Muhammad Ali Blvd.

GETTING AROUND Bounded by I-64, which runs east–west, and I-75, which runs north–south, these expressways have exits for LaGrange,

Shelbyville, and Crestwood—but take the back roads to see them in style. While the downtowns are tiny, you'll still need a car, because the only public transportation is a few commuter bus routes into Louisville.

MEDICAL EMERGENCY Baptist Hospital Northeast (502-222-5388; www.baptistnortheast.com), 1025 New Moody Lane, LaGrange. This full-service hospital serves patients primarily from Oldham, East Jefferson, Henry, Trimble, and Carroll Counties.

ALCOHOL If you are looking for alcohol in this region, you might need to plan ahead. The communities in this section spread across several counties, each with its own version of the law. Jefferson County is a wet county, so alcohol sales are permitted everywhere. In Henry County, which is moist, you will find alcohol within the city of Eminence and the Smith-Berry Winery. Oldham and Shelby Counties are considered limited, which means that certain restaurants can sell alcohol by the drink. So if you want a glass of wine with dinner, call the restaurant first to see which county they are in and what the law is in their neck of the woods.

✳ To See

✑ **Yew Dell Gardens** (502-241-4788; www.yewdellgardens.org), 6220 Old LaGrange Rd., Crestwood. Call for directions or check their website

YEW DELL GARDENS

Nick Kremer

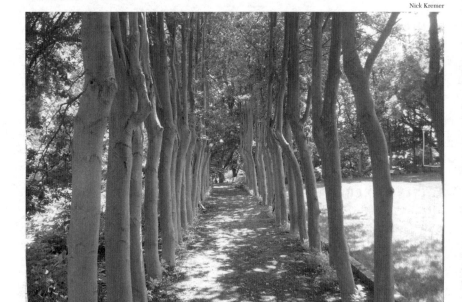

for a map, as some Internet mapping systems are incorrect. Summer hours (Apr.–Nov.) Mon.–Sat. 10–4, Sun. noon–4. Winter hours (Dec.–Mar.) Mon.–Fri. 10–4. This spectacular 33-acre garden is certainly not your run-of-the-mill collection of geraniums and marigolds. This is the former home of Theodore and Martha Klein, horticulturalists who ran a successful nursery on the property for more than 40 years. Now run by a nonprofit organization, their collection of more than 1,100 species of trees, shrubs, and flowers is breathtaking. Wander through the themed gardens, which include roses, dwarf conifers, hollies, and evergreens. Also on site are a relocated log cabin, a stone castle, and a tobacco barn. They have classes and demonstrations throughout the year, but you can also just take a self-guided walking tour. Bring your iPod and download the guided tour so you can follow it without the guide. $7 adults, $5 seniors; under 12 free.

Smith-Berry Vineyard and Winery (502-845-7091; www.smithberry winery.net), New Castle. Walk the grounds of the vineyard and then stop by the tasting room (Tue.–Sat. 10–6) to taste the benefits of harvesting grapes by hand and fermenting them in small distinct lots. Smith-Berry hosts concerts during the summer where you can kick back and relax with some great music and homegrown wine.

Rob Morris Home (www.discoverdowntownlagrange.org), 110 Washington St., LaGrange. Open by appointment only. Tour this beautiful home, which was once owned by Rob Morris, the poet laureate of Freemasonry and founder of the Order of the Eastern Star. The two-story white-clapboard house, which was built in 1840, was home to the Morris family from 1862 through the 1890s. Furnished with several pieces of the Morris family furniture, the home also features artifacts of Morris's life and pieces of history from the Order of the Eastern Star.

Oldham County Historical Society (502-222-0826; www .oldhamcountyhistoricalsociety .org), 106 N. 2nd Ave., LaGrange. Open Tue.–Sat. 10–4, Sun. noon–4. Housed in three pre–Civil War buildings, this museum does a good job re-creating Oldham County's past.

OLDHAM COUNTY HISTORICAL SOCIETY
Deborah Kohl Kremer

✳ To Do

GOLF Henry County Country Club (502-845-2375; www.hccc.com), 2200 Campbellsburg Rd., New Castle. Quite the gathering place for Henry County residents, this semi-private club features an 18-hole, par-71 course. An excellent value: You pay one greens fee and golf from dawn to dusk. So load up your cooler and try to beat one local's personal record of 54 holes in one day.

Clear Creek Golf Course (502-633-0375), 717 Burks Branch Rd., Shelbyville. This 9-hole par-4 executive course is perfect for beginners but gets high recommendations from serious duffers, too. Carts are available, but it's a nice course to walk. Call for a tee time on holidays and weekends.

Weissinger Hills Golf Course (502-633-7332; www.weissingerhills.com), 2240 Mount Eden Rd., Shelbyville. With a clubhouse as nice as the 18-hole, par-72 course, you might want to stay awhile. This scenic course also offers friendly staff and a well-stocked pro shop.

SCUBA Falling Rock Park Scuba Diving Park (502-939-5049), Fendley Mill Rd., Oldham County. Open Sat.–Sun. May–Oct. This former rock quarry is now a 50-foot diving lake. Pay one fee and dive all day. Loaded with fish, sunken boats, and even an old school bus, all for your diving pleasure.

TOURS Spirits of LaGrange Ghost Tours (502-356-3293; discover lagrange.org/ghosts). Tours available the fourth Saturday of each month. Reservations necessary. Get to know some former residents of LaGrange on this 1½-hour lantern-lit walking tour. The expedition covers about 12 city blocks and is led by an entertaining and knowledgeable tour guide. No children under 12. $15 per person.

✳ Green Space

Guist Creek Lake (502-647-5359), 11990 Boat Dock Rd., Shelbyville. Primarily known for its stock of largemouth bass, hybrid stripers, catfish, crappie, bluegill, and rockfish, it is a fisherman's dream. During the summer months, the lake also has an area set aside for water-skiers. A fully stocked marina on site offers gas, bait, snacks, and fishing licenses. They also have a boat ramp and some small motorboats available for rent. A campground is available Mar.–Nov. with primitive sites as well as pull-through RV camping with electric and water hookup.

Lake Jericho Recreational Area (502-743-5205). This 137-acre lake located in Henry County offers bank fishing for largemouth bass, bluegill, crappie, and catfish. They also have a 62 RV camping sites with electric and water hookups. Throughout the property there are tent sites available, too. The fishing lake is open year-round, but camping is only available Apr.–Oct.

✴ Lodging

The Bluegrass Country Estate B&B (502-222-2009, 877-229-2009; www.bluegrasscountry estate.com), 1226 Bluegrass Pkwy., LaGrange. For those traveling with a horse, this B&B will pamper you as well as your equine traveling companion. Although innkeeper Cheryl Sabin refers to her inn as a bed & breakfast, it is more like a luxury retreat that you won't want to leave. Inside the gorgeous home are five well-appointed guest rooms loaded with horse decor and antiques, making them warm and inviting. But wait until you try the beds. Each room features a top-of-the-line Swedish sleep system that practically cuddles you into dreamland. It might be the best night of sleep you have ever had. Even though you won't want to get out of bed, wait till you see what else Cheryl has available. There is a fabulous home gym, a heated pool and hot tub, and a theater room with a giant screen, hundreds of movies, and a popcorn machine. More draws to this room are the comfy reclining theater chairs and the personalized Hollywood photographs featuring movie legends like Don Ameche and Ava Gardner. These original photos belonged to Cheryl's mother, who worked in the commissary at Paramount Pictures in the 1950s and '60s. Listen to her fascinating stories over gourmet omelets and scones or pecan waffles, just two of her oft-requested breakfast specialties. $$$

Colonial Hill Inn (502-558-4504; www.colonialhillinn.zoomshare.com), 316 E. Cross Main St., New Castle. Innkeeper Tina Stambaugh considers her B&B to be a retreat destination, where people come to unwind and unplug. For that reason, you won't find a television in every room. This 1830s Greek Revival home offers two antiques-laden guest rooms that feature a welcome basket and homemade cookies upon your arrival. Tina is happy to accommodate special requests, like a favorite dessert in the evening or acknowledgment of a special occasion. Wander along the walking path that winds through the home's 22 acres. For breakfast, enjoy the deluxe continental array that always features Tina's signature scones. $–$$

✴ Where to Eat

DINING OUT ♿ **Claudia Sanders Dinner House** (502-633-5600; www.claudiasanders .com), 3202 Shelbyville Rd., Shelbyville. Tue.–Sun. 11–9. When the wife of Colonel Sanders decided to open a restaurant, she put her own chicken on the menu. The chicken dishes are "finger-lickin'" . . . but Mrs. Sanders knew how to make southern favorites like hot brown, country ham and biscuits, and Kentucky pie with pecans and chocolate chips, too. $–$$

🍸 **Westport General Store** (502-222-4626; www.westport generalstore.com), 7008 KY 524,

Westport. Serving dinner Thu.–Sat. 5–10. Head west of LaGrange a few miles and you'll come to the tiny burg of Westport, where this store has been in business almost continuously since Westport formed in 1780. The wood plank floors, wood-burning stove, and old black-and-white photographs really add to the ambience. Yet their southern-style (with a hint of upscale) menu options are what bring people back time and again. You can't find dishes like black-eyed peas, collard greens, and fried bologna sandwiches alongside filet mignon and bison rib eyes just anywhere. Nice dessert selection, too. $$–$$$

The Science Hill Inn (502-633-2825; www.wakefieldscearce.com), 525 Washington St., Shelbyville. Tue.–Sun. 11:30–2:30, Sat 5:30–7:30. More than 100 years ago, young ladies of a certain pedigree attended the Science Hill Inn to learn social graces. Today the upscale dining room has an air about it that makes you try harder to use your manners. So put the cloth napkin on your lap, get your elbows off the table, and carefully browse the southern-inspired menu. With choices like shrimp and grits, Kentucky hot brown, and country ham and pimiento cheese sandwiches, the decisions are tough, but your final decision will be a good one. The entrées are first-rate, and the dedicated servers will keep your table supplied with hot corn bread pone during your visit. $$

♈ **Old Stone Inn** (502-722-8200; www.old-stone-inn.com), 6905 Shelbyville Rd., Simpsonville. Serving lunch Thu. and Fri. 11–2, dinner Mon.–Sat. 4–10. Completed in 1818 and built from local limestone, the Old Stone Inn is a historic gem located in Shelby County. Touring the building and admiring the construction is worth a stop alone, but while you are there you have to experience their wonderful southern-inspired menu. Dive into Grandma Mary's chicken livers, southern-fried chicken, or their bourbon barrel pork chops for a real treat. Side dish options include southern greens, okra, and grits, reminding you that you are south of the Mason-Dixon line. They also serve more standard fare like burgers, sandwiches, and salads, which are all good, too. If the weather is nice, eat out on the patio and soak in that country air. $$–$$$

EATING OUT Our Best (502-845-7682), 5728 Smithfield Rd., Smithfield. Open for lunch and dinner Tue., Wed., Thu., and Sun. 11–8. They stay open until 9 PM on Fri. and Sat. Breakfast is served on weekends only, Sat. and Sun. 8–10:30. Slightly off the beaten path, about 8 miles east of LaGrange, you'll find this cozy hometown eatery. Housed in the former Smithfield Milling Company, Our Best serves up old-fashioned favorites like fried chicken, bean soup, and fried corn bread. One of their signature dishes is the fried green tomatoes, which you can have as a side dish or on a BLT, which they call BLGT. The creaky wood floor and enormous collection of business cards tacked to the walls add to the ambience. $–$$

& **Red Pepper Deli** (502-225-0770), 103 E. Main St., LaGrange. Mon.–Fri. 10:30–6, Sat. 10:30–4. Known for their huge portions; you won't go away hungry. Their impressive lineup of homemade soups and salads, as well as sandwiches all served on fresh bread, make it hard to choose. $–$$

One Nineteen West Main (502-222-1246; onenineteenwestmain .com), 119 W. Main St., LaGrange. Open every day from breakfast through dinner, this family-owned and -operated gem features home-cooked meals and tons of choices.

Salads, sandwiches, and entrées like pork chops and salmon means there is something for everyone. Check out the cute menu names to reflect the train-running-through-the town motif. $–$$

Big R's BBQ Shack (502-222-0058), 213 S.1st St., LaGrange. Mon.–Thu. 11–2, Fri and Sat. 11–8. Wander about a block farther down Main Street and you'll find a barbecue lover's dream. When you smell the slow-roasted barbecue, you will know you are at the right place. Featuring baby back ribs, pulled pork sandwiches, and pulled chicken and brisket sandwiches, all swimming in sauce and lip-smacking good. Their potato salad is so good, some people are tempted to order it as an entrée. $–$$

Serendipity (502-222-4216), 116 E. Main St., LaGrange. Mon.–Sat.

SERENDIPITY

Paul Kremer

10–5. Serendipity is a darling mix of café, gift shop, and tearoom. Stop in to browse their unique collection of home decor items and country-inspired art, then have a seat and enjoy a warm bowl of soup, a grilled sandwich, or a cup of tea. Everyone gets treated to a piece of scone to whet their appetite. $–$$

Ϋ **Irish Rover Too** (502-222-2286; www.theirishroverky.com), 117 E. Main St., LaGrange. Open Tue.–Thu. 11–9, Fri. and Sat. 11–10. With a perfect combination of Irish favorites transformed into American bar food, this pub is a perfect choice for a group trying to please several appetites. Nowhere else in LaGrange will you find a Welsh rabbit sandwich, a salmon burger, shanagarry fish cakes, or an order of bangers and mash. For those not feeling so Irish, they have a big hearty cheeseburger, stuffed pork loin, and a flavorful chicken salad sandwich. Nice assortment on their kids' menu, too. Save room for an Irish-cream-liqueur-laced cheesecake or bread-and-butter pudding that is soaked in whiskey-caramel sauce. Yes, you do have room for it. $–$$

Ϋ **Siegs on the River** (502-228-1922; www.siegsontheriver.com), 1902 Victory Lane, Prospect. Open Mon.–Thu. 11–10, Fri. and Sat. 11–11, Sun. 10–10. Cutoffs and flip-flops are welcome. Eat outside on the floating wharf and enjoy watching the boats go by as you feast on casual selections like chicken fingers, wraps, and sandwiches and burgers. The food is good, the prices are right, and dining on the river makes you feel like you're on vacation. Live music on the weekends. $–$$

SNACKS ♧ ∮ **Morgan Drug Store** (502-255-3540), 325 US 42, Bedford. Open Mon.–Fri. 8–6:30, Sat. 8–2. Closed Sun. About 9 miles east of Campbellsburg, you will find the tiny community of Bedford. Although it is off the beaten path somewhat, it's worth your while to slip back in time to this old-time soda fountain that has been serving up treats to Trimble County natives for more than 50 years. The malts, shakes, and ice cream cones are still hand dipped the way they always have been, but the real draw is that this is probably the only place in Kentucky where you will find a nickel Coke. Yes, they really are a nickel. $

Q&A Sweet Treats Bakery & Dessert Café (502-265-0550; qasweettreats.com), 211 S. 1st St., LaGrange. Open 7–6 during the week; until 8 PM on Fri. and Sat. Closed Sun. and Mon. Known for their baked-fresh-daily Italian bread, this crusty bit of heaven comes out of the oven every afternoon, so locals can pick up a loaf for dinner. But while you are here, you won't want to miss out on their unbelievable cookies, scones, and bread-of-the day selections. You won't be disappointed. $

✳ Selective Shopping

Cherry House (502-425-7107; www.cherryhouse.com), 2419 S. KY 53, LaGrange. This furniture business started out selling cut glass and handmade solid cherry furniture in a small showroom in 1969. Today you can browse through several homes and buildings, where you'll find furniture displayed as it would be in your house. The Cherry House is widely regarded as the premier resource for upscale, yet affordable, fine home furnishings.

Wakefield Scearce Galleries (502-633-4382; www.wakefield scearce.com), 525 Washington St., Shelbyville. Closed Sun. Housed in a former all-girl academy known as Science Hill, these galleries concentrate on British antiques, mint julep cups, and fine silver. The historic building also features smaller shops offering fine clothing, linens, and silk flowers.

The 1887 Corner Store (502-222-4454), 101 E. Main St., LaGrange. This building, which has been lovingly restored to its 1880s grandeur, is one of the first things visitors see when arriving in historic downtown LaGrange. The warm and inviting shop is full of gift items you'll want to keep for yourself. They have pottery, linens, home decor items, and an assortment of upscale pieces for your home.

Karen's Book Barn and Java Stop (502-222-0918; karensbook barn.com), 127 E. Main St., LaGrange. Order up a coffee, cappuccino, or fresh fruit smoothie and wander through this cozy shop bursting with both new and used books.

✎ **The Treasured Child** (502-225-9646; www.thetreasuredchild .com), 115 E. Main St., LaGrange. The sign out front says COME IN AND PLAY, and they mean it. This independently owned toy store has shelves and shelves of wonderful toys for the kid in everybody. The story is so inviting, you really will want to play for a while.

The Gathering Room Quilt Shoppe (502-222-1044; www .gatheringroomquiltshop.com), 109 E. Washington St., LaGrange. Closed Sun. and Mon. Just browsing through this 1880s-era home and looking at all the quilts, patterns, and fabric makes you want

THE GATHERING ROOM QUILT SHOPPE
Deborah Kohl Kremer

to start stitching. One whole room is dedicated to Civil War reproduction fabrics and patterns, inspiring to both quilters and non-quilters.

✷ Special Events

Weekends, May–July:
🍴 ✎ ♿ **Highland Renaissance Festival**, Eminence. Spend a day steeped in the Renaissance period of the Dark Ages around the 15th and 16th centuries. See jousting demonstrations, knights in shining armor, and period-appropriate musical acts. Wear a costume from that era in history and you'll make friends quickly. They have food like turkey legs but also festival-type fare to appeal to the whole family.

July: 🍴 ✎ ♿ **Annual Harvest Showcase and Farmer's Market**, Henry County Fairgrounds. Although it feels a lot like a county fair, this huge farmer's market is really a way to bring goods from the garden to the table. Agriculture is the main attraction, with chefs cooking up the homegrown products like meat, honey, and produce. There are also kids' games like Thimble in the Haystack, a husband-calling contest, and a tractor pull. Spend the day and feel like a local.

Western Kentucky 6

Western Kentucky

© The Countryman Press

KYEGii1 Western Kentucky

INTRODUCTION:
WESTERN KENTUCKY

Western Kentucky differs from the rest of the state geographically, because it's primarily flat. Vast open plains, giant farms, and dense wooded areas blanket Kentucky's lower left quadrant. Its beauty differs from the rugged mountains in the east and rolling bluegrass plains of central Kentucky, but it is beautiful all on its own.

The Ohio, Cumberland, Rough, Green, and Tennessee Rivers make up the myriad waterways that allowed this area to grow and prosper as Kentucky's settlers moved west. Now, 200 years later, it is these same rivers, along with the human-made Kentucky Lake and Lake Barkley, that bring people to the area. Although the flatboat has been replaced by luxury houseboats and the dugout canoe has evolved into a speedboat with a water-skier hanging on the back, it is the same water and shoreline that help the area flourish.

Western Kentucky is twangy bluegrass music, succulent barbecue restaurants, intricately stitched quilts, and the aforementioned water-related recreation. Yet although these are major factors in the area's character and charm, they merely scratch the surface. You have to go there, meet the people, and participate in these activities before you really understand what makes Western Kentucky special.

OWENSBORO AND HENDERSON

Located just about 30 minutes apart via US 60, you'll find the two river cities of Owensboro and Henderson. Although both are delightful on their own, they each deserve a place in Kentucky's history, as well as your vacation travels.

The third largest city in Kentucky, **Owensboro** is located on the banks of the Ohio River. The area is known for its famous barbecue and bluegrass music, but that's certainly not all this river city has to offer. They have a fine collection of museums, parks, and golf courses, as well as a lively downtown. But somehow everything seems connected to the bluegrass or the barbecue.

Let's start with the bluegrass connection. Owensboro was the birthplace of Bill Monroe, known as the Father of Bluegrass, so residents know and understand this music. Locals claim that if it weren't for Monroe, there would be no genre of music called bluegrass. So it seems natural that the International Bluegrass Music Museum is in Owensboro. This is where you can learn all about Monroe and other pioneers in the industry. It is also home to the Bluegrass Music Hall of Fame.

Now on to the barbecue connection. Folks in this town know how they like their barbecue. It's not something that comes out of a can, and it's not something that people would refer to as "Sloppy Joes." It is a meal of various kinds of meat, preferably mutton, served with, depending on the restaurant, trademark sauce. Locals grow up going to one of these barbecue joints, and that is where they go for barbecue their whole life. They are a loyal bunch. So whether you are going to Moonlite Bar-B-Q, George's Bar-B-Q, Ole South Barbeque, or Old Hickory Bar-B-Q, you'll be getting a real authentic Owensboro barbecue. You might need to try them all so you can be a fair judge.

The river city of **Henderson** is a favorite stop for the paddle-wheel riverboats like the *Mississippi Queen* and the *American Queen* because Henderson is a perfect example of a darling, small Kentucky town. The city, home to about 27,000 people, has a nice park area along the river, which gently rolls into the downtown area.

Henderson's most famous former resident, John James Audubon, who spent most of his life painting birds, is honored in the downtown area with bird sculptures scattered about. He is also remembered at Audubon State Park, where you'll find camping, trails, a nature center, and a collection of his original artwork.

Another famous resident was W. C. Handy, aka the Father of the Blues. To preserve his memory and honor his lifelong achievements, Henderson stages its free W. C. Handy Blues & Barbecue Festival on the riverfront each June.

GUIDANCE Owensboro-Daviess County Tourist Commission (270-926-1100, 800-489-1131; www.visitowensboro.com), 215 E. 2nd St., Owensboro. Open 8–4:30 weekdays. Located in a refurbished historic building right in the heart of downtown. Lots of information, maps, and advice here, and it also houses the Hometown Hero Hall of Fame (see below). **Henderson County Tourist Commission** (270-826-3128, 800-648-3128; www.hendersonky.org), 101 N. Water St., Suite B, Henderson. Open weekdays 9–5. The Henderson Welcome Center is located in a replica of a historic riverfront railroad depot and has all the brochures and advice you could ever need. It is also the site of the Henderson Historical Society, so it is like a mini museum covering Henderson's past. Stop in and look around.

OWENSBORO VISITORS CENTER
Deborah Kohl Kremer

GETTING THERE The area is served by the **Evansville Regional Airport** (www.evv airport.com) just 12 miles away from Henderson. This airport offers commuter flights to connecting airports. **Greyhound Bus** (270-821-3086; www.greyhound .com) serves the Madisonville and

Western Kentucky region. The station is located at the Red Cardinal Inn, 4765 Hanson Rd., US 41N, Madisonville.

GETTING AROUND Owensboro Transit System (270-687-8570; www.owensboro.org). Runs several route around the city, Mon.–Fri. 6–7, Sat. 8–4. Check the website for route maps. The **River City Trolley** loops around to all the Owensboro attractions, restaurants, and shops. Tue.–Sat. 9–5, Sun. 1–5. The trolley does not operate during the months of Jan., Feb., and Mar. Running several routes through Henderson is the HART Bus System. They do not have a website, but you can call 270-831-1249 for a schedule or pick one up at the Henderson County Tourist Commission.

MEDICAL EMERGENCY Owensboro Mercy Health System (877-888-OMHS; www.omhs.org), 1006 Ford Ave., Owensboro. Serving 11 counties in Western Kentucky and Southern Indiana, this hospital provides medical services to the regional community. **Methodist Hospital** (270-827-7700; www.methodisthospital.net), 1305 N. Elm St., Henderson. Originally known as Henderson Hospital, it was built in 1946 and has 160 beds.

ALCOHOL Both Daviess County, home to Owensboro, and Henderson County, home to Henderson, are wet counties, which means alcohol is available at bars, restaurants, and liquor stores.

✳ To See

🐾 ♿ **Hometown Hero Hall of Fame** (270-926-1100; www.visitowensboro .com), 215 E. 2nd St., Owensboro. Open weekdays 9–4. Attached to the visitors center, you'll find information about local residents who have made it to the big time via sports, movies, television, and politics. The Owensboro area is the former home of the Everly Brothers, Johnny Depp, and America's mom, Florence Henderson. Free.

HOMETOWN HERO HALL OF FAME
Deborah Kohl Kremer

🐾 ✎ **Sassafras Tree**, 2100 block of Frederica St. (US 431), Owensboro. See this 100-foot-tall tree, which is thought to be the world's largest.

♿ **International Bluegrass Music Museum** (270-926-7891;

Deborah Kohl Kremer

INTERNATIONAL BLUEGRASS MUSIC MUSEUM

www.bluegrass-museum.org), 117 Daviess St., Owensboro. Tue.–Sat. 10–5, Sun. 1–4. This museum is dedicated to preserving the history of bluegrass music and the artists who created the whole genre. As a native from the Owensboro area, legendary Bill Monroe, along with his Blue Grass Boys Band, are celebrated in an impressive exhibit. Hands-on displays, photos, and memorabilia from the early days of bluegrass through today are all featured as well. $5 adults, $2 students; under 6 free.

OWENSBORO AREA MUSEUM OF SCIENCE & HISTORY

Deborah Kohl Kremer

✍ ♿ **Owensboro Area Museum of Science & History** (270-687-2732; www.owensboromuseum.com), 122 E. 2nd St., Owensboro. Mon. 10–8, Tue.–Sat. 10–5, Sun. 1–5. Kids can have fun while learning at the PlayZeum, an indoor playground for children under 10. They get to crawl through tubes and bridges and play on a riverboat and in tree houses. You'll also find science-based exhibits, and a gallery depicting local racing history and motor sports. $3 adults; under 2 free.

&ch. **Owensboro Museum of Fine Art** (270-685-3181; www.omfa.museum), 901 Frederica St., Owensboro. Tue.–Fri. 10–4, weekends 1–4. Lovers of fine art will appreciate a tour of Kentucky's second largest art museum, just behind Louisville's Speed Art Museum, in Owensboro. From pieces dating back to the 15th century through an impressive permanent collection of folk art and stained glass, the museum covers everything. Also on site is a 1909 Carnegie Library and the John Hampden Smith House, a pre–Civil War mansion. Voluntary admission fee.

Bill Monroe Birthplace (270-274-9181; www.visitohiocountyky.org), 6210 Blue Moon of Kentucky Hwy. (US 62E), Rosine. Open Mon.–Sat. 9–5, Sun. 1–4. About 40 miles south of Owensboro you can pay homage to one of the area's favorite sons. Take a guided tour of the birthplace of Bill Monroe, the Father of Bluegrass Music. The home, where Bill was born in 1911, is full of Monroe family memorabilia. Included with the furnishings are photographs of Uncle Pen, who was the subject of one of Bill's most beloved songs. Monroe, who is the only musician to be inducted into the Rock 'n' Roll, Country, and Bluegrass Music Halls of Fame, created the unique genre of music that today is known as bluegrass. Just down the road a bit is the cemetery where Bill and Uncle Pen are buried, if you'd like to pay your respects. Free, but donations are appreciated.

Ruby Moon Vineyard & Winery (270-830-7660; www.rubymoonwinery .com), 9566 US 41A, Henderson. Open Mon.–Thu. 11–6, Fri. 11–8:30,

OWENSBORO MUSEUM OF FINE ART

www.kentuckytourism.com

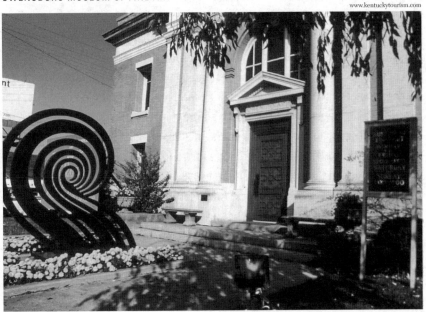

BILL MONROE, THE FATHER OF BLUEGRASS MUSIC

When William Smith Monroe was born on September 13, 1911, in tiny Rosine, Kentucky, the world of music did not know what it was in for. Bill, who grew up on the family farm in Ohio County, near Owensboro, would grow up to be known as the Father of Bluegrass Music, in honor of the music genre he created.

He was the youngest of eight children, and the Monroe family's members all seemed to have a musical spark. His mother, Malissa, and her brother, Pendleton Vandiver, are credited with keeping the family instruments humming. Being the youngest, Bill was coerced into learning the mandolin, which was not his choice. But with older siblings already claiming the prized guitar and fiddle, he took what he could get.

By the time Bill was a teen, his parents had passed away and his older brothers and sisters had moved on. So he lived with various family members before settling down with Pendleton, whom he, and now the world, knows as Uncle Pen. Bill accompanied Pen to fiddle-playing gigs and learned the instruments, as well as songs and melodies that he pulled from his entire professional life. One of Bill's most legendary songs, called "Uncle Pen," was written in 1950 and is on an album released in 1972.

Bill headed out of Kentucky in 1929 in search of work. He worked briefly at an oil refinery in Indiana with his brothers. In their spare time they formed a musical group called the Monroe Brothers. The boys played at local parties and dances and even did a few live radio broadcasts that reached several states. Their unique sound got noticed by RCA, and they signed a recording contract in 1936. They recorded more than 60 songs in the next two years, including the hit single gospel song "What Would You Give in Exchange for Your Soul?"

Although the group disbanded in 1938, Bill never forgot his roots. Following a move to Little Rock, Arkansas, he found some fellow musicians and formed a group called the Kentuckians. This did not last long, so Bill moved on to Atlanta, where in keeping with his humble beginnings he formed the Blue Grass Boys, the first edition of a group of musicians whose sound would change the music world forever.

The combination of vocal harmony, fast tempo, and unique mar-

www.kentuckytourism.com

BILL MONROE BIRTHPLACE

riage of violin, banjo, and mandolin grew into the genre of bluegrass music—named for the band, who were named for the commonwealth—that we know today.

The Blue Grass boys recorded hits in the 1940s such as "Wicked Path of Sin," "My Rose of Old Kentucky," "Little Cabin Home on the Hill," and Monroe's most famous song, "Blue Moon of Kentucky," which was recorded by Elvis Presley in 1954. It was on the flip side of "That's All Right," Elvis's first 45 with Sun Records. Although Monroe intended for the song to be a ballad, Presley put his own spin on it. Monroe liked the Elvis version so much, he re-recorded it with a hint of rock and roll himself.

According to Bill Burden, 74, who grew up near Rosine, Bill Monroe is the typical story of a local boy who made it big and remembered his roots. Burden recalled his family gathered around the radio on Saturday nights in the 1940s to listen to Monroe on the *Grand Ole Opry*.

"We saved our batteries so we knew we would be able to listen to the whole show," he said. "Bill would always mention that he was from Rosine on those shows. He was our star."

Burden said Monroe would come back to the area fairly frequently, even performing at the Rosine Barn Jamboree with the U.S. Navy Band, in 1995, just a year before he passed away.

"He did us a favor then, and another one by being buried here with his family," said Burden. "Anyone who wants to know more about blue-grass music needs to come to Ohio County and visit the family home and the Rosine Cemetery, where they can pay their respects."

Monroe has been inducted into the Rock and Roll Hall of Fame, the Country Music Hall of Fame, and the Nashville Music Writers Hall of Fame; he received a Grammy Lifetime Achievement Award. He was the inaugural inductee into the International Bluegrass Music Hall of Honor, which is in the International Bluegrass Music Museum in downtown Owensboro.

"Bill Monroe and the Blue Grass Boys established a sound that was new. At first it was considered hillbilly or country, but it was so distinctive that it became its own subset," said Forest Roberts, curator of the museum. "He was the true pioneer, and now most of the museum, in some way, leads to Bill Monroe."

Sat. 11–6. Owners Jamie Like and Anita Frazer are proud of their award-winning wine and invite visitors to tour the vineyard and then stop for a sample. Wine tasting is free if you make a purchase, and you will once you taste their wonderful flavors.

✱ To Do

GOLF Ben Hawes State Park Golf Course & Driving Range (270-685-2011), 400 Boothfield Rd., 4 miles west of Owensboro. This course has 27 holes: an 18-hole course and a par 3 course with 9 holes. The front 9 was built on flat terrain and the back 9, on hilly. The Pro Shop offers pull carts, golf cars, and rental clubs.

Golfland U.S.A. (270-683-4963; www.golflandusa.net), 1864 Old Calhoun Rd., Owensboro. They have a pro shop, an 18-hole miniature golf course, batting cages, and a go-cart track. Bring the whole family for a day of fun.

Panther Creek Golf Course (270-785-4565), 4641 Hwy. 1514, Utica. This 18-hole, par-70, regulation-length public course offers 5,990 yards of golf from the longest tee.

Players Club of Henderson (270-827-9999; www.playersclubof henderson.com), 800 Wolf Hills Blvd., Henderson. With 13 lakes and more than 90 bunkers, this public 18-hole par-72 course can challenge even the best golfers. They also have a pro shop and Players Pub, a sports bar and grill right off the 18th green.

RACEWAY Windy Hollow Raceway Park (270-785-4300; www.windy hollowspeedway.com), 5141 Windy Hollow Rd., Owensboro. The park includes a 0.25-mile drag strip and D-shaped dirt stock-car track. Check the website to see the racing schedule.

THOROUGHBRED RACING Ellis Park Race Course (800-333-8110; www.ellisparkracing.com), 3300 US 41N, Henderson. Live racing July–Labor Day; simulcast races from other tracks year-round. Check the website for schedules and post times. Come out and enjoy Kentucky's only thoroughbred track that doesn't feel like it's in Kentucky. Originally built in 1922, Ellis Park is located on the shores of the Ohio River. Strangely enough, it's on the north side of the river, so it appears to be part of Indiana. But based on some long-drawn-out story about an earthquake and Kentucky's borders and the edges of the river, you just have to know that you are still in Kentucky. Don't let the fact that they use Indiana's 812 area code throw you off, either. A day of studying the race card can make you hungry, so while you're there, make reservations to eat at the **Sky Theater Restaurant**. They have a fantastic view of the track and finish line. It is an all-smoking restaurant, though—something to keep in mind if you don't care for smoke.

WALKING TOURS Audubon Sculpture Tour and Historic Walking Tour. Scattered about Henderson's downtown area are life-sized bird sculptures. These fabulous pieces of art were created by Kentucky sculptor Raymond Graf from John James Audubon's portfolio. Your tour includes Central Park, which is thought to be the oldest city park west of the Allegheny Mountains. Explore the downtown and see prime examples of 19th-century architecture in the homes, buildings, and churches. Get a map at the tourism office, or download from the website, so you don't miss anything.

AUDUBON SCULPTURE

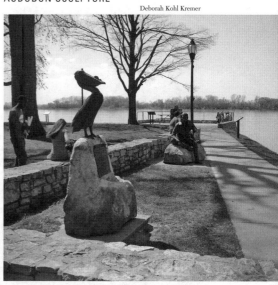
Deborah Kohl Kremer

✳ Green Space

Pinecliffe Gardens (270-281-9791), 6745 Foster Rd., Philpot. You've never seen a garden like this. This daylily and hosta farm has more than 1,500 varieties on display. Although peak bloom season is the second and third weeks of June, the gardens are a nice place to visit all through the summer.

Western Kentucky Botanical Gardens (270-852-8925, 270-993-1234), 25 Carter Rd., Owensboro. Open to the public Mon.–Fri. 9–3. With six established gardens—Butterfly, Rose, Daylily, Iris, Herb, and Fruit & Berry—this small piece of Eden is chock-full of blooms you can enjoy and display ideas you can use in your own garden. Wander through and take in the glorious sights and smells.

Adkisson Greenbelt Park (270-687-8707). The 15-mile-long Greenbelt Park was designed to encircle the city of Owensboro. The 10-foot-wide paved surface is perfect for walking, running, skating, or bicycling.

Yellow Creek Park (270-281-0436), 5710 KY 144, Owensboro. Nestled along the wooded banks of Yellow Creek, the park offers 119 acres of recreation including plenty of softball fields, picnic shelters, nature trails, basketball courts, tennis courts, fishing, and a playground. They also have a disk golf course that is recognized by the Professional Disc Golf Association.

Audubon Mill Park, N. Water St., Henderson. Right alongside the Ohio River is this charming park. It features park benches where you can enjoy a take-out lunch, statues of James Audubon and some of the birds that he studied, and fabulous views of the river. The park sits on the land where

AUDUBON MILL PARK

Deborah Kohl Kremer

www.kentuckytourism.com

AUDUBON STATE PARK AND MUSEUM

Audubon ran a gristmill, one of several business ventures he participated in while living in Henderson. Some of the foundation stones are still on site, as is a huge stone from the mill.

STATE PARKS 🎐 ✎ ♿ **Ben Hawes State Park** (270-684-9808; www .parks.ky.gov), 400 Boothfield Rd., off US 60, 4 miles west of Owensboro. Situated on a former mining village. There are still nine buildings that were part of the Rudy Mines, which operated from 1820 to 1950. Enjoy 300 acres, a 2-mile nature trail, mountain bike trails, an archery range, a playground, and a picnic shelter.

✎ ♿ **John J. Audubon State Park and Museum** (270-826-5939; www .parks.ky.gov), 3100 US 41N, Henderson. John James Audubon, renowned naturalist and artist, lived in the area 1810–19, and it was here that he spent time searching for wild birds and sketching them. The park offers 6.5 miles of trails through the nature preserve and even backcountry hiking. For recreation they offer fishing, a 9-hole golf course, tennis, and paddle boats. The on-site museum includes memorabilia from Audubon's life and a nature center with hands-on exhibits. Museum hours: Mar.–Nov., daily 10–5; Dec.–Feb., Wed.–Sun. 8–4:30. Although there is no lodge, this park offers six rental cottages plus 69 campsites with utilities. Campgrounds are open year-round, although the water at sites is turned off during winter months. No reservations accepted.

✳ Lodging

L&N Bed & Breakfast (270-831-1100; www.lnbbky.com), 327 N. Main St., Henderson. This 100-year-old Victorian home features soaring ceilings, a hand-carved staircase, stained-glass windows, and welcoming fireplaces. Close to the railroad bridge, the occasional train can lull you to sleep in one of the four gracious guest rooms. Innkeepers Norris and Mary Elizabeth Priest make sure you enjoy your stay. Norris loves magic and might do a trick if you ask. $

Victorian Quarters (270-831-2778; www.victorianquartersbb.com), 109 Clay St., Henderson. Overlooking the Ohio River, this Italianate home was built in 1865. The house is fully restored to its original days, with authentic antique furniture in each of the three cozy guest rooms and common areas. $

CAMPING Diamond Lake Resort and Campground (270-229-4900), 7301 Hobbs Rd., located 11 miles west of Owensboro on KY 56. It is worth the drive to this wooded park with 270 campsites on 157 acres. This resort is full of family fun: fishing, swimming, a go-cart track with carts for all ages, and even a paintball field.

Windy Hollow Campground Recreation (270-785-4150; www.windyhollowcampground.com), 5141 Windy Hollow Rd., Owensboro. Not just a 110-site campground, they have all kinds of fun

things to do. There's a swim lake with waterslide and a sandy beach, as well as a fishing lake stocked weekly with farm-raised catfish. Grill up your catch on their 40-foot barbecue pit.

✳ Where to Eat

In Owensboro

Famous Bistro (270-686-8202), 102 W. 2nd St. Open for lunch and dinner every day. In this land of barbecue, this is the place to go for a slightly upscale Mediterranean or Greek meal. Try the gyros and spanakopita for an authentic treat. $

☿ **Eat @ Bill's Restaurant** (270-852-8120; atbills.com), 420 Frederica St. Serving lunch Tue.–Fri. 11–2, dinner Tue.–Sat. beginning at 5. Closed Sun.–Mon. Well known in culinary circles, chef and author Bill Hughes has brought his passion to Owensboro by opening Eat at Bill's. The menu is quite a collection of regional favorites with a few tricks to make them not-so-typical, like the seafood shepherd's pie, salmon caribe with jerk spices, and the simply delicious sweet potato black bean burrito. Save room for dessert: Bill puts his signature rum sauce on his bread pudding for a taste you won't find anywhere else. Full wine menu, too. $–$$

☿ **Briarpatch Restaurant** (270-685-3329; www.brpatch.com), 2760 Veach Rd. Open Sun.–Mon. for lunch 11–2. Open every day for dinner 5–9:30. This locally owned steak house has been around since 1971. In addition to steaks, they have a large assortment of soup and salad bar items, as well as a full bar service and fine wines. Save room for dessert: They offer the Official Kern's Kitchen Derby Pie direct from Louisville. $

♈ **Miller House** (270-685-5878), 301 E. 5th St. Offering lunch Tue.–Fri. 11–2; dinner seating begins at 5. Sun. brunch 10–2. Closed Mon. They have something for every taste, with elegant dining in a gorgeously restored historic home. Eat on the classy wraparound porch or head downstairs to Spirits bar for pub grub and beer. $$

Bee Bops (270-663-0623), 122 W. 2nd St. Open Mon.–Sat. 6 AM–9ish. Dig out your mom's poodle skirt and saddle shoes and head over to this '50s-style diner. Although they make a fantastic breakfast, most locals head here for the burgers. Lots of chrome so you can slick back your hair. $

In Henderson
♈ **Wolf's Tavern & Restaurant** (270-826-5221), 31 N. Green St. Open daily for lunch and dinner. This family-style restaurant has really friendly service. Try their famous Kentucky hot brown or their bean soup. They are true blue, which means they offer drink specials when the Kentucky Wildcats play. $

Hunan (270-827-2229), 1765 S. Green St. Open daily for lunch

and dinner. Whether you are in the mood for Chinese, Mandarin, or Szechuan, you'll enjoy your meal at Hunan. They have reasonably priced lunch specials and a buffet on Sunday. Try the Hunan chicken, hot-and-sour soup, or garlic chicken; all are local favorites. $

Thomason's Barbecue (270-826-0654), 701 Atkinson St. Call ahead for hours. This small stand-alone restaurant has just a few tables and a counter because most people order their barbecue to go. Thomason's barbecues everything: pork, mutton, beef, spare ribs, baby back ribs, chicken, ham, and turkey. Grab a few bottles of their barbecue sauce—or, as they call it, "dip"—before you go. You'll want more of that flavor once you get home. $

♈ **Rookies Sports Bar** (270-826-1106; www.rookiesrestaurant.com), 117 2nd St. Open Mon.–

ROOKIES SPORTS BAR

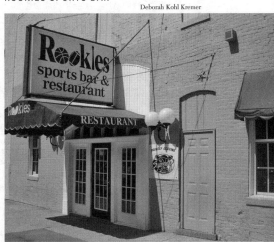

Deborah Kohl Kremer

OWENSBORO BARBECUE

Owensboro proudly proclaims to be the Bar-B-Q Capital of the World. Although they can't agree on how to spell it—you'll see *BBQ*, *Barbeque*, *Barbecue*, and *Bar-B-Q*—you will find hickory-smoked meats slow-roasted for hours and accompanied by a secret sauce at the acclaimed restaurants in town. The meats, be they mutton, pork, chicken, or beef, are served up on a plate of hamburger pickles, fresh onions, and a few slices of white bread. This is how barbecue is served in this part of the country, so roll up your sleeves and dig in.

Mutton, which is lamb, is also a staple on the menu of these barbecue restaurants. Although you can order it sliced or chopped and soaked in sauce, it is the primary ingredient of burgoo, another dish that claims Owensboro as its home. Burgoo is a thick stew full of meat (usually mutton, but other meats can be substituted), vegetables, and spices; it resembles a similar porridge made by sailors in the 1700s. The name either came from a sailor with slurred speech who was trying to say "bird stew" or was derived from the word *bulghur*, which is wheat that was added to the pot. It's also sometimes called poorman's stew or roadkill soup. The jury is out as to why burgoo is primarily found in this part of Kentucky and nowhere else in the country, but while you are here, you need to try some. There seems to be no official recipe for burgoo, just an inclination to add all the meat and veggies you have on hand to a large pot and cook for about 12 hours. The seasonings and spices vary from restaurant to restaurant, so try it wherever you are, because you are in for an unexpected treat.

& **Moonlite Bar-B-Q Inn** (270-684-8143; www.moonlite.com), 2840 W. Parrish Ave. Open Mon.–Sat. 9–9, Sun. 10–3. Moonlite is largest and perhaps best-known barbecue restaurant in Owensboro, and maybe Kentucky. In business since 1963, the huge dining room and a parking lot full of tour buses are your first tip-offs that this is a popular tourist attraction. The Bosley family have been running Moonlite for three generations now, and they say the secret to their fine barbecue is simply the hard work and 12 hours of slow-roasting that goes into the process. They must be doing something right, because they serve up 10,000 pounds of barbecue a week. They offer an enormous buffet during lunch and dinner hours, and it is the perfect way to get a sampling of the fine mutton, pork, chicken, and

Deborah Kohl Kremer

MOONLITE BAR-B-Q

beef barbecue they are known for. The meat, cooked over hickory wood and dunked in a vinegar-based dip as it cooks, is served without sauce. Their famous tomato-based sweet barbecue sauce is available on the tables, so you can add a lot or a little, based on your tastes. Luckily for you, the sauce is also available in the gift shop area near the checkout and online for real emergencies. This sauce is addicting; you might want to stock up before you leave. $–$$

& **George's Bar-B-Q** (270-926-9276), 1362 E. 4th St. Open Mon.–Sat. 7 AM–8 PM. Closed Sun. This is the place to go for stick-to-your-ribs burgoo and barbecued mutton slow-roasted over hickory and sassafras wood. In business since 1955, the folks at George's seal their meats in a vinegar-based dip that is mopped onto the barbecue as it smokes. Order your mutton "off the pit"—which means sauceless—or slathered in its natural gravy. Either way you're in for a treat. Stop by for breakfast, too. Their country ham is smoked out on the pit for an entire day before it ends up on your plate, alongside your fried eggs, pancakes, or omelet. $

& **Ole South Barbeque** (270-926-6464), 3523 KY 54E. Open Tue.–Sat. 6 AM–8 PM, Sun. and Mon. 6–2. This homey restaurant is known around town for their mutton, pork, and beef brisket, which are all cooked slow in a pit and then covered in their homemade sauce. And even though it's a barbecue restaurant, they have usually have quite a breakfast crowd that come in for Ole South's huge portions. $

♿ **Old Hickory Bar-B-Q** (270-926-9000), 333 Washington Ave. Open 9–9 every day. Before you even enter Old Hickory, you see the massive pile of chopped hickory wood stacked up against the building. Looks like they are preparing for a long winter, but actually they're just keeping the home fires burning so they can barbecue their meat over the open flame as they have since 1918. Back then, Pappy Foreman, an Owensboro blacksmith, hung up his horseshoeing tools and started roasting mutton over an open pit, selling it to locals. It became all the rage, and now this family-run business is into their fifth generation. Their dedication to cooking exclusively on hickory wood is evident when you breathe in that strong hickory-smoked scent wafting through the dining room. They are primarily known for their Western Kentucky barbecue chopped mutton and melt-in-your-mouth pork, but they also have awesome potato salad and blackberry cobbler. This casual restaurant is always packed with locals, which oughta tell you something. If you don't have time to dine in, they offer a to-go counter with barbecue by the pound and even bread, buns, pickles, and, of course, jars of their Old Hickory sauce. $–$$

OLD HICKORY BAR-B-Q

Deborah Kohl Kremer

Thu. 4–11, Fri.–Sat. 4–2. The kitchen closes at 10 PM. With 27 TVs scattered around, you're not going to miss one play of the big game. While you're here, you might as well eat. They have everything from Buffalo wings and potato skins to filet mignon and pork chops. $

Downtown Diner (270-827-9671), 122 1st St. Call for hours. Located in an old dairy building right in the heart of town, this is the place to go for burgers, fried green tomatoes, and typical diner fare. Not fancy but very friendly. $

Bon-Tin Mini Mart (270-826-1207), 2036 Madison St. Call for hours. Not much to look at, as far as ambience is concerned, but this little diner can crank out the fried chicken. If the colonel were alive, even he would come here for a meal. Side dishes like potato salad, coleslaw, and onion rings all get rave reviews, as well. If you are not a smoker, you might want to make your order "to go." $

SNACKS Darlene's Bakery (270-831-1804), 1321 2nd St., Henderson. Open weekdays 6–5:30, Sat. 6–2. Cakes, pies, cookies, bagels, doughnuts, yep, they make it all, plus they are wide awake at 6 AM, even if you're not. $

&. ((·)) **Planters Coffeehouse** (270-830-0927; planterscoffee house.com), 130 N. Main St., Henderson. Open for lunch weekdays. Housed in an old bank building, this is a cute place to

stop for a coffee or light lunch. Even though the vault is gone, you'll still find the original wood-work, bank railings, framed sav-ings account statements, canceled checks, and financial-looking stuff all around. Order the chicken salad sandwich if you can't decide. $

&. ((·)) **Crème Coffee House** (270-683-7787; cremecoffeehouse .com), 109 E. 2nd St., Owensboro. Open Mon.–Thu. 7 AM–9 PM, Fri.–Sat. 7 AM–10:30 PM. Stop into this coffee shop for a strong café mocha and enjoy the charm of this

CRÈME COFFEE HOUSE

Deborah Kohl Kremer

historic building with high tin ceilings, exposed brick walls, and a comfy conversation pit in the back room. Wake yourself up with a gourmet coffee, specialty drinks, desserts, soups, and panini sandwiches. $

&. (ᵞ) **Bridgeview Coffee** (270-830-949), 327 2nd St., Henderson. Open every day from about 6 AM until about 6 PM. Wide selection of coffee drinks, plus a full menu of soups and deli sandwiches.

Tea Café and Gift Shop (270-827-7779; teacafehenderson.com), 325 3rd St., Henderson. Serving lunch Tue.–Fri. Relax with a cup of tea and a pimiento cheese sandwich in this cute shop. The menu changes weekly, so check the website. They also have all kinds of tea supplies and Kentucky Proud merchandise.

Andria's Candy (270-684-3733; chocolate-candy.com), 217 Allen St., Owensboro. Mon.–Fri. 10–5, Sat. 11–5. Making candy since 1959, they have melt-in-your-mouth chocolates and bourbon balls. Stop in for a treat.

✳ Entertainment

Henderson Fine Arts Center (270-850-5324; www.haaa.org), 2660 S. Green St., Henderson, offers a wide range of professional performances in its 1,000-seat auditorium with an enormous stage. The gallery hosts changing art exhibits year-round.

RiverPark Center (270-687-2770; www.riverparkcenter.org),

101 Daviess St., Owensboro. Hosting more than 1,000 events each year, the RiverPark Center is home to the Owensboro Symphony Orchestra, as well as musical concerts and Broadway touring productions.

✳ Selective Shopping

Baker's Rack (270-684-6130), 2690 Frederica St., Owensboro. Owned by the Baker family, this darling gift shop is known for their distinctive brown-and-white-spotted wrapping paper. When you see a gift wrapped like this, you know you're in for a real treat. They specialize in Waterford crystal, Vera Bradley bags, and unique jewelry.

Kentucky's Best (270-683-2733), 5000 Frederica St., Towne Square Mall, Owensboro. Featuring products made in Kentucky such as Louisville's Hadley Pottery, Frankfort's Candleberry Candles, and Kim Cabbage hand-painted gourds from Sacramento, Kentucky. They also have some items from Owensboro artisans as well as Kentucky-made candy, sauces, and honey.

Memories Past and Present Antique and Gift Shop (270-844-0014; www.henderson memories.com), 324 N. Elm., Henderson. Wed.–Sat. 10–5. Visit their amazingly clean and organized showroom filled with gifts, home decor, vintage jewelry, hats, gloves, glassware, china, and decorative items and furniture from the past.

Gabbi's Boutique (270-827-1567; www.gabbisboutique.com), 137 2nd St., Henderson. Offers one-of-a-kind, uniquely designed, and hand-sewn fashions for dogs. Bring your dog while you shop for food, treats, collars, leashes, toys, and gifts. Closed Sun.

Homefolks Hardware & Gifts (270-827-5745), 120 N. Elm St., Henderson. Shop for a hard-to-find tool or even a hard-to-find gift in this old storefront, complete with creaky wood floors and authentic tin ceiling.

Owensboro Antique Mall (270-684-3003), 500 W. 3rd St., Owensboro. With about 50 booths, you are sure to find a little bit of everything. They have furniture, glassware, toys, and collectibles. Open seven days a week.

✳ Special Events

May: 🍴 ✎ ♿ **International Bar-B-Q Festival** (www.bbqfest.com). Recognized as one of the top 100 events held in the United States each year. Owensboro has become known as "the Bar-B-Q Capital of the World." Each year for about 30 years, Owensboro has welcomed about 80,000 people to the downtown riverfront to enjoy "two days of barbecue heaven." Experience live bands, carnival rides, pageants, a car show, and backyard barbecue competitions while enjoying the hickory-smoked chicken, pork, beef, and mutton.

June: 🍴 ✎ ♿ **International Blues Music Museum** presents River of Music Party, better known as "ROMP" Bluegrass Festival (www.bluegrass-museum.org/riverof

BAR-B-Q FESTIVAL

www.kentuckytourism.com

music). Performances held at the International Bluegrass Music Museum, Yellow Creek Park, and the River Park Center, Owensboro. Four days of blues performances, musical workshops, and even a bluegrass film festival. This is a huge gathering of blues musical performers and fans.

🏵 ♬ ♿ **W. C. Handy Blues & Barbecue Festival** (www.handyblues.org). This weeklong festival celebrates the life and legacy of Henderson resident and "Father of the Blues" William Christopher Handy. Held on the riverfront each year, this free festival is one of the largest blues festivals in the nation. The opening day of the festival is highlighted by the "Taste of Henderson Barbecue," where you can enjoy barbecue of all varieties and listen to some of the hottest names in blues.

THE HOPKINSVILLE AREA

Tucked into the rolling farmland of Southwestern Kentucky is the town of **Hopkinsville**. Although it appears small in size, the 30,000 residents of this city and nearly 80,000 residents of surrounding Christian County know the huge benefits of the area.

Several places in this region are named for an indigenous plant, the pennyroyal or pennyrile, depending whom you ask. Both names are accepted, and the plant itself is a member of the mint family. It has been used as everything from an upset stomach remedy to an insect repellent, but the jury is still out on whether it is a medicine or a toxin. So if you see any, don't eat it. Whether the plant is good or bad, the Pennyrile Forest State Resort Park is a wonderful place to kick back and unwind. Situated on a secluded lake, the park offers lodging, camping, and various outdoorsy recreations.

In the 1830s, Hopkinsville was a campground for the Cherokee along the Trail of Tears, a route of forced western migration for Native Americans. This brutal trail took the lives of many Natives, and today you will find a park that includes the grave sites of two chiefs, White Path and Fly Smith. In September, Hopkinsville hosts the annual Intertribal PowWow in the park. This event includes storytelling, music, and Native Americans in full regalia. To the north of Hopkinsville, you'll find Madisonville, a quaint town full of antiques shops. Keep heading north and you will end up in Historic Hanson, a postage-stamp-sized town featuring a business district housed in buildings dating back to the 1890s. Stroll along the sidewalks and visit local artists and antiques dealers in their shops. To the south is Oak Grove, which is known as the "Hometown of Fort Campbell." The U.S. Army's 101st Airborne Division, better known as the Screaming Eagles, calls Fort Campbell home.

Come to Hoptown, as it's known to locals, for its small-town charms and get a sprinkling of history and nature while you're there.

GUIDANCE **Hopkinsville/Christian County Convention & Visitors Bureau** (800-842-9959; www.visithopkinsville.com), 2800 Fort Campbell Blvd., Hopkinsville. Just 16 miles to the south is the city of Oak Grove. Contact the **Oak Grove Tourist Commission** (270-439-5675; www.oak groveky-tourism.com) for information on the goings-on there. They are located in a log cabin replica right off Exit 89, I-24, leading into town.

GETTING THERE The closest airport is just over the border in Tennessee. The **Nashville International Airport** (615-275-1675; www .nashintl.com) is 70 miles from Hopkinsville. **Greyhound Bus** (270-821-3086; www.greyhound.com) serves the Western Kentucky region. The station is 35 miles away, located at the Red Cardinal Inn, 4765 Hanson Rd., US 41N, Madisonville.

GETTING AROUND Hopkinsville is a small town and doesn't have public transportation, but if you need a ride, you can call **Haddock Blue Line Cab** (270-886-3262).

MEDICAL EMERGENCY **Jennie Stuart Medical Center** (800-887-JSMC; www.jsmc.org), 320 W. 18th St., Hopkinsville. Founded by Dr. Edward Stuart in 1913 and named for his deceased wife, whose savings were used to build the hospital. This is a respected medical center serving Western Kentucky and Northern Tennessee. It began with just 12 beds; today JSMC is a thriving 194-bed state-of-the-art hospital.

ALCOHOL Hopkinsville is the seat of Christian County, a wet county that allows alcohol sales everywhere.

✳ To See

🐾 ✐ &. **The Trail of Tears Commemorative Park** (800-842-9959; www .trailoftears.org), US 41 (Pembroke Rd.), Hopkinsville. This historic park is one of the few documented sites of the actual trail and campsites used during the 1830s forced removal of the Cherokee people from their southeastern homelands across the Mississippi River to Oklahoma. More than 13,000 Cherokee camped here and received provisions for their forced migration. This park is the burial site for two Cherokee chiefs who died during the removal, Fly Smith and White Path. There is also a heritage center on site, housed inside a log cabin that dates back to this time period. Here you will find more information about the trail as well as the Cherokee people. Stop by the park anytime; the center is open Thu.–Sat. 10–2.

🐾 ✐ &. **Pennyroyal Area Museum** (270-887-4270), 217 E. 9th St., Hopkinsville. Weekdays 8:30–4:30, Sat. 10–3. Housed in the town's historic post office, which dates back to 1914, this museum portrays the history of

Southwestern Kentucky through exhibits of antique clothing, toys, and local memorabilia. They also feature rotating exhibits by local artists. The newest addition to the museum is the Charles Jackson Circus Museum, featuring an extensive collection of circus memorabilia. Even the floor is made of sawdust to give it the feel of the big top. Admission $5.

🦫 ✪ ♿ **The Woody Winfree Fire-Transportation Museum** (270-887-4270), 217 E. 9th St., Hopkinsville. Open most days 10–4, but call first to make sure. Just across the street from the Pennyroyal Area Museum, housed in the original city fire station, is a unique museum. It features historic fire trucks, automobiles, carriages, wagons, and various firefighting memorabilia. The building's original 22-foot brass pole has been returned to its home, along with the city's first fire truck. The museum features several historically significant fire trucks, automobiles, wagons, and buggies. Admission $5.

🦫 ✪ ♿ **Jefferson Davis State Historic Site** (270-889-6100; parks.ky.gov), US 68E, Fairview. Open May 1–Oct. 1. Visit this towering 351-foot concrete obelisk honoring Jefferson Davis, the president of the Confederacy during the Civil War, who was born on this site in 1808. Visitors can take an elevator to the observation deck for a panoramic view of the countryside. While there, you can learn more about Davis in the visitors center museum. They also have picnic shelters, a playground, and a gift shop. The admission fee includes an elevator ride to the top of the obelisk and access to the small museum.

🦫 ✪ ♿ **The Don F. Pratt Museum** (931-431-2003; www.fortcampbell.com), 5702 Tennessee Ave., Fort Campbell. Open Mon.–Sat. 9:30–4:30. This museum offers artifacts and memorabilia related to Fort Campbell and the 101st Airborne Division, better known as the Screaming Eagles. The exhibits really tell the stories

VIEW FROM THE JEFFERSON DAVIS OBELISK

Deborah Kohl Kremer

well. A new facility, Wings of Liberty Military Museum, is scheduled to open in the next few years. It will feature an 80,000-square-foot museum, as well as an IMAX theater. Free.

Lone Oak House Museum (270-719-9462), 317 E. 16th St., Hopkinsville. By appointment only. Visit this gorgeous and historic home that dates back the 1830s.

✒ ♿ **Christian Way Farm** (270-269-2434; www.christianwayfarm.com), 19590 Linville Rd., Hopkinsville. Open for tours on Sat., or call for an appointment during the week. Tour this working farm and learn what it takes to keep a 350-acre spread going. The Corley family welcome guests to help with chores or to take part in one of their educational programs, like "growing hamburgers and french fries." $5 per person, children under 2 free.

✷ To Do

ATV PARK Greasy Creek ATV Park (270-584-0304; greasycreekatv .com), 2515 Richland Manitou Rd., Madisonville. Open weekends; check the website or call for hours. With more than 400 acres of woods, trails and even some swampland, its an off-roader's dream. They also have nine lakes and primitive camping available, so bring your tent and rod-and-reel.

GOLF Cherry Grove Golf Course (270-466-3610), 1006 Dixie Bee Line Hwy., Trenton. This 18-hole, par-71 public golf course has a natural creek running through it, so watch for ducks and beavers. There is also a driving range and putting green.

The Links at Novadell Golf Course (270-886-1101; www.novadell .com), 500 Nova Dell Way, Hopkinsville. This links-style 18-hole championship course sits on the rolling terrain of former Kentucky farmland. Practice your game on the 10-acre driving range, 8,000-square-foot putting green, and practice bunker.

SCUBA Pennyroyal Scuba Blue Springs (270-885-2585; www.penny royalscuba.com), 602 Christian Quarry Rd., Hopkinsville. Open Wed.– Thu. 10–4, Fri. 10–6, Sat. 8–6, Sun. 8–5. With the nearest ocean about 700 miles away, if you're in the mood to scuba dive, you'll need to stop here. This former quarry has been turned into a diving destination with more than 40 sunken attractions in its crystal-clear water. Diving ranges from 5- to 130-foot depths. They also have a full line of rental gear. Rates vary.

WALKING TOUR Historic Downtown Walking Tour (270-498-5180). Grab a map at the Hopkinsville/Christian County Convention & Visitors

Bureau and get started. You can enjoy the intricately detailed historic architecture and see landmarks such as the Old Fire Station and Clock Tower, Carnegie Library, and Christian County Courthouse as you stroll along the shops and eateries that give Hopkinsville its small-town charm.

✳ Green Space

Tie Breaker Park and Aquatic Center (270-890-0730; www.tiebreaker park.com), 9503 Eagle Way Bypass, Hopkinsville. Open in the summer months. This park features a softball complex, sand volleyball courts, a paved walking trail, and a playground and picnic area. The new water park has twisting tubes, a lazy river, and a splash zone interactive playground, along with a poolside café. Don't forget the sunscreen.

Jeffers' Bend Environmental & Botanical Gardens (270-886-6719; jeffersbend.org), Metcalfe Lane and US 41, Hopkinsville. Formerly a water treatment facility, this 40-acre park is perfect for bird-watching and 2.7 miles of nature trail hiking.

STATE PARK ✐ ♿ **Pennyrile Forest State Resort Park** (800-325-1711), 20781 Pennyrile Lodge Rd., Dawson Springs. Located within the 14,648-acre Pennyrile State Forest, this park has all the amenities you need for a relaxing vacation. They have 14 miles of nature trails, tennis and golf courses, and swimming, boating, and fishing in Pennyrile Lake. It was named for the tiny pennyroyal plant found in the woodlands surrounding the park; this plant gives off a minty smell and is used in medications and herbal remedies. Stay at the **Pennyrile Forest State Park Lodge**, the rustic stone lodge high atop a cliff overlooking the shores of Pennyrile Lake. The lodge features 24 comfortable rooms, all with a view of the lake. For even more serenity, 12 private one- and two-bedroom cottages are tucked away in the surrounding woods. Watch for wildlife, which is abundant. There is also a 68-site wooded campground offering utility hookups, a dump station, showers, restrooms, and laundry. Open Mar. 1–Oct. 31.

✳ Where to Eat

Woodshed Pit Bar-B-Que & Restaurant (270-885-8144), 1821 W. 7th St., Hopkinsville. Open Mon.–Sat. 10:30–8. Even though it's a little bit off the beaten path, it's worth your effort to find this spot. The ribs are awesome, but they also have specials on catfish and prime rib. Start your meal with some of their flavorful Kentucky burgoo and end it with one of their signature fried pies. They have all kinds of flavors—Oreo, chocolate, coconut, peach—so you might want to order more than one. $

Y **Difabio's Casapela** (270-825-1900; www.difabios.com), 17 W. Center St., Madisonville. Open for dinner Wed.–Sat. An authentic Italian eatery with seafood, steak, and chicken entrées in addition to Italian favorites. This family-run restaurant makes you feel like a relative from the moment you arrive until you polish off your three-layer cappuccino cheesecake. $

The Crowded House (270-825-1178), 26 W. Center St., Madisonville. Light breakfast and lunch served Mon.–Fri. 7–2:30; dinner Wed.–Sat. 5–10. Lunch features gourmet sandwiches and paninis, while dinner is heartier fare. Eat indoors or out. $

Ferrell's Snappy Service (270-886-1445), 1001 S. Main St., Hopkinsville. Open 24/7. This is a true burger joint. No fries, no shakes, just a counter, seven stools, and the best burgers around. In business since 1936, this is a true Hoptown landmark. If you want a side dish, grab a bag of chips, or just order more burgers. $

Ms. Ann's Tea House (270-874-2922), 1507 S. Main St., Hopkinsville. Tue.–Sat. 11–2. Reservations necessary. You'll think you are just going to get a cup of tea, but when you arrive and see the tempting treats on the menu, you'll be staying for lunch. Salads, sandwiches, and quiches, all made from scratch. Amazing array of tea choices, too.

Las Fuentes Mexican Restaurant (866-421-1417; www.las fuentesmexicanrestaurant.com), 3119 Canton Pike, Hopkinsville. Mon.–Thu. 11–10, Fri. and Sat. 11–10:30, Sun. 11–9:30. Serving the area for more than 10 years, the menu offers both Mexican American fare as well as true south-of-the-border dishes. $

* Entertainment

The Alhambra Theatre (270-887-4023; www.pennyroyalarts .org), 507 S. Main St., Hopkinsville. The majestic Alhambra opened in 1928 for both live stage shows and silent movies. Renovated in 2008, the restored 780-seat proscenium facility now offers live theater and musical performances. Check the website to see what's showing.

* Selective Shopping

Gracious Me (270-886-8090; www.graciousme.com), 4537 Fort Campbell Blvd., Hopkinsville. Closed Sun. Stop in and see owner Sherry Calhoun and find out what's new. Her shop offers china and crystal, picture frames, and gift ideas from well-known names like Lenox and Noritake, as well as Olivia Mullin and Gorham.

Legacies Military Keepsakes (931-431-2003; www.fortcampbell .com), 5702 Tennessee Ave., Fort Campbell. Located inside the museum dedicated to Fort Campbell, this shop has all kinds of military gifts and souvenirs like shirts, hats, decals, and even Christmas ornaments.

ART GALLERIES Pennyroyal Arts Council (270-887-4295; www.pennyroyalarts.org), 425 E. 9th St., Hopkinsville. Housed in the late-1800s L&N Depot downtown, they feature monthly exhibits by a variety of local artists.

Brushy Fork Creek Studio and Gallery (270-424-5988; www .brushyforkcreek.com), 1550 Pleasant Green Hill Rd., Crofton. Featuring the award-winning art of Paul and Patricia Ferrell. They both produce bowls, lamps, and vases, but Paul specializes in woodturnings and Patricia in pot-tery. They also raise organic blueberries and herbs on their farm. Please call for hours.

✳ Special Events

September: ❦ ✐ ♿ **Intertribal PowWow at the Park**. This annual gathering of Native Americans commemorates the beauty and integrity of their people. This public festival features Native American crafts, storytelling, demonstrations, and an Indian dance competition.

THE LAND BETWEEN THE LAKES REGION

This region is truly one of a kind. This is the only place in the United States designated as a National Recreation Area, which is just a smidge below national park status. The area encompasses more than 170,000 acres and 300 miles of undeveloped shoreline. The largest island peninsula in the nation, it was created with the impounding of the Tennessee River on the west and the Cumberland River on the east. The creation of the dams brings flood control, hydroelectric power, and about two million visitors to the region each year. Kentucky Lake, which was created in 1944, is one of the largest human-made lakes in the world and contains about 160,000 acres of water. It is home to Kentucky Dam Village State Park, Kenlake State Park, and numerous marinas and docks.

When the Cumberland River was dammed in the early 1960s, it formed the 118-mile-long Lake Barkley, which was named for local resident and 35th vice president of the United States Alben Barkley. Lake Barkley State Park sits on one of the fingers of this huge 60,000-acre lake.

The actual land between the lakes is a huge recreational forest, where visitors can commune with nature. With the creation of the lakes, families and entire communities were removed from the land by eminent domain. The lakeside towns of Eddyville and Kuttawa were moved to higher ground; the original villages are now under 50 feet of water. The only thing that remains is the family cemeteries; some 250 of them are still undisturbed on the Land.

The Land itself has no commercial development, billboards, or fast-food restaurants, so plan ahead. The only major road, called The Trace, runs the entire 69 miles of the Land from north to south. You'll find three helpful visitors centers along the way, as well as a few attractions that you won't want to miss. To the north is the Nature Station, an educational place to learn about the real natives to the area. In the middle you will find the Elk and Bison Prairie, the Golden Pond Observatory, and the

Planetarium. On the south end is Homeplace 1850, where you can get a taste of how life was back then. Besides this, the rest of the Land is pure wilderness and recreation. There are five campgrounds with about 1,000 sites, 100 miles of horse trails, 200 miles of hiking trails, five beaches, and loads of access ramps and docks for boating and fishing.

There's no place like the Land Between the Lakes anywhere else in the United States. Come see for yourself what it is like and take time to enjoy nature at its finest.

GUIDANCE Kentucky's Western Waterlands Visitors Center (800-448-1069; www.kentuckylakebarkley.travel), 721 Complex Dr., Grand Rivers. This visitors center is located right off I-24 at Exit 31. They have all the information, maps, and brochures you will need for your stay in this area.

For information specific to the Land Between the Lakes, stop in the **visitors center** (800-LBL-7077; www.lbl.org) located just off US 68 in the middle of LBL. This center has exhibits explaining the origins of LBL and also has a gift shop.

GETTING THERE Greyhound Bus (270-442-2706; www.greyhound .com) serves Paducah, which is about 40 miles from Eddyville. The station is located at 301 N. 4th St., Paducah. The closest commercial airport is the **Nashville International Airport** (615-275-1675; www.nashintl.com). It is about 100 miles from the northern areas of the Land Between the Lakes Region. There is also the **Barkley Regional Airport** (www.barkley regional.com), which serves private and charter planes.

GETTING AROUND The area has quite a few unmarked roads leading to marinas and lodging near the lakes. Several restaurants and attractions in the area recommend calling for directions, as some Internet map sites won't get you there. So get a good local map at the visitors center and call ahead if you're not sure.

Classic Carriage Service (270-825-1657), Grand Rivers. Take a romantic horse-drawn carriage ride all around the cute city of Grand Rivers. Service runs Fri. and Sat. nights, 4–10 (weather permitting). Board your carriage in front of **Patti's 1880s Settlement** (270-362-8844, 888-736-2525; www.pattis-settlement.com), 1759 J. H. O'Bryan Ave., Grand Rivers.

MEDICAL EMERGENCY There are several hospitals in the area of the Land Between the Lakes. The visitors center recommends the Paducah hospitals: **Western Baptist Hospital** (270-575-2100; www.western baptist.com), 2501 Kentucky Ave., and **Lourdes Hospital** (270-444-2444; www.lourdes.com), 1530 Lone Oak Rd. Both hospitals can be reached in less than an hour from the Land Between the Lakes area.

ALCOHOL This region sprawls across five different counties, with five different laws regarding alcohol sales, so check maps to see which county you are in before ordering a drink. Marshall County is dry, but allows alcohol by the drink in restaurants. Trigg County, whose largest city is Cadiz, is a dry county that does not allow alcohol sales anywhere. Lyon County is a dry county, but you can purchase alcohol by the drink at certain restaurants in Kuttawa. In Livingston County, alcohol sales are prohibited everywhere within the borders. In Calloway County, alcohol sales are prohibited except at certain restaurants in Murray, where you can order a drink by the glass.

✳ To See

🐾 ✎ ♿ The acres and acres of actual land situated between the lakes is mostly forest. There are a few attractions on this land, and you get to each of them by following The Trace, which is the main road running north–south through it. **The Homeplace** (800-525-7077; www.lbl.org). Open daily Mar.–Nov.; call for hours. Spend the day at this working farm that has been restored to represent the 1850s. Although it is located just over the border in Pryor Hollow in Tennessee, it is part of the Land Between the Lakes recreational area. The tour includes 16 cabins with interpreters in period clothing demonstrating chores and activities from that era. Small fee. **The Nature Station** (800-525-7077; www.lbl.org). Open daily Mar.–Nov.; call for hours. Stop in to learn about the wildlife in the area. The station has an indoor discovery center with both live and stuffed animals and a staff to tell you all about them. Outside, the backyard is home to rescued animals that can't make it on their own. Stop by and see the bobcat, vultures, coyotes, and even a majestic bald eagle. Small fee. **Elk and Bison Prairie** (800-525-7077; www.lbl.org). Open year-round from dawn to dusk. Enjoy the 700 acres of rolling meadows from the comfort of your car. It's the perfect place to watch the buffalo roam, or in this case elk and bison. Just follow the winding road and see these huge animals in their native environment. Small fee per car. **The Golden Pond Planetarium and Observatory** (800-455-5897; www.lbl.org). Open daily Mar.–Dec.; call for hours and showtimes. Take a trip to outer space without leaving your chair. Learn

BISON RELAXING ON THE PRAIRIE
Ellie Kremer

www.kentuckytourism.com

ADSMORE HOUSE

about stars, planets, and even space exploration during the daily planetarium shows on the 40-foot screen. Small fee.

The Adsmore House Museum (270-365-3114; www.adsmore.org), 304 N. Jefferson St., Princeton. Tue.–Sat. 11–4, Sun. 1:30–4. Located about 30 miles east of Grand Rivers. You'll be tempted to don your hoop skirt or top hat to tour this stately antebellum home. Built around the mid-1850s, the home is full of period furniture and memorabilia that belonged to the original owners. Located on the property is a restored log building, used as a gun shop, that dates back to 1844. $7 adults, $6 seniors, $2 ages 6–12; under 6 free.

❧ **Wrather West Kentucky Museum** on the campus of Murray State University (270-809-4771; www.murraystate.edu), N. 16th St. and University Dr., Murray. The museum is open weekdays 8:30–4 and Sat. 10–1. Highlighting the development of Western Kentucky and the Jackson Purchase with art, mementos, and artifacts of days gone by; exhibits cover everything from Daniel Boone to World War II. Housed in the first permanent structure on Murray's campus, the building, which dates to 1924, is on the National Register of Historic Places. Enjoy the campus while you're here. Murray is home to about 10,000 students. Free.

GOLF Marvel Golf Club (270-354-9050), 466 Bay Hill Dr., Benton. This Palmer-designed 18-hole, par-71 championship golf course lies on the western shores of Kentucky Lake. After you shoot 18, stop in the southern-plantation-style clubhouse to relax. They also have a pro shop and full-sized driving range.

Arrowhead Golf Course (270-522-8001; www.arrowheadgolf.com), 183 Arrowhead Club Dr., Cadiz. With four sets of tees and a wide variety of teeing areas, you can make this 18-hole course as difficult or easy as you want. Designed by Gary Roger Baird, it is sculpted from forested hills and dramatic rock formations along the winding Little River.

HORSEBACK RIDING Wrangler's Camp (877-444-6777), located in central LBL along Lake Barkley and Ford's Bay. Offering 100 miles of trails in the secluded area, which is laced with creeks and streams. Bring your own horse or rent one of theirs.

OFF-ROADING Turkey Bay OHV (800-LBL-7077). Get directions at the LBL Visitors Center. A true off-highway vehicle area, not just for ATVs and motorcycles; full-sized 4x4s and even dune buggies are welcome. They have approximately 100 miles of OHV trails that cover a variety of terrain and offer something for every skill level.

STATE PARKS 𝒮 ♿ **Lake Barkley State Resort Park** (270-924-1131; 800-325-1708; www.parks.ky.gov), 3500 State Park Rd., Cadiz. With 120 rooms, most with private balcony and lake view, you'll love the surroundings. They also have cottages, cabins, and a 78-site campground available. Enjoy the fitness center, indoor and outdoor pools, sand beach, tennis courts, hiking trails, and even a trapshooting range. Rent a boat or park your own at the nearby marina. Eat at the **Windows on the Water Restaurant** with floor-to-ceiling windows offering a panoramic view of the lake while you dine on good old country cooking like fried chicken, catfish, and meat loaf. $–$$

𝒮 ♿ **Kentucky Dam Village State Resort Park** (270-362-4271; 800-325-0146; www.parks.ky.gov), 113 Administration Dr., Gilbertsville. Located adjacent to the giant dam that created these massive lakes, you'll find the aptly named Kentucky Dam Village. **The Village Inn Lodge** offers a private patio or balcony in all of their 72 rooms. They also have 68 very nice cottages, some with up to four bedrooms. For more lodging options, try one of their 219 paved campsites. Rent just about any kind of boat at the marina, swim at the lodge pool, hike on the nearby trails, or test your skills on the 18-hole championship golf course. Try the **Harbor**

Lights Restaurant, serving all three meals every day, with fantastic views of the dam and marina. $–$$

✍ ♿ **Kenlake State Resort Park** (270-474-2211, 800-325-0143; www .parks.ky.gov), 542 Kenlake Rd., Hardin. Surrounded by serene gardens and the magnificent lake, this 48-room lodge is really inviting. They also have one- to three-bedroom cottages that offer lake, wooded, or golf course views and include decks and screened-in porches. If you want to camp, they have a 90-site campground, too. **The Aurora Landing Restaurant** overlooks both the gardens and the lake. They feature well-known Kentucky dishes like hot brown, as well as some Italian-inspired entrées. Open for all three meals, seven days a week. They have walking trails, tennis courts, and a full-service marina where you can rent boats and Jet Skis. $–$$

WATER PARK ✍ **Venture River Water Park** (270-388-7999; www .ventureriver.com), 280 Park Place, Eddyville. This water park has all the makings of a fun day in the sun. Whether you want to float along Old Man River or take in the excitement of speed slides and giant water flumes, you're sure to have a good time. They have an area just for the little ones as well as a large area to just lie out and catch rays.

✳ Lodging

BED & BREAKFASTS

✍ ♿ **The Rose of the Lake Bed and Breakfast** (270-362-3233; www.bbonline.com/ky/rose ofthelake), 293 Lawson St., Grand Rivers. They have a pool and hot tub as well as four comfy guest rooms and a two-bedroom cottage. $–$$

Aire Castle Bed and Breakfast (270-354-5004; airecastle.com), 435 Salem Chapel Rd. N., Benton. This lovely home offers three guest rooms, all with private bath and one with a private entrance. Innkeepers Mike and Ann are eager to make your trip a memorable one, offering deals on multiple nights and willing to make arrangements for families traveling together. They also have an in-ground pool

and serve up a delicious breakfast. Stained-glass art is their passion; check out the website to learn more about classes and workshops available. $$

✍ **Journey's End Bed and Breakfast** (270-388-5117; www .journeysendbb.com), 121 Spring Hill Dr., Eddyville. Right on the water, they offer a dock, a screened-in porch, a butterfly garden, and private boat parking. This nice B&B features the Anchor Room, a standard guest room. They also have the Morning Glory Family Suite, with two bedrooms and a kitchen, and the Eagles Nest, which is a lake-view studio apartment that sleeps four. $

Futrell House (270-522-9214; futrellhouse.com), 125 Main St.,

Cadiz. Just steps from some fabulous antiques shops is this cozy B&B. Innkeeper Gary Polete will greet you at the door of this historic Queen Anne home that was built in the 1870s. It is the perfect place to unwind, relax, and rejuv. The three-guest-room home features a fireplace in one of the rooms and a cozy sitting room, full of books, on the second floor that lures everyone in. Gary serves up what he calls a Full Fancy Breakfast every morning. Among his signature items are cheddar and grits casserole, hot cinnamon rolls, and breakfast potatoes. $$

Maple Hill Bed and Breakfast (270-388-4963; maplehillbb.com), 13 Maple Hill, Eddyville. This historic 1850s home is filled with antiques but has all the modern amenities that guests are looking for. The home has four beautiful guest rooms, each with a fireplace and claw-foot tub. Innkeeper

Sherri Rickard offers a full breakfast each morning. $$

RESORT MARINAS ♪ **Green Turtle Bay Marina** (800-498-0428; www.greenturtlebay.com), Grand Rivers. Located on Barkley Lake and at the canal that connects to Kentucky Lake, they offer luxury one- to four-bedroom condos. The marina offers boat rentals including Jet Ski rentals, fishing boats, pontoons, and houseboat rentals. Stop by the marina store, the Ship's Chandlery, a 3,000-square-foot nautical store with the latest fashions, home decor items, books, and marine parts and supplies. $$$

♪ **Buzzard Rock Resort and Marina** (800-826-6238; www.buzzardrock.com), 985 Buzzard Rock Rd., Kuttawa. Try a two-bedroom cottage or a one-bedroom resort unit; either way you'll have comfy digs and a deck

GREEN TURTLE BAY MARINA

www.kentuckytourism.com

LIGHTHOUSE LANDING MARINA

with a lake view. At the marina you can rent a fishing or pontoon boat, fill up on fuel, and stock up on food and fishing supplies at the marina store. $–$$

✒ (ᵞ) **Lighthouse Landing Marina and Resort** (270-362-8201, 800-491-7245; lighthouse landing.com), 320 W. Commerce Ave., Grand Rivers. Situated right on Kentucky Lake, they offer 200 open slips for boats up to 42 feet in a well-protected harbor. They rent everything from sailboats to kayaks. Cute cottages, from one to three bedrooms, sit lakeside. They are fully equipped for your get-away. They have lake views, air-conditioning, and gas grills; some even have WiFi. $

✒ **Eddy Creek Marina Resort** (270-388-2271; 800-626-2300; www.eddycreek.com), 7621 KY

93S, Eddyville. Situated on 102 acres of lakeside property, this resort offers motel-style rooms and log cabins for your lodging. They also have an outdoor pool and a sand beach. The marina opens at 6 AM, so you can get an early start on the lake. They rent fishing and pontoon boats and have all the things you need to head out. $–$$$

CAMPING ✒ 🐾 **Prizer Point Marina and Resort** (800-548-2048; www.prizerpoint.com), 1777 Prizer Point Rd., Mile Marker 55 on Lake Barkley, Cadiz. Whether you want to sleep in a tent condo, cabin, bungalow, or tree house, this is the place to come. They offer lakeside camping as well as boat rentals (try the pontoon with a slide off the back, known as the Slidezilla). Their restaurant, **The**

Landing, serves breakfast, lunch, and dinner right on the water. Family-friendly activities include soccer fields, volleyball, a game room, hiking and biking trails, mini golf, and a swimming and splash pool. There is even a huge "iceberg" floating in the lake, perfect for climbing up and jumping off. Cottage $

✳ Where to Eat

DINING OUT The Brass Lantern Restaurant (270-474-2773; www.brasslanternrestaurant.com), 16593 US 68E, Aurora. Open mid-Feb.–Dec. for dinner only, starting at 5 PM. Closed Mon. and Tue. Western Kentucky's first three-star restaurant. Fine dining with options like lobster tail, grilled pork tenderloin, and salmon. Try the homemade soups, which change with the seasons. They also have fried oysters and signature grasshopper pie. $–$$

♂ ♪ ♿ **Patti's 1880s Settlement** (270-362-8844, 888-736-2525; www.pattis-settlement.com), 1759 J. H. O'Bryan Ave., Grand Rivers. Patti's is open every day 10:30–8 (Jan.–Mar.) or 10:30–9 (Apr.–Dec.). The restaurant is famous for its cozy and casual ambience, but it can seat hundreds of diners in intimate dining rooms. Servers are dressed like they just came off the prairie, and they do a great job of making you feel welcome. If you go to Patti's, you have to try the flower pot bread, which comes with strawberry butter, and the 2-inch-thick pork chops. Don't leave without ordering a slice of mile-high meringue pie. You'll be glad you did. The Settlement includes gift shops, a playground, and even an animal park with sheep, peacocks, llamas, and pigs. You can also play a round of miniature golf or get married in their wedding chapel. $–$$

EATING OUT ♟ The Buzzard Rock Café at the Buzzard Rock Resort and Marina (800-826-6238; www.buzzardrock.com), 985 Buzzard Rock Rd., Kuttawa. Serving all three meals, they open at 7 AM every day. This bar and restaurant is a favorite of locals, as it is the only wet spot on the lake in this otherwise dry part of Kentucky. The restaurant serves home-cooked meals as well as their own big ½-pound Buzzard Burger. It is huge, so come hungry. $

Broadbent's (270-388-0609; www.broadbenthams.com), 257 Mary Blue Dr., Kuttawa. Open every day. Known as the Pride of Trigg County, they have been following a family tradition of curing country ham, bacon, and sausage for over 80 years. They serve sandwiches, ice cream, and pies, but try some of the hand-rubbed, hickory-smoked meats like pepper bacon, sun-dried tomato bacon, and maplewood-smoked cinnamon bacon. $

♪ **Willow Pond Catfish Restaurant** (270-388-4354; www.willowpondcatfishrestaurant.com), 124 US 62W, Eddyville. Open seven days a week, but call for seasonal hours. All guests get a free bowl of their signature hush puppies, and that's just the start. They are known for their pond-raised catfish fillets, shrimp, frog legs, and tilapia, but they also have grilled steaks, chicken and pork chops, burgers, and a kids' menu. Dessert choices are unbeatable: homemade cobblers, cheesecakes, and their signature items, double chocolate brownies bites and French coconut pie. This is a nice, homey, casual place to eat. $

Echo Charlies (270-388-2271; www.eddycreek.com), 7612 KY 93S, Eddyville. Enjoy the fabulous lake view 6 AM–9 PM seven days a week during peak season. Stop in for a breakfast omelets, if you're there before 11 AM, or grab a salad or a burger and fries. They also have a huge selection of entrées like grilled yellowfin tuna, strip steak, and hickory-smoked molasses pork tenderloin. Very casual and relaxing. $

Brenda's Kitchen (270-545-3334; brendas-kitchen.com), 21234 Marion Rd., Fredonia. Mon.–Fri. 6 AM–2 PM, Sat. 6 AM–11 PM. Brenda's slogan is, "Where the coffee is hot and the gossip is free," and that about sums it up. Except that she forgot to add "and the food is good." Because it is. Brenda serves a lot of pork barbecue, breakfast all day, and some amazing pecan pie. Not at all fancy, and that is the way the locals like it. $

Ⴤ **The Oasis Southwest Grill** (270-388-0777; www.theoasis southwestgrill.com), 42 Days Inn Dr., Kuttawa. Mon.–Thu. 11–11, Fri. and Sat. 11–midnight, Sun. 11–9, Sun. brunch 11–2. Whether you want a rib eye, sirloin, or filet, all their aged steaks are charbroiled over a mesquite flame. Slow-roasted prime rib, served au jus, is available on Fri. and Sat. after 4 PM; get it while you can. Eat outside on the patio or inside in the fun dining room. Enjoy free peanuts, too. $$

Lite Side Bakery and Garden Cafe (270-362-4586; www.liteside bakery.com), 2115 Dover Rd. (KY 453), Grand Rivers. Open Wed.–Sun. 7–3 year-round. Owners Bob and Irene have been serving up healthy breakfasts, lunches, baked goods, and picnics since 1994. Try an enormous Belgian waffle or fresh cinnamon rolls for breakfast or a veggie burger or quesadilla for lunch. Well known for their muffins; try one of their 37 flavors (18 are available each day). $

Parcell's Deli and Grille (270-527-9300; www.parcellsdeli.com), 165 US 68E, Benton. Open 10:30–7. Closed Sun. Run in for sandwiches, box lunches, desserts, and even hand-dipped ice cream, milk shakes, and floats. They have good deli sandwiches and salads, and interesting burgers, like the Reuben burger and the pizza burger. Try one of their daily specials like the chicken cordon bleu sandwich. $

Nelson Pharmacy (270-527-3616; www.nelsonpharmacy.net), 1112 Main St., Benton. Open weekdays for lunch only. Just a few minutes from the Kentucky Lake area, you'll find this local drugstore complete with a soda fountain. Everyone in town stops by for a hand-dipped ice cream cone, an old-fashioned float, or a creamy milk shake, but the lunches deserve a nod, too. Order up some homemade soup, burgers, or chili dogs; they're all quite tasty. But if you want to eat like a local, it's Nelson's taco salad that fills up that lunch counter every day. $

In Murray
HRH Dumplins (270-753-0000), 305 S. 12th St. Open Mon.–Sat. 10–4. Homemade bread really makes the sandwich; that's why they make it fresh daily. In fact, everything is homemade and delicious. They are known for their desserts, so think ahead while ordering. Big apple dumplings and yeast rolls served with honey butter are just two of the favorites. $

Victors Sandwiches (270-753-7715; victorssandwiches.com), 1301 Main St. Mon.–Fri. 11–8, Sat. 11–5. Closed Sun. In business for nearly 30 years, Victors knows about sandwiches. Although they have burgers, pizza, and Mexican choices, first-timers need to stick with a sandwich. They have more than 90 choices on their extensive menu—and if you can't find one you like, then make one up. They'll help you out. Good service, fresh ingredients, fun varieties. $

Jasmine (270-761- 8424; crave jasmine.com), 506 N. 12th St. Mon.–Sat. 11–9:30, Sun. 11–9. Delicious Thai dishes and sushi that is as scrumptious as it is beautiful. Each roll is a work of art. $

Ⓨ **Nick's Family Sports Pub** (270-762-0022; nicksmurray.com), 616 N. 12th St. If you are really hungry, maybe you can accept one of Nick's food challenges, like eating a massive 30-inch pizza with three of your friends in 30 minutes. But if you are just regularly hungry, you are sure to find something of normal size on their menu. Steaks, pastas, pizza, wings, wraps, and sandwiches—they have something for everyone, plus you can watch the big game on all their TVs. Full bar. $$

Matt B's Main Street Pizza (270-759-1234), 1411 Main St. Closed Sun. When you are in Murray, swing by Matt B's for great food, served in big portions, at a great price. Luckily, it is in walking distance of campus, so you might appreciate the chance to burn a few calories on your way back. Matt B's sells pizza by the slice for less than $3, and MSU students know it is so big, it eats like a meal. They also have a legendary calzone that can feed at least two people for around $5. Crowded at lunch, so go early. $

Los Portales (270-767-0315), N. 12th St. Open for lunch and dinner. This place serves really good Tex-Mex, at really low prices. Good salsa and fajitas. $

✴ Entertainment

Badgett Playhouse (888-362-4223; grandriversvariety.com), 1838 J. H. O'Bryan Ave., Grand Rivers. The Badgett Playhouse is home to Branson-style musical performances with a professional cast of singers, dancers, and a live band. Check the website to see what's showing.

✴ Selective Shopping

Newsom's Old Mill Store (270-365-2482; www.newsomscountry ham.com), 208 E. Main St., Princeton. Closed Sun. A part of downtown Princeton since 1914, this old country store is home of the nationally renowned Col. Newsom's Aged Kentucky Country Hams. You'll find some modern-day products, but they still have the same counter used by the Newsom's almost 100 years ago. Stop in for seeds, plants, produce, preserves, relishes, sorghum, salad dressings, and, of course, a ham or two.

ANTIQUES Red Door Antique Mall (270-388-1957; www.thered doorantiques.com), 35 US 641N, Eddyville. Specializing in a unique blend of country farm antiques and country primitives, all in a 7,000-square-foot showroom. Open seven days a week.

Days Past Antiques (270-362-4683), 1555 J. H. O'Bryan Ave., Grand Rivers. Housed in an all-log building, this cute shop specializes in quilts, antique furniture, and pottery. Stop in to see what's new. Open seven days a week.

OUTLET MALLS Shops at Eddyville (812-524-0917), 385 Outlet Ave., Eddyville. Just a few shops but, it's the kind of place you can slip in and browse around for a bargain. Stores for women's clothes, home decor, and even socks for the whole family.

✴ Special Events

August: ✤ ✿ ⚅ **Hot August Blues Festival**. This two-day festival features blues performers from around the world. Performances take place at the amphitheater at Kenlake State Resort Park in Aurora, but you can listen from your boat, too.

October: ✤ ✿ ⚅ **Hunters Moon Fall Festival** and **Grand Rivers Storytelling Festival**. These two festivals could be enjoyed on their own, but they run simultaneously, so why not catch both of them? The Hunters Moon Fall Festival features beauty pageants, street dances, craft shows, Taste of the Lakes, and a parade filled with floats and bands. The Grand Rivers Storytelling Festival features entertaining stories from professional, nationally acclaimed storytellers. Enjoy a variety of lively tales of Grand Rivers folk life. Both festivals are held in the downtown area of Grand Rivers.

THE PADUCAH AREA

A delightful mix of old and new, **Paducah** is the perfect example of a small Kentucky town that has successfully spruced itself up and put itself back on the map. Besides its flourishing, historic downtown, city leaders have created a growing arts community, centered in Paducah's Lowertown, that blends itself right in. You can feel the artsy vibe as soon as you arrive.

Since the creation of the Paducah Artists Relocation Program in 2000, the city has brought in more than 70 artists who are now full-time residents. The program includes both cultural and financial incentives for the artists to set up homes and studios in a 26-block section of Lowertown, once the city's most run-down neighborhood, now its prime attraction. All the artists who now call Paducah home say that this energizing

PADUCAH TOWN CENTER

Deborah Kohl Kremer

community, so rich in residents who produce textile, fiber, paint, and glass art forms, makes this the place they want to live.

This river city is protected by floodwalls that not only keep rising waters out when necessary, but also show off a bit of the artistic bent of the city with the fabulous hand-painted murals by Robert Dafford. After perusing the giant murals, each a life-sized chapter into Paducah's past, head down to the river shore to take in the confluence of the Tennessee and Ohio Rivers. The rivers flow together, making a wide, calm portion of the Ohio as it flows westward and merges with the mighty Mississippi about 50 miles downstream.

Undoubtedly the biggest draw to Paducah is the National Quilt Museum of the United States. This one-of-a-kind museum displays more than 150 quilted works of art in an ever-changing gallery. Whether you are an avid quilter or know nothing about the art form, it should be a mandatory stop while in town. This ages-old craft, which started as a way to make warm blankets and grew into an intricate form of stitching and storytelling, can simply take your breath away. As home to this national museum, Paducah rolls out the red carpet each April to quilters and admirers alike for the American Quilter's Society Quilt Show and Convention, which draws upward of 30,000 people each year.

As you poke through the antiques shops, tiny diners, and artists' workshops of Paducah, don't forget to give a nod of appreciation to the leg-

PADUCAH VISITORS CENTER

Deborah Kohl Kremer

endary Chief Paduke. According to legend, Paduke was the hospitable chief of the Chickasaw Indians, a tribe that called the area, then known as Pekin, home in the early 1800s. He was well known for welcoming settlers to the area as they arrived on flatboats on the Ohio River and encouraging good relations between the Native Americans and these early pioneers. The community grew and prospered until around 1827, when William Clark, part of the famed Lewis and Clark adventure team, arrived with plans to lay out a city. Chief Paduke and his tribe graciously left the area, and Clark got to work creating the city grid that is still evident today. In a move of appreciation to the chief and his tribe, Clark renamed the city Paducah. A statue of the chief stands proudly at 1818 North 19th Street at Jefferson Street.

GUIDANCE The Paducah–McCracken County Convention & Visitors Bureau (270-443-8784, 800-723-8224; www.paducah-tourism.org), 128 Broadway, Paducah. Open weekdays 9–4. On your way through Paducah's historic downtown district, swing in for maps and brochures. **Whitehaven Mansion/Welcome Center** (270-554-2077), US 45, just off I-24 Exit 7. Open 24 hours for travelers; tours of the home offered daily between 1 and 4. Come in for brochures and maps and get a free tour of the 1860s antebellum home that houses the welcome center. The Corinthian-columned white Classic Revival house is stunning. Whitehaven, Kentucky's only welcome center located in a formerly private home, showcases memorabilia of Paducah's native son Alben Barkley, who served as vice president under Harry Truman.

GETTING THERE Paducah is located right off I-24, 137 miles from Nashville, Tennessee, and 176 miles from St. Louis, Missouri. To arrive by commercial air, your best bet is **Nashville International Airport** (615 275-1600; www.nashintl.com). It's about 130 miles from downtown Paducah. **Barkley Regional Airport** (www.barkleyregional.com), which is in Paducah, serves private and charter planes and makes connections to larger commercial airports. You can also get there by bus. **Greyhound Bus** (270-442-2706; www.greyhound.com) serves the Paducah and Western Kentucky region. The station is located at 301 N. 4th St., Paducah.

GETTING AROUND Paducah is easy to get around by car or by foot if you're in the downtown area. Look for a downtown trolley in the summertime that loops through the charming downtown area, stopping at all the popular attractions.

MEDICAL EMERGENCY Western Baptist Hospital (270-575-2100; www.westernbaptist.com), 2501 Kentucky Ave., Paducah, and **Lourdes Hospital** (270-444-2444; www.ehealthconnection.com/regions/lourdes),

1530 Lone Oak Rd., Paducah. Both offer an array of services to fill any medical need.

ALCOHOL McCracken County is one of those counties that is moist, not quite wet but not quite dry, either. Primarily, the county is dry, serving no alcohol, but within the county are five wet precincts. One of those precincts is the city of Paducah, where you can buy alcohol within the city limits.

✳ To See

In Paducah

&. **The National Quilt Museum** (270-442-8856; www.quiltmuseum.org), 215 Jefferson St. Open Mon.–Sat. 10–5; Apr.–Oct., the museum is also open Sun. 1–5. Prepare to be amazed at the 150 modern-day quilts on display. Each a work of art, they look like they were created with paintbrush on canvas rather than needle and thread. The lighting and display techniques allow you to get up close to see the intricate stitches and tiny pieces of fabric used to create these masterpieces. There are also reader boards alongside each quilt so you can learn about the artist and how the work came to be. The display quilts are housed in three galleries, and the exhibits change throughout the year. No cameras allowed, and don't think about touching them, even though you'll want to run your fingers over this beautiful fabric. The museum also offers workshops throughout the year and has a gift shop full of quilt-related books and non-quilt-related pieces of art. $11 adults, $9 seniors, $5 students; under 12 free.

NATIONAL QUILT MUSEUM

Deborah Kohl Kremer

Deborah Kohl Kremer

WALL TO WALL MURALS

&. **Paducah Wall to Wall Murals** (270-554-3589; www.paducahtourism
.org). These gorgeous life-sized floodwall murals depict Paducah's past.
Hand painted by legendary artist Bob Dafford, the 48 panels are so lifelike, you feel like you can walk right into them. Stroll along Water Street
and take in their beauty while learning about Paducah at the same time.

&. **William Clark Market House Museum** (270-443-7759; market-
housemuseum.com), 121 S. 2nd St. Mon.–Sat. noon–4. This darling
museum tells the story of Paducah
inside a historic building that used
to be an open-air market. Evidence of the market stalls is still
apparent, complete with old photos so you can envision what the
place looked like when horses and
buggies were parked out front.
The museum has 4,000 square
feet of rotating exhibits that do a
good job of painting the picture of
Paducah's growth and challenges.
Adults $4.

MARKET HOUSE MUSEUM

Deborah Kohl Kremer

**Lloyd Tilghman House and
Civil War Museum** (270-575-
5477), 631 Kentucky Ave. Open

Wed.–Sat. noon–4, Apr.–Nov., and by appointment. Tour the home of Confederate general Lloyd Tilghman, which dates back to 1852. Exhibits focus on the role of Western Kentucky during the Civil War and General Tilghman's efforts to keep the state neutral. Small fee.

The Paducah Railroad Museum (270-519-7377; www.paducahrr.org), 200 Washington St. Open Fri. 1–4 and Sat. 10–4 or by appointment. Enjoy an interesting display of authentic railroad memorabilia, maps, and photos. $3.

✳ To Do

In Paducah

CARRIAGE RIDES **Annie's Horsedrawn Carriage Rides** (270-210-6095), weekends. Meet at the gazebo across from the convention and visitors bureau, take in a 20-minute tour of the river and floodwall murals, and get a feel for the town.

GOLF **Paxton Park Golf Course** (270-444-9514; www.paxtonpark.com), 841 Berger Rd. This 18-hole, par-71 course is a favorite of local residents. They have a pro shop, driving range, and snack bar. If you forget your clubs, they have rentals available, too.

PAINTBALL **Paducah Shooters Paintball Field** (270-443-3758; www.pssguns.com), 3919 Cairo Rd. Open weekends 10–5. Located next to their Shooters Supply store, you can pick up all your paint gun necessities and head out for a round of paintball wars.

RACEWAYS **Paducah International Raceway** (270-898-7469; www.paducahinternationalraceway.com), 4445 Shemwell Lane. Enjoy high-profile NASCAR events, like late-model stock-car and sprint-car racing, on the 3/8-mile clay track.

Bluegrass Downs (270-444-7117; caesars.com), 32nd and Park Ave. Live racing from the end of Apr. to early June. Simulcasting Wed.–Sun. 11:30–8:30. This track is home to live thoroughbred racing and harness racing, so come out and pick a winner. Throughout the year, intertrack wagering is available from Kentucky's other tracks.

WALKS Pick up a map at the convention and visitors bureau, 128 Broadway, and walk along the historic downtown. You'll enjoy the ages-old architecture, the revitalized historic buildings, and vibrant floodwall murals. The map will even take you to Lowertown so you can find all the artists and their studios.

✳ Lodging

In Paducah

INNS ♿ **1857's Bed and Breakfast** (270-444- 3960; www.tribe carestaurant.net), 127 Market House Square. This building, which is listed on the National Historic Register, was built in, you guessed it, 1857. Located above Tribeca Restaurant, they offer two guest rooms on the second floor and a giant guest room that covers the entire third floor of this old building. The 12-foot ceilings and old hardwood floors blend beautifully with modern necessities and antique furnishings. They offer a private deck, complete with outdoor Jacuzzi and continental breakfast each morning. $–$$

The Egg and I Guest Suites (270-443-6323; www.eggandiarts .com), 335 N. 6th. Located in a pre–Civil War home in the Lowertown district, the two guest rooms are above The Egg & I Fine Art & Crafts Gallery. Each room offers a queen-sized bed and a sitting room with a pullout sleeper sofa. Both rooms feature giant showers, measuring about 4 by 6 feet, so you can spread out and enjoy yourself. $

Fox Briar Inn at RiverPlace (270-443-7004; foxbriarinn.com), 100-C Broadway. You won't believe you're still in Kentucky. This refurbished historic building houses loft-style apartments, making you feel like you are in New York City. Located atop the storefront restaurants and shops of Broadway, you'll find these open, airy apartments complete with

FOX BRIAR INN SITS ATOP THE STOREFRONTS.

Deborah Kohl Kremer

exposed brick, 12-foot ceilings, and creaky hardwood floors. Each apartment, which can be rented for the night or long term, is decorated with cool contemporary furniture, whirlpool tub, and utensil-stocked gourmet kitchen. They even have washer and dryer. $$–$$$

Fisher Mansion Apartments (270-443-0716; www.fisher mansion.com), 905 Jefferson St. You can walk to everything from this convenient location in Lowertown. Fisher Mansion offers one- and two-bedroom furnished apartments for the same price as a motel room; the rooms are perfect for both long- and short-term stays. The 1,000-square-foot apartments are completely furnished and offer linens, tableware, and all the comforts of home. $$

✳ Where to Eat

In Paducah

DINING OUT ♈ **Ristorante di Fratelli** (270-442-7054; www .difratelli.net), 211 Broadway. Open for dinner Tue.–Sat. Fine dining, Italian-style. Enjoy the charm of the renovated historic downtown building while indulging in the elegant surroundings and upscale menu choices, featuring fresh fish and fine cuts of steak in addition to the authentic Italian options. Everything is made from scratch, and it shows. $$–$$$

♈ **Martin Fierro Argentinean Grill and Rodizio** (270-408-1300), 314 Broadway. Open for dinner Tue.–Thu. 5–9, Fri.–Sat. 4–10. Carnivores take note: This is a meat restaurant. Although they do have an impressive salad bar, don't waste too much time there, because the focal point is the Latin American meat. Served by authentic gauchos, skewered sausage, chicken, pork, and steaks that have been marinated and grilled to perfection start appearing at your table and keep on appearing until you've had your fill, which might be a while. Try everything. $$–$$$

♈ **Whaler's Catch** (270-444-7701; www.whalerscatch.net), 123 N. 2nd St. Open for lunch and dinner Mon.–Sat. Whaler's, as it is known to the locals, has been serving up market-fresh seafood since 1977. The building itself was built in 1878 and has housed everything from a distillery to a furniture warehouse to a union hall. The weathered brick facade and ornamental accoutrements add to the turn-of-the-century charm. This three-story building offers two levels of dining with seating for about 400. The first floor is a bit more casual and rustic, while the second floor has larger tables, six of them with large window views. Don't miss the 24-foot hand-carved mahogany bar that is a prominent feature in the dining room. This bar, which was built around 1863, is said to have been brought up from New Orleans by barge and called a roadside tavern in Cairo, Illinois, home. The legend goes that Ulysses S. Grant was actually served at this bar during the Civil

Deborah Kohl Kremer

WHALER'S CATCH

War. The building is on 2nd Street in historic downtown Paducah. Whaler's has added an open-air double gazebo-like dining area and bar called the Crow's Nest. Named for the lookout location on sailing ships, it's built on stilts that rise two stories above the street level, offering patrons a great view of the Ohio River. This area, which is naturally just open during the summer months, features live bands on weekends and can seat 150 people.

Whaler's Catch is known for their great seafood. One of the most popular entrées is the Boiling Bag, which is basically a bag made of cheesecloth, stuffed full of shrimp, crawfish, crab legs, and oysters. Diners can't wait to see what's inside. The menu really sticks to its promise of "A Taste of New Orleans." Appetizers like fried alli-

gator, deep-fried okra, and oysters on the half shell are all very popular. Soup choices carry out the hint of New Orleans with offerings such as red beans and rice, jambalaya, and étouffée—fresh shrimp or crawfish and vegetables cooked in a roux to make a thick stew. That hint of New Orleans shows itself again on the dessert menu, with beignets and Bourbon Street bread pudding options. $$

♉ **d. Starnes at RiverPlace** (270-442-2122), 108 Broadway. Open Mon.–Sat. for lunch and dinner. Known for hickory-smoked barbecue shoulders, this is where locals go for authentic Western Kentucky meals. They've been a Paducah staple for more than 50 years, so obviously they are doing something right. Try the homemade corn bread muffins with a piping-hot bowl of soup. Or skip the meal and go straight for the coconut cream pie, which you know was made fresh that morning. $–$$

EATING OUT ⑂ **Max's Brick Oven Café** (270-575-3473), 112 Market House Square. Open Mon.–Thu. 5–10, Fri.–Sat. 5–11. Reservations are a good idea. Located in a converted warehouse, this hip restaurant uses architectural salvage items, like shutters, windows, and woodwork, to add to the ambience. The menu features delicious selections of gourmet pizza and sandwiches from their massive brick oven. Eat outside in the courtyard if the weather is warm. Live music sometimes on the weekends. $–$$

Tribeca Mexican Cuisine (270-444-3960; www.tribecarestaurant .net), 127 Market House Square. Open Tue.–Fri. for lunch 11–3,

Deborah Kohl Kremer

TRIBECA MEXICAN CUISINE

dinner 5–9; Sat. noon–9. This is the place to go for authentic fresh Mexican entrées served up in a fun, casual atmosphere. Order up a margarita and spicy enchilada, and save room for their famous cheesecake burrito. $–$$

Bob's Drive In (270-443-6493), 2429 Bridge St. Open Mon.–Thu. 10–9, Fri. and Sat. until 10. Known as the oldest drive-in restaurant in Kentucky, Bob's has thick creamy milk shakes and a nice selection of burgers. $

SNACKS Kirchhoff's Bakery and Deli (270-442-7117; kirch- hoffsbakery.com), 114–116 Market House Square. The bakery opens at the crack of dawn; the deli is open for lunch Mon.–Sat. Established in 1873, Kirchhoff's has been serving Old World and arti-

KIRCHHOFF'S BAKERY

Deborah Kohl Kremer

san breads, pastries, and cookies to the people of Paducah for generations. In addition to their fine bakery items, they offer a deli, with loaded sandwiches served on fresh-baked breads. Although they have fresh salads and homemade soups, you would be missing out if you didn't have a grilled sandwich on their focaccia or sourdough bread. $

The Chocolate Factory (270-442-5222; www.chocolatefactory ky.com), 109 Market House Square. Open weekdays, 9–5, Sat. 10–5. If the name alone doesn't make your mouth water, the smell of all the delicious chocolate will. This old-time candy shop, featuring jars of homemade chocolates

and a fudge counter full of assorted must-try flavors, is pure heaven. It's owned by two sisters who have been making chocolates all their lives—and these ladies know what they are doing. Try the chocolate caramel fudge, the English toffee bark, or a tiger butter cup: white chocolate mixed with peanut butter, with dark chocolate swirled in. $

✴ Entertainment

In Paducah
The Maiden Alley Cinema (270-441-7007, 800-442-7002; www.maidenalleycinema.com), 112 Maiden Alley. Open Thu.–Sun. Located at the end of a brightly lit alley, this is where to

THE CHOCOLATE FACTORY

Deborah Kohl Kremer

go to see recently released international and domestic art films that are never on the bill at the big-screen megaplex.

The Market House Theatre (270-444-6828, 888-648-7529; www.mhtplay.com), 132 Market House Square. Enjoy fine community theater in this historic 240-seat building. Check the website to see what this talented bunch is working on.

♿ **Luther F. Carson Four Rivers Center** (270-450-4444; thecarsoncenter.org), 100 Kentucky Ave. Enjoy live Broadway shows, the Paducah Symphony Orchestra, and even rock concerts at this 1,800-seat theater. Check the website to see who's showing.

✱ Selective Shopping

In Paducah
The Kentucky Oaks Mall (270-444-0440; www.kentuckyoaks mall.net), 5101 Hinkleville Rd. With 12 anchor stores and 96 specialty shops, they probably have anything you need. The mall also has eight restaurants and a movie theater.

ANTIQUES American Harvest Antiques (270-442-4852; www .american-antiques.net), 632 N. 6th St. This shop is loaded, really loaded, with cards, books, furniture, and all kinds of old stuff.

Jeremiah's Antique Mall (270-443-3991), 226–229 Broadway St. Closed Sun. Right in the heart of downtown, you'll find this shop

full of both American and European antiques.

Just English Antiques (444-8454), 212 Broadway St. Closed Sun. A not-so-ordinary collection of antiques from across the pond.

ART GALLERIES AND STUDIOS Yeiser Art Center (270-442-2453; www.theyeiser .org), 200 Broadway St. Open Tue.–Sat. 10–4. What began in the 1950s as an attempt to create Paducah's first art museum has emerged into a contemporary gallery that exhibits work by American, European, African, and Asian artists. Included in the permanent collection are works by Henri Matisse, Mary Cassatt, Salvador Dalí, and Francisco Goya as well as regional artists. Free.

Wildhair Studios (270-444-6115; www.wildhairstudios.com), 201 Broadway St. Open every day. The word *whimsy* comes to mind as soon as you enter this fun shop. Owner Sue Edwards keeps her studio well stocked with Paducah souvenirs, quilting-related T-shirts, humorous gift cards, and really fun jewelry.

In Lowertown
Bryerpatch Studio (270-444-8040; www.bryerpatch.com), 502 N. 5th St. You have to see this studio of Caryl Bryer Fallert, three-time winner of the Best of Show award at the American Quilter's Society Annual Convention. Caryl's work can be found in museums and private collections

CARYL BRYER FALLERT OF BRYERPATCH STUDIO

Deborah Kohl Kremer

around the world. Take in her exquisite collection of quilts on display, or peruse the collection of fabrics that she hand dyes and paints for use on her own quilts. She has bolts and bolts of brightly colored fabric and it is all for sale, in case her work has inspired you. If you have time, you might be able to fit one of her quilting workshops into your visit.

The Egg and I Fine Arts and Crafts (270-443-6323; www.egg andiarts.com), 335 N. 6th. Visit with artists Steve and Carol Gabany and see their inspiring art created by carving ostrich, emu, and duck eggs. They painstakingly carve through the shell to expose the various layers underneath, resulting in treasured pieces of art. They also offer fine beaded jewelry.

Gallery 5 (270-444-2020; www .renzulliart.com), 803 Madison St. (entrance is on 8th St.). Open Wed.–Sun. Dr. William Renzulli, a physician and artist, showcases his artwork, which he creates from pastels, watercolors, and acrylics. The results are bold, colorful, and imaginative paintings.

Mentor House Gallery (270-442-1635; www.mentorhouse gallery.com), 332 N. 6th St. Open Wed.–Sun. noon–5. Okay, so you'd be hard-pressed to miss this 18-foot-tall giraffe sculpture right smack-dab in the middle of their front yard, so watch for it as you come down the street. Artist Paulette Mentor, herself a relocated artist, has brought her dramatic acrylic paintings to town. Her gallery features her own work as well as dramatic art glass, sculptures, and unique pieces from artists around the country.

Aphrodite Gallery (270-444-6871; www.julieshawdesigns.com), 503 N. 7th St. Open Wed.–Sun. noon–5. See owner Julie Shaw's amazing designs of intricate, gem-laden jewelry pieces.

Coco's Art Gallery (270-415-5662; cocosgallery.com), 430 N. 6th St. Fine contemporary art by Coco Babenco. Call Coco to see her works in person.

Studio Miska (270-442-5266; fredafairchild.com), 627 Madison St. Visit the gallery and studio of artists Freda Fairchild and Cricket Alexander, who are mother and daughter. Studio open on Friday and Saturday; call for times or appointment.

Dixie Leather Works (270-442-1058; www.dlwleathers.com), 306 N. 7th St. Open Mon.–Fri. 10–5. With 38 years devoted to the art of leatherworks, owner Phillip Phillips can make anything from a guitar strap to a reproduction of a regulation field medical case from the Civil War. Dixie Leather Works created countless pieces for museum displays and battlefield reenactors. They've had had cameo appearances in blockbuster movies like *The Alamo* and *Gettysburg*, and TV shows like *Dr. Quinn Medicine Woman*. They also produce and sell handmade leather purses, briefcases, and trunks. This interesting shop has all kinds of fascinating leatherworks that you didn't know existed. It also smells fantastic in there.

✳ Special Events

April: ♿ **American Quilter's Society Annual Quilt Show and Contest**. Since 1984, quilters have been gathering for this annual quilt show where they can view a juried exhibit of some of the finest quilts from around the world, as well as see the latest in wares from quilt supply dealers. More than 30,000 quilters arrive each spring, and Paducah rolls out the red carpet for them. Events are held all over the city to coincide with the quilt show.

May: ♞ ✄ ♿ **Lowertown Art and Music Festival**. Held every Memorial Day weekend right in the streets of Lowertown. Live music on stages throughout the district provides the backdrop for the artists who are demonstrating and displaying their art forms. Painters, sculptors, and even yoga instructors fill the booths along the streets, inviting you in to see what they do and how they do it.

Summer months: ♞ ✄ ♿ **Downtown After Dinner** (800-723-8224). For some hometown fun, head for the middle of town on Saturday nights all summer long. The streets are full of live music, car shows, cloggers, and street artists who all come out 7–10 PM each week. Perfect for both travelers and people who call Paducah home. You'll feel like a local before the night is through.

INDEX